Political economy of financial integration in Europe

D1386078

MANCHESTER
UNIVERSITY PRESS

European Policy Research Unit Series

Series Editors: *Simon Bulmer and Mick Moran*

The European Policy Research Unit Series aims to provide advanced textbooks and thematic studies of key public policy issues in Europe. They concentrate, in particular, on comparing patterns of national policy content, but pay due attention to the European Union dimension. The thematic studies are guided by the character of the policy issues under examination.

The European Policy Research Unit (EPRU) was set up in 1989 within the University of Manchester's Department of Government to promote research on European policies and public policy. The Series is part of EPRU's effort to facilitate intellectual exchange and substantive debate on the key policy issues confronting the European states and the European Union.

Titles in the series include:

The regions and the new Europe   ed. Martin Rhodes

Mass media and media policy in Western Europe   Peter Humphreys

The European Union and member states   ed. Dietrich Rometsch and Wolfgang Wessels

The governance of the Single European Market   Kenneth Armstrong and Simon Bulmer

Political economy of financial integration in Europe

The battle of the systems

Jonathan Story and Ingo Walter

Manchester University Press

Published by Manchester University Press
Oxford Road, Manchester M13 9NR, UK

British Library Cataloguing-in-Publication Data
A catalogue record for this book is available from the British Library

ISBN 0 7190 4312 3 *hardback*
ISBN 0 7190 4313 1 *paperback*

First published 1997

01 00 99 98 97   10 9 8 7 6 5 4 3 2 1

Printed in Great Britain
by Biddles Ltd, Guildford and King's Lynn

Contents

List of figures and tables	*page* vii
Preface and acknowledgements	ix
List of abbreviations	xi
1	European diplomacy, institutions and the Financial Area	1
2	Politics and economics of European macroeconomic convergence	32
3	The EU in search of union	75
4	Financial system benchmarks: efficiency, stability and competitive performance	105
5	Financial structure and corporate control	136
6	The politics and markets of German financial services	162
7	The politics and markets of French financial services	189
8	The politics and markets of UK financial services	224
9	Building the European Financial Area	250
10	The battle of the systems	275
	Epilogue	313
	Index	326

Figures and tables

Figures

2.1 Macro-financial linkages: one-country model   *page* 37
2.2 Macro-financial linkages: two-country model   41
2.3 The snake, 1972–1978   47
2.4 OECD inflation, 1965–1994   51
2.5 Monthly Treasury bill rates, 1988–1993   52
2.6 Nominal effective exchange rate, 1992–1993   53
2.7 Purchasing power parity and actual exchange rates, 1980–1995   56
2.8 Public opinion surveys of the single market initiative   64
2.9 The Maastricht criteria   68
2.10 Inflation and long-term interest rates, 1996   70
2.11 General government deficit and gross public debt, 1996   71
3.1 Economic and monetary union, 1996–2004   97
3.2 The Economic and Monetary Union time-line, 1988–2003   99
4.1 Financial intermediation dynamics   109
4.2 Efficiency in financial intermediation   112
4.3 Integration of global financial markets   115
4.4 Initial depth of financial development, 1960, versus future growth, 1960–1989, for selected countries   116
4.5 Universal bank organisation structures   123
4.6 Comparative household asset deployment in the USA, Europe and developing countries, 1995   126
4.7 Regulatory tradeoffs, techniques and control   128
5.1 National regulations and financial policy communities   137
5.2 Alternative corporate control structures   139
6.1 Household wealth by investment in Germany, 1950–1988(%)   173
6.2 Non-financial corporate financial structure in Germany, 1970–1993   178
6.3 German crossholding structure, 1993   184
10.1 Selected French crossholdings, June 1995   287

Tables

4.1 The US financial services sector, 1950 *page* 113
4.2 The US financial services sector, 1995 113
4.3 Percentage shares of assets of financial institutions in the United 124
States, 1860–1993
5.1 Legal and regulatory restraints on corporate control in the United 152
States, the United Kingdom, Japan and Germany
5.2 Estimated comparative pattern of ownership and agency 153
relationships in the United States, the United Kingdom, Japan
and Germany
5.3 Differences in the structure of the boards of large non-financial 154
firms in the United States, the United Kingdom, Japan and
Germany
6.1 Market shares of bank groups in percentage of all bank turnover, 167
1960–1989
6.2 Structure of share ownership in Germany, 1960–1990 174
11.1 Global wholesale banking and investment banking, 1995 321
11.2 Global wholesale banking: market concentration, 1990–1995 322

Unless noted otherwise, the sources for all figures and tables are the authors.

Preface and acknowledgements

Few aspects of the great European experiment in economic integration that began in 1956 has been as difficult and fraught with political conflict as the creation of a single financial market. Close to a half-century after the launch of the European Union (EU), the financial sector in Europe remains surprisingly fragmented. National currencies remain, and some are likely to be around well into the next century. Bond and equity markets in Europe are far from seamless. Efforts at macroeconomic convergence have encountered one setback after another, often handing enormous windfall gains to those betting on the lack of credibility of the established course. The whole process has been extremely slow, painful, and beset with pitfalls as the common interest came up time and again against vested national interests and, quite simply, different ways of doing things. The financial market conditions that exist in what is by far the largest unified pool of capital resources in the world, the United States, still seem far off.

Yet progress has been made, often with two steps forward and one step back, and often against great odds. The gains in terms of improved resource allocation, improved growth and improved social welfare are inordinately difficult to measure, but they doubtless exist. The founding fathers of the EU recognised that financial integration is a key part of the march to economic union, and they were right. How difficult and time-consuming that would be, no one could have foreseen.

In this book, we trace the political, financial and economic steps towards financial union in Europe with a focus on the political economy of the process – notably the dynamics of a Europe of sovereign states reflecting deep-seated differences in ideas about how financial institutions ought to be organised, how financial markets ought to be regulated, how companies ought to be governed and what the relationships between banks (and insurance companies) and non-financial firms ought to be, and how the role of the state ought to be played out. These differences are reflective of very different and entrenched national histories, yet they must be reconciled, ultimately through convergence on a unified European financial system, or in the more immediate future through agreed processes of supervision over a confederal regime rooted in the inherited national financial systems but tied one to another through multiple channels and exchanges.

Accordingly, we consider the political diplomacy of financial integration in the first chapter of this book, followed by a discussion of the economic mechanics and political process of the kind of macroeconomic convergence that is a prerequisite to financial integration. The third chapter analyses the package of measures introduced alongside the financial area initiative – notably, social policy, monetary union and a common foreign and security policy – that the French and German leaderships conceived of as indispensable features of a completed EU. We then turn to the financial sector itself, with a discussion of optimum financial-system design and its relationship to the performance of the real sector of the economy through the process of corporate governance and control. These processes have been conditioned by the different national financial-market and regulatory histories, and separate chapters are devoted to three very different approaches in Germany, France and the United Kingdom. These approaches, we argue, are locked into a battle that will ultimately determine the financial landscape in Europe, the contours of which we consider in the final two chapters. The epilogue contains a succinct discussion of what we believe to be the key lessons.

Work on this book began in 1993, after the excitement of the EU's 1992 single-market initiatives had abated and in the run-up to the ratification of the Maastricht Treaty. The book's gestation, thankfully shorter than our subject's but longer than we anticipated, was due to the care we hope to have taken in avoiding repetition of erroneous canards, such as the shopworn thesis of bank power in Germany and the even more erroneous but widely held view in Great Britain and elsewhere that the Tory government's financial market reforms were 'de-regulatory'. We argue that one of their main features was to have subordinated the whole financial system to statutory regulation, in some instances for the first time. Collaboration between a political scientist and an economist has also required us to align our different thoughts and paradigms – an exchange much facilitated by convivial discussions in pleasant venues in France and the United States. We have benefited from discussions with many colleagues during the course of this project, with Yakov Amihud, Roy Smith, Jean Dermine and Douglas Webber deserving special mention. INSEAD helped with financial support, and we are grateful to John Butterfield for helping with some parts of the research. Ann Rusolo aided us immeasurably with completion of the final manuscript. Any errors of omission or commission, of course, are our own.

Jonathan Story   Ingo Walter
Fontainebleau, France   New York

Abbreviations

AAA	bond rating (highest quality grade awarded by the rating agencies)
AFB	Association Française des Banques
AFBD	Association of Futures Brokers and Dealers
AFEC	Association Française des Etablissements de Crédit
AG	Aktiengesellschaft (German joint-stock company)
AGF	Assurances Générales de France
AIBD	Association of International Bond Dealers
AMB	Aachener und Münchner Beteiligungsgesellschaft
ATM	automated teller machine
BCCI	Bank of Credit and Commerce International
FCE	Banque Française de Commerce Extérieure
BfG	Bank für Gemeinwirtschaft
BHA	Banco Hispano Americano
BIS	Bank for International Settlements
BNCI	Banque Nationale de Commerce et d'Industrie
BNP	Banque Nationale de Paris
BOSS	order-routing system of the Deutsche Terminbörse
CA	Caisse Nationale du Crédit Agricole
CAC	system of computerised quotation
CAC-40	French stock-market index
CAD	Capital Adequacy Directive
CAP	Common Agricultural Policy
CB	Commission Bancaire
CBV	Counseil des Bourses de Valeurs
CdC/CDC	Caisse des Dépôts et Consignations
CEO	Chief Executive Officer
CEPS	Centre for European Policy Studies
CET	Comité des Etablissements de Crédit
CFA	Communauté Financière Africaine (African Financial Community)

CFTC	Commodity Futures Trading Commission
CL	Crédit Lyonnais
CMT	Conseil du Marché à Terme
CNA	Conseil National des Assureurs
CNC	Conseil National de Crédit
CNEP	Comptoir National d'Escomptes de Paris
COB	Commission des Opérations du Bourse
COC	Comité des Organisations Professionelles du Crédit
COFACE	Compagnie Française pour le Commerce Extérieur
COMECON	Council for Mutual Economic Assistance
CPSU	Communist Party of the Soviet Union
CRB	Comité de la Réglementation Bancaire
CREST	British securities clearance and settlement system
CSI	Council for the Securities Industry (UK)
DAX	Deutscher Aktienindex (German share price index)
DG Bank	Deutsche Genossenschaftbank
DGB	Deutscher Gerwerkschaftsbund (German association of labour unions)
DTB	Deutsche Terminbörse (German futures market)
DTI	Department of Trade and Industry (UK)
DWZ	Deutsche Wertpapierdatenzentrale GmbH
EBRD	European Bank for Reconstruction and Development
ECB	European Central Bank
ECJ	European Court of Justice
ECOFIN	Council for Economic and Finance Ministers
ECSC	European Coal and Steel Community
ECU	European Currency Unit
EDC	European Defence Community
EFTA	European Free Trade Area
EIB	Europeans Investment Bank
EMA	European Monetary Agreement
EMI	European Monetary Institute
EMS	European Monetary System
ENA	Ecole Nationale d'Administration
EPC	European Political Cooperation
EPRU	European Policy Research Unit
EPU	European Payments Union
ERM	Exchange Rate Mechanism
ESCB	European System of Central Banks
EU	European Union
EUA	European Unit of Account
Euratom	European Atomic Energy Community
EUROLIST	list of European quoted companies
Europartners	an alliance of European banks

EUROQUOTE	a financial information system
FDES	Fond de Développement Economique et Social
FDI	foreign direct investment
FECOM	European Monetary Cooperation Fund
FFSA	Fédération Française des Sociétés d'Assurance
FIMBRA	Financial Intermediaries, Managers, and Brokers Regulatory Association (UK)
FSA	Financial Services Act (UK)
G-7	Group of Seven (leading industrial nations)
GAN	Groupement d'Assurance Nationale (French insurance company)
GATT	General Agreement on Tariffs and Trade
GDP	Gross Domestic Product
GmbH	private limited-liability company (Germany)
GZS	Gesellschaft für Zahlungssysteme
HSBC	Hong Kong and Shanghai Banking Corporation
IBF	International Banking Facility
IBIS	Inter-bank Information System (Germany)
IBRD	International Bank for Reconstruction and Development
Id	International Dealership
IDIS	Inter-Bourse Data Information System
IFSE	International Federation of Stock Exchanges
IMF	International Monetary Fund
IMRO	Investment Management Regulatory Organization
INSEAD	Institut Européen d'Administration des Affaires (European Institute of Business Administration)
IOSCO	International Organisation of Securities Commissions
IRPT	interest-rate parity theorem
ISD	Investment Services Directive
ISE	International Stock Exchange (of the UK and the Republic of Ireland)
ISRO	International Securities Regulatory Organisation
JMB	Johnson Matthey Bankers
KISS	price information system of the Deutsche Terminbörse
LAUTRO	Life Assurance and Unit Trust Regulatory Organization (UK)
LIFFE	London International Financial Futures Exchange
MATIF	French futures and options exchange
MIB	Marketing Investments Board (UK)
Minitel	French interactive telephone information system
MITI	Ministry of International Trade and Industry (Japan)
MoF	Ministry of Finance (Japan)
NASDAQ	US over-the-counter securities market
NASDIM	National Association of Securities Dealers and Investment Managers

NATO	North Atlantic Treaty Organization
OECD	Organisation for Economic Cooperation and Development
OEEC	Organisation for European Economic Cooperation
OFT	Office of Fair Trade (UK)
OPEC	Organization of Petroleum-Exporting Countries
OTC	Organization for Trade Cooperation
Paribas	a French merchant bank
PIA	Personal Investment Authority
PIPE	Price Information Project Europe
PPP	purchasing power parity
RELIT	automatic settlement system
REX	German government securities index
RIE	Recognised Investment Exchange
RONA	system to channel orders automatically
SBD	Second Banking Directive
SBF	Sociétés des Bourses Françaises
SDB	Sociétés de Bourse
SDR	Special Drawing Rights (IMF)
SEA	Single European Act
SEAQ	Stock Exchange Automated Quotations
SEC	Securities and Exchange Commission (USA)
SFA	Securities and Futures Securities Association Authority
SIB	Securities and Investments Board (UK)
SICAV	Société d'Investissements à Capital Variable
SMH	Schröder, Münchmeyer, Hengst & Co. (Germany)
SNECMA	French manufacturer of aircraft engines
SPD	Socialdemokratische Partei Deutschlands (Social Democratic Party of Germany)
SRO	self-regulatory organisation
TAURUS	Transfer and Automated Registration of Uncertified Stock
TBTF	too-big-to-fail (with reference to banks)
UAP	Union Assurance de Paris (French insurance company)
UBAF	Union des Banques Arabes et Françaises
UCITS	Undertakings for Collective Investment in Transferable Securities (EU financial directive on unit trusts, October 1989)
UN	United Nations

1

European diplomacy, institutions and the Financial Area

Both the Single European Act (SEA), launching the European Union's (EU) internal market programme and the Maastricht Treaty – signed on February 7, 1992 and aiming to create a single currency by 1999 at the latest – were initiated in the early 1980s when Europe and Germany were still divided along the lines of the Cold War. It was only in April 1983, twenty-five years after the Rome Treaty came into effect, that the European Commission submitted proposals for an internal market in financial services.[1] These later entered into Lord Cockfield's White Book of June 1985, and were negotiated under the new rules for EU procedures introduced in the SEA, which was ratified finally by all member-state parliaments in 1987. The proposals found expression in a series of directives and regulations voted upon by the Council in the course of 1986–93.

The EU Finance Ministers decided on June 13, 1988 to liberalise capital movements by July 1, 1990, with some exemptions until 1994 for the poorer countries, and an escape clause for the benefit of France and Italy. At the European Council meeting in Hanover on June 27–28, the heads of government agreed to set up a committee to study monetary union. These three initiatives – (1) completing the internal market, (2) liberalisation of capital movements, and (3) monetary union – formed part of a broader strategy pursued by Commission President Jacques Delors to advance the EU towards political union.

What could account for the long delay in the EU moving towards an internal market in financial services, and why should the proposal have been made public in April 1983? A proximate cause was that the three initiatives formed part of a broader Western strategy to dismantle non-tariff barriers, and to promote market and political interdependence among the three great pillars of the world economy in Western Europe, the United States and Japan. Consolidating a large internal market within the territory of the EU was conceived as a prerequisite for the Commission and the member states together to strengthen their negotiating position on trade with the United States and Japan. The strategy soon confronted two countervailing forces: (1) the anticipation of a large internal market contributed to accelerate inward and outward investment by corporations – an area where the Commission's powers were practically non-existent; and (2) as soon as the European public became aware, in the course of 1988, that their particular habits could be challenged by the creation of the single market, they mobilised to protect themselves or to project their special interests into EU legislation. Opening up the markets within Europe kindled parochial concerns and ran parallel to the globalisation of corporate strategies. The growing din of protectionist voices in Europe thus preceded the fall of the Berlin Wall. Legislation on the internal market threatened national standards or traditions. Member states and their corporations protected their discretionary powers with regard to investment decisions.[2]

There were thus two key dimensions to the familiar structure of European diplomacy.

- The states held a dual membership. They were signatories to the EU treaties, and they were participants in the world system of states. This dual membership was evidenced by the diversity of multilateral institutions in Europe, with different functional tasks, overlapping responsibilities and distinct memberships. These had been spawned by the states over the preceding decades in their efforts to reconcile the pursuit of national interests and to secure European peace and prosperity. They fashioned a dense fabric of multilateral overlay to the traditional bilateral form of European diplomacy. The institutional fabric which wove the Atlantic Community into the continental dimension of Western Europe betrayed the complex layers of partial accords between Europe's sovereign states, tying them through cumulative treaties to each other and to the rest of the world.
- The ambition to achieve a European union among constitutional states with their own preferences, extra-European attachments and ideas to defend and to promote required the consent of public opinions with their own collective memories and references. European political constituencies consistently supported the idea of European cooperation, but repeatedly showed their reservations whenever the member states in the EU sought to disturb their national ways, and to break out of the dreary round of incrementalist measures by big leaps into uncertain futures. EU legislation on financial services, as a prime example, was thus a negotiated product of the clash of ambitions and inhibitions among the states and interests which negotiated it. This chapter traces the history of the long negotiations within the multilateral context of European politics and diplomacy.

The Western alliance and European integration: 1944–1969

Western European integration was originally entwined in the institutional fabric emerging from the wartime alliance between Great Britain and the United States. The ideals of national self-determination, individual freedoms and access to world markets proclaimed the crusade around which the Grand Alliance formed in January 1942. The 'special relationship' between London and Washington was cemented by the creation of the combined chiefs of staff along with a number of economic boards, and culminated in the creation of the United Nations organisation, as well as in the regional economic and security arrangements of the late 1940s. The Bretton Woods institutions were brought into existence in 1946–47, in order to avoid repetition of the currency experience of the inter-war years.[3] The aims of the International Monetary Fund (IMF) were to foster financial stability and expansion of international trade for the sake of high levels of national employment and economic activity, along with the General Agreement on Tariffs and Trade (GATT), signed in 1947. Convertibility of currencies as an IMF cornerstone was intended to foster transactions on current account. In the event of a 'fundamental disequilibrium' in current payments, member states could choose between devaluation, internal retrenchment, or temporary financing agreed upon with the IMF. The International Bank for Reconstruction and Development (IBRD) was to provide long-term funds for the reconstruction of the industrialised regions ruined by war.

In effect, the United States acted as the world's banker. Congress had insisted that its approval would be required for any change in the dollar's parity. This measure altered the sense of the IMF statutes to avoid rigidity in exchange rates and gave Congress the final say in any multilateral realignment of parities with respect to gold, as stipulated in the statutes. The dollar subsequently became the world's key currency, pegged to gold at $35 per fine ounce and exchangeable among central banks at the official IMF rates of exchange. The statutes included no practical measures that could be taken against chronic surplus countries, the United States being the only candidate for that condition in 1945. On the contrary, US business clamoured to break open British Commonwealth export markets, while the Administration cancelled lend-lease and demanded – in the terms of the December 1945 Anglo-American loan agreement – that the pound sterling make an early return to full convertibility. When external convertibility (for non-residents) came in 1947, the continental Europeans rushed from sterling into dollars to protect the value of their reserves and to keep their economies running. Sterling convertibility was suspended in August that year. British trade was then directed more forcefully to the Commonwealth countries, which accounted for nearly two-thirds of British exports and imports until the early 1960s. Trade among Western European countries on the Continent grew much faster.

Meanwhile, the United States moved to support Europe's economic reconstruction, as part of the emerging policy to contain the Soviet Union. In June 1947, Secretary of State George Marshall launched the idea of a long-term US undertaking to grant aid in support of a cooperative regional effort in Europe. 'Its purpose', Marshall declared, 'should be the revival of a working economy in the world so as to permit the emergence of political and social conditions in which free institutions can exist'.[4] Following the Paris conference of July–August 1947, the Organisation for European Economic Cooperation (OEEC) was set up in April 1948, with sixteen member states. Stalin ordered

Prague and Warsaw to desist from participation in the Marshall Plan. The United States contributed the dollars, and accepted a degree of European protection against its exports. US diplomacy only resumed the push for freer trade on world markets in the late 1950s, once continental European central banks had rebuilt their reserves.

In 1961, OEEC membership was expanded to include the United States, Canada, Australia and New Zealand. Japan and Spain joined subsequently. The OEEC later became the Organisation for Economic Cooperation and Development (OECD), indicating the dual trend of Western economies to promote national economic growth simultaneously with global market integration among industrialised countries.

The other strand of US containment policy incorporated Western Europe as a US protectorate. In March 1947, President Truman announced US aid to anti-communist forces in Greece and Turkey, promising to 'support free peoples who are resisting attempted subjugation by armed minorities or by outside pressures'.[5] Following the Czechoslovak Communists' seizure of power in Prague in February 1948, Britain, France and the Benelux countries signed the Brussels Treaty pledging mutual military aid and economic cooperation. This was only a prelude to involving the United States directly in Europe's defence.

The Washington Treaty, setting up the Atlantic alliance, was signed in April 1949. It specified a general commitment by the United States, Canada and the ten European founding members (Belgium, Britain, Denmark, France, Iceland, Italy, Luxemburg, the Netherlands, Norway and Portugal) to come to their mutual protection. Outbreak of war in Korea in 1950 hastened the creation of an Atlantic command structure, a post which was successively occupied by American generals responsible to the US President. The Atlantic Council, attended by Foreign and Defence Ministers, was presided over by a European secretary-general. Greece and Turkey joined in 1952. West Germany was admitted in 1955, and Spain became a member in 1982.

In order to facilitate the coexistence of the sterling area with a managed system of commercial payments in Western Europe, British diplomacy in 1950 supported the creation of a European Payments Union (EPU). The EPU operated as the agent for European central banks through the Bank of International Settlements (BIS), set up in 1929–30 in Basle, Switzerland, to deal with the payments problems in respect of Germany's reparations under the Versailles Treaty following World War I. The US Federal Reserve attended the regular BIS meetings. Every month, each central bank settled accounts and extended credits to other central banks. At the end of each month, the central banks notified debit or credit balances to the BIS, which kept the general accounts for the whole operation. The balances were settled in gold, dollars or in credits extended by countries in trade surplus (e.g. West Germany) to those in deficit (e.g. France). The greater the debt, the more had to be repaid in dollars and gold. This arrangement helped overcome the prevailing network of bilateral clearing arrangements, as well as to maintain the absolute fixity of parities, and included Western

Europe, the French franc zone, and the whole sterling area, i.e. monetary arrangements covering about four-fifths of global trade. The mechanism thereby discriminated against the dollar, prompting US diplomacy to push for unilateral convertibility. The EPU was dissolved in December 1958, thereby ending the notion of a distinct monetary zone for Europe. Private foreign-exchange markets, centred on London, came to substitute for the official clearing mechanism.

French diplomacy under the Fourth Republic sought to go beyond cooperative diplomacy, dear to London's interests. Supporters of European unity had been disappointed by the intergovernmentalism of the Council of Europe, set up in May 1949 by ten founding states. The Council was based at Strasburg to symbolise Franco-German reconciliation, and came to be identified specifically with the European Convention of Human Rights, signed in November 1950. But for those who saw nationalism as the source of Europe's terrible wars, the Council's emphasis on cooperation between states was entirely inadequate.

The first initiative to bring European resources under a common authority was the European Coal and Steel Community (ECSC), launched in May 1950 by France's Foreign Minister, Maurice Schuman. The two industries covered by the ECSC were brought under a supranational authority, in exchange for which a common market was established in those sectors. It was followed by a French proposal for a European Defence Community (EDC), encapsulated in the Paris Treaty signed in May 1952. Both proposals were presented as major steps to Franco-German reconciliation, and were immediately welcomed by Chancellor Konrad Adenauer of West Germany as satisfying German national aspirations for equality of treatment. Great Britain declined the offer to join in both institutions out of hostility to supranational ideals.

The battle of beliefs between the protagonists of supranationalist or federalist institutions for a united Europe, and those who favoured cooperation between sovereign states, became a constant theme of the following decades in European affairs. Supranationalists contended that common institutions had to be sufficiently powerful in order to master Europe's diversity, and to allow Europe to assume its place in world affairs as a single entity to be taken seriously. The federalists favoured common institutions, whose tasks would be those which could not be effectively handled by the states or by their national authorities alone. Intergovernmentalists argued that only the democratically-elected representatives of the states could negotiate on behalf of their peoples. The force of the intergovernmentalist arguments seemed vindicated when French opinion turned against the EDC, which was rejected by the National Assembly in August 1954. The result was a British scheme for German participation in the North Atlantic Treaty Organization (NATO). The Federal Republic was admitted into the Atlantic alliance in May 1955, and its nascent armed forces were placed under NATO command.

The failure of the EDC was interpreted by the pragmatists as suggesting more flexible methods in pursuit of the desired objective of eventual European union.

Hence the accommodations to national susceptibilities included in the European Atomic Energy Community (Euratom) and Rome Treaties, signed in 1957 by France, the Federal Republic, the Netherlands, Belgium, Luxemburg and Italy. The Treaty of Rome came into effect in 1958. It stipulated an institutional structure composed of Commission, Council of Ministers, Parliament and Court of Justice. Majority voting in the Council of Ministers was restricted to Commission proposals on market liberalisation. Commission powers were not extended into the fields of non-tariff barriers, taxation or money. Western European security matters, after the EDC saga, were left to NATO and to the United States.[6]

While the Commission could aspire to transform the European state system in the long term, it had to work with states, corporations and associations to transform the markets. This meant that the 'spillover effect' operated in two directions.[7] The expectation that a customs union in the EU would lead to political unity might be awakened when steps were taken towards an integrated market, which in turn would create further demands to proceed in the same direction. A customs union could create conditions to integrate commodity as well as capital markets. An integrated market, in turn, could create demands for a single currency so that investors bear no currency or exchange-rate risk, and all firms face equal conditions in their access to a common pool of savings. Monetary union, in turn, requires political integration – which is only possible if the member states are prepared to abandon to a significant degree their separate macroeconomic policies.

It is when the process is seen by the member states as close to fruition that the temptation to turn back is greatest. The process may thus operate in reverse, from a refusal or postponement of monetary union back to an explicit avowal of autonomous credit policies, to a rejection of the customs union as a goal, and retrenchment from freedom in product markets. Since its inception in 1958, the EU has moved uneasily along this spectrum between integration and the assertion of national identities.

Financial and monetary integration were seen by many of the EU's founders in the 1950s as a necessary component of the overall process of economic integration. Even so, nowhere was there mention of monetary union as a goal. Independent currencies were considered as too closely identified with matters of national sovereignty. The Rome Treaty was negotiated in an environment of (1) exchange controls left over from the post-war reconstruction period, (2) the Bretton Woods system of pegged exchange rates, as well as (3) national, fragmented and (from the viewpoint of the proclaimed goal of an integrate EU internal market) domestic financial policies.

The Rome Treaty's principal stated objective was the creation of a customs union. The Commission was charged with sole responsibility for establishing the Common External Tariff (CET), thereby becoming a crucial negotiating partner for the United States on trade liberalisation. The Rome Treaty envisioned, in addition to the establishment of a customs union and a common commercial policy towards third countries, 'the elimination, as between Member States, of customs duties and of quantitative restrictions'[8] on the free movement of persons, services and capital. In the course of the transition period – which was to last from 1958 to 1970[9] – restrictions were to be reduced in four key areas related to financial services.

- Articles 52 to 58 provided for the right of establishment so that the self-employed or enterprises based in one member state could set up operations in another. In banking, measures to coordinate legislation had to be taken by unanimity.[10] Non-EU banking companies in the EU were 'to be treated in the same way as natural persons who are nationals of the Member States'.[11]
- Articles 59 to 66 provided for the freedom to supply services across national frontiers. The liberalisation of banking and insurance services was to be introduced alongside 'the progressive liberalisation and movement of capital'.[12] To this effect, the Commission was to set out a general programme,[13] to be implemented by means of directives.
- Consideration of EU monetary integration first took place alongside negotiation of the European Monetary Agreement (EMA) in 1955–58, which was intended to liberalise exchange controls. It preceded the full restoration of external convertibility on current transactions at the end of 1958, and by 1961 adherence by the EU member countries to IMF Article VIII on exchange-control liberalisation. Articles 66 to 73 of the Rome Treaty entailed a binding commitment to abolish restrictions on capital movements related to current payments only. The Treaty stipulated only that each member state work towards liberalisation of exchange controls as quickly as practicable. In the course of the transition period, member states were progressively to abolish 'between themselves all restrictions on the movement of capital belonging to residents of the Community, and to eliminate any discrimination based on nationality, to the extent necessary to ensure the proper functioning of the common market'.[14] To this end, the authorities were 'to endeavour to avoid' introducing new exchange restrictions, and to grant exchange permits as liberally as possible.[15]
- Finally, the Treaty required that member states act in the 'common interest' when formulating and executing exchange-rate policies.[16] A major concern of those drawing up the Rome Treaty was that currency convertibility, together with continued autonomy in national economic policy, should not lead to exchange depreciations. Currency realignments threatened to restore the protectionist measures negotiated away in creating the Common Market. Hence the emphasis placed on the need to coordinate economic and monetary policies,[17] and to proscribe an alteration of exchange rates, 'which seriously distorts conditions of competition'.[18] But member states retained their powers 'to take the necessary protective measures'[19] in the event of a sudden crisis in their external accounts. The Treaty thus implied the joint pursuit by the member states of compatible policies for economic growth and price stability, with currency realignments accepted only as a last resort.

Notably, the drafters of the Rome Treaty left monetary, credit, insurance and exchange-rate policies firmly in the hands of the national finance ministries and central banks. The Commission and Council were to be closely associated in the coordination of economic policies, and in the liberalisation of financial services. The Council of Ministers approved two directives on the liberalisation of capital movements on May 11, 1960[20] and on December 18, 1962.[21] Both accompanied a relaxation of capital controls in France and Italy. Capital flows were classified into four broad categories, each with their special provision.

- Transactions in the first category comprised direct investments, and were liberalised unconditionally.
- A second category referred to trading in securities listed on stock exchanges. These, too, were to be liberalised 'unconditionally' and traded on 'free' exchange markets as long as governments 'endeavour to avoid' excessive discrepancies between free and official rates.
- The third category included the issuance and placement of new securities, especially collective investment instruments, which were to become a major growth area with the development of unit trusts and pension funds. Transactions in this category were subject to conditional liberalisation. Member states could retain or reintroduce controls on new securities issues in the interest of national economic policy.
- The final category included transactions in medium- and long-term loans that were subject to similar safeguard clauses in the Treaty's chapters on the free provision of services and on the balance of payments.

In December 1961, the Council adopted a general programme for the abolition of restrictions on the freedom of establishment,[22] and of freedom to provide services in the EU,[23] in conformity with Article 54 of the Treaty. The programme distinguished between services to which regulations concerning the free movement of goods, capital and persons did not apply, and services relating to the movement of capital. Services involving capital movements had to be liberalised at the same time as movements of capital.

The Commission then suggested that eventual monetary union would require permanently fixed exchange rates,[24] and advanced a number of institutional proposals. On April 13, 1964 the Council adopted these suggestions, as well as a broad commitment to price stability. At the same time, the Commission submitted a draft directive to liberalise restrictions on the issuance and placement of foreign shares on national markets, but nothing came of the proposal. As the main source of supply of capital in the six EU member countries at the time, Germany pushed for an unconditional abolition of restrictions, but the French Finance Ministry wanted to keep control over new issues on the domestic market and to promote Paris as the main financial centre in the EU.[25]

The programme's first directive came into force in August 1964, and provided for the abolition of restrictions on reinsurance business. This directive only sanctioned the status quo, since reinsurance and the coverage of large risks was already internationalised, and only needed a legal cover. But discussions dragged on the insurance of individuals and companies. Debates turned around the interpretation of the Treaty as to whether the freedom to provide services was complementary or subsidiary to the freedom of establishment, whether home or host country law should prevail, and whose tax rates were to be applied. The result was that it took nine years – until July 1973 – before the freedom of establishment in non-life insurance was secured.

The EU's legislative record on financial services for the transition period thus yielded a very modest harvest indeed. The main accomplishments were the two directives of 1960 and 1962 on liberalisation of capital movements, the reinsurance and non-life directives of 1964 and 1973, and a motor-insurance directive of 1972 under which policies were to provide cover across the EU.

European diplomacy's long march to the internal market

By the time of the EU summit of heads of state and government at The Hague in December 1969, the concept of cooperation between member states within the EU had prevailed over the more ambitious aims of creating a federal Europe, to which the states would be subordinate. The timetable to achieve the customs union and dismantle internal tariffs and quotas was partially completed in 1968, with the establishment of the EU's agricultural policy and the moves in the GATT to reduce the EU's external tariffs. Meanwhile, France's repeated vetoes of Britain's bid to enter the EU prompted the creation in 1961 of the European Free Trade Area (EFTA), composed of Britain, the Scandinavian countries, Finland, Austria, Switzerland and Portugal. EFTA established a small secretariat at Geneva, with the task of promoting intra-EFTA tariff reductions on manufactured goods. France also stressed the right of member states to use their veto on EU market policy, but agreed to fuse the institutions of the ECSC, the Rome Treaty and Euratom, thus creating a single Commission, Council, Parliament and European Court of Justice (ECJ) for the European Communities.

By the late 1960s the feuds over Europe's future shape between the protagonists of an Atlantic partnership, a federal Europe, or a Europe of the states had resulted in a delicate set of compromises. Europe of the late 1960s was a complex fabric of interdependent markets, and a mosaic of states cooperating in a complex of overlapping forums. The Soviet Union's control over its satellites in Eastern Europe remained precarious, based mainly on force. The communist parties of Western Europe sought to distance themselves from Moscow's policies in Eastern Europe, while making common cause with Moscow in promoting a policy of peaceful coexistence from within the Western European states. France's detachment from NATO in 1966 left Germany with a pivotal role in establishing the framework of European security, predicated on a recognition of the outcome of World War II. The United States, disillusioned with the turn of events in Western Europe, moved towards acceptance of Europe's and Germany's division, while expanding its presence in the Gulf and edging towards a deal with China to contain the Soviet Union in Asia.

At the Hague summit in 1969, Chancellor Brandt balanced his diplomatic overtures towards Moscow by backing French proposals to 'deepen' the EU through the establishment of a European Monetary Union, based on stable exchange rates. In the more turbulent currency conditions from 1968 on, member states had applied the safeguard clauses of the Treaty to restrict capital outflows, while the EU agreed on a directive – of particular concern to Germany – whereby national authorities could impose unilateral restrictions on capital inflows which jeopardised monetary stability.[26] The EU then launched a second, more serious attempt at monetary union, sketched in the Werner Plan and presented to the Council in October 1970.[27] But in August 1971, President Nixon ended the dollar's convertibility into gold. To preserve currency stability, EU leaders at their Paris summit in October 1972 sketched an ambitious programme to establish a full European economic and monetary union by 1980. Their aspirations were undermined by divergent national economic policies, and by the decision of the German Bundesbank to terminate currency intervention to support the dollar, allowing the DM to float upwards with smaller country currencies in tow. Within two years, all the major European leaders of the time were either dead or out of office.

At the Hague, Chancellor Brandt and President Pompidou had also agreed to widen the EU's membership to incorporate Britain. But British entry in effect served to strengthen the trend to a reinforcement of the Council of Ministers in EU affairs. The Commission became engaged in a never-ending series of trade negotiations with outsiders seeking to preserve market access to an enlarged EU through membership, associate status or preferential trade agreements. The negotiations, which spanned the period from 1969 to 1985, absorbed EU energies, disrupted the compromises of the 1960s on which its partially unified external trade and farm policies had been based, and altered the weighting of the EU – first to the north, with the extension of EU membership from six to nine (including Britain, Denmark and Ireland), and then to the south, following the political transitions out of dictatorships in Greece, Spain and Portugal. Greece joined in 1981, while negotiations with Spain and Portugal were concluded in March 1985. The further expansion of the EU from ten to twelve member states threatened either to bring the cumbrous EU mechanisms to a halt, or to oblige the organisation to resort to an extension of majority voting.

The summit at The Hague in December 1969 also marked a more purposeful move towards a specifically European society of states,[28] characterised by a sharing of common interests and values and by complex political and market interdependence with the rest of the world. As Germany's Ostpolitik matured, so France edged away from being the champion of state sovereignty and national independence towards being a champion of a pooled exercise of sovereignty within the institutions of the EU. German diplomacy ran in parallel, with a view to moving to state unity and national self-determination. Reconciliation of

French and German foreign policies within the EU took the form of a strengthening of intergovernmental cooperation, already exemplified in the Franco-German Treaty of 1963, which set the mould for regular consultations among EU foreign ministries.

The Hague meeting also marked the first step to establishing the summits of heads of state and government on a regular basis, leading to the creation in December 1974 of the European Council. The Council helped to incorporate the heads of state and government into the EU's business, with the Commission as the other head of a tandem governance structure. It subsequently led to direct elections to the European parliament, the launching of the European Monetary System (EMS) in March 1979, as well as the enlargement negotiations.

A central purpose of the European Council was to set a European agenda in the summits of industrialised countries, initiated at Rambouillet in November 1975. The discussions at Rambouillet confirmed the dollar's status as the world currency, and paved the way for the ratification in January 1976 of the modified Articles of Agreement of the IMF. The Special Drawing Rights (SDR), as numéraire, was to be valued not in gold but in terms of a basket of currencies where the dollar weighed one-third. Governments were to counter disorderly conditions in foreign-exchange markets essentially by giving priority to domestic price stability in their national economies. This did not preclude major subsequent swings in exchange rates, notably between the DM and the dollar. Summit efforts to reconcile divergent national economic policies ranged from the June 1978 Bonn accord – intended to reflate the German economy – to the May 1985 Bonn summit, which presented an ambitious package of agreed microeconomic measures.

One of the EU's many weaknesses was its poor economic performance. Growth rates, which stood at about 5 per cent in the 1960s, fell to 3 per cent between 1974–79 and to 1 per cent in the early 1980s. While the United States created 15 million and Japan 4 million net jobs from 1973 to the early 1980s, none were created in Europe. There were four major explanations of the phenomenon.

- One view traced the roots of chronic European unemployment to the conservative nature of macroeconomic policies pursued by the German Bundesbank, as relayed through the exchange-rate mechanism to all countries whose currencies were tied to the DM. Growth rates in the rest of Europe were thus kept far below potential.
- Another view emphasised the structural impediments to factor movements embedded in the national legislations of the member states. The wage explosion that followed the oil shock of 1973–74 was accompanied by a surge in social security expenditures and labour legislation that raised the cost to employers of hiring labour.
- A third opinion stressed the trend in the EU towards a decline in savings rates, and a switch to greater private and government consumption, which both rose relative to the United States and Japan. By the early 1980s, government outlays

in Western Europe were in the range of 45 per cent of national income, as against one-third or less in the United States and Japan.
• A fourth view traced the problem to the fall-off in corporate investment and profitability, accompanied by a decline in extra-European market shares and a weakening in the EU's market position in high-technology sectors.

The Commission's principal allies in reviving the Rome Treaty's promise of a unified EU internal market were European businesses, particularly those represented in the Round Table of European Industrialists. The time seemed ripe to challenge the national producer coalitions which had supported the unanimity rule on decisions relating to non-tariff barriers in Article 100 of the Rome Treaty in 1957. As markets expanded in scope and sophistication, these coalitions had become more heterogeneous. Some sacrifice of autonomy by member states within the bounds of the EU could strengthen its combined influence over economic developments around the world.

There was also a mix of motives in the EU member states' support for Commission proposals to finally implement the Rome Treaty's promise of a single internal market. The British government saw an opportunity to promote free-market ideals as a positive contribution to the common enterprise. The Netherlands stayed loyal to its traditional attachment to the ideal of European union. Belgium, Luxemburg and Italy looked for a more determined lead from Brussels as a means to promote reforms at home, while welcoming the culmination of Spain's lengthy entry negotiations to the EU as providing a new impetus to Community affairs. But the major stimulus to support for the Commission's aspirations came from Germany and France. The German and Italian foreign ministers, Genscher and Colombo, presented their plan for a 'European Act' to the European Parliament in November 1981. The main idea was carried over by the German Christian Democrat–Liberal coalition government, formed in March 1983 at the height of the crisis in the Atlantic Alliance over the installation of the Cruise and Pershing missiles. President Mitterrand came to Kohl's aid in his domestic struggle against the Social Democrats and, in his speech to the Bundestag, declared France's backing for the installation of the missiles.

However, President Mitterrand's domestic economic policy of extensive nationalisations, reflation and income redistribution was at odds with any forceful French lead in the EU. The moment of truth came in March 1983, when Mitterrand decided to ditch his initial policies. He opted for the franc's stabilisation within the EMS, rejecting counsel to move to national protectionism. During its Presidency of the EU in early 1983, the new government in Bonn established its EU credentials at the Stuttgart European Council, where the heads of government subscribed to a Solemn Declaration on European Union, indicating an intention to extend EU deliberations into 'the economic and political aspects of security', as well as into the cultural or foreign policy areas. Bonn made the successful completion of the Spanish entry negotiations a precondition for the release of additional funds for the EU budget. The move underscored Germany's status as Europe's prime economic and political power. It obliged member states to speed agreement on control of farm surpluses, to conclude Spain's EU entry negotiations in March 1985, and to win member-state support for the Commission's internal market programme – from which Germany had most to gain. The Genscher–Colombo plan lent its name to the Single European Act (SEA), amending the Rome Treaty, and agreed upon at the Luxemburg European Council of February 1986.

Mitterrand's substitute policy – announced in two key speeches in early 1984 at The Hague and at Strasburg – was European unity. This implied a prior agreement on agricultural policy reform, Spain's EU entry and new funding for the EU budget. French–Spanish bilateral negotiations paved the way for the conclusion of Spain's entry negotiations in March 1985. The subsequent European Council meetings witnessed the EU's relaunch. France, and French public opinion, became a champion of European integration. France's Finance Minister, Jacques Delors, who had launched the French financial system on far-reaching reforms, took over the Presidency of the Commission in January 1985.

The Single European Act, finally ratified by all member-state parliaments in June 1987, both amended the Rome Treaty and incorporated into it the institutions and practices that had already developed alongside the drawn-out negotiations. It may be seen as an expression of the Community's practice of 'cooperative federalism',[29] in that the intergovernmentalism of the European Council and EU foreign policy were incorporated officially among Community institutions. Cooperation in fiscal, monetary, as well as security issues were evoked. The first two fell expressly within the rule of unanimous voting, while European security policy was made primarily within NATO. The SEA had strengthened federalist elements in the Community. It fully associated the Commission with the proceedings on European Political Cooperation (EPC), and confirmed the SEA's status as a twin pillar alongside EPC in the elaboration of the EU's external policies. It extended majority voting in the Council of Ministers to include financial services, capital markets, and transport legislation concerning the internal market that had previously fallen solely under the unanimity rule. This opened wide areas of discretion for the Commission, which could frame policies in such a way as to bring them under the majority voting rule. A new procedure allowed the European Parliament to amend a Council position. The European Parliament also had an effective veto over new applicants for membership, and especially over the ratification of trade agreements with third countries (SEA, Articles 7 and 9).

The Act, in short, strengthened the Commission within the EU structure, and reinforced the EU as a negotiating partner for third parties. The states retained the legislative power in the Council of Ministers.

The Commission's campaign for the internal market: 1973–1988

The internal market programme was also rooted in a prolonged campaign by the Commission, as co-equal partners of the Council, to overcome the EU's stagnation following the events of 1973–74. Financial services lay at the heart of the effort. A draft directive on freedom of establishment and the provision of services presented by the Commission had finally been adopted in June 1973[30] by the Council of Ministers of the recently enlarged EU of nine, including Denmark, Ireland and the United Kingdom. But different national legislations on licensing, market access or prudential measures remained effective barriers to the creation of a common market for credit. As the Commission's directive indicated, liberalisation measures would remain without effect unless national laws were altered. Indeed, the Commission had earlier presented a draft directive in June 1972 that aimed to create a single banking market at one stroke,[31] which represented a first attempt to create an EU-wide regime for universal banks and proposed bank control by home rather than host-country authorities, together with close coordination between bank regulatory authorities of national EU credit markets. It received support in principle from Germany, the Netherlands, Belgium and Luxemburg, but was opposed by Italy and France, jealous of their discretionary powers over credit. The City of London was viscerally opposed to any EU harmonisation which would enmesh it in EU laws, biased toward German-style universal banks. The draft was withdrawn by the Commission at the end of 1973, and replaced by a new document more amenable to British susceptibilities.

In 1974, the ECJ handed down judgements whereby all financial institutions enjoyed the right to establish and provide services anywhere in the EU after the end of the transition period in January 1970. Yet this was far from fact. The EU directives of the 1970s on banking and insurance had sanctioned the right of establishment but failed to provide for the freedom of cross-frontier provision of financial services. The first non-life insurance directive came into effect in early 1976,[32] and was followed after a time-lag by the first life insurance directive, finally adopted in March 1979.[33] EU insurers could set up in another member state, but they were to be subject to the regulatory requirements of the host country, while home-country regulators retained the responsibility for ensuring the firm's solvency. These provisions severely restricted EU-wide business for London's insurers, especially Lloyd's of London, and served to protect domestic markets in France and Germany.

In December 1977, the Council adopted the First Banking Directive,[34] which provided freedom for EU banks to set up branches in member states. The objective was to facilitate the extension of Treaty freedoms. But authorisation for establishment was required of host-country authorities, who retained powers to supervise branch activities under national legislation. As all member states – with the exception of the United Kingdom – required branches to maintain endowment capital, the incentives to exploit the opportunities provided by the legislation were minimal. This was illustrated in the list of financial institutions published by the Commission in fulfilment of the terms of the First Banking Directive: of the 9,434 credit institutions recorded in the EU, 429 were classified as foreign banks, only 107 of which had their parent company based in a member state.[35] Governments proved reluctant to grant licences to other member-state banks under the Directive's terms.[36]

The main innovation flowing from these directives was to institutionalise cooperation procedures through the creation of a Bank Advisory Committee, composed of senior civil servants from the member states as well as from the Commission, and of the EU Permanent Conference of Insurance Regulators. This linked Commission and member states intimately in the initiation of legislation. An alliance for liberalisation was thus struck between the Commission and the United Kingdom and Dutch governments, both eager to open EU markets to their insurers and banks. A draft non-life insurance directive, first presented in 1975, had been shuffled around the EU institutions before being elevated in 1981 to the Council during the presidencies of the Netherlands and the United Kingdom, but no agreement could be reached. Without a legal battle, the matter seemed blocked until 1986, when the two states would resume the presidency. The British Commissioner, Christopher Tugendhat, therefore seized the opportunity offered by member states which had failed to comply with the Rome Treaty and with a 1978 directive on mutual reinsurance[37] to take France, Germany, Denmark, Ireland, Italy and Belgium to the European Court of Justice in the course of 1983 and 1984.

Coordination between EU supervisory authorities and central banks took on a new dimension with the introduction of the European Monetary System (EMS) in March 1979. The EMS represented a return to jointly-managed exchange rates, with the French franc in particular entering the DM zone. Yet restrictions on capital movements were retained under the Rome Treaty's safeguard terms, so that the EU in the late 1970s moved to open product markets under a system of restricted financial flows. In parallel, the Commission resumed tentative efforts to ease the many restrictions on national capital markets. A code of good conduct on transactions in transferable securities was introduced,[38] with a view to its serving as a framework for future national and EU legislation. Closer links were also fostered by the Commission between national capital markets.[39] The Council subsequently adopted directives in 1979,[40] 1980[41] and 1982,[42] dealing with the terms of admission, the listing of particulars, and the periodic publication of information for access to capital markets. But few parliaments had ratified them,[43] when the Commission in April 1983 issued its proposal to the Council for a broad move to financial integration, covering banking, insurance and capital markets.[44]

A central element of the Commission's thinking on opening up the internal market was encapsulated in the principle of mutual recognition and found its way into the June 1985 White Book, setting out in detail the measures to eliminate internal barriers to trade within the EU by January 1, 1993. The Commission had elaborated the principle of mutual recognition, based on an ECJ ruling of February 1979.[45] The landmark case involved Cassis de Dijon, a French liqueur manufacturer that had been excluded under the German *Branntweinmonopolgesetz* from commercialisation in the Federal Republic on account of its excessively low alcoholic content. The Court's judgement in *Rewe-Zentral* versus *Bundesmonopolverwaltung für Branntwein* was, in fact, cautious, specific and the subject of much subsequent legal debate. A further judgement in June 1980 prompted the Commission to issue a statement to the member states in October, whereby a product may be freely exported to another EU member state when it has been produced and commercialised in accordance with the regulations of the exporting country. This principle opened a chink in the states' armour of non-tariff barriers to internal trade, and provided the Commission with the legal means to challenge the previous ponderous method of harmonisation based on unanimity in the Council of Ministers.

The implication of this 'new approach' was that national norms and regulations be brought into alignment with one another. The ground rule was that national regulations could no longer serve a priori as non-tariff barriers. The multiple decisions of producers and consumers seeking to arbitrage the rents derived from different regulatory systems would substitute for the elusive search for harmonisation, and provide an incentive for governments to link their public policies to each other. In other words, the new approach was predicated on allowing businesses to exploit to the maximum the diversity of the European state system. It represented a shift towards a general policy for a federation of distinct states and national markets, rather than an effort to impose harmony as a step to a single unified state and market.

Changes in political conditions in Bonn in October 1982 and President Mitterrand's decision in March 1983 to end his experiment in nationalisation, reflation and income redistribution provided a more propitious environment for Commission initiatives. At the European Council of December 1982 in Copenhagen, the Commission submitted a report on the state of the internal market that included the proposal to liberalise financial services. At the same time, the heads of state and government agreed to create an Internal Market Council to accelerate matters. At Stuttgart in June 1983, the European Council concurred that completion of the internal market should be an urgent priority. This victory for an EU market-liberalisation strategy was confirmed at Brussels in March 1985, when the European Council called on the Commission to draw up 'a detailed programme with a specific timetable'. At Milan in June, the Italian Presidency won majority support for an intergovernmental conference to negotiate a draft treaty for European union.

The programme for completion of the internal financial services market was spelled out in the 1985 White Book presented by the Internal Market Commissioner, Lord Cockfield, to the European Council at Milan. Freedom was the principle which was to predominate in the provision of financial services. According to the White Book, 'experience has shown that relying on a strategy based totally on harmonisation would be over-regulatory, would take a long time to implement, would be inflexible and would stifle innovation'. A genuine common market could not be realised by 1992 if the Community relied exclusively on Article 100 of the Rome Treaty. The new approach, as applied to the financial services area, was therefore predicated on three key principles.

- Harmonisation would be conceived in terms of minimum requirements.
- Member states would accept the principle of mutual recognition of each others' national regulations.
- The home-country principle would prevail, whereby a business conducted in any one of the member states would be subject to home-country regulations, whatever national regulations were applied by the regulatory authorities of the host country.

This meant, in effect, that negotiations over the details of financial services liberalisation in the EU would turn around the degree of (minimal) harmonisation required and the areas of discretion left to national authorities on the basis of mutual recognition of each others' regulatory systems. The legislative process was to be guided by the concept of mutual recognition, whereby member states were to accept each others' actions within their respective jurisdictions in order to safeguard the interests of the public – notably in such matters as licensing, supervision and the restructuring of financial institutions. The Commission also emphasised the notion of a 'financial product', the home-country authorities being best placed to exercise control. Capital movements were to be liberalised, with use of the Treaty's safeguard clauses restricted to measures of last resort. Cross-border provision of financial services was to be ensured by the removal of barriers to entry in national markets. To this end, the White Book listed twenty-seven draft directives.

The SEA (Single European Act) was elaborated at the three European Councils of Brussels, Milan and Luxemburg in the course of 1985 and early 1986. Revision of the Rome Treaty had to await the states' final agreement at the Luxemburg Council of February 1986. The SEA referred to 'the progressive realisation of economic and monetary union'. Its brief reference to economic and monetary union was the result of an understanding reached between Chancellor Kohl and President Mitterrand at Luxemburg in December 1985 that France would agree to liberalise foreign-exchange controls if Germany would renew its recognition of monetary union as a goal.

Both Kohl and Prime Minister Thatcher considered liberalisation as a pre-condition to progress on the internal market. This is where they parted company. Kohl was ready to discuss monetary union. Thatcher was adamantly against it. The Act noted that the Paris summit of October 1972 had approved 'the objective of the progressive realisation of economic and monetary union', and it alluded to the Rome Treaty's Article 102a, referring to 'further development in the field of economic and monetary policy'. This major difference was compounded by the Thatcher government's proposal of an Action Programme for Employment and Growth[46] which, with Irish and Italian backing, championed the freeing of labour markets and stood in stark contrast to the Commission's preferences for social protection. It was promptly scotched by an alliance between Commission President Delors and the early 1987 Belgian Presidency.

The SEA's principal feature, though, was Article 8A, modifying Article 100 of the Rome Treaty and enshrining a commitment of the states to achieve 'a progressive establishment of the internal market by December 31, 1992'. It introduced qualified majority voting in the Council of Ministers for legislation concerning the internal market, including financial services and capital markets. This modified – but did not alter – the wording in Article 57.2, that unanimity was to be required on matters relating to 'the protection of savings, in particular the granting of credit and the exercise of the banking profession . . . . The effort of harmonisation must principally deal with the establishment of a minimum of common rules concerning the protection of users of services and supervision by the home country'.[47] The aim was also to establish rules of mutual recognition of financial techniques, to avoid standardisation by administrative means.

The Council celebrated commitment to the protection of savings by adoption on December 20, 1987 of a directive coordinating provisions for business in collective investment funds (unit trusts), initially advanced in 1976.[48] The Commission then proposed a two-stage process to free capital movements.[49] The first stage entailed modification of the directives of 1960 and 1962, and was adopted by the Council in November 1986.[50] Trade in securities was thereby eased, along with access to stock markets. The second stage, presented by Delors in October 1987, involved the implementation of Article 67 of the Rome Treaty. The directive was adopted during the Finance Ministers' Council in Luxemburg in June 1988[51] and was the central measure which Delors used to link the internal market to all aspects of the broader EU programme.

The full policy of market liberalisation was launched in 1986. The Dutch and British presidencies in 1986 cooperated closely with the Commission on pressing ahead on the internal market. Spain and Portugal's full entry to the EU was one factor prompting US diplomacy – in close alliance with the British and Dutch – to promote another round of trade negotiations in the GATT, finally agreed upon at Punta del Este, Uruguay, that September. The Uruguay Round of GATT negotiations, running in parallel to the EU's internal market programme, included financial services for the first time. In December 1986, the ECJ delivered its much-awaited judgements on insurance.[52] In essence, the Court found in favour of the cross-border provision of services, but endorsed restrictions for 'imperative reasons relating to the public interest'. The judgements provided a new legal basis for the Commission to revive the stalled programme on insurance directives, and signalled the EU insurance market was opening for business. That month, thirteen directives were adopted, indicating the acceleration of legislative activity for the internal market and freedom to provide services across the EU.[53]

The long march to implementing the unrestricted provision of services across the EU thus took much longer than the drafters of the Rome Treaty had anticipated. The main contribution of the directives of the 1970s was to sanction the right of establishment subject to host-country control, and to develop cooperative procedures for certification of suppliers. In the 1980s the home-country principle was elaborated and introduced into the EU legislation through the 1983 directive on consolidated supervision and the 1986 directive on annual and consolidated accounts for banks extended the principle of home-country control, while the ECJ's rulings ended the deadlock on insurance. A return to more stable exchange rates among EMS participants provided a propitious background to resume efforts to open up national capital markets. And that in turn required that France, Italy and Spain move to complete liberalisation of capital movements, having been unwilling to subscribe to the liberalisation measures implicit in the White Book without the Treaty's revision in the form of the SEA. Freer financial markets within the EU would have to be accompanied by moves to ensure 'the cohesion and specificity'[54] of the European financial space.

The EU's infrastructure of committees and the Financial Area

The rush of EU legislation on financial services between 1986 and 1993 was made possible by an infrastructure of committees created over the previous decades. Three permanent committees acquired prominence.

- Only the Monetary Committee was mentioned in the Rome Treaty. It was 'to report regularly' on the EU's monetary condition, and to deliver opinions, 'even on its own initiative'.[55] Member states and the Commission were to appoint two members each to the Monetary Committee, generally the head of the country's treasury and the deputy governor of its central bank. This numerical superiority of the member states' representatives in the Monetary Committee thus duplicated the primacy of the states in financial matters. Initially, its tasks were to advise on the liberalisation of capital movements, balance of payments and monetary policy. Over time, its status evolved along with the extension in scope of EU competences, and the salience of financial affairs.[56] Even so, governments continued to take policy decisions unilaterally, despite agreements in principle on consultations prior to currency realignments.
- The central role of the states was confirmed by the Council's decision in 1960 to institute periodic meetings of Finance Ministers, thereby creating the Council for Economic and Finance Ministers (ECOFIN) as a central institution in EU governance. The Commission then suggested that eventual monetary union would require permanently fixed exchange rates,[57] and a Committee of Central Bank Governors to coordinate monetary policy, alongside a Budgetary Committee to supervise economic policy.[58] On April 13, 1964 the Council adopted these institutional suggestions, as well as a broad commitment to price stability. Half of the Monetary Committee's members attend the Committee of Central Bank Governors, which meets in Basle. The

presidents of these two committees are elected by their members every one and two years, respectively.

- An Economic Policy Committee was created in 1974 out of a merger of previous committees, to deal with the EU budget in the negotiations leading up to the launch of the EMS in 1978–79, and in the debates of the early 1980s on the United Kingdom government's net contribution to EU coffers. The Monetary and Central Bank Governors Committees only emerged as key institutions with the development of the EMS, and the exigencies of daily management of the ERM. Convergence of member states' economic policy and performance on price stability provided the central understanding, which bound the small group of officials who came to constitute Europe's monetary élite.

EU negotiations during 1986–88 on the liberalisation of capital movements revealed the two committees' significance to the Commission. The Council's adoption of the directive in June 1988 on the free movement of capital could not have been secured without their sanction.[59] The committees' reports bore the Bundesbank's firm imprint. There was to be no deviation from the principle of *erga omnes*,[60] meaning no distinction between liberalisation of capital flows within the EU and free capital movement with the rest of the world. The Bundesbank also insisted on restricting access to national capital markets in order to preserve control over monetary policy. This exception to the rule of free access meant weaker-currency EU countries could argue for retaining a safeguard clause against destabilising capital flows. The two committees were to be 'closely associated' in implementing this procedure.[61] Nor was there any agreement among the member states about Germany's obligations to support other currencies in the event of speculative capital flows.

At the Madrid summit of June 1989, it was agreed to revamp the infrastructure of the two committees in preparation for the move to the first stage of monetary union on July 1, 1990. The presidency at that point passed to France, and differences between the French and German perspectives on monetary union became quickly apparent. The Commission proposed modest institutional changes to improve consultative procedures.[62] The German Finance Ministry insisted on the autonomy of a strengthened Central Bank Governors Committee, while Delors and the French Finance Ministry championed a greater role for discretionary fiscal policy. The Finance Ministers in November 1989 agreed to revise the 1964 measure creating the Central Bank Governors Committee, and the 1974 procedures to facilitate 'convergence'. The new measures to improve the coordination of economic and monetary policy among the EU Twelve were to come into effect on July 1, 1990. Finance Ministers were to meet twice a year, with the president of the Central Bank Governors Committee in attendance to analyse the EU's economic condition. The Monetary Committee would discuss multilateral surveillance of each country's policies. These guidelines added little and concealed much. The central ambiguity was the division of powers between central banks and finance ministries.

For Delors, the creation of a common financial space was to be accompanied by closer cooperation between finance ministries, central banks and bank supervisory authorities.[63] This had already been institutionalised in the first banking directive of December 1977, with the creation of the Bank Advisory Committee, composed of three representatives from central banks, bank supervisory authorities and relevant ministries of the member states, and three representatives from the Commission. Like the Monetary Committee, the Bank Advisory Committee elected its senior officers – who have invariably come from the boards of the central banks – and many of their personnel are interchangeable. The Bank Advisory Committee meets twice a year, and is intimately involved in making EU legislation. It serves as an additional sounding-board for ideas and a debating-forum for policy initiatives.[64] Its main work has focused on the development of prudential measures to strengthen control over EU financial institutions. In turn, the Committee is supported in an advisory capacity by the European Banking Federation, which brings together the national banking federations.

The EU Council and the Bank Advisory Committee ensured that powers of implementation of new banking and financial laws would stay with the states. On 13 July 1987, the Council decided[65] that powers could be exercised by the Commission alone, or by the Commission with the help of a committee according to one of three procedures. The third of these procedures applied to financial services and entailed a regulatory committee. There were two procedural variants, which would follow from the Council's failure to vote on a contentious measure after a period of three months. In variant (a) the Commission's policy option is adopted. In variant (b) the Council decides against by a simple majority of votes. The Council regularly preferred variant (b), the result of which was to confirm the Bank Advisory Committee's powers in the implementation of the own-funds directive;[66] in licensing procedures connected with the second banking directive;[67] and in supervision of the banking-solvency ratio directive.

Once the main elements of the new EU banking regime were in place to serve as a precedent, the Commission felt able to propose a regulatory committee for insurance. The Commission proposed an 'a' category committee, but the Internal Market Council voted in December 1991[68] a 'b' category for the new Insurance Committee. Its functions were defined as similar to those of the Bank Advisory Committee, but the Commission's powers were even more constrained. It presides over the Insurance Committee, composed of delegations from national federations of insurance companies, but may not formulate implementational measures unless the Committee votes in favour on the basis of a qualified majority. If the Commission continues to disagree, it may submit a proposal for the Council to vote on a qualified majority. Either way, a minority coalition of states could block legislation.

Agreement proved even more difficult to achieve in the case of securities markets. Investment services were at the core of competing interests and traditions in European capitalism. A Contact Committee between stock-exchange regulators had been formed in 1978, with a view to organising a network of supervisory associations. The Commission followed this up with a colloquium in 1980 titled 'Towards a European Stock Exchange', and started working with the recently created Committee of Stock Exchanges, which later created a Capital Market Committee to 'influence the design of the legislative framework for the European capital market'.[69] A draft investment services directive was finally presented in December 1988 and then modified in 1990. Commissioner Leon Brittan then suggested an *ad-hoc* reflection group to find a compromise. The Council adopted legislation in the course of 1992, but the powers of the committee proposed to assist the Commission were advisory only, and essentially limited to the mutual exchange of information.[70] Its formation required the definition of tasks between existing authorities within the member states and the development of a common language on which to base future legislation for the EU.

All this institutional activism prompted a proliferation of umbrella organisations. Commercial, savings, cooperative and mortgage banks came under the wing of the COC – the Comité des Organisations Professionelles du Crédit – instituted in Brussels with the help of the Commission in 1979. Like the insurance and stock-exchange lobbies, the COC split along both national and functional lines, leaving public officials far-reaching discretion to modify legislation, preserve national powers, promote domestic reforms, or export legislation applied in banking to insurance or investment services. There were also the consumer lobbies and Eurofiet (the umbrella union organisation for financial services), the former favouring and the latter wary of financial deregulation fervour.[71] Lobbies also offered their expertise, used their combined blocking power to delay unwanted legislation and strengthened cross-border alignments to underpin coalitions in the Council, or to appeal to a broader public in favour of financial stability. Given the internationalisation of markets, they were also tied into such organisations as the International Federation of Stock Exchanges (IFSE) and the International Organisation of Securities Commissions (IOSCO).

The EU's infrastructure of committees was rooted in the bureaucracies of the member states. They were therefore tied into the broader span of international organisations, such as the United Nations (UN), the BIS, the Council of Europe, the OECD or the GATT, where the Commission was also represented in its prime Treaty role as sole representative of the EU in external trade relations under Article 113. Alongside the umbrella organisations in Brussels were the member states' diplomatic delegations in Brussels, and the embassies and delegations from the United States, Japan and the EFTA countries. Conversely, the Community was represented by its own delegations in Washington, DC and in Tokyo, as well as its delegation in Geneva – which was assisted by a committee appointed by the Council and composed of national officials of the member states to track the Commission in the exercise of its trade negotiation powers.[72] Bank regulators and the umbrella organisations were the most solidly anchored by the time negotiations on the internal market got under way. At the other end of the spectrum were financial services, into which banks, insurance companies and investment houses and their regulators were crowding under the dual impact of deregulation of domestic markets and the clear trends toward global-isation.

A brief history of the European Financial Area

With such a preponderant lock of the EU member states on the legislative and implementation process, there could be little surprise that the negotiations over market-opening measures were often very heated indeed. Bank regulators formed a confederal regime. Insurance regulators lagged, but edged away from purely national regimes. Investment services proved the least susceptible to EU institution-building, being controlled first and foremost by public officials, with lobbies in an often national supportive role.

National institutions, traditions and interests remained vigorous, as exempli-fied by the EU states' resistance to abandon powers in matters of taxation, money or defence. In each country there were strong currents of resistance to a policy of internal market liberalisation which could be readily stoked by ambi-tious projects for union that threatened to undermine national identities. Major divisions between EU member states plagued the development of common foreign and trade policies *vis-à-vis* the rest of the world.

In opposition to the states' reservations was their commitment in harness with the Commission to achieve the initial programme outlined in the White Book and the SEA. The new vision for the EU was above all a political programme to associate the twelve member states in a common task for the future. As in the past, the protagonists of a European federation or of a Europe of the states coop-erating together could not agree about the ultimate goal. The EU was thus embarked on an open-ended process, indeterminate in outcome, inviting all par-ticipants to fashion the future to their own distinct preferences. Initially, the process was restricted by the programme's focus on business. As the Commission stated, 'a key condition of success is the credibility of the process, the assurance that in the medium term the environment will undergo a transformation that will oblige all firms . . . to adopt a European strategy'.[73] In practice, businesses were invited to consider that, even if the programme was not implemented in all its legislative guises, competitors could assume that it would be and thereby required risks to be taken as if the internal market was a near-certainty. Not least, the whole programme became a media phenomenon, with a date – 1992 – holding the promise that something significant was going to happen by December 31 of that year. It thereby resurrected the Community method of writing a detailed timetable, holding over the heads of governments a deadline to which all manner of expectations could be pegged.

By 1993, the rules governing the EU market for financial services were to a large extent on the Community books. With liberalisation of capital movements serving as a catalyst linking all domains of financial services and monetary union, the EU process spun a seamless web of legislation.

- Freedom of capital movements was seen as one of the main conditions for the creation of the internal market, in that its achievement would assure 'an optimal allocation of European savings'. With the adoption in June 1988 of the directive on the liberalisation of capital movements, all barriers were to be dropped from July 1990, with escape clauses, and delays for Ireland and Spain until 1993, and Portugal and Greece until 1995. Liberalisation of capital movements pressured governments to bring tax levels and structures more into line, which proved particularly controversial in view of the distinct tax regimes of the member states.
- Lord Cockfield presented the flagship second banking coordination directive[74] in January 1988. It received its first hearing in Council in November, at the height of controversy over reciprocity clauses on treatment of subsidiaries from non-member countries. That was resolved in April 1989, involving a deal on the content of reciprocity and a key flanking directive on own-funds.[75] Freedom of establishment subject to the surveillance of the host country's authorities was already in place. In June 1989, the Commission moved to a liberal definition of the single Community banking licence, whereby an accredited institution in one country would be free to set up and conduct business in all other member states. Foreign banks already installed inside the EU would be subject to the same rules as home-country institutions. While this opened the door to US and Japanese banks in the EU, the Commission's position was that EU financial institutions setting up in foreign markets would be supported in demands for equivalent treatment to home-country firms.
- The own funds and solvency[76] directives provided the necessary harmonisation of bank supervision standards and introduced mutual recognition of licensing procedures. The Second Banking Directive (SBCD) was finally adopted in December 1989. Further changes were made on consolidated accounting[77] in order to accommodate bank groups whose parents were not credit establishments, and recommendations put forward in 1986 for banks to limit large exposures were modified into a more binding directive[78] so as to avoid contagion of risk in the event of a bank failure. The collapse in 1991 of the Bank of Credit and Commerce International (BCCI) drew attention to the problems of supervising a banking business with stated assets of $20 billion, branches operating in over seventy countries, and holding companies in Luxemburg and the Cayman Islands. The operating leadership was located in London, and the principal shareholders in Abu Dhabi. The BCCI affair prompted the Community to enact legislation against money-laundering[79] in the hope of promoting closer coordination in the struggle against organised crime, drugs and terrorism.
- The insurance fraternity proved less well organised than the bankers. It took until June 1991 to agree on annual and consolidated accounting standards.[80] Insurance brokers had to rest content with an inadequate 1976 directive[81] on cross-border services. The Council finally voted for an insurance committee in December 1991, fourteen years after the bankers had acquired theirs. Even so, the directive on non-life insurance, adopted in June 1988, established a more

open insurance market, accompanied by protection for consumers. The Commission then promulgated a second directive on life insurance, voted by the Council in November 1990,[82] which drew on the freedom of investors to place their funds anywhere in the EU. The Council voted similar directives for motor insurance, providing coverage across the whole EU, closer coordination of guarantee funds, and more security for small policyholders than for 'large risks'. In late 1989, the Commission launched a 'third generation' of insurance directives on the basis of principles elaborated in the SBCD. This led to the adoption of the third life insurance directive in June 1992 and the third non-life insurance directive in November 1992. No agreement was reached on pensions, and the Commission's draft directive was shelved in 1994.

- Financial services proved the least amenable to legislative activism. Trust between Europe's financial centres was a scarce commodity. Competition prevailed over cooperation. Tax regimes differed. Ideas diverged about the role of capital markets. When the Council adopted the directive on collective investment instruments in December 1985,[83] only Denmark and the Netherlands had implemented the earlier EU legislation of 1979, 1980 and 1982.[84] Fears of a freer market in collective investment instruments also prompted a number of amendments before its introduction in October 1989. The draft investment services directive, presented by the Commission in December 1988,[85] was finally adopted in December 1992. It was accompanied by a battle royal over the capital adequacy of investment firms, as well as rules concerning the issuance of bonds, insider trading, and transmission of information between financial centres. Disputes spilled over into policies covering mergers and acquisitions, competition law and social policy.

- Freeing up of continental markets for corporate control was to be furthered by many of the measures included in the Commission's financial services proposals. These included agreed standards on banks' minimal capital, disclosure rules for major shareholders, and limits on banks' stakes in non-financial firms. Financial liberalisation pointed to the need for an EU-wide competition policy. Commission proposals, held up in Council for fifteen years, were renewed in 1987 as the transborder merger wave gathered force on the back of the global stock-market boom. The main thrust of the Commission's position was to ask for powers to vet mergers in advance in order to enforce EU competition law, and also to oppose national discrimination against share purchases by investors from other parts of the EU.

- The Commission presented its proposal for a European Social Charter in September 1988, laying out principles for employment policy, free movement of workers, training and labor participation rights. The latter was the most divisive, and lay at the heart of the perennial debates on a European Company Statute to coexist with national company laws. Management would be able to choose between three formulas: (a) the German co-determination model; (b) the French practice of a 'comité d'entreprise'; and (c) a collective-bargaining model.

So what caused the prolonged delay between the Rome Treaty in 1957 and the 1986–93 legislation on a single market in financial services? An initial answer points to new directions taken in Bonn and Paris, following the switch in Bonn in late 1982–83 from a liberal–social democrat to a liberal–Christian democrat coalition, and President Mitterrand's *grand tournant* of March 1983 when he opted for the franc to stay in the European Exchange Rate Mechanism (ERM). The decision ended his short-lived experiment to harness the inherited state-led credit system to a policy of economic expansion, and opened the way to extensive financial market reforms. Chancellor Kohl's new government embarked on a pro-business platform to shift financial resources back from the government to the private sector. In the United Kingdom, Prime Minister Thatcher's radical government launched 'the City revolution',[86] following the decisive victory of the Conservative Party in the June 1983 general election. Currency misalignments combined with high interest rates had killed off companies at an alarming rate across Europe, and European savings were flowing to the United States in search of higher returns.

Delays in creating an internal market for financial services in the end stemmed from their political sensitivity in each of the member states. When the Rome Treaty was negotiated the financial services industry stood at the heart of national politics, too closely identified with national ambitions and national sovereignty to be lightly tampered with. National financial systems were the product of Europe's history in the early twentieth century, when savings in large part came from the wealthier classes, who placed deposits in the commercial banks or invested in securities markets. The mutual savings banks and cooperatives serviced the farm, small-business or working-class communities, and accounted only for a fraction of total banking activity. But the two world wars demonstrated that financial systems could be hitched to state purposes while savings were decimated by inflation, notably in Germany and France. The banking acts of 1934 and 1941 in both countries served as the foundation for legislation in the post-war decades that protected national financial markets, allowed for bank financing of reconstruction, and later of corporate expansion. Insurance markets were even more protected, with both French and German law making it a criminal offence for insurance policies to be sourced abroad. Securities issues supplied only a fraction of corporate funds in both countries, and served mainly to finance government needs. As international business expanded, 'offshore' markets were created with government encouragement in London and Luxemburg to circumvent national regulations. Commission proposals for a financial area were thus a bid to shift from national regulatory regimes to an EU-wide regime.

This shift could not have been accomplished without the maturing of Europe's society of states. After the fallow years of EU integration in the 1960s, the states associated the Commission, the ECJ and then the European Parliament in a complex polity, composed figuratively of a number of circles, linked one to another. At the centre was the Franco-German relationship, structured institutionally around the 1963 Treaty and the European Council. The second layer was composed of the member states and the EU's institutions. The third layer was composed of the Council of Europe, the Helsinki Accords on European security and cooperation, and the UN. The fourth layer was formed by the BIS, the OECD, the GATT and NATO in which the member states were variously represented, alongside the United States, Canada, Japan and much of the rest of the world. The 'relaunch' of the EU in the early 1980s was carried out against the complex dynamics and relationships built into this polity. The Commission proposals for a financial services would not have been possible without the jurisprudence of the ECJ, the demands by central banks for consolidated accounting and capital adequacy filtered through the BIS, the build-up of the EU's infrastructure of committees, or the internationalisation of financial flows, itself related to the foreign and domestic policies of the major industrialised states.

In all areas, filtering a market policy through a multi-state political system proved an arduous undertaking. As the legislative train slowed after 1993, more sober assessments could be made. The proclaimed objective of the White Book had been to facilitate cross-border business. But bank transfers between countries were reckoned to cost anywhere from ten to twenty times more than domestic transfers,[87] prompting the Commission to launch a programme which the professionals reckoned would take up to ten years to implement.[88] Regulations covering investment services were condemned by Knud Sorenson, President of the European Banking Federation, 'as likely to prove very difficult to implement in the coming years'.[89] Not least, the gaps and deficiencies of the regulatory framework became evident before the ink had dried on the EU's legislation. The harsh verdict of the secretary-general of the Banking Federation, Umberto Burani, was that the home-country principle – supposedly the centrepiece of the financial services programme – 'has been introduced in no legislation'.[90]

The three EU financial services initiatives were launched prior to the fall of the Berlin Wall on November 9, 1989, when European affairs were conducted within the familiar context inherited from World War II and the *de-facto* post-war settlement hinging on the presence of the United States in the heart of Europe. But they were negotiated as Germany moved to state unity, and as the competition among wartime allies for the loyalty of the German people became more acute. Gorbachev's common European home competed as a vision for the future of a neutral and non-nuclear Germany with Reagan's vision of a world free of nuclear weapons and Washington's iron will for a Germany bound into NATO. In the course of 1990, the familiar dialectics between East and West, the two Germanies and the two Europes gave way to an unfamiliar landscape of a wider Europe and a united Germany. The military threat faded, to be replaced by the multiple disorders on Europe's expanding periphery that accompanied the collapse of the party-states. With the disappearance of the Soviet Union, Western unity was challenged as familiar landmarks vanished.

Yet the ambition to achieve 'an ever closer union' within the EU was driven by a powerful combination of state and corporate interests. In the past, efforts at

European integration had become ensnared in the toils of debate between the supporters of a Europe of the states and the champions of a federal or suprana-tional Europe. Little had been achieved relative to the promise. The novelty of the SEA was that the member states agreed to concentrate on achieving a unified internal market by mutual recognition of their diverse ways of conducting busi-ness. Simply doing things differently would no longer be an excuse for protec-tion. The objective was to open up national markets, and – according to the calculations in the Cecchini report popularising studies undertaken for the Commission – would help to 'raise the Community's GDP by 4% to 7%'.[91] The implications were immense. The EU's force of attraction had pulled Britain, and then Spain into its orbit. Austria, Finland and Sweden joined in 1995. The EU – as the inner core of Western Europe – accounted for 45 per cent of world trade. Add to that the EU's declared ambition to move to a single currency by the year 1999 at the latest, and there could be no longer any hiding the fact of Europe's bid to become a world power on a footing of near-equality with the United States.

Notes

1 'Communication de la Commission au Conseil sur l'intégration financière de la Communauté', COM (83) 207, April 1983.
2 Thomas Bourke, 'EC–Japan Relations 1985–93: The impact of foreign direct invest-ment on regional political integration', doctoral thesis, European University Institute, Florence, September 1995.
3 See Ragnar Nurske, *International Currency Experience* (New York: League of Nations, 1944).
4 Cited in Ernst H. van der Beugel, *From Marshall Aid to Atlantic Partnership: European Integration as a Concern of American Foreign Policy* (Amsterdam: Elsevier, 1966), p. 51.
5 Cited in Peter Marion Jones, *The Fifteen Weeks* (New York: Harcourt, 1955), p. 22.
6 For an early account, see Finn B. Jensen and Ingo Walter, *The Common Market* (Philadelphia, PA: J. P. Lippincott, 1965).
7 Hans O. Schmitt, 'Capital Markets and the Unification of Europe', *World Politics*, Vol. 20, January 1968, pp. 228–44.
8 Article 3(a).
9 Article 8.1.
10 Article 57.2.
11 Article 58.
12 Article 61.2.
13 Article 54.1.
14 Article 67.1.
15 Article 68.1.
16 Article 107.2.
17 Article 105.
18 Article 107.2.
19 Article 109.1.

20 Journal Officiel (henceforth J.O.) 43, 12.7.1960.

21 J.O. 9, 22.11.1963.

22 J.O. 36/62, 15.1.1962.

23 J.O. 32/62, 15.1.1962.

24 European Economic Community, Memorandum of the Commission on the Action Program of the Community for the Second Stage (Brussels, October 24, 1962), p. 67.

25 *The Economist,* July 4, 1964.

26 J.O. LO91, 18.4.1972.

27 EC Commission (1970), 'Economic and Monetary Union in the Community' (Werner Report), *Bulletin of the European Communities,* Supplement No. 7.

28 Hedley Bull, *The Anarchical Society: A Study of Order in World Politics* (London: Macmillan, 1980).

29 Simon Bulmer and Wolfgang Wessels, *The European Council: Decision-Making in European Politics* (London: Macmillan, 1987).

30 J.O. L194, 16.7.1973.

31 Paolo Clarotti, 'La Coordination des législations bancaires', *Revue du Marché Commun,* No. 254, February 1982, pp. 68–88.

32 J.O. L228, 16.8.1973.

33 J.O. L63, 13.3.1974.

34 77/780 J.O. L322/30, 17.12.1977.

35 J.O. C296, 16.11.1981.

36 Information P, 25.4.1985.

37 J.O. L151, 7.6.1978. The directive sought to reserve mutual insurance to industrial risks, defined as risks 'which require by their nature and importance the participation of several insurers for their guarantee'. France and other member states used this absence of precision to unilaterally fix the threshold figures of mutual insurance.

38 J.O. L212/37, 20.8.1977.

39 CE Informations, 15.1.1980; 8.12.1980.

40 J.O. L66, 16.3.1979.

41 J.O. L100, 17.4.1980.

42 J.O. L48, 20.2.1982.

43 CE Note d'Information, June 1983.

44 COM (83) 207, April 1983.

45 See Christian W. A. Timmerman, 'La Libre Circulation des Marchandises' in *Trente Ans de Droit Communautaire* (Collection 'Perspectives Européennes', Brussels: Commission des CE, 1982), pp. 283–5, 295–6. Also Jean Claude Masclet, 'Les articles 30, 36 et 100 du Traité CEE à la lumière de l'arret "Cassis de Dijon", Cour de Justice des CE, 20 Février 1979', *Revue trimestrielle de Droit Européen,* No. 4, 1980, pp. 611–34; A. Mattera, 'L'arret "Cassis de Dijon": une nouvelle approche pour la réalisation et le bond fonctionnement du marché intérieur', *Revue du Marché Commun,* No. 241, November 1980, pp. 505–14.

46 Chris Brewster and Paul Teague, *European Community Social Policy: Its Impact on the UK* (London: Institute of Personnel Management, 1989), pp. 94–9; 'Résolution du Conseil du 22 décembre 1986 concernant un programme d'action pour la croissance de l'emploi' (86/C 340/02).

47 'Programme for the Liberalisation of Capital Movements' COM (86) 292 final, 23.5.1986.

48 J.O. C171, 26.7.1976.

49 COM (86) 292 final, 23.5.1986.

50 J.O. L332, 26.11.1986.

51 J.O. L178, 8.7.1988.

52 220/83 (Commission, United Kingdom, Netherlands/France, Italy, Belgium, Ireland); 252/83 (Commission, Netherlands, United Kingdom/Denmark, Belgium, Ireland); 205/84 (Commission, Netherlands, United Kingdom/Federal Republic, Belgium, Denmark, France, Ireland, Italy); 206/84 (Commission, Netherlands, United Kingdom/Ireland, Belgium, Denmark, France).

53 The directive on consolidated accounts for banks served as a precedent for a similar draft directive for insurance: J.O. C131, 18.4.1987.

54 COM (86) 292 final, 23.5.1986.

55 Article 105.2.

56 Andreas Krees, 'The Monetary Committee of the European Community', *Kredit Und Kapital*, Vol. 20, No. 2, 1987, p. 266.

57 European Economic Community, Memorandum of the Commission on the Action Program of the Community for the Second Stage, p. 67.

58 *Bulletin of the European Economic Community*, Supplement, July 1963, pp. 3–4.

59 CE Informations, 15.7.1986.

60 *Europolitique,* No. 1401, April 30, 1988.

61 Vassili Lelakis, 'La libération complete des mouvements de capitaux au sein de la Communauté', *Revue du Marché Commun*, No. 320, September–October, 1988, pp. 441–9.

62 *Europolitique,* No. 1525, September 23, 1989.

63 *Europolitique,* No. 1303, October 31, 1987.

64 Tomasso Padoa-Schioppa, president of the Bank Advisory Committee, presented the official report and argument for the internal market in *Le grand marché unique: efficiacité, stabilité, équité* (Paris: Economica, 1987).

65 J.O. L197, 18.7.1987.

66 *Europolitique,* No. 1436, December 14, 1988; *Les Echos,* December 13, 1988; *Europolitique,* No. 1481, March 18, 1989.

67 *Wall Street Journal*, June 20, 1989.

68 J.O. L374, 13.12.1991.

69 Rudiger von Rosen, executive vice-chairman of the German Stock Exchange to the Mid-Atlantic Club of New York, April 29, 1989, 'The Future of the European Stock Exchange System Approaching 1992'.

70 Title VI, 'Authorities Responsible for Authorization and Supervision', in the Investment Sources Directive (ISD), J.O. L141/43, 11.6.1993; Article 9 in the Capital Adequacy Directive (CAD), J.O. L141, 11. 6. 1993.

71 *Europolitique,* No. 1375, January 27, 1988.

72 Gérard Nafilyan, 'La coordination au sein du GATT', in Constantin Stephanou (ed.), *La Communauté et ses Etats membres dans les Enceintes Internationales* (Paris: PUF, 1985), pp. 38–52.

73 Economie Européenne, Commission des Communautés Européennes, *1992: la nouvelle économie européenne*, No. 35, March 1988, p. 31.

74 J.O. L386, 30.12.1989.

75 J.O. L124, 5.5.1989.

76 J.O. L386, 30.12.1989.

77 J.O. C315, 14.12.1990.

78 J.O. C123, 9.5.1991.
79 J.O. L166, 28.6.1991.
80 J.O. L374, 31.12.1991.
81 J.O. L26, 31.1.1977.
82 J.O. L330, 29.11.1990.
83 J.O. L375, 31.12.1985.
84 *La Tribune de l'Expansion*, November 20, 1985.
85 COM (88) 778 final-doc., C.3–47/89.
86 Maximilian Hall, *The City Revolution: Causes and Consequences* (London: Macmillan, 1987); W. A. Thomas, *The Securities Market* (London: Philip Allan, 1989).
87 *Europolitique,* No. 1803, October 14, 1992.
88 'Interview avec Umberto Burani, Secrétaire Générale sortant de la Fédération Bancaire', *Europolitique,* No. 1858, May 12, 1993.
89 *Europolitique,* No. 1851, April 17, 1993.
90 *Ibid.*
91 Cited in Jacques Delors, préface to *1992: Le Défi, Nouvelles données économiques de l'Europe sans frontières* (Paris: Flammarion, 1988), p. 34.

2

Politics and economics of European macroeconomic convergence

European states have never found ready agreement on the appropriate exchange-rate regime for their interdependent economies. The longest period of European monetary stability lasted for about four decades prior to the outbreak of war in 1914, when the major powers subscribed to a gold standard. Attempts to reintroduce a gold-based regime after 1918 foundered on turbulent post-war conditions. After 1945, the US in effect provided the anchor to the international financial system, which was run along the principles agreed on at the Bretton Woods conference in 1944. But divergent economic policies across the major trading industrial countries set in around the mid-1960s, leading to a withdrawal of the US from its self-appointed role. European efforts to maintain a regional zone of monetary stability reasserted themselves time and again, through failure after failure, from the brief attempt at monetary union in the early 1970s, through the Bremen summit of 1978 and the Maastricht Treaty of February 1992. These were accompanied by the emergence of a massive German trade surplus, and the Bundesbank's *de-facto* role as central bank of Europe.

The following sections examine the pre-1971 history and performance of European exchange-rate policies; discuss the preconditions for a stable exchange-rate regime; comment on the emergence of Germany's trade surpluses; then analyse the two decades from the failure of the attempt at monetary union in the early 1970s to the creation of the EMS in March 1979, and the prolonged period of the 'hard franc', wherein the French government rejected Bundesbank requests to revalue the DM within the ERM parities. This lasted until the currency crises of 1992 and 1993.

Negotiations about the 'accompanying measures' to the internal market – as monetary union, labour-market policy and EU foreign and security policy came to be termed – were opened in early 1986 and culminated in the Maastricht Treaty. They are discussed in Chapter 3. As in the negotiations for the European financial area and in the post-1971 conduct of exchange-rate policy – the focus of the first two chapters of this book – different state interests and preferences were injected into the search for monetary and political union.

From the gold standard to the breakdown of the Bretton Woods system

In retrospect, the longest period of relative stability in exchange rates lasted from the early 1870s until the outbreak of World War I in August 1914. Great Britain returned to full convertibility of sterling into gold at the end of the Napoleonic wars, and had its position confirmed as the prime international financial power by the combined effects of the policy of free trade, its head-start in industrialisation, the growth of an open financial centre in London and abundant capital available for investment around the world. The newly created German Empire adopted gold as its monetary unit in the early 1870s, and moved off a bi-metallic standard that included silver. The resulting sale of silver undermined the French-led Latin Monetary Union, and brought the French government around to suspending silver coinage in 1878. The United States and Austria-Hungary joined the gold standard the following year, and Russia did so as well in 1893. The major states in the global system prevailing at the time thereby subscribed to a common regime, which in principle ensured a guarantee of convertibility between gold and domestic currencies at fixed rates, and a free market for gold imports and exports. Gold flows compensated movements in other categories of national balances of payments, and contracted or expanded domestic money supplies, prices and incomes.

This prolonged period of stability in Europe prior to 1914 acquired mythical proportions in the turbulent post-war years. The protagonists of a return to pre-war conditions emphasised the 'automaticity' of a regime which had ensured the rapid expansion of trade and investment, with minimal interference by governments.[1] After 1918, however, trade and payments were hampered by the severe dislocations of war, budgetary imbalances, discord over debt repayments, and a patchwork of misaligned currencies. Central banks acquired the habit of holding their reserves in foreign exchange as well as in gold, and this cut the link between reserves and domestic money supplies, while providing easy credit for those countries, such as Britain, whose currency was widely used abroad as official reserves.

The precarious edifice of post-war reconstruction collapsed in the years 1929–31, when the contraction of credit in the US markets spread to Germany and central Europe. At the London World Economic Conference of June 1933, France sought to restore an unbiased monetary standard before removing trade barriers. Britain wanted to restore freer trade as a prerequisite to a stable international monetary regime. President Roosevelt dealt the conference a mortal blow in his administration's statement that countries were better advised to give priority to their own economies than to fixed currency values.

In 1945 the US, as sole world power and with European acquiescence, instituted a gold-exchange standard under Bretton Woods rules which consecrated the gold-linked dollar as the world's principal reserve instrument and trading currency. As long as the US was ready to have the dollar function as the anchor of the system's stability, the European states could reconstruct their economies, restore external convertibility, and expand into the high-growth period of the 1960s. Tariff reduction transformed Western Europe into a far more open economy. Cheap oil stoked world growth, and extended the dollar's primacy as the key currency. But growing balance of payments disequilibria and increasingly frequent currency revaluations, combined with cross-border liberalisation of financial transactions, suggested that the preconditions for a durable fixed exchange-rate regime were increasingly being violated.[2]

Cautious fiscal and monetary policies were slowly abandoned in favour of more ambitious plans to stimulate growth. The 1948 currency reform in West Germany and the realignment of European currencies in 1949 laid the stable domestic conditions for Germany's subsequent expansion. Between 1950 and 1969, the accumulated German balance of payments surplus amounted to DM180 billion.[3] Once the EPU had been put aside in 1958, the Federal Republic's permanent trade surpluses in Europe could no longer be offset by official recycling mechanisms. In parallel, Europe shifted from the dollar scarcity of the immediate post-war years to a massive dollar overhang as the United States moved to overall deficit in its balance of payments. One way of reducing the transatlantic and intra-European trade imbalances was to stimulate demand in surplus countries, and the OEEC proved an appropriate forum for disseminating the gospel of stimulative deficit spending. Governments proved attentive, as evidenced by Bonn's adoption of a Stability and Growth Law in 1967, empowering the government to plan for expansionist growth beyond the one-year fiscal cycle written into the Federal Republic's constitution. Electoral shifts across Europe brought centre-left parties to power. Budgets slipped into permanent deficit, and inflation rates ratcheted upwards. These strains on national markets were duly translated into pressures on exchange rates.

Governments countered growing competition on international markets by elaborating national industrial policies. High rates of employment shifted the balance of power in labour markets away from management towards trade unions. Governments conceded a host of benefits for people in work, providing disincentives for employers to hire. Parties across the political spectrum demanded a greater state role in credit allocation, worker codetermination in industrial and financial enterprises, or wage-earner funds run by trade unions. Union membership expanded, along with militancy with respect to higher wages. With corporate profits falling as tariffs declined, European states began to promote 'national champions', notably in high-technology sectors. Government procurement was used as a means to defray research and development costs and to keep national corporations in business. Cross-shareholding between companies was fostered to act as a barrier to foreign takeovers. Funding for national governments and corporations was typically shifted away from fiscal budgets to captive national capital markets. Meanwhile, the Eurodollar markets provided abundant sources of funds for multinational corporations, which governments scrambled to attract through tax holidays or interest-rate subsidies.

International trade negotiations over politically sensitive agricultural markets became acrimonious. The United States in 1955 refused to have agricultural products included in GATT negotiations. This opened the way for France, under President de Gaulle, to take the lead in a continental peasant coalition to establish a protectionist agricultural policy that threatened to exclude US farm exports from the lucrative West German and other EU markets. De Gaulle used US demands for trade liberalisation to push through French policy to establish a Common Agricultural Policy (CAP).[4] Within the EU, France forcefully used its veto right to trade an opening of markets for manufactured goods in exchange for German implementation of the CAP. This entailed the establishment of common farm prices, EU preference for local producers, a common farm budget, and provisions for export subsidies on third markets. The key cereal price was established below the cost of production in Germany, but considerably above French levels. The result in the longer term was to have output grow faster than consumption, moving the EU towards self-sufficiency by the end of the 1970s. Fear of exclusion from a continental trading bloc drove Britain to sacrifice the Commonwealth agricultural system. Sterling, which had held its parity against the dollar since 1949, was devalued in 1967.

The 1960s also witnessed a replay of the late 1920s, when the Bank of France had objected to the expansion of national currencies in foreign-exchange reserves as inflationary.[5] The continental European states, in comfortable surplus, urged Britain and the United States to reduce domestic consumption, while the latter sought to reduce EC trade discrimination against their exports. As neither side was ready to concede, dollars and sterling accumulated in central bank reserves and irrigated the nascent offshore currency markets in London. In February 1965, de Gaulle attacked the whole monetary system as highly inflationary, and called for a return to payments discipline based on agreed rules.[6] The Anglo-American response was to push for an increase in world liquidity through the creation of Special Drawing Rights (SDRs) for central banks on the IMF. But the Anglo-American payments deficits continued, with consumption in the United States fuelled by budget deficits, compounded by expenditures on the Vietnam War. The war's unpopularity was gauged by President Johnson's refusal to ask Congress to finance the military effort through taxation. Attempts by the US Federal Reserve to manage the economy through manipulation of interest rates only served to accentuate flows in and out of national monetary systems. France began converting its dollar holdings into gold, while Germany desisted after US warnings against following the French example.

Monetary diplomacy in the 1960s gave the BIS a further lease of life, after laying the EPU to rest in 1958. At its monthly meetings, the Western world's central bank governors discussed means to preserve exchange-rate parities and deal with the growing volume of capital flows across frontiers. The EU's Monetary and Central Bank Governors Committees were little more than accessories. The main transactions were between each of the member states and the United States.

With its gold stock shrinking further, the United States in March 1968 arranged with its major European partners – in France's absence – to signal the *de-facto* non-convertibility of dollars into gold. Capital flows became more precipitate, moving Western Europe away from fixed parities embodied in a series of currency realignments between the pound sterling, the franc and the DM in the years 1967 to 1969. European governments faced an uncomfortable series of choices between: (1) absorbing dollars in reserves at the risk of inflating the domestic money supply; (2) recycling the dollars into US Treasury bonds, and into the burgeoning Eurodollar markets; or (3) having their currencies revalued either through negotiations or by letting the international markets set the price.

The whole edifice was brought down in August 1971, when Richard Nixon refused to have the US economy contract and announced the dollar's non-convertibility into gold. The end of the gold-exchange standard was not followed by floating rates, but rather by widened intervention margins (from 1 per cent to 2½ per cent on either side of the parity rate) under the Smithsonian Agreement, which lasted until 1973. Even before that too collapsed, the Europeans set about creating a regional fixed-rate regime, beginning in 1972.

As noted in the previous chapter, the Werner Report in 1970 had already proposed creation of a single European currency, complete liberalisation of capital movements, freedom of establishment for financial institutions, a common central banking system essentially modelled on the US Federal Reserve System, and a centralised, EU economic policy-making body politically responsible to the European Parliament. Many of the Werner Report's recommendations found resonance in an EU Council resolution adopted in March 1971 for gradual narrowing of intervention margins among the EU currencies, which was subsequently instituted in the form of the EU currency 'snake' in March 1972. This involved limiting intra-EU exchange-rate margins to 2¼ per cent on either side of fixed reference rates, while the EU countries as a group maintained a margin of 5 per cent against the dollar under the Smithsonian Agreement of December 1971.

The strong bias in favour of exchange-rate stability had shown through much of the early discussions leading up to and following the signing of the Treaty of Rome. Perhaps more than some other countries like the US or Japan, therefore, the end of the Bretton Woods system in 1971 and the subsequent collapse of the Smithsonian Agreement in 1973 created a schizophrenia in European exchange-rate policies. On the one hand, governments sought to manage their national currencies in the light of changing circumstances. On the other hand, repeated European initiatives were mounted for global and regional exchange-rate stability. The following chapter deals with the most ambitious effort to achieve monetary union, launched in the mid-1980s. Here we consider the economic mechanics of exchange-rate stability.

The mechanics of a fixed or stable exchange-rate regime

The essential preconditions for a fixed or stable exchange-rate regime may be explained in terms of the basic mechanics of macroeconomic convergence.

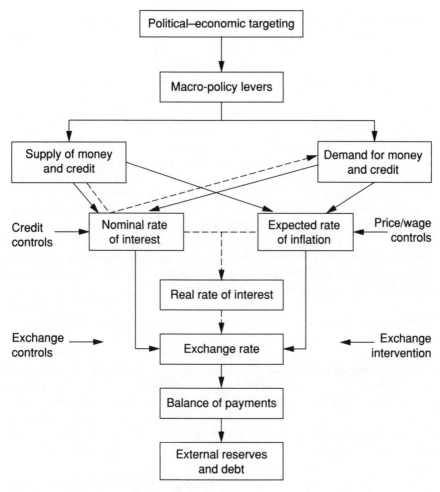

Figure 2.1 Macro-financial linkages: one-country model

These are quite straightforward, and can be seen in Figure 2.1. Modern international economics teaches that the exchange rate is linked to two sets of economic drivers, one in the financial sector and one in the real sector, wherein the former is quantitatively far more significant than the latter.

First, the exchange rate, which is defined as the national currency of one country denominated in the national currency of another, is closely tied to the level and structure of interest rates in the two countries through the interest-rate parity theorem (IRPT). If interest rates in one country rise relative to rates in the other, the currency of the first country will appreciate in the foreign exchange market against the currency of the second, as transactions flow through the market to take advantage of the interest-rate differential and, at the same time, are covered through forward contracts to safeguard the home-country value of the principal and interest proceeds at the end of the investment period. These are classic *currency swaps*, and the market for these transactions is both broad and deep. At equilibrium, any remaining interest-rate differential will exactly equal the cost of the swap, net of transaction costs and residual risks such as the imposition of exchange controls or other sovereign measures threatening completion of contracted transactions (transfer risk) and failure of banks acting as intermediaries in the transaction (counterparty risk).

Second, the exchange rate tends to be linked to the development of prices of goods and services in the two economies. If one country has significantly higher inflation than another, a fixed exchange rate over a long period would create a significant trade deficit (the currency becomes overvalued) which must be matched by equal capital inflows. Failing that, the currency will eventually depreciate. Purchasing power parity (PPP) suggests, therefore, that over extended periods of time currencies will follow their underlying relative purchasing powers in terms of real goods and services, although international financial flows that are vastly greater in magnitude may bring about significant and sometimes extended displacements from this relationship.

Third, the linkage of the exchange rate to *both* prices and interest rates can be combined in terms of the relationship of the exchange rate to expected relative *real* interest rates. The expected real interest rate is the difference between the nominal interest rate and the expected inflation rate, which will define the purchasing power of principal and interest proceeds at the end of the investment period. If the expected real interest rate in a country is low relative to another, it is likely that its currency will be correspondingly weak, unless there are mitigating country-risk differentials. Note that expectations play an important part in this story – expectations about real interest rates and about the exchange rate itself in response to new economic or political information provided to the market.

In turn, interest rates and expected inflation rates are related to two sets of factors at work in national economies, which can be summarised in Figure 2.1 as the supply of money and credit and the demand for money and credit. Each has a dual linkage to the nominal interest-rate and inflation expectations.

First, the supply of money and credit, all else equal, is negatively related to the nominal interest rate, so that a sustained increase in the monetary base should result in a drop in interest rates, while monetary tightening should cause rates to rise. This linkage tends to be rather immediate, since banks, securities firms and others exposed to interest-rate movements have a vital interest in attempting to anticipate movements in monetary aggregates and react rapidly to their expectations in this regard.

Second, the supply of money and credit should, all else equal, have a positive linkage to inflation rates. In some environments, especially national economies operating with excess capacity and sticky prices (such as multi-year labour contracts), the inflation effects of monetary developments may be rather sluggish, perhaps taking eighteen months to two years in some of the industrialised countries. In others, especially economies with limited supply capacity operating at full-tilt, or in countries with experience of high and variable rates of monetary growth which people have grown accustomed to anticipating, the inflationary impact may be much more rapid. The linkage of inflation to monetary growth has, of course, been subject to intense debate among economists over the years, and requires a good deal of knowledge about national economic structures and the formation of expectations to diagnose.

Third, the demand for money and credit is positively related to the overall level of economic activity. Assuming a constant money and credit supply and an expanding level of GDP, for example, one would expect interest rates to rise, while a recession in economic activity should be associated with an easing of interest rates. If one is concerned about interest rates, therefore, one has to look both to factors affecting the demand for money and credit and to factors affecting the supply of money and credit. This is typically what money-market economists spend their time doing.

Fourth, in the absence of any change in the supply of money and credit, the level of prices ought to be negatively related to the level of real economic activity. If output rises with a constant money supply, all else equal, the price per unit of output should fall. This might be regarded as something of a conceptual linkage, since economic expansion usually leads to an accommodating rise in the monetary base on the part of the national central bank.

In terms of the mechanics in Figure 2.1 therefore, an increase in the supply of money and credit alone should cause a country's currency to depreciate, assuming nothing else happens, since it would be associated with lower nominal and expected real interest rates. A significant rise in consumer spending, on the other hand (again if nothing else happens), should be associated with an appreciation of the currency, since nominal and real interest rates would be expected to rise.

Finally, one can incorporate policy variables into Figure 2.1. The supply of money and credit may be subject to various kinds of shocks, such as international capital flows or seasonal factors, which the central bank might want to counteract using standard monetary policy tools such as open-market purchases or sales of eligible securities, lending to banks on a secured or unsecured basis, changing bank reserve requirements, etc. On the other hand, it might use these same tools to bring about changes in the supply of money and credit, either in an expansionary manner to stimulate economic activity and employment, or in a contractionary way to counteract inflation. In either case, monetary policy will tend to have an impact on nominal and real interest rates and hence on the exchange rate. Fiscal policy may be used in an expansionary effort using tax cuts, public expenditure increases, etc., to stimulate the real sector of the economy, which in turn would cause interest rates to rise and the currency to appreciate. Of course, both types of policy may be used simultaneously in an attempt to achieve politically important macroeconomic objectives, while at the same time avoiding the kinds of undesirable side-effects that are always at the root of the policy-maker's dilemma.

The structure of institutions and the policies of public officials are important in discerning the possible direction of policy and its execution. It may make a great deal of difference whether or not the central bank is autonomous in relation to those elected officials who call the shots politically, and who far more often than not have the tendency to call for monetary expansion in an effort to cut unemployment – probably the most important economic statistic of concern to politicians. How effective the central bank is in resisting such pressure tends to have a great deal to do with what happens to interest rates and exchange rates.

Lastly, in terms of Figure 2.1, policy-makers may be tempted to resort to direct controls in credit markets (e.g. interest-rate ceilings) or in the real economy (e.g. price and wage controls) to deal with undesirable economic performance when there is no ability or willingness to address the underlying causes using monetary or fiscal policies. Such measures are indeed 'symptom-targeted', and generally represent only temporary palliatives as an excuse for fundamental policy inaction, while at the same time causing significant distortions in resource allocation and often creating parallel or black markets for capital and for goods and services whose prices are subject to control.

With respect to the exchange rate itself, the authorities may also intervene directly in the market if they are unable or unwilling to alter monetary or fiscal policies to attain a particular exchange-rate objective. First, they may impose exchange controls, distorting capital and/or trade flows and in many cases creating a black market in foreign exchange, or they may engage in sterilised intervention, that is, the central bank steps in to buy or sell its own currency in order to achieve a particular exchange-rate objective and then proceeds to neutralise the impact of the intervention by means of domestic monetary policies. In such cases the central bank either gains or loses reserves, and the country encounters a balance of payments surplus (undervalued currency) or deficit (overvalued currency). This in turn leads to a change in the central bank's external reserve position, increasing it in the former case and eroding it in the latter. Since reserves represent a stock of liquidity, external balances of the central bank eventually become impaired in the case of a balance of payments deficit. In the case of a balance of payments surplus, excess reserves accumulate which may carry a significant opportunity cost for society.

What has all this to do with the mechanics of stable exchange rates, and for the search for monetary union in Europe? The answer may be found in Figure 2.2. If an exchange rate between two currencies (such as the DM and the franc) is to be locked in over time under a fixed-rate regime, it is obvious that there must also be convergence in expected real interest rates, that is, in nominal interest rates and over the longer term in expected rates of inflation. This convergence can be brought about at any inflation of interest rates that are politically acceptable to participating countries. But the point is that it must come about sooner rather than later if the exchange-rate link is to have credibility. If it does not, one

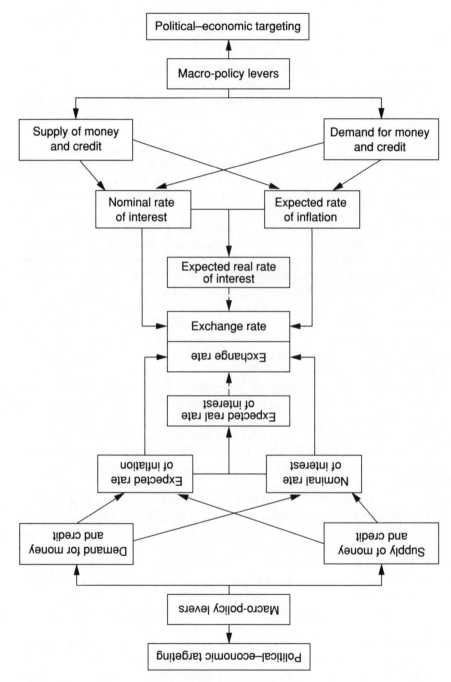

Figure 2.2 Macro-financial linkages: two-country model

country will run a balance of payments deficit and lose external reserves while the other will run a balance of payments surplus and gain external reserves, a process which can continue only until the first country's reserve holdings or capacity to borrow externally becomes impaired. At that point, either the fixed exchange-rate relationship will come apart or the two countries will have to bring domestic inflation and interest rates into alignment, usually under crisis conditions.

Convergence of interest rates and exchange rates necessarily means, in terms of Figure 2.2, that monetary policy convergence will have to be brought about as well, which probably means that the charters of the central banks of countries pursuing a fixed exchange-rate regime will have to be very similar to each other, particularly in terms of insulation from political pressures to expand the supply of money and credit.

Finally, locked-in exchange rates in terms of Figure 2.2 mean convergence in fiscal policies as well, partly because countries pursuing different tax and spending policies would tend to exert different pressures on the demand for money and credit, which in turn would exert pressure on the exchange rate, and partly because budget deficits bring pressure on central banks to purchase government securities in the market, which then would bring monetary policies targeted on maintaining fixed rates out of alignment. So whereas absolutely identical tax rates and budget balances are probably not necessary – as is the case among the states in the United States – a substantial degree of fiscal convergence is unavoidable in efforts to achieve fixed exchange rates.

Convergence along the lines just described almost certainly requires a high degree of political consensus among countries pursuing a fixed exchange-rate regime. There has to be consensus about how monetary policy is conducted and the political mandate of the central bank (notably its degree of independence from the political pressures of the moment). There has to be consensus as well about fiscal policies. And there has to be consensus about economic policy priorities.

At the limit, of course – as under EMU – there is only one central bank and one monetary policy, and only one federal or confederal budget and fiscal policy, with all member states having to finance any budgetary deficits in the single capital market, very much like the states and municipalities of the United States (and European municipalities today). Their securities will be subject to default risk, they will be rated by the bond-rating agencies, they will be priced accordingly in terms of the interest rates at which they will sell, and their acceptability by domestic and international investors will be determined accordingly. In short, they will no longer be truly 'sovereign' instruments, since they will no longer be purchasable by a domestic central bank that no longer exists, so that participating countries' fiscal affairs will be subject to strict market discipline, just as is the State of New Jersey or the City of New York are today.

The basic mechanics of monetary convergence thus allows us to go quite far in assessing the political requisites and the validity of the view of many commentators on fixed-rate regimes over the years, including the Bundesbank's long-standing position that effective progress toward EMU is non-credible without far-reaching political integration. Absent this prerequisite, the system will inevitably come under stress and periodically come apart, which is of course what has happened repeatedly at great taxpayer cost (and speculator benefit) over the years in Europe.

Managing the export surplus

Germany's traditional industrial prowess was reflected in the nearly unbroken record of trade surpluses. Between 1970 and 1993, its accumulated trade surplus amounted to over DM1,420 billion.[7] Western Europe absorbs 70 per cent of total exports, and is the overwhelming source of the cumulative surplus. The heart of Germany's strong position is quality engineering, notably in machinery and transport. The Federal Monopoly Commission reckoned that 100 of Germany's largest companies accounted for one-half of total exports,[8] with eighty-eight of the largest companies run as joint stock companies and the three large banks and Allianz[9] as major shareholders – a stakeholding source of the surplus which was a main target of the 'liberal camp' in the negotiations on the European financial area, discussed below. Put another way, one-quarter of per-capita income in Germany derives from export sales of goods and services. Banks and insurance companies are major beneficiaries of this German export interest. It is an important source of lending and premium income, and sustains Germany's savings as a proportion of disposable income. It fosters their close relations with companies through provision of export finance and advice. All work closely with the Ministries of Economics, Finance and Foreign Affairs in administering the Hermes export insurance scheme, covering about 10 per cent of total exports.

Germany's trade surpluses were nonetheless accompanied by a gradual decline in real growth rates. The economy grew at an annual average of 8 per cent in the 1950s; 5 per cent in the 1960s; and 1 per cent from the 1970s through to 1987, followed by the boom of 1987 to 1991. Expansion of the business-sector capital stock slowed from 6 per cent per annum in the 1960s to under 3 per cent in the 1980s. Growth in labour productivity in German manufacturing fell to 1.3 per cent per annum, against a 2.9 per cent average in Western Europe as a whole and 4.2 per cent in the United States.[10] The general government debt rose from 18 per cent to 46 per cent of GDP between 1973 and 1993. The public accounts were in balance only in one year (1989). There was a steady transfer of real and financial resources within Germany towards the public sector and Germany became one of the four leading government bond markets in the world.

Externally, the large merchandise trade surpluses were reduced by the considerable outflows on the services account – notably from tourism and financial services. But German producers also lost shares in world markets, and in the 1980s came to depend for between 40 per cent and 60 per cent of the trade surplus on EU markets. As long as general government deficits were held within limits, as in

1985 and 1990, earnings on current account could cover them and produce a surplus for recycling on capital account. The Bundesbank, furthermore, contributed to restrained domestic consumption by maintaining high real interest rates. Countries whose currencies were pegged to the DM imported the interest-rate structure set by the Bundesbank. This helped keep down growth in Europe as a whole down. With German unity, the pattern of external financing shifted to capital inflows.

Whether Germany ran a trade-generated current account surplus or was a net capital importer, the Bundesbank had regularly to control the inflationary effect on the domestic money supply. To prevent an explosion of lending the Bundesbank had to clamp strict reserve requirements on banks, and encourage them to channel unwanted funds abroad. The banks duly recycled earnings from exports or from foreign currency inflows to the DM zone, through the bank subsidiaries in Luxemburg. Between 1972 and 1978, the balance-sheets of German banks in Luxemburg increased sixfold.[11] Luxemburg also offered freedom from Bundesbank controls on lending.

The DM began its prolonged appreciation in 1969. As foreign direct investment picked up, banks followed corporate business abroad. International markets were growing faster, and provided a cheaper source of funds. The banks' capacity to place securities denominated in DM waxed, along with the credit and market risks to which the banks were exposed. Yet the DM's emergence as the world's second trading and reserve currency also raised the banks' dependence on the Bundesbank, and its external reserves, as a lender of last resort. This dependence had become evident in July 1974 when the Herstatt Bank was unable to meet its obligations. Following the crisis, the Bundesbank and the German commercial banks subscribed capital to the Liquidity Consortium Bank to provide funds to banks in trouble, limits were placed on bank exposure on foreign exchange markets, and tightened regulations on bank credits were introduced in the 1976 amendment to the Credit Law.

Germany became a key currency country, in tandem with the rise in government debt. The Bundesbank kept tight control over the domestic bond market through the Central Capital Market Committee, set up in 1957. Under its supervision, the big banks were made sole lead managers of new issues and drew up the monthly calendar of bond sales – a subcommittee was created in 1968 to regulate issues on the EuroDM bond market.

Government debt exploded after 1973, rising from 18 per cent to 48 per cent of GDP by 1980. In 1975, the Bundesbank found allies in the state governments run by conservative parties to restrain federal government spending by the liberal–social democrat government in Bonn. But there was little the Bundesbank could do to prevent state banks lending to state governments. The clash between the Bundesbank and banks came in 1976–78, when the banks' operations in Luxemburg[12] intermediated a steady flight into the DM[13] as Latin American countries and OPEC member states switched their dollar holdings to DM through the Euro–DM asset purchases. As German banks in Luxemburg continued to add exposure, the Bundesbank and the Finance Ministry demanded extended controls over the lending of German banks registered there.[14] The Finance Ministry had to wait until the June 1983 EU directive on consolidated accounting and the banks' scare over the collapse in November 1983 of the Luxemburg subsidiary of Schröder, Münchmeyer & Hengst Co. (SMH),[15] to further strengthen control over bank audits, tighten up on lending provisions, and have banks raise additional capital. The amendment to the Credit Law came into effect in January 1985.

Germany's huge trade surpluses also provided the funds to engage in cheque-book diplomacy in support of its Ostpolitik, designed to ease and eventually overcome the pains of national division. German banks' participation in the recycling of funds to developing countries following the oil price hikes of 1973–74 was therefore geographically selective. They provided 8.7 per cent of the total bank credits to the twenty-five major borrower states,[16] but their lending activity was focused on Council for Mutual Economic Assistance (COMECON) neighbours and on Organization of Petroleum-Exporting Countries (OPEC) member states. Reticence became more pronounced following the collapse in late 1978 of the Shah's Iran, in which corporate Germany had invested heavily, and the growing financial problems afflicting Turkey, Yugoslavia and Poland. German banks raised provisions against bad debts, and sought (against Bundesbank opposition) to have the responsibility for impaired loans taken over by international organisations, such as the IMF and the IBRD.[17] Bank share-holders, too, mobilised against loans to politically controversial states, such as South Africa, or Poland, following the imposition of military rule in 1981. Only loans backed by government – as in the case of DM2 billion in loans during 1983–84 to East Germany[18] – received the Bundesbank's blessing. Lending blossomed afresh as Germany bought its way to unity in the years 1988 to 1991 through Soviet bond issues on German capital markets,[19] generous bank credits,[20] and the extension of Hermes credit guarantees for exports.[21]

European exchange-rate policies: 1974–1989

The history and performance of European exchange-rate policies may be divided into three periods.

- 1974 to 1980 saw lax monetary conditions being applied around the industrialised world.
- The decade of the 1980s witnessed the emergence of the Bundesbank as Europe's *de-facto* central bank.
- The 1990s were overshadowed by the problems associated with German unity. The turn of the two decades in 1979–80, and again in 1989–90, saw fundamental shifts in world financial and political circumstances.

European financial-market relationships were also fashioned by the broader world context, where the US dollar continued to occupy an unrivalled position.

It was a chastened Europe which emerged in 1974 into a world of floating exchange rates. That winter, oil-producing countries raised prices by a factor of 3.5 in dollar terms. In January 1974, all restrictions were ended on foreign loans by US banks. This opened the way to the recycling of funds through the Eurodollar markets to oil-importing countries in balance of payments difficulties. In September, the Federal Reserve Board initiated an expansion of the US money supply. The banks' sovereign lending to Latin America and in Eastern Europe grew by leaps and bounds. The United States also concluded agreements with Iran and Saudi Arabia on weapons sales and on the placement of their dollar surpluses in US Treasury bonds. Then in 1975, US brokerage commissions were made negotiable and a number of other liberalisation moves followed. Both the federal government and corporations sought to use the new competitive conditions to reduce the cost of funds. The subsequent five-year boom in the United States was sustained on a diet of fiscal deficits and easy money. It was the depreciation of the dollar, and the upward pressure on the DM in the winter of 1977–78 that convinced Chancellor Schmidt of the urgency of tying the DM into a stable exchange-rate regime in partnership with France.

The events of 1973–74 had highlighted, as the Commission pointed out at the time, the EU's 'weaknesses and dependence'.[22] Lack of internal currency stability during the decade could be clearly traced to divergent macroeconomic and labour-market policies – strains caused by oil-price shocks as well as by the aforementioned monetary policy shocks emanating in particular from the United States (see Figure 2.3). The Federal Republic was confirmed as Europe's foremost exporter, industrial power and key currency country. France dropped out of the joint float with the DM against the dollar in January 1974. Neighbouring small countries hitched their currencies to the DM, as a means of exerting a price-discipline on their economies. The 'snake' came to consist of a DM-bloc of relatively strong currencies, those of Germany, the Netherlands, Belgium, Luxembourg and Denmark. In Italy, Britain, France and the smaller European countries, government deficits leapt, inflation rose to double digits, and wage costs soared. When the dollar fell in late 1977, the Bundesbank entered the markets in force to keep the currency from appreciating, prompting a rapid growth of the DM as an international reserve currency.

As mentioned, Germany's trade surpluses were accompanied by a pronounced decline in growth rates, while key currency country status was the counterpart to the rise in government debt. This was the root of the OECD's 'locomotive' theory: Germany's contribution to international cooperation on economic policy would be to stoke the engine of domestic growth, promote imports, and thereby stimulate supply in other Western European economies. At the Bonn summit of June 1978, Chancellor Schmidt agreed to such stimulation of the economy as part of a wider G-7 package. But the fall of the Shah of Iran and the subsequent rise in oil prices in 1979, combined with a pick-up in German growth, precipitated the German economy into an unaccustomed current account deficit. The DM began to weaken so that rising import prices on the domestic markets

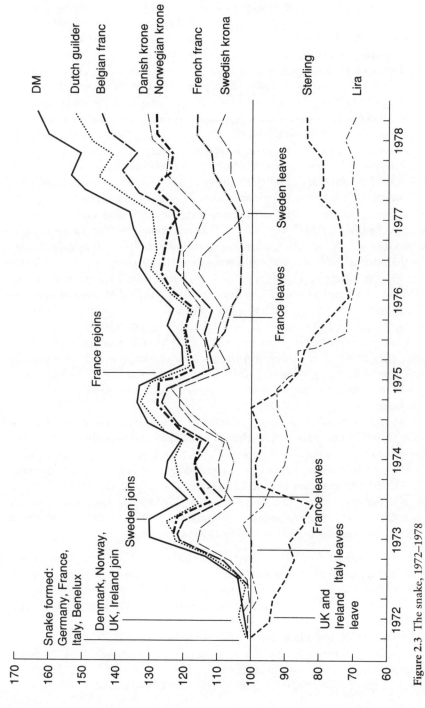

Figure 2.3 The snake, 1972–1978

Source: International Monetary Fund; Datastream.

(notably oil) drove up the general price level. As world interest rates rose, savings began to flow out of Germany in search of higher remuneration elsewhere.

After much delay, the Bundesbank in February 1981 drove up German interest rates in order to stabilise the economy. The Bundesbank concluded from the experience of 1978–81 that reserve-currency status required Germany to run a current-account surplus, in order to avoid a loss of confidence in the DM by foreign asset-holders.[23] It furnished an additional reason to pursue price stability as a top priority. Reserve-currency status provided Germany the privilege of paying its foreign bills in its own currency, and brought Germany into competition with other governments to draw on world savings.

Meanwhile, the Federal Republic had found a new partner in France to establish 'a zone of monetary stability' in Europe.[24] The French government had opted in January 1974 for more inflationary growth, with a view to preventing a Left-wing victory in the forthcoming Presidential elections. But German imports were sucked in by French consumers. This confronted the French government with a difficult choice between continuing the growth-devaluation cycle, widening the external deficit, or reducing French economic activity to a pace set by the Bundesbank's preferences. It was only when a reflationary package in September 1975 led to a renewed run on the franc in March 1976 that President Giscard d'Estaing decided to edge back to a hard-currency policy. Prime Minister Barre was appointed to implement it. His central objective was to bind the franc to the DM, thereby importing into France the virtues of 'the German model'. But it was only with the election victory over the Socialist parties in March 1978 that the conservative French government had a freer hand to join Bonn. The European Monetary System (EMS), conceived as a Franco-German initiative in April 1978, was launched in March 1979.

The EMS amounted to an organisation of foreign-exchange markets on the basis of stable but adjustable exchange rates. The common discipline, it was hoped, would encourage a convergence of domestic economic policies. Annual policy guidelines were formulated for members by the Council of Ministers (1974). A European Unit of Account (EUA) was created for intra-EU central bank settlements (1975), and was superseded in 1978 by the European Currency Unit (ECU). The Bremen summit creating the EMS effectively recreated a regional Bretton Woods. The four-point EMS programme involved:

• Establishment of the ECU as a weighted basket of member-country currencies.
• Implementation of an exchange-rate mechanism (ERM) limiting currency fluctuations to 2¼ per cent in relation to a bilateral parity grid based on the ECU, with no established reference rates between the ECU and non-ERM currencies.
• Creation of a European Monetary Cooperation Fund (FECOM) to which participating governments contributed 20 per cent of their gold and US dollar holdings in exchange for ECU balances, intended to be used in very short-term financings of intervention in order to maintain EMS parities.

- Design of a fiscal transfer mechanism to ameliorate intra-EU payments disequilibria and facilitate payments adjustment.

Italy was granted a 6 per cent fluctuation band in the EMS to make allowance for its chronic financial difficulties. Britain retained its option to join, but showed no willingness to make parity changes for sterling a matter of EU concern. The FECOM was indefinitely delayed for a 'more opportune moment' at the European Council meeting in Brussels in December 1980. In effect, the Bundesbank registered its reservations about having to intervene to support weaker currency countries,[25] and the ERM soon became an extended DM-zone incorporating the franc and lira. The Bundesbank opposed development of the ECU on the grounds of its composition as an index of currencies and thus softer than the DM.[26]

Postponement of FECOM was called for also by changed circumstances. The fall of the Shah of Iran in the winter of 1978 precipitated the second surge in oil prices. In May 1979, the British Conservatives were returned to power with a programme to sweep away the state-directed policies that had hampered the British economy since 1945. Tight monetary conditions were imposed. In June, the leaders of the main industrialised countries agreed that the 1978–79 oil price rises would not be accommodated by easy credit, as was done in 1974. The Federal Reserve Board tightened monetary policy in October, setting the pace for a world-wide rise in interest rates.[27] Debtors were figuratively strangled by the high interest rates. Euromarket rates jumped to a new high and volatile plateau of around 16 per cent in 1980 and 1981. Borrowers faced real long-term interest rates of 7–8 per cent. OECD countries initiated a competitive race to attract funds. OPEC countries were less prepared to invest in dollars after the 1970s depreciation, and looked for alternatives. In March 1980, both Germany and Japan modified domestic regulations to increase the attractiveness of investments denominated in yen and DM.

With the Reagan administration's inauguration in January 1981, foreign exchange intervention to keep the value of the dollar as agreed in 1979 was ended. The dollar soared as the high interest rates prompted by an expansionary fiscal and tight monetary policy pulled in funds from abroad. Corporate investment picked up. The solitary US boom of 1982–85 rescued the world from severe recession, but the United States – politically gridlocked into massive federal budget deficits – became the world's main debtor. Meantime, the strong dollar raised the oil bill for energy-dependent countries, and helped widen US trade deficits with the rest of the world. Financial outflows from Japan into the US bond markets helped sustain imbalances in savings and investment between the two economies. High dollar interest rates increased debt burdens of developing countries. The American thirst for world savings was fully revealed in 1984 with the removal of the US withholding tax on interest earned by non-residents on US securities. At the same time, the Treasury demanded that capital restrictions on yen be lifted, triggering a flow of funds into the US from Japan, easing momentarily the problems of financing the federal deficit and forgoing financial interdependence between the United States and Japan. The German government also ended the withholding tax on securities to keep DM savings home, while the French Socialist government embarked on its own major reforms of the financial system.

The launching in March 1979 of the EMS had been a true Franco-German initiative. France was assured stable exchange rates, without which the important yearly setting of farm prices in the CAP, for example, would have been impossible to sustain. German industrialists won on price competitiveness in world markets as the DM was tied to weaker currency countries and less prone to revaluation against the dollar. Domestic *and* external policies of Germany became the central consideration for European neighbours. There were two special features of this arrangement.

- As mentioned, the Bundesbank set a priority on the German economy running a trade surplus, while no longer discouraging the growth of the DM as a reserve currency. Unlike the United States or Britain, reserve currency status was not to be a way of financing German corporate or government requirements through volatile short-term capital flows. As will be seen in the chapter on the German financial system, this choice was rooted in the specific features of German corporate financing.
- The Bundesbank came to hold a dual status as the *de-jure* central bank for the Federal Republic, while operating as Europe's *de-facto* monetary manager. As such, the Bundesbank had a special relationship with the United States and Japan. The Bundesbank could opt for stabilisation or expansion, in either concordance or non-concordance with the United States as the world's central banker. These two sets of policies (stabilisation/expansion) and relations (concordance/non-concordance) postulate four situations for the Bundesbank on monetary and exchange-rate policy.

First, in February 1981 the Bundesbank countered the rise in US interest rates by raising its own lending. The Bank of Italy followed suit in March. The Socialist government elected in France in April and May had to raise interest rates from 12 per cent to 18 per cent, in order to stabilise the franc. This condemned President Mitterrand's moderate reflation of 1981–83 to failure. The French current account deficit tripled. In March 1983, after prolonged negotiations with Bonn and Frankfurt, France decided to keep the franc within the ERM. The franc was devalued, and a stabilisation policy introduced. Still, the track-record of the EMS in actually achieving convergence was decidedly mixed through the early to mid-1980s, despite the fact that the period represented a relatively benign economic environment within which to begin to move towards monetary convergence. As Figure 2.4 shows, inflation differentials among the principal ERM countries narrowed significantly in the 1980s and continued to do so in the 1990s, as German inflation rates edged up. By contrast, inflation in the principal non-ERM member countries continued to decline.

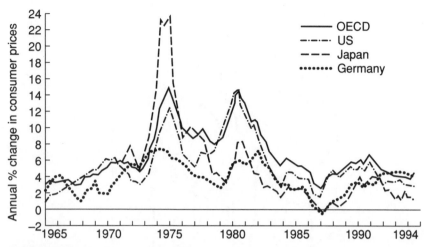

Figure 2.4 OECD inflation, 1965–1994
Source: Datastream.

Interest differentials declined as well during the 1980s but widened again after 1992 following the currency crisis of that year, as Figure 2.5 shows.

Divergence of ERM exchange rates continued during the decade after 1978, involving a total of eleven currency realignments (see Figure 2.6); ample testimony to the difficulty in achieving substantive macroeconomic policy coordination among the ERM countries during this period, especially in the monetary sphere. The eleventh realignment was negotiated acrimoniously in January 1987.

Second, the ERM arrangement was always irksome for Germany's EU partners. During the 1983 crisis, Finance Minister Delors bludgeoned the German government into a reluctant upward realignment of the DM, while complaining of the 'arrogance and incomprehension' of German financial circles.[28] The Bundesbank invariably let the burden of adjustment fall on the deficit country, for fear of having to buy up surplus lira or francs. Any continuation of the EMS would therefore sanction and further solidify the supremacy of the Bundesbank. The main argument for replacing the Bundesbank by a European Central Bank (ECB) was presented by the Deputy Governor of the Bank of Italy, Tomasso Padoa-Schioppa – governments could not enjoy simultaneous stability of exchange rates, freedom of capital movements and autonomy in monetary policy.[29] The ending of capital controls would converge interest rates in the national and Euro-markets. That meant a choice between sticking to fixed exchange rates and allowing the burden of adjustment to fall on domestic labour costs, or the pursuit of national growth strategies which would entail a widening of the bands within the ERM, and more frequent currency realignments.[30] There was also the option adopted by President Carter in 1978 of orchestrating a

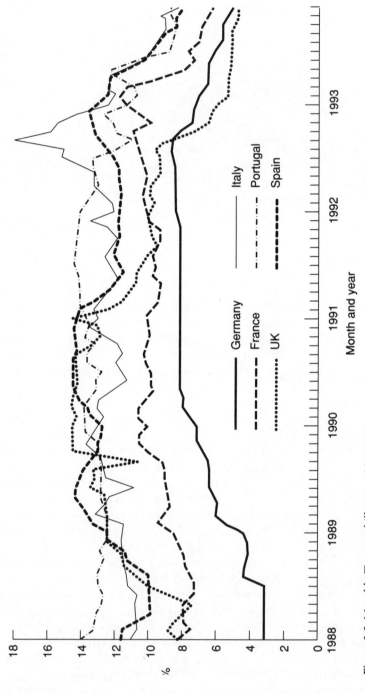

Figure 2.5 Monthly Treasury bill rates, 1988–1993
Source: International Monetary Fund.

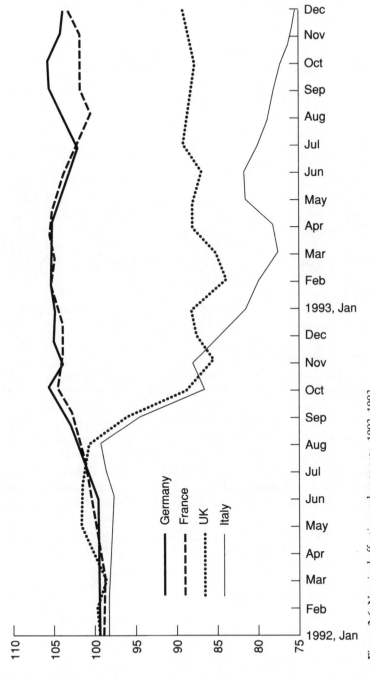

Figure 2.6 Nominal effective exchange rate, 1992–1993

Source: J. P. Morgan.

combined set of G-7 expansionary policies in surplus countries and more coordination on exchange rates.

But Bonn and Frankfurt were both agreed that a repetition of the experience following the June 1978 Bonn summit had to be resisted. Paris, Rome and London therefore turned to the United States to prod Germany into a more accommodating macroeconomic policy. Agreement proved easier to achieve among the G-7 on exchange rates than on national economic policies. At a meeting of the G-5 Finance Ministers in the New York Plaza Hotel in September 1985, the second Reagan administration sought the cooperation of the other industrial countries in order to jointly manage the dollar downwards. There ensued a general lowering of interest rates, a surge in the yen and a decline of the dollar against the DM. At a meeting in the Louvre in February 1987, the leading financial powers struck a deal. West Germany and Japan pledged to boost growth, while the United States promised to cut its budget deficit – and US Secretary of Treasury Baker promised to stop 'talking the dollar down'.[31]

Within the EU, in the Basel–Nyborg Agreements of September 1987 a partial accord was reached whereby the EU central banks were to lend to each other in order to defend agreed-upon currency values before reaching the 2¼ per cent mandatory intervention limit under the ERM. The Bundesbank initially denied any obligation. But the world equity market crash of October 19, 1987 accompanied by angry exchanges between Bonn and Washington exposed the Federal Republic's isolation, counselling closer cooperation with ERM partners. France, too, was affected by the crash. The government suspended trading in equities, and its privatisation programme ground to a halt. Fiscal restrictions in France were slightly eased, and Germany's monetary targets were exceeded. Bonn and Paris cooperated through the financial disorders of November 1987. At the Franco-German summit that month, it was agreed to introduce an Economic and Financial Policy Council, within the bounds of the 1963 Franco-German Treaty. The Council was launched in January 1988. The Bundesbank immediately expressed reservations about an initiative that threatened to put the Bundesbank in a minority and subject it to the authority of Finance Ministries.

Third, a number of factors favoured the European boom of 1988–90, and helped lubricate relations between the Bundesbank and its European partners and the United States. A growth rate of 4–5 per cent for the two years had been helped by a significant drop of oil prices in 1986 and the abundance of international liquidity. Spain's entry into the EU opened a protected market to suppliers. After the eleventh realignment in the ERM in January 1987 France refused to agree to the DM's revaluation so that Germany's competitively-priced capital good exports expanded into EU markets at ever more advantageous prices. Business self-financing reached an all-time high in Germany, reducing the impact of higher real interest rates on corporate cost of capital. The partial liberalisation measures of the mid-1980s paid off in France, with a boom on stock markets and in corporate profits. Monetary conditions were eased, narrowing French interest and inflation differentials with the Federal Republic. The British government, meanwhile, had introduced a series of tax-cutting budgets, and moved to financial market deregulation. House-ownership was encouraged on liberal financial terms. The result was both a consumer boom and a growing trade deficit with continental Europe. Corporate investment in Europe surged, encouraged by the optimism surrounding the launching of the '1992' programme of EU market liberalisation, even as world financial markets recovered quickly from the October 1987 crash.

Finally, the European boom of 1988–90 culminated in the German 'unification boom', and ended in tears as EU member states pursued incompatible policy objectives. The ERM's subsequent travails were aggravated by the aforementioned trend towards a fixed exchange-rate regime across Europe in the second half of the 1980s. In Great Britain, control over domestic monetary aggregates had been abandoned by a Tory government bent on financial deregulation to sustain the City of London's standing as Europe's premier trading market. The Treasury's policy of pegging sterling to the DM at a rate of 1:3 led to a surge in the money supply as the Bank of England in 1988–89 bought up DM and dollars to keep the exchange rate, with the result that inflation once more rose to double digits. After much internal strife, the Conservative government opted to borrow the DM's external discipline by bringing the pound into the wider ERM band in October 1990. In Spain, unit labour costs continued to rise at over 6 per cent annually, contributing to the government's decision to enter the ERM's narrow band in June 1989. Sweden attached the krone to the ERM in the course of 1991 for similar motives and in preparation for its bid to join the EU. Fiscal imbalances in Belgium, Italy, the Netherlands, Denmark, Greece, Portugal and Ireland were rooted in party politics and political culture, only marginally susceptible to discipline through a hard currency zone linked to the DM. Nonetheless, the lira entered the ERM's narrow band in January 1990.

There were, of course, a number of advantages to the ERM. The correlation of exchange rates among ERM participants was much higher than between members and non-members. And the periodic currency realignments within the ERM effectively had prevented the sort of exchange-rate displacement against relative purchasing power in the ERM cross-rates that has been so troublesome in the case of the United States, Japan and the United Kingdom. As shown in Figure 2.7(a), the dollar–DM exchange rate deviated dramatically from the corresponding hypothetical rate based on the relative purchasing power parities (PPP) of the national currencies during the 1980–91 period. This was also true of the sterling–DM and yen–DM rates depicted in Figures 2.7(b) and 2.7(c). On the other hand, the franc–DM, guilder–DM and lira–DM rates remained closely aligned to bilateral PPP relationships throughout this period, as shown in Figures 2.7(d), 2.7(e) and 2.7(f). For a composite view, it is useful to compare the DM–ECU against the dollar–ECU PPP relationships in Figures 2.7(g) and 2.7(h). Note the dramatic differences in medium-term PPP overshooting around a PPP

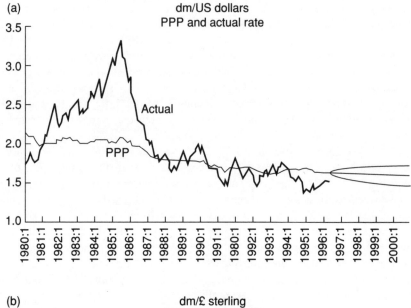

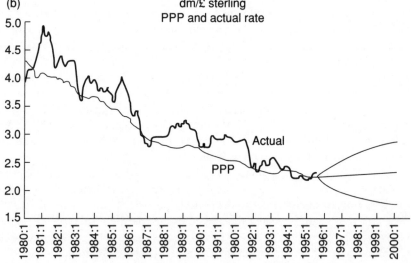

Figure 2.7 Purchasing power parity and actual exchange rates, 1980–1995
Source: Swiss Bank Corporation.

anchor, and hence the potential for distortions attributable to real exchange-rate shifts.

Medium-term real exchange-rate volatility creates significant risk exposures for those engaged in international trade and investment activities. Those exposed to medium-term exchange-rate movements find it difficult and costly to

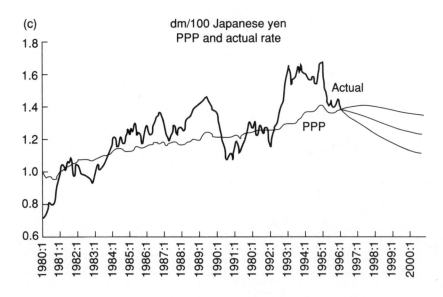

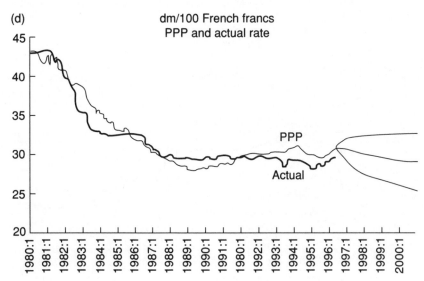

Figure 2.7 (continued)

hedge using available financial instruments and markets. Instruments for controlling exposure are either entirely absent over the maturities involved, illiquid, or exceedingly costly. By substantially driving out medium-term exchange-rate instability, the EMS-based combination of policy coordination and timely exchange-rate realignments may have effectively reduced intra-EU transaction costs facing business and industry, and made a significant contribution to

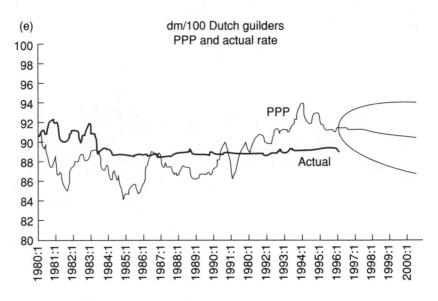

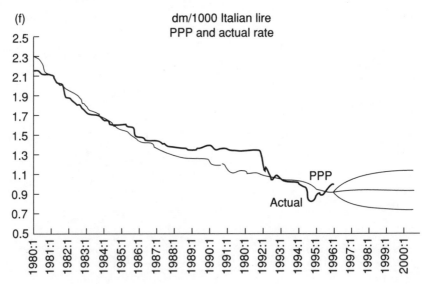

Figure 2.7 (continued)

economic integration during the 1980s and 1990s, despite the failure to achieve
full policy coordination or fixed exchange rates. A test of this proposition would
be whether intra-EU trade volumes would have risen as much if there had been
no ERM-based reduction in medium-term instability of member countries' currencies. However, such a hypothesis is difficult to test, given a host of other
factors that influence trade flows.

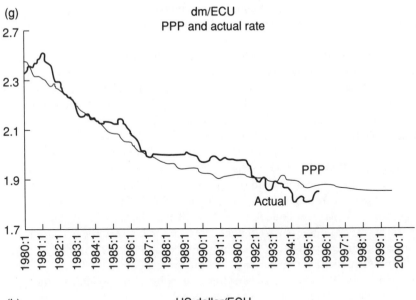

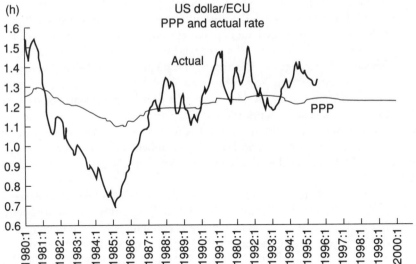

Figure 2.7 (continued)

German unity and tensions in the ERM

At issue was not the ERM's functioning so much as the decision not to negotiate a realignment once German unity was under way. This was the result of an alliance between President Mitterrand, bent on defending France's 'hard franc' policy, and Chancellor Kohl. While the Bundesbank had approached Paris in

October to allow the DM's revaluation, Secretary of State Tietmeyer, who had presided over the EU negotiations on the financial area and was appointed that winter to the Bundesbank Council, was quoted as saying that Bonn did not want to revalue the DM against the franc.[32] Chancellor Kohl confirmed this after meeting President Mitterrand in the context of the regular Franco-German talks early in November 1989. Following the breaching of the Berlin Wall on November 9, Bonn turned to discuss the forthcoming, prolonged transition process in East Germany. In his November 28 ten-point programme for German unity, Kohl had talked of creating 'confederative' structures to foster the process of unification. But on February 6, 1990 Kohl unilaterally announced an early merger at a DM–OstMark exchange-rate of 1:1. General elections in East Germany were brought forward from May to March 18, 1990. Haste, said Kohl, was justified by the 'globally dramatic situation'. The negotiations for the Unification Treaty were completed by May 18, and the State Treaty laying down the terms for economic, social and monetary union between the two Germanies was ratified by the two parliaments in June 1990.[33]

German monetary union came into force on 2 July. The Treaty preamble referred to economic union as a step towards political union, and affirmed that EU law would apply after German national unity had been achieved. The Bundesbank was to take over full power in the monetary union. The GDR was politically merged into the Federal Republic through the use of Article 23 of the Basic Law, which had served to allow the Saar to vote its return to Germany in 1955. This came into effect on October 3, and the first general elections for the all-German parliament were held on December 2, 1990, yielding a victory for the incumbent coalition parties. Kohl had won in part by promising not to raise taxes to finance the cost of unification. A German Unity Fund, initially capitalised at DM115 billion, would issue Bund-backed bonds.[34] Three mini-budgets in March, May and October raised Federal government financing requirements, which the OECD reckoned would be over 4–5 per cent GNP for 1991 through to 1995.

As soon as Germany began to move towards unity, Bonn had asked Paris to agree to the DM's upward alignment. Paris refused, since this would have been a *de-facto* devaluation of the franc. Germany's economic policy was equally self-centred. Unity expenditures without commensurate taxation promised to keep growth rates up, and pull in imports, reducing the German trade surplus. Financing unity through the issue of Bund bonds on the international capital markets also attracted funds away from the US Treasury bond markets. From April 1990 on, G-7 exchange-rate coordination inherited from the Louvre accords weakened. The dollar floated down, as the Federal Reserve moved to lower interest rates in response to lower domestic growth and fears of financial fragility. Over the year, the dollar lost 13 per cent against the DM, and 9 per cent against the yen. Weaker currency countries in the ERM therefore were squeezed between higher interest rates and more intense US competition on product markets.

Through 1991, the Bundesbank became increasingly concerned with its shrinking credibility on global financial markets. Inflation rates exceeded 4 per cent. Its discretionary powers had been consistently under attack. The February 1987 Louvre accords had obliged it to intervene heavily on the foreign-exchange markets, while Paris refused to agree to any further revaluations of the DM within the ERM. The Bundesbank had been informed only at the last moment about the creation of the Franco-German Finance Council. There followed the difficulties of monetary control under conditions of near-fixed exchange rates in the ERM, battles between the Bundesbank and the Finance Ministry backed by Paris and Rome over the introduction of withholding tax on interest earnings in the EU during the winter of 1988–89, and the threat from French plans to have the EU Finance Ministers play a greater role in economic policy coordination. The new Länder government insisted on full representation on the Bundesbank board, potentially influencing its policies. And Chancellor Kohl repeatedly overrode the Bundesbank in the first half of 1990 over German unity, ignoring the central bank's warning that German unity would have to be paid by either a rise in taxation or a rise in interest rates. The epic struggle indicated the significance attached in Germany to preserving influence over monetary policy and the scale of political misgivings in the new Germany about abandoning powers to a future ECB. Governor Pöhl took early leave of his post in October 1991.

The Bundesbank faced the following alternatives.

- One option was for the Bundesbank to endorse a European System of Central Banks (ESCB), as France was insisting, thereby ending the permanent struggle to reconcile domestic priorities with pressures from other European governments to determine monetary and exchange-rate policies for Europe as a whole. But such an initiative could only be contemplated if the German guardians of currency stability could be assured that the ESCB's record would be as good and preferably better than their own.
- A second option was to allow the DM to appreciate in the ERM and against the dollar. Realignment in the ERM would help keep inflationary pressures down in Germany via cheaper imports. But this would tend to postpone convergence of inflation rates among ERM members, as the price for German goods in local currencies rose for European purchasers. Allowing the DM to rise against the dollar would pull up the currencies in the ERM, thereby increasing their competitive disadvantage in dollar markets. In any event, France was opposed to a realignment.
- A third option was to allow German inflation rates to rise with a view to easing the costs of reunification. In effect, German monetary policy remained expansionary in years following reunification. Higher taxes, coupled with a surge in wage demands by trade unions, brought price increases and challenged the Bundesbank to defend its cherished reputation at home and abroad as a guardian of currency stability.
- A fourth option was to impose a dose of European stabilisation as the

Bundesbank drove up interest rates to keep domestic inflationary pressures under control. This highly conflictual option could be mitigated to the extent that the urgency of reconstruction in the new federal states could be expected to pull in imports from other EU suppliers. But high interest rates in a fixed-rate system would increase the debt service charges facing European governments, while exerting a deflationary pressure on business activity across the Continent.

It was the combination of doubts in international markets about the DM and the Bundesbank's monetary stance that combined with negative expectations about Germany's exposure to unstable conditions in Central and Eastern Europe and the costs of unity. Externally, there was also a consolidation of the US position in the Gulf following Iraq's defeat in early 1991. The dollar/DM interest-rate gap widened. By the summer of 1991, German ten-year interest rates were three points over US rates. From October on, international investors moved into the DM as it became evident where the Bundesbank's priorities lay, and the US administration once again gave priority to domestic growth over the dollar's external value. In December 1991, the German discount rate stood at 8 per cent, and the US rate at 3.5 per cent. This differential of 4.5 per cent in favour of the DM marked a swing of eight percentage points from early 1988 – when negotiations on the ECB were launched – and Europe lurched to a fixed exchange-rate system. The Bundesbank nonetheless saw fit to raise rates again in December 1991, and once more in July 1992 to the highest levels since 1931. This left the other European countries no option – short of massive currency realignments – but to give absolute priority to policy convergence based on price stability.

This constellation of interest rates and exchange rates helped to widen the gulf between political leaders and their public opinions across Europe. Scepticism about the EU's internal market programme had been building up for some time. In October 1987, 46 per cent of those polled across the EU member states expressed indifference or relief if the EU were scrapped, falling to 42 per cent by June of 1992. In France, abstention rates in the EU Parliamentary elections of June 1989 totalled 51 per cent of the electorate. The British public was hardly alone in its lack of enthusiasm for European union. One opinion poll showed that 40 percent of Germans saw their model state as Switzerland, with the United States, France and Britain attracting 6, 8, and 2 per cent of the respondents respectively.[35]

Greatest overall support for the EU came from Italy and Greece, the two countries with the worst record in implementing the single-market legislation. Portugal, Spain, Ireland and Greece – as major recipients of EU structural funds – recorded high satisfaction with the benefits of their country's EU membership. German citizens remained relatively supportive, although those German citizens judging that the country had benefited from EU membership fell from a peak of 61 per cent polled in December 1990, at the time of the first nation-wide elections since November 1932, to 48 per cent by June 1992. This sharp decline paralleled the rise in anxiety in Germany at the anticipated costs of unity, and above all at the prospect of 'losing the DM' as the symbol of the Federal Republic's success. The most notable change, however, came in France, which had traditionally been the principal protagonist of European union. By June 1992 48 per cent of those polled expressed indifference or relief if the EU were scrapped, placing the French public alongside the Belgian, British and Danish as the least supportive of the EU.

This disenchantment was best registered in the *Eurobarometer* question as to whether the single market was a good thing. The peak of 57 per cent of respondents in October 1987 fell progressively by thirteen points to 44 per cent in June 1992 (Figure 2.8). The most spectacular declines in support were registered in the EU's six founding members, with Belgium, France, Germany, Luxemburg and The Netherlands recording levels of support well below the average of June 1992. While these trends reflected distinct national political agendas and priorities, they nonetheless revealed a number of shared concerns. Initial enthusiasms waned as the implications of the programme became more widely appreciated.[36] Higher-income earners with advanced educational pedigrees consistently backed the internal market to a notably greater extent than the more numerous lower-income groups. At the national level, satisfaction at the way democracy worked rose sharply through the process of unity in Germany, and brought Chancellor Kohl a third electoral victory in the general elections of December 1990. But this satisfaction contrasted sharply with the lack of satisfaction with government demonstrated in Italy, Britain and France.[37]

By early 1992, few European governments were immune from their electorates' displeasure. The Euroboom had been precipitated back into Eurorecession by the rise of interest rates across the region, and the shocks emanating from German unity. Unemployment was once more on the rise, with all governments tempted to offset the decline in consumer demand by a surge in fiscal spending. Kohl's popularity had slumped as the Chancellor edged away from his commitment not to raise taxes. The French Socialist governments, in office since the general elections of spring 1988, were rapidly losing electoral support. Prime Minister Thatcher had championed the cause of limiting the EU's agenda to achieving the internal market, but had to resign in November 1990, as Tory party leaders took fright at the plunge in the party's popularity at home and the Prime Minister's isolation in European discussions on further moves to monetary and political union. Her successor, John Major, nonetheless brought the party to a fourth successive victory in the general elections of April 1992, against a Labour Party which had espoused the EU's social policies as the best means to reintroduce social democracy to the country. In Italy's elections that month, the Christian Democrat vote fell further and then plummeted as political reforms were accelerated by Mafia assassinations and a popular backlash against pervasive political corruption involving the entire spectrum of Italian political life. These were the conditions in which the Danish government submitted the Maastricht Treaty to referendum by the electorate.

There was another dimension to the ERM saga in 1992 and 1993. Various capitals were competing to host the future seat of the ECB. Germany's campaign

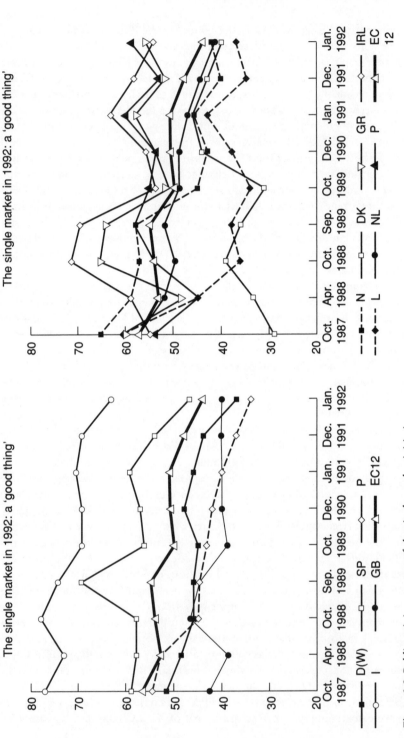

Figure 2.8 Public opinion surveys of the single market initiative
Source: Eurobarometer.

was launched in January 1992, when Kohl made an official visit to Frankfurt for the first time in his ten years as Chancellor. He pledged to bring the ECB to Frankfurt, and backed Finance Minister Waigel's strategy to make the Finanzplatz Deutschland first among continental competitors. The 'big three' German banks then threw their weight on to the scales in a public relations campaign, proclaiming monetary union as a logical consequence to the internal market,[38] and contrasting Germany, as Europe's rising power, with Britain's decline.[39] In June 1992, Prime Minister Major urged London's claim to the ECB.

On June 2, 1992, the sceptical Danish electorate voted against ratification of the Maastricht Treaty, prompting President Mitterrand to announce a French referendum for September. Initially, polls registered an ample majority in favour, but as the summer wore on and the Treaty's opponents mustered their arguments, the French began to turn against the government's economic policies in general. As German long-term interest rates rose, French rates had been pulled up in their wake, including short-term rates. As only 30 per cent of corporate loans were long-term, havoc was wreaked in the French corporate sector.

World financial markets, dominated by institutional investors, scented blood, in the belief that a currency realignment was pending for the first time since 1987. Speculators sold lira, sterling and pesetas, while a weak dollar added to the strains by encouraging further switches into the DM. When EU Finance Ministers met on September 5, 1992, Germany's partners demanded that the Bundesbank cut interest rates, tempting Governor Schlesinger at one moment in the proceedings to get up and leave the meeting. He was restrained by Finance Minister Waigel, but he refused to concede.

Chancellor Kohl could not afford to see Mitterrand defeated in a crucial referendum by a *de-facto* alliance of the Bundesbank with international speculators. Bonn therefore had the Bundesbank intervene with the Banque de France in a massive effort to support the franc.

That weekend, Chancellor Kohl attended a Bundesbank meeting where the Governor reportedly asked the Chancellor to negotiate a realignment within the ERM, which probably would have tilted the balance in favour of the Treaty's opponents in the French referendum. Fortunately for relations between Bonn and Paris, the lira and pound were more vulnerable to speculative attack than the franc. A Bundesbank leak to the press that an ERM realignment was desirable was followed by a minimal cut in the Bank's lead interest rate. On September 16, the British government raised interest rates in a vain attempt to stem the rush out of sterling. The ERM central banks, with the Bundesbank to the fore, threw tens of billions of dollars into the market to no avail. The pound and the lira quit the ERM that night. The peseta devalued. Only massive Franco-German intervention saved the franc from devaluation on September 23, after the pro-Maastricht camp in France had won the referendum by a whisker. But the markets continued to scent blood as German interest rates stayed high. Finland and Sweden, as well as Spain and Portugal, had to devalue or leave the ERM. The Danish krone and Irish punt hung on.

The Bundesbank then insisted that the pound sterling could only rejoin the exchange-rate mechanism at a price agreed by all. As the British government was not prepared to have Germany determine sterling's 'correct' value, and had in any case not yet signed up to the third phase of monetary union, London was effectively out of the running to host the ECB.

The Bundesbank had not been defeated in its determination to escape the straitjacket clamped on it by France. Its chance came with the landslide victory of the French conservative parties in the April 1993 elections, and the devastating verdict meted out to the socialist governments of 1988–93 for presiding over the most reactionary set of economic policies since the early 1930s. In the years 1931 to 1936, French governments had clung to the gold standard and a hard franc, and had gone down to defeat at the hands of the left. Mitterrand's socialists now stood condemned for similar reasons. Following a period of calm when Denmark in May re-voted in favour of the Treaty – after having been granted special opt-out conditions from monetary union and a common EU security policy – speculation against the franc picked up in July. How could the French square be circled between the hard franc and an official unemployment rate of over 12 per cent (and rising)? Finance Minister Alphandéry announced in a radio broadcast that he had 'taken the initiative to ask his German counterparts to come to Paris' to discuss the lowering of interest rates. Finance Minister Waigel had the meeting cancelled.[40] Sensing a Franco-German rift, the markets turned once more against the franc. The Banque de France abandoned support of the franc on July 30. In negotiations, France suggested that the DM exit the ERM, thereby leaving the franc as the anchor.

On August 2, 1993 the Monetary Committee in effect conceded a Bundesbank victory by agreeing to have the fluctuation bands widened to 15 per cent either side of the central rates. This relieved the Bundesbank of an implicit obligation to intervene on exchange markets in favour of weak currencies, while it satisfied the French that the wider bands would increase the foreign exchange risk to speculators.

There would be no concealing that the two victors in this drama were the Bundesbank and the world financial markets. Ever since the Bremen summit of 1978, the Bundesbank had resisted demands of weaker countries to support their currencies in the foreign-exchange markets. For their part, the world financial markets had demonstrated that they stood as judge and jury over the policies of governments and the performances of national economies. Global foreign-exchange trading was centred in London, New York and Tokyo which (with Switzerland, Hong Kong and Singapore) amounted to over 100 times the daily average of world exports of goods and services. In political terms, this meant that market judgements prevailed over exchange-rate alignments that were not in conformity with the markets' own judgements. In terms of economic policy, the events of 1992 and 1993 effectively left the ERM in a shambles, the consequence of attempting to maintain non-credible exchange-rate relationships in the absence of the requisite degree of macroeconomic policy alignment.

The breakdown in the exchange-rate mechanism was not unwelcome to the Bundesbank. At the level of symbolic politics, breakdown showed that it alone was 'the Bank that rules Europe'.[41] More prosaically, the Bundesbank was relieved that it no longer had to support other currencies in the exchange-rate mechanism at the risk of losing control over the German money supply. The reward came at the October 1993 EU summit at Brussels, when Kohl won the vote of the majority of member states to locate the ECB in Frankfurt. Consecration of German primacy was celebrated when the new Governor of the Banque de France made his first public testimony to the Bundestag in March 1994, a few days before doing so to the National Assembly in Paris.[42]

The Maastricht Treaty and the ERM

At the end of 1991 there seemed little doubt that the EU was committed (post-Maastricht) to pressing ahead to full economic and monetary union and hence macroeconomic policy convergence by the end of the 1990s. This was to be the 'glidepath' which the member states would follow on convergence to union. But the mix of German unity and public reactions in to the terms of the Maastricht Treaty during 1992 and 1993 brought home to electorates across the EU what EMU actually meant for the conduct of macroeconomic policy in the member countries. Consequently, deriving implications of the macroeconomic environment for financial markets prospects requires at least two alternative assumptions: (a) full convergence by 1999 along the lines agreed to at Maastricht; and (b) non-convergence in various forms, ranging from a 'two-speed' process separating the DM-linked bloc from the rest to continuation of regime in basically its current form. The Maastricht convergence criteria are listed in Figure 2.9.

There are a host of open questions and issues to be considered, including the following:

Under any fixed exchange-rate regime, the burden of international financial adjustment falls disproportionately on deficit countries which are under pressure from erosion of external reserve holdings and therefore obliged to pursue deflationary monetary and/or fiscal policies. Surplus countries can afford to run up extensive reserves, assuming they are able to sterilise the effects on the domestic money supply. Surplus countries also bear a potentially significant opportunity cost by holding excess reserves, to be sure, but are under no immediate pressure to adjust through monetary and/or fiscal expansion. Macroeconomic policy coordination is therefore mandatory in order to increase the perceived fairness in sharing adjustment burdens. Such a regime is credible only if exchange rates are fixed and inviolable.

Under the auspices of the ECB, member countries' monetary and intra-EC exchange-rate policies would have to be increasingly aligned during the transition. But the ECB's powers remained somewhat uncertain. An integrated financial market would make substantially greater portfolio diversification for investors possible across financial instruments and currencies, but at the same time reduce

- Be a member of the EMS for two years prior to entry without having experienced 'severe foreign exchange tension'.

- Average inflation (Consumer Price Index) in the 'trial period' (1997) not to exceed the average of the three best-performing members by more than $1^1/_2$ percentage points (forecast 3.1%).

- Exhibit a long-term government bond yield not to exceed the average of the three best performing members by more than 2 percentage points.

- Be judged as not running excessive budgetary imbalances: defined as either a deficit below 3% of GDP or heading 'decisively and credibly' in that direction.

- Achieve a ratio of debt to GDP below 60% or heading 'decisively and credibly' in that direction.

Figure 2.9 The Maastricht criteria

the potential *gains* from international portfolio diversification. If investors actively manage portfolios in ways that include acting in anticipation of currency realignments, it could lead to 'currency substitution' and monetary instability. Disparate monetary policies would clearly place pressure on the parity grid, yet convergence of national interest-rate structures is based on the assumption that the agreed currency bands (with a few exceptions) would hold. This is exactly what happened in the 1992 ERM crisis.

Since the 1960s, financial market participants had been sceptical of the integrity of fixed-rate regimes that lack strong evidence of monetary discipline. If investors were convinced that the EU parity grid rates would be defended, no incentive would exist for destabilisation. Consequently, national authorities would be forced to intensify economic policy coordination and to narrow inflation differentials, and possibly to move to a single currency as quickly as possible, producing an increase in volatility of long-term interest rates versus short-term rates, and reducing speculation.

How and where would the ECB conduct its monetary policies? Practices varied widely among member countries on the use of reserve requirements (and their implicit taxation aspects), central-bank repurchase operations and advances to credit institutions, and open-market operations. Would the relationship of the national central banks to the ECB be comparable to the regional Federal Reserve Banks to the Board of Governors in the United States? Which markets would be used to conduct securities and forex operations, and could these be centralised or decentralised through the creation of multiple ECB dealing rooms? How and when would ECB-eligible paper be classified and market techniques specified?

What would be the ECB's stance on global exchange rates after the single currency had been achieved? Monetary and exchange-rate policies are inseparable, so that the EU countries, through their new European central bank, would have to take a stand by the end of the 1990s on the exchange-rate regime governing the international economy as a whole. If history is a guide, pressure could be expected towards greater exchange-rate stability and, consequently, broad-gauge alignment of global interest rates and inflation rates.

Most countries have seen government tax and expenditure policies fall into relative disuse as techniques of active macroeconomic policy, due to both market integration and increased political and economic rigidities. In the EU context, free internal trade ensures that national tax and expenditure policies tend to spill over on to partner countries and reduce domestic macroeconomic policy usefulness. Moreover, with fully integrated financial markets, domestic interest rates become less responsive to fiscal deficits as capital inflows prevent crowding-out of domestic private-sector borrowers. Fiscal deficits will have an impact on the interest rate environment faced by all. Together with the impact of differential fiscal burdens on the location of EU economic activity, such considerations will make it necessary to achieve substantial harmonisation of fiscal measures and to expand the EU system of fiscal transfers among member countries.

As noted earlier, the degree of residual fiscal independence after EMU may be akin to that of the states within America. Unless the future EU central bank defines all national debt issues to be eligible for purchase in the conduct of its monetary policy, countries will no longer be able to monetise debt. EU bonds may be viewed as a similar quality to US Treasury bonds, with associated (collective) central government backing. In the event of a common foreign and security policy, the EU, in centralising the budget requirements for public goods such as defence, will eventually be issuing its own supranational securities, but 'local' bonds (denominated in the common currency) issued to finance 'local' expenditures such as education and roads will likely be viewed as similar to US municipal bonds. As a result, countries that run budget deficits may find that their debt will be rated less than highly. Indeed, credit-risk tiering will develop across the sovereign bonds issued by (local) EU country governments, similar to that observed for corporate and US municipal bonds.

National, as well as municipal governments, will thus have to compete in private markets. To attract investment capital to national debt issues under such circumstances, national governments will be encouraged to do all they can to reduce transaction costs, as well as tax and other impediments to investment. This may include encouraging improvements in domestic clearance and settlement facilities, or removing barriers to the use of international clearing and settlement facilities by cross-border investors, or both. Financing needs for ready cross-border investment may compete with demands for protection of domestic infrastructure or formalities believed to improve tax enforcement in the definition of public policy in this area. Selective regulation of pension funds, insurance companies or other institutional investors may of course force them to take

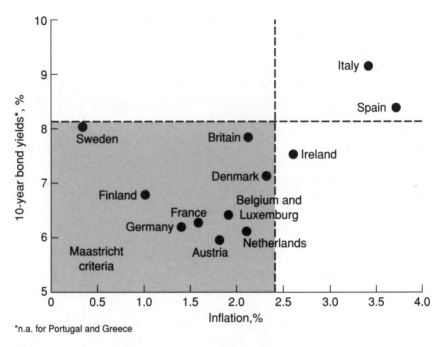

*n.a. for Portugal and Greece

Figure 2.10 Inflation and long-term interest rates, 1996
Source: National statistics; J. P. Morgan; ABN AMRO; Hoare Govett.

disproportionately large allocations of national government issues. But EU initiatives, especially in the pensions field, and the need to maximise performance should, over the long term, reduce the ability of governments to force investment in their own paper. This, in turn, may add to the factors forcing public issuers to compete more actively for international investment. And as local currencies disappear and a single integrated capital market emerges, the intra-EC Eurobond market should become irrelevant for both investors and issuers.

Using an array of monetary and fiscal indicators, Figure 2.10 indicates the 'readiness' of individual EU countries for Stage Three of monetary unification based on inflation and interest-rate convergence. With the exception of Italy and Greece, both criteria are satisfied or are close to being satisfied by most of the EU member countries. The extent of fiscal divergence in government deficits and debt levels for the various EU countries is depicted in Figure 2.11. Here all countries except Luxemburg were out of compliance as of mid-1996.

Summary

As the foregoing discussion suggests, achieving further macroeconomic convergence in the EU pivots on the credibility of EU members' pursuit of common fiscal and monetary policies. Progress on both fronts will be reflected in financial

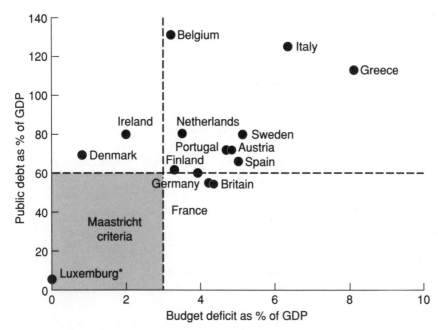

Figure 2.11 General government deficit and gross public debt, 1996
Source: European Commission.

market conditions and their reading of various national political circumstances. Completely free internal financial flows in the absence of economic policy coordination could be potentially destabilising. But progress towards a common currency and unified economic policies would serve as the catalyst for creating a single financial market, at the same time influencing a wide range of market activities.

These include: (a) the ability to profit from intra-ERM exchange-rate realignments and the need on the part of traders, borrowers and investors to hedge against them via currency swaps, futures and options; (b) the alignment and ultimate convergence of interest-rate patterns across the EC, possibly coupled to greater interest-rate stability, gradually reducing and ultimately eliminating opportunities for fixed-income arbitrage across EU financial markets and (assuming enhanced stability) eroding the need to hedge and the economic value of interest-rate derivatives; and (c) the location and nature of central bank intervention in fixed-income and foreign exchange markets in the pursuit of monetary and exchange-rate policies, and the role of the ECB as an ultimate investor in eligible securities. Each has critical implications for markets, investor and issuer behaviour, as well as trading activity, and hence the market for infrastructure services.

Moreover, EMU commitments may have profound and 'unintended' effects on weaker EU securities markets such as those of Spain, Greece and Portugal and possibly Italy, Ireland, the United Kingdom and Belgium as well. This is because, in order to maintain fixed exchange rates, weaker (non-anchor) countries have to raise interest rates, tighten fiscal policies by raising taxes and/or institute price/wage controls. The first two policies can have important securities market implications. High interest rates add to a country's debt burden and can crowd out private-sector borrowers. One possible outcome may be to force non-government borrowers in 'weaker' currency countries to raise funds across borders in strong currency countries such as Germany by using currency swap-driven transactions.

To the extent that investors hold expectations that various EU countries will seek devaluations or revaluations of their currencies within the ERM or exit ERM, as occurred in 1992, we would expect to see a volatile and varying risk premium impounded in the long-term bond rates of weaker EU countries and possibly a negative risk premium (reflecting potential revaluations) in strong-currency countries. As a result, in the period leading up to full monetary union and fixed exchange rates there is likely to be a relative increase in the volatility of long-term rates over short-term rates across the EU. Thus, monetary convergence is not inconsistent with a growing demand for derivative securities and synthetic instruments that permit long-term bond risk to be hedged. As long as there is continued uncertainty regarding the final values of exchange-rates on full monetary union, importers, exporters and investors will try to hedge their exposures as best they can.

In short, currency convergence requires convergence in expected real interest rates, which in turn requires convergence of nominal interest rates and expected inflation rates. This in turn requires convergence of monetary policies and far-reaching convergence of fiscal policies. A high degree of political unification is doubtless a final prerequisite for convergence of these critical policy variables. This has been the position of the Bundesbank all along, and it is anchored either in the ambitious conditions written in to the Maastricht Treaty or in the explicit terms for the Treaty's completion in the 1996–7 intergovernmental conference.

Notes

1 Committee on Currency and Foreign Exchanges after the War, First Interim Report (Cd 9182, London: HMSO, 1918), pp. 3–4.
2 Henry Nau, *The Myth of America's Decline: Leading the World Economy into the 1990s* (New York: Oxford University Press, 1990).
3 Figures from Bernard Keizer, 'Les Choix de la République Fédérale d'Allemagne', *Economie et Statistique*, No. 102, July/August 1978, p. 78.
4 Frank Roy Willis, *France, Germany and the New Europe, 1945–1967* (Stanford, CA: Stanford University Press, 1965), pp. 312–65.
5 Jacques Rueff, *Oeuvres Complètes. De l'Aube au Crépuscule, Autobiographie* (Paris: Plon, 1977), pp. 259–74.

6 Guy de Carmoy, *Les Politiques Etrangères de la France* (Paris: La Table Ronde, 1972), pp. 469–71; Edward Kolodziej, *French International Policy Under de Gaulle and Pompidou: the Politics of Grandeur* (Ithaca, NY: Cornell University Press, 1974), pp. 176–221.

7 OECD, Statistics of Foreign Trade, Series A.

8 German Monopolies Commission 1973–1983, *Summaries of the First Five Biennial Reports* (Baden-Baden: Nomis, 1987), p. 15.

9 *Ibid.*, p. 153.

10 OECD Economic Surveys, *Germany*, 1994, p. 77.

11 'Bank authorities want greater transparency abroad', *International Herald Tribune*, April 18, 1979.

12 'Closer Scrutiny of Euromarkets Sought', *Financial Times*, August 9, 1979.

13 OECD Economic Surveys, *Germany*, 1979, p. 29.

14 'Closer Scrutiny of Euromarkets Sought'.

15 'Fierce Debate on Likely Reforms', *Financial Times*, August 30, 1983.

16 'Die Auslandsstützpunkte sind wichtig', *Frankfurter Allgemeine Zeitung*, May 21, 1985.

17 'Firm Bundesbank Line on Third World Debt', *Financial Times*, April 15, 1983.

18 'East Germany's Friendly Face Wears a Warning Scowl', *Financial Times*, June 3, 1984.

19 'Soviet Union in DM 500 Billion Bond Issue', *Financial Times*, July 27, 1988.

20 'Kohl's Moscow Visit Promises Trade Rewards', *Financial Times*, October 21, 1988; 'Kohl in Caucasus with Gorbachev', *Financial Times*, July 16, 1990.

21 'Gone But Not Forgotten', *Financial Times*, September 30, 1994.

22 Quoted in Alfred Grosser, *Les Occidentaux, les Pays d'Europe et les Etats Unis depuis la Guerre* (Paris: Fayard, 1973), p. 356.

23 'Opportunities to Grasp', *Financial Times*, June 23, 1981.

24 Peter Ludlow, *The Making of the European Monetary System* (London: Butterworth, 1982).

25 In his letter to the German government in November 1978, Bundesbank Governor Emminger indicated that Bonn and Frankfurt were agreed that a 'definitive' regulation for the EMS would require a change in the Rome Treaty, and that a crucial aspect of Germany's stability policy was to place '*a limit on the intervention responsibilities*' of the Bundesbank (Emminger's italics). In Otmar Emminger, *D-Mark, Dollar Währungs-krisen, Errinerungen eines ehemaligen Bundesbank-präsidenten* (Stuttgart: Deutscher Verlag, 1986).

26 (My translation.) 'The Bundesbank is opposed to indexation of prices. As the ECU is composed on an index of currencies, its full development as a reserve currency would oblige the Bundesbank to buy one ECU for about DM2, without counterpart. The Bundesbank has bought only dollars, as a counterpart to its special relation with the United States' (Bundesbank press release).

27 David Calleo, *The German Problem Reconsidered: Germany and the World Order, 1870 to the Present* (Cambridge: Cambridge University Press, 1978).

28 'Double Delight in Paris, But No Thanks', *Financial Times*, March 31, 1983.

29 An early rendering of this position is to be found in Tomasso Padoa-Schioppa, 'Les marchés européens de capitaux entre la libération et les restrictions', deuxième symposium des banques européennes, Milan 1982: Europe-monnaie et politique européennes–Perspectives européennes (Commission des Communautés européennes, 1984). Mimeo.

30 Charles Wyplosz, 'Le système monétaire européen sur la sellette', *Le Figaro*, May 23, 1989.
31 *Financial Times*, February 23, 1987.
32 *Le Monde*, October 19, 1989.
33 In Bonn, the text was ratified by the Bundestag on June 21, 1990, by 445 for, 60 against and one abstention. The Bundesrat voted the Treaty a day later. The Volkskammer voted 302 for and 82 against.
34 In a May 15, 1990 communiqué the Bonn Finance Ministry put German savings deposits at DM280 billion, and DM120 billion capital exports. On average, Länder governments raised DM80 billion per annum. The Fund would need DM20 billion in the first year. This communiqué was preceded by rumours that the issues could attract Japanese savings, drawing on the world's limited pool.
35 *Suddeutsche Zeitung*, January 4, 1990.
36 E. Noelle-Neumann, 'Europa das unbekannte, unbeliebte Wesen?', *Frankfurter Allgemeine Zeitung*, December 19, 1988.
37 This was noted in the study *Pulse of Europe: A Survey of Political and Social Values and Attitudes* (Washington, DC: Times Mirror Center for the People and the Press, September 1991), p. 66.
38 'Absage an die kritischen Thesen zu Maastricht', *Neue Zurcher Zeitung*, June 17, 1992.
39 'Frankfurt: Germany's financial capital prepares to meet the Single Market', Commerzbank advertisement, *The Economist*, December 17, 1992.
40 'Les frictions se multiplient entre la France et l'Allemagne', *Le Monde*, June 24, 1993.
41 David Marsh, *The Bundesbank: The Bank that Rules Europe* (London: Heinemann, 1992).
42 'Odd couple's testing tiffs', *Financial Times*, March 24, 1994.

3

The EU in search of union

The SEA was drawn up in a divided Europe, where the Federal Republic was *primus inter pares* but not a prospective dominant power, overshadowing its neighbours or its major EU partners. Its inspiration was liberal in that it enshrined in Article 8A a commitment of the states to achieve 'a progressive establishment of the internal market by December 31, 1992', as specified in the White Book. The promise was spelled out in the Commission's study on 'the costs of non-Europe', published in popular form in spring 1988 during the German EU Presidency.[1] The main target of the programme was business.[2] Growth would accompany the measures, along with the creation of between 1.8 and 5 million jobs. Inevitably, though, greater emphasis on market forces would lead to an initial loss of jobs inherent to a process of corporate rationalisation and restructuring. The Act therefore considerably extended the Commission's ability to exploit the legal limits of its powers in matters of social policy.[3] Reference was also made to economic and monetary union, the result of an understanding between Chancellor Kohl and President Mitterrand reached in Luxemburg in December 1985, that France would agree to liberalise foreign-exchange controls if Germany would renew its recognition of monetary union as a goal.

There were thus three key 'accompanying measures' to the EU's internal market programme.

- Monetary union was seen by the Commission President Delors as a vital complement to the internal market.
- Both Kohl and Mitterrand agreed on the need for the internal market to be underpinned by a common social policy.
- Bonn was eager to develop a common EU foreign and security policy, as support in Germany for the Atlantic alliance and for its policy of nuclear deterrence waned with the development of the European peace movement in the early 1980s.

This chapter therefore traces the revival of the 'accompanying measures' in the years leading up to the keystone German presidency of the EU in early 1988, examines the concepts behind monetary union and the debate on fiscal policy and labour markets, follows the three dimensions of EU policy through to early 1990, presents the policy rationales of the three major European states, and presents the unfinished business of the Maastricht Treaty.

The revival of the accompanying measures

Commission President Delors had played a central part in the effort to revive EU policy following the elation of the early 1970s. Delors's personal history as a Catholic trade unionist presents a varied path, from experience in the Bank of France, an active role in Prime Minister Chaban-Delmas's efforts to introduce a 'New Society' programme during his administration from 1969 to 1972, to membership of the French Socialist Party delegation to the first directly elected European Parliament, and finally as Mitterrand's first Minister of Finance from 1981 to 1984, with the change in government that July. Delors had been the central figure in the March 1983 negotiations with the Bundesbank, leading to the decision to keep the franc in the ERM and stabilise the French economy, ending the hopes of reducing the nation's unemployment rates through the gentle expansionary policies of the preceding two years.[4] This experience confirmed his conviction that the only answer to stagnation in France lay in a relaunch of the EU.[5] In his opening speech to the European Parliament in January 1985, Delors proposed accompanying the internal market with a strengthening of the EMS, expansionary EU economic policies, and creation of a 'single European social space'. Maintenance of western Europe's welfare policies was vital to ensure continued popular support for the internal market programme.[6]

Delors's inheritance was one of near complete impasse in both social and monetary affairs. The EC's Social Action Programme, initiated under Chancellor Brandt's patronage at the October 1972 Paris summit and launched by the Council in June 1974, had barely withstood the swing towards a greater emphasis on markets in economic policy across Europe from the mid-1970s onwards. The programme had focused on: (1) the achievement of full and better employment; (2) the improvement of living and working conditions; and (3) the more active participation of social partners in community life and in corporate decisions. An assessment a decade later,[7] when a modest second programme was launched under the French EU Presidency in June 1984, could record only scant achievements. There were three dimensions to the first Delors Commission's efforts to end the stalemate.

- He won the backing of employer, union and public enterprise representatives in Brussels for an expansionary EU economic policy.[8]
- The Commission attempted to revive the proposals for worker participation, but the July 1986 Council of Ministers under the British EU Presidency postponed the issue until 1989.[9]
- The Belgian Presidency proposed a 'plinth' of fundamental social rights, to accompany the move to the internal market.

The matter then moved to the bottom of the Community agenda, until settlement of the EU's budgetary problem at the Brussels special European Council of February 1988.

The impasse on monetary union was more readily overcome with the change in policy orientation in France and the revitalisation of support within the EU. The French government was the main protagonist, backed by the European Parliament. Adoption of the SEA in 1986 pointed to completion of the internal market, but it also fully associated the Commission with the proceedings on EPC and pointed to further development of a common social policy, as well as economic and monetary union. Between 1985 and 1987, the French Treasury entertained hopes that the G-7 countries would support a concerted management of exchange rates. But following the eleventh realignment in the ERM in January 1987, Prime Minister Chirac's government adopted the hard-franc policy, the source of which was rooted in France's revolution in public financing, analysed in Chapter 7. There followed the September 1987 Nyborg agreements, and the creation in January 1988 of the Franco-German Treaty Economic and Finance Council.

As France unfurled its policy to tie the Federal Republic into a strengthened EU, Gorbachev's appointment as Secretary-General of the Communist Party of the Soviet Union (CPSU) in March 1985 was transforming Germany's position in central Europe. The 1980s heralded a sharply modified world order. The rapid emergence of the dynamic economies in the Asian Pacific, led by Japan, prompted a 'new thinking' in Washington and Moscow on the need to restructure world politics, and to release resources from the supply of military hardware in the production of civilian goods and services.[10] Paris, London and Bonn had reinforced defence ties in 1986–87, as the two world powers edged towards agreement on partial nuclear disarmament. Gorbachev's proposals in February 1987 to dismantle intermediate-range missiles in Europe as separate and distinct from discussions on the US and Soviet strategic arsenals were listened to attentively in Washington. Pressure to agree was brought to bear on the NATO allies, particularly Germany. Kohl reluctantly conceded. Washington then asked Bonn to renounce partial control of short-range nuclear weapons based in Germany, and the way was cleared for the Washington Treaty of December 8, 1987 between Gorbachev and Reagan. The Treaty meant the removal of intermediate-range nuclear weapons that the Soviet Union feared, while leaving in place 'battlefield' nuclear weapons for eventual use on German soil.

The Washington Treaty of December 1987 opened the way for a removal of intermediate nuclear weapons installed in Europe in the mid-1980s. The Treaty, and the accelerating decompression of communist party-state rule in central–eastern Europe, transformed Germany's international context. As the Bavarian leader Franz-Josef Strauss wrote, Kohl's August 1987 decision to abandon the Pershing short-range missiles deprived Germany in effect of nuclear cover, and reduced the Bundeswehr to the status of a colonial army.[11] Whether or not the judgement was deserved, it reflected a weakening of Germany's commitment to the formulas for Western security devised in the Atlantic alliance during the 1960s.

France was particularly sensitive to these developments. The Chirac government revived the dormant WEU in October 1987, when its member states reiterated the principles of NATO strategy predicated on nuclear deterrence. These were promptly undermined by the Washington Treaty. Prime Minister Chirac's government then revived the military provisions in the 1963 Franco-German Treaty by setting up the Franco-German Security Council in January 1988. The Council paralleled the Economic and Finance Council. A 4,200-man Franco-German brigade was created. Then Mitterrand won the Presidential election against Chirac in May 1988.

Implications of monetary union

Monetary union was regarded by many as an integral part of the political developments and a logical extension of the process of economic integration. At its most fundamental level, of course, it was intended to eliminate national currencies and exchange rates among the participating countries. As a consequence, monetary union eliminates associated transaction costs. Making payments between a French buyer and a German seller, or between an Italian borrower and a Dutch lender, for example, would in principle involve no greater costs than comparable transactions between comparable parties in a single country. This clearly would reinforce the basic idea of a common market in goods and services, and parallels the 1992 single-market initiative to clean up remaining market distortions.

Beyond that, monetary union would make possible for the first time a unified market for money and capital, one which would be increasingly seamless with respect to debt and equity instruments. No longer would companies issuing securities have to worry about various pockets of investors separated by foreign-exchange risk, nor would investors have to worry about asset allocations across currency zones, where they would face not only the possibility of exchange-rate changes but also different directions in economic policies and their subsequent impact on relative asset values. Capital would be allocated in an optimal way on the basis of the underlying risks and returns, which (like regional free trade) provides an immediate booster-shot by allocating this scarce resource more efficiently on an EU-wide basis, reflected in turn in a higher level of GDP. At the same time, a unified capital market could be expected to help raise the rate of savings and investment, technological change, and other determinants of economic growth. By continually feeding capital to viable industries and denying it to industries that have lost their competitive advantage at global market prices, a single capital market could thus be expected to accelerate the rate of economic growth in a global competitive context – sometimes called *dynamic* benefits of monetary union.

Both the static and dynamic capital-allocation benefits of monetary union are

hypothetical unless there is parallel institutional development of financial intermediaries that ensures vigorous and contestable competitive conditions within
the integrated market. For this reason it was important that the Second Banking
Directive and the Investment Services Directive, along with the Capital
Adequacy Directive, develop in tandem with, and perhaps ahead of, the move
towards monetary union. It is important that the financial intermediation infrastructure is in place at the time of monetary union in order to obtain the
maximum leverage from this development.

As noted earlier, monetary union means a single financial market in which all
borrowers except the sovereign (the EU as a whole) must compete on an even
footing. The European Central Bank (ECB) presumably can only purchase EU
debt instruments in order to assure adequate growth of the money supply and,
under such circumstances, only the EU as a whole can finance deficits by having
its debt monetised (purchased and held by the central bank). Nations like Spain,
Italy or Germany could continue to finance budget deficits or infrastructure
development by issuing debt, but this debt would have to compete on an even
footing with all other types of debt in the market, including that issued by
corporations, banks, financial and non-financial institutions, regional governments and municipalities, etc. All debt would be evaluated by potential investors
and much would be rated by independent rating agencies like Moodys and
Standard & Poors in terms of default risk, which in turn would be reflected in
the interest rates associated with individual financings. Governments of EU
member states would thus be on a relatively short leash, and this would have to
be clearly reflected in their fiscal policies. As noted earlier, the ability of EU
member states to run budgetary deficits would be akin to that of the federal
states in the United States. The bond markets would demand prompt corrective
action in the event of irresponsible fiscal conduct, and this would be signalled by
interest-rate changes and/or the success or failure of new issues. Monetary union
and the absence of national central banks, in short, requires bringing fiscal policies under significantly greater discipline.

Finally, monetary union would have significant implications for industrial and
labour-market policies as well. First, the ability of governments to support
uncompetitive industries would be constrained by virtue of the fiscal discipline
imposed by monetary union, favouring privatisation and winding-down of the
kinds of massive government subsidies that have been the hallmark of industrial
policy in a number of European countries. Second, industrial adjustment to
changing competitive conditions may well accelerate as the fluidity of capital
increases, creating turmoil in labour markets and requiring much greater
occupational and locational mobility of the labour force. Labour policy will
have to accommodate this by lubricating the adjustment process in ways that
support rather than retard it. In other words, the disciplines imposed by unified
capital markets under conditions of monetary union are decidedly uncomfortable, and require rethinking a broad range of policies associated with the deployment of productive resources in Europe.

EU policy from the German Presidency to German unity

When public discussion on EMU was renewed in 1987, two key ideas were in circulation. Mooted in a memorandum by French Finance Minister Balladur, the first notion focused on the inequity of Germany setting monetary policy for others. It provided the thrust for the creation in January 1988 of the Franco-German Economic and Financial Council in parallel to the Defence and Security Council modifying the Elysée Treaty of 1963. The Council was to meet three times a year and be attended by the respective Economics and Finance Ministers, as well as the two central bank governors. The second proposal, advanced in Rome, was for all EU currencies to join the ERM, and for an ECB to be set up as the central coordinator for a European currency policy.[12] In this way, the German economy would not continue to make 'structural gains' through the DM's undervaluation, while Britain would not be able to gain from capital-market liberalisation, 'without being subject to the restrictions (membership in the ERM) placed on domestic economic policies'.[13]

The German EU Presidency of early 1988 proved to be the point on which all elements of European policies converged.[14] Bonn was instrumental in negotiating a long-term budget package, satisfying the demands of Spain for more funds to the poorer regions in the EU. Bonn thereby increased its contributions to the EU budget by nearly 50 per cent. With the SEA ratified, the Commission presented the directives for the European financial area, of which the SBCD formed the core, and announced the guiding principles for 'social Europe'.[15] Jacques Delors launched his crusade for the Community's 'social dimension' at the European Trade Union Congress's meeting in Stockholm in May 1988.[16] There were to be three initiatives in the field. The first was for a 'plinth of guaranteed social rights'. The second was the revival of the social dialogue, and notably the right of workers to permanent education. The third entailed the revival of the European Company Statute, which successive Commissions had advanced since 1968 with a view to facilitating incorporation under EU law. On June 13, the EC Finance Ministers decided to move to liberalisation of capital movements, as the prerequisite to a more efficient allocation of European savings.[17] At the European Council of Hanover on June 27 the EU political leaders heeded Foreign Minister Genscher's idea and appointed a committee to study a move to monetary union. They also promised to stress 'the social aspects of progress towards the objectives of 1992'.

The whole programme had built up a seemingly unstoppable momentum, with the Commission President forecasting that within a decade up to 80 per cent of the major Community policy decisions would be taken in Brussels. The committee on monetary union was composed of the eleven central bank governors and three 'wise men' – Miguel Boyer, former Finance Minister and President of Spain's Banco Exterior; Alexandre Lamfalussy, Director-General of the BIS; and Professor Niels Thygessen, of the University of Copenhagen. Commission President Delors was given the chair, and the Committee's secretary was

Tomasso Padoa-Schioppa of the Bank of Italy. Delors presented the committee's report in April 1989. The conditions for union were spelled out as entailing fixed exchange rates, complete freedom of capital movements, a single financial services market and a common monetary policy. The ECU was seen as having 'potential' as a common currency. The process of moving to monetary union was gradualist, as already proposed in the Werner Report of 1970, and was to involve three stages. (Article 236 of the Rome Treaty required ratification procedures for any major institutional changes.)

- The first stage would come into effect on July 1, 1990, and involve central bank governors in presenting finance ministries with recommendations for a closer convergence of macroeonomic policies and performance. This meant a strengthening of the 1964 Central Bank Governors' Committee, the Monetary Committee, and the 1974 economic policy 'convergence' procedures in the EU.
- The second stage would start on an unspecified date with the entry into force of a new treaty establishing the European System of Central Banks. The Bank would have a President and a Directorate, nominated for periods of five to seven years, and responsible for exchange-rate, monetary and macroeconomic supervision. There would be precise but not binding rules relating to the size of budget deficits. A start would thus be made on a common monetary policy, and to reduce the margins of currency fluctuation within the EMS.
- The third stage, also starting on an unspecified date, would lead to 'irrevocably fixed' parities and would be sealed by the transfer of most economic and monetary policy powers to the Union. National currencies would be replaced by a single currency. The stage would only be embarked upon once all of the policy instruments had been tried and tested. The instruments for the internal market would be an efficient competition policy, common rules governing takeover bids and corporate control, a set of common fiscal policy goals and close monetary policy coordination.

At the June 1989 European Council meeting in Madrid, Prime Minister Gonzalez used the EU Presidency to find compromises. Little accord was reached on social policy. However, the Commission had presented its proposal for a European Social Charter in September 1988, laying out principles for employment policy, free movement of workers, training and participation rights. In April 1989 the Commission approved a modified version, requesting the heads of government to approve it in the form of a solemn declaration. This would also entail a mandate for the Commission to produce an action programme for detailed proposals on worker rights by mid-1990. But at Madrid, the conference communiqué placed social policy within the purview of national governments.[18] On monetary union, it was agreed that the Delors report was to provide the basis for future discussions. The first stage was to start on July 1, 1990, and EU institutions were to make 'complete and adequate' preparation for an intergovernmental conference that would establish the timetable and substance for the later stages. But Chancellor Kohl was reluctant to concede a deadline, so that

President Mitterrand failed to have December 31, 1992 agreed to as the ultimate deadline for deliberations.

France then took over the rotating EU Presidency. 'I am a determined supporter of political Europe and seek to bring about economic and monetary union, an obligatory passageway',[19] Mitterrand declared. The Finance Ministers duly agreed on revision of the 1964 measure creating the Central Bank Governors Committee, and reaffirmed the 1974 procedures. A catalogue of proposals for treaty changes was drawn up.[20] But Mitterrand failed to get Kohl's support to hold an intergovernmental conference in the second half of 1990. Kohl, however, did bow to French wishes against any realignment in the ERM. Both agreed, too, to back the Commission's final suggestion for social policy. The French EU Presidency had the text adopted at the Social Affairs Council of October 30, with Britain withholding its signature. A general Social Charter was adopted by the European Council at Strasbourg in December 1989, and accompanied by an 'action programme' comprising twenty-six articles. In January 1990, the Commission started to issue draft directives.[21]

Meanwhile, as German unity was accelerating, the Bush administration's prime concern was to ensure Germany's Western anchorage, and to resist temptation by Moscow's blandishments for a neutrality status in Europe. Public opinion polls in Germany showed active support for Gorbachev's policies and reinforced Bonn's determination to defend national interests. A more assertive Germany had appeared in the course of 1989. In April, Chancellor Kohl created a new cabinet in Bonn, marking a sharp swing to the right to woo conservative voters tempted to vote for the Republicans, an extreme nationalist party. President Bush welcomed Germany as a 'partner in leadership', opted for progress in the conventional arms talks being held in Vienna, and joined NATO allies in expressing support for the right of the German people to self-determination.[22] As the events in central and eastern Europe unfolded, the White House came out in support of intensified efforts of the EU to unite. 'German unification should occur', Bush stated, 'in the context of Germany's continued commitment to NATO and to an increasingly integrated European Community'.[23]

As the Communists' hold in central–eastern Europe crumbled, President Bush, Chancellor Kohl and President Mitterrand appeared of one mind that there was no alternative to European union. But Kohl announced his ten-point reunification programme unilaterally, without any direct reference to a united Germany's frontiers with Poland. Differences between Paris and Bonn were patched up by a successful Franco-German summit that set the agenda for the EC Strasburg summit of December 8–9, 1989. At the summit, the EU heads of state and government reiterated support for the German people to 'refind unity through free self-determination', and Bonn concurred in Paris's request that a new intergovernmental conference be held prior to the German elections in 1990, with a view to incorporating monetary union into the Treaties.[24] Germany's western orientation seemed confirmed with Kohl's statement in Paris in January that 'our common aim must be to build up the EU as the kernel of a future European peace order'.[25]

Kohl then opted for a fast track to German unity. On February 1, 1990, Moscow offered German unity in return for neutrality. Bonn and Washington promptly reached broad agreement on the timetable for German unity within NATO. On February 6, Kohl overrode the Bundesbank's advice and offered East Germans a 1:1 exchange rate in order to stem the flow of emigration westward.

The EU's importance for France's embrace of Germany was underlined when Kohl and Mitterrand proposed political union in April 1990. Their common message to the Irish EU Presidency called for the intergovernmental conferences to include the establishment of common foreign and defence policies. At the Dublin summits of April and June 1990, political union discussions and monetary union talks were set to begin in December, and to end one year later under the Dutch Presidency in December 1991.

Unlike monetary union talks, those on foreign and security policy were open-ended, and the differences among the states over what to do in a fluid situation were too great to bridge effectively. At the same time, the difficulties facing the Commission in promoting its plan for EMU became evident at the Finance Ministers' meeting at Ashford Castle, Ireland on March 31 and April 1, 1990. The German position was clearly in favour of an independent ESCB, whereas the French position favoured an equal status for Finance Ministries in the making of EU economic and monetary policy. Nor, as the negotiations leading to the Maastricht Treaty were to indicate, was there much agreement on social policy. These differences were rooted in the different policy rationales of the three major states.

Germany united in the EU

The 1980s witnessed Germany's emergence as Europe's pre-eminent economic and political power. As Europe's prime exporter, Germany's interest was to promote the removal of national hindrances to trade and investment in the EU. At home, however, initial public support for the EU's internal-market policy waned as the liberal market implications became more widely appreciated,[26] prompting Chancellor Kohl to lend emphatic support to trade-union demands for protection against 'social dumping'.[27]

Kohl's pivotal domestic ally for the EU's social policy was the trade unions. The pact was cemented in April 1988, at a meeting between Chancellor Kohl, Labour Minister Blum and Deutscher Gewerkschaftsbund (DGB) President Breit. German social standards were to be preserved, with social policy being given equal weight with economic objectives in the creation of a single EU market. At the National Europa Conferences of December 1988 and August 1989,[28] the Chancellor hammered home his message. The idea of the social-market economy had won widespread acceptance across the EU. Germany's main advantage in international competition was its record of stability, and he would resist any turn in EU policy that promoted social dumping. He advised German employers to aggressively promote Germany's labour-management participation practices in the EU as a whole. The unions attended the European conferences, and extended their European alliances, while reaching agreement with the German employer organisations in June 1989 in favour of a Social Charter.[29] The nine-point plan of government, employers and unions subsequently formed the heart of the Commission's action programme.[30] The German unions led the campaign during the French EU presidency for binding social legislation, and sought to promote worker rights for consultation and collective bargaining, notably with respect to the debates on the European Company Statute.

Germany's domestic imperative for an EU social policy that protected the fabric of the social market economy was duplicated in monetary policy. The tone of Bonn's position on monetary union had been set by a February 1988 resolution of the German cabinet. 'The longer term goal is economic and monetary union in Europe, in which an independent European Central Bank, committed to maintaining price stability, will be able to lend effective support to a common economic and monetary policy.'[31] On repeated occasions thereafter, Germany's conditions for agreeing to an ECB were spelled out. Foreign Minister Genscher summarised German demands – priority accorded to price stability, political independence, no inflationary financing of government deficits, and a federal structure in the manner of the institutions of the Federal Republic or the United States.[32] There were to be restrictive and binding rules on government spending. Prior to union, price levels had to converge on a stable and low norm. The conditions for an ECB would have to be strict.[33]

Nor did the Bundesbank share the French government's sense of urgency to hasten the move to monetary union. A favoured Bundesbank analogy was that the creation of an ECB should 'crown' a long process, and that demands from Paris and Rome for an end to asymmetry in the ERM meant first building the 'roof' through a move to common policy-making.[34] The Bundesbank and the Finance Ministry sang in unison on the vexed question of the transition out of the status quo – an ECB had to 'succeed at the first attempt'.[35] The intermediary Stage Two of the Delors Report would have to go, and an immediate jump made into Stage Three. The Delors report was too vague about the conditions of the second and third stage and placed too much emphasis on policy coordination. Experience after 1990 with German unification suggested that tying two economies with different productivity rates together in one currency, or to permanently fixed exchange rates, implied potentially massive transfers.[36] There was little support from German taxpayers to pay for federal German transfers to the new Länder, and next to none to have Germany continue to act as European paymaster within the EU.

Not least, asking the Germans to abandon the DM was bound to drive up their price for cooperation in the EU. As Pöhl admitted, the passage that he found most attractive in the Delors report referred to 'the role played by the DM as anchorage point for monetary and intervention policies of the participants'.[37] If a political decision was taken to end DM hegemony, the only way was the creation of an authentic currency by an ECB.[38] There was no place for the ECU, which – as a basket of currencies and softer than the DM – could not serve as a satisfactory reserve asset. Nor was there a true substitute for the DM, as the German people would be 'sacrificing a hard currency on the European altar without knowing what we would get in return'.[39] If public support was to be assured for such a bold step, the ECB would have to be located in Frankfurt.[40] It would have to make monetary policy for the EU as a whole, deploy all modern monetary instruments, and have the monopoly of money creation, and undivided power over exchange-rate policy, binding on all members.[41] The interests of individual financial centres, such as London, would have to be subordinated to the ECB's paramount goal of price stability,[42] using Bundesbank methods. The Bundesbank would take over the management of open-market operations, with a permanent place on the ECB committee and rotation for the rest.[43]

This structural propensity of Germany to protect its domestic arrangements by projecting them as non-negotiable demands into the international arena also influenced the government's ideas about the achievement of state unity and the transformation of European security in the course of 1990. Bonn's vision for the new Europe was illustrated in the two July 1990 communiqués from the London NATO summit, and from the bilateral meeting of Helmut Kohl and Michael Gorbachev in the Caucasus. Germany, in the first communiqué, was to remain in the alliance of free democracies, while being 'associated with the growing political and economic integration' of the EU, notably in the affirmation of an European security identity.[44] In the second communiqué, 'a reunited Germany, exercising its unlimited sovereignty, may freely decide which alliances or blocs it wants to belong to'.[45] Which Germany was it to be: a Western-anchored or a national Germany? The answer was *both*. For Germany, the imperative of establishing a peace system in Europe along the lines of the Helsinki Final Act represented a task – in the words of President von Weizäcker – 'that the Germans have for all Europe, thanks to their weight and geographic position'.[46]

The combination of the related moves to German unity and self-determination, along with integration in Western Europe and the creative disintegration of the liberated countries of central–eastern Europe, thus pointed to two contradictory forces at work in the Europe of the 1990s. First, the problems confronting the wider Europe in its transition to a more integrated economy and an effective peace system far outweighed the resources available to any one country. This applied with particular force to Germany, whose urgent and immediate task was to manage a successful transition to a reunited country. Second, fear of a dominant Germany had been a determinant factor in the precipitate rush to bind Germany into a European Union. Yet German political leaders could anticipate that they would be able to convince national opinion that the sharing of sovereignty within a new and untried European political entity was worthwhile only if the new Europe conformed in large measure with German preferences. In other words, the price for surrendering the sovereignty so recently acquired was for Europe to be forged in a German likeness.

Germany's terms for the EU were already evident prior to reunification. For price stability to be established across the EU, labour-market institutions would have to adapt to the German model. The ECB would have to be on Bundesbank lines. Upgrading the Central Bank Governors Committee was a step in this direction. Pöhl was confirmed in his new capacity as President of the Committee in March 1990, and used his new platform to reaffirm Germany's intent that the conditions for an ECB would be strict.[47]

Germany's terms could not but escalate. Were German public opinion to grow confident in a recently confirmed national identity, France's strategy to bind Germany into a European Union, as sketched at Maastricht, would entail paying an ever higher political price. As German reticence about Maastricht rose, the German leadership's terms would harden. Germany was being asked to abandon monetary sovereignty. In exchange, nothing short of a federal Europe was acceptable. The future ECB had to be located in Frankfurt. Its market operations would be decentralised, and not located primarily in London. All central banks would have to be politically independent agents of the ECB. Meanwhile, member states had to meet the Treaty criteria for convergence. That spelled stabilisation across Europe, a marked stiffening of public finance across the Continent, and a sharp decline in public support for European union. Yet it was far from clear that Germany could meet the Maastricht criteria by 1996 or 1998, given the budgetary problems associated with the transfers to the new Bundesländer.

France: social protection, monetary union and German unity

President Mitterrand's two EU presidencies witnessed the partial redefinition of French policy to embrace Germany in the EU. But France, like Germany, proved reluctant to alter its domestic arrangements. The catalyst for change were the financial market reforms, initiated by Jacques Delors during his years as Finance Minister and analysed in subsequent chapters. The limits to a French liberal-market policy became evident during Prime Minister Chirac's administration in 1986–88. Despite privatisation of state properties, the continuities in French economic policies and performances were more notable than the changes.[48] The Chirac government emphasised commitment to preserving social policy arrangements, in view of the electorate's sensitivity to any cutbacks.[49] Newly privatised corporations were protected against hostile takeovers by cross-shareholdings. Sales of state properties were frozen by Mitterrand after his re-election in May 1988, as champions of 'a social-democratic, humanist future for Europe', 'based on liberal economic policies combined with generous social ones'.[50] This included retention of the social security system, and defence of the trade unions' role in its administration. Initial enthusiasm in France for the internal market was turning to a wider concern about its possible effects.[51]

France's domestic imperative to maintain social cohesion was compounded by linkage to the external imperative to anchor Germany in the EU. Mitterrand's victory in the May 1988 Presidential elections thus opened the prospect of a Franco-German deal. France, Prime Minister Rocard declared in his programmatic speech to the National Assembly, 'will make progress in the European (social) space a condition of progress registered in other areas'.[52] But whereas Germany emphasised price stability as the objective, France saw the purpose of the internal market, the ECB and the social 'plinth' in favour of workers' rights in an expansionary EU fiscal policy.

One of the main battle lines during negotiations on monetary union was drawn between France and Germany on the relative roles of finance ministries and central banks. The German Finance Ministry insisted on the autonomy of the strengthened Central Bank Governors Committee. During the French EU Presidency of late 1989, it was agreed that the finance ministers were to meet twice a year – with the President of the Central Bank Committee in attendance – to analyse the EU's economic condition. Despite intervening agreements, the French stuck to their original preferences. A government communiqué, rejecting 'the delegation of sovereignty to a technocratic institution',[53] stated that the economic governance of a united Europe would have to be predicated on the Council of Ministers and answerable to the European Parliament. The principle of the primacy of elected over unelected officials in EU macroeconomic policy was later reiterated forcibly by President Mitterrand. 'Those who decide economic policy, of which monetary policy is only one instrument, are the politicians elected by universal suffrage, the heads of state and government who make up the European Council.'[54]

During the Irish EU Presidency of early 1990, differences among member states became apparent in the opposition expressed to the proposal of centralised control of national budgets, and to an increase in resources denoted to the EU budget, as well as in the differences over the constitutional distribution of powers between the ECB and the Finance Council. These included the powers and voting rights of the ECB Board members, their accountability to the Council of Ministers or to the European Parliament, and the necessary 'coordination' of economic policy. It was agreed that the ECB would have sole rights to issue the currency and define monetary policy, but France insisted that exchange-rate policy was to be set by finance ministers.

The differences were settled essentially on German terms under the Italian EU Presidency of the second half of 1990. The first stage of EMU took effect on July 1, followed by German monetary union. In October, the Bundesbank circulated an unofficial paper entitled 'Compromise Proposal for the Second Stage of EMU' among other central banks, proposing a tough set of preconditions before any move to the second stage.[55] 'It is in the interest of Germany, but also of its partners, that the German currency remains a haven of stability', the Governor stated.[56] Further differences over the timing and content of Stage Two were finally overridden when Chancellor Kohl announced on French television his accord with a Spanish proposal of January 1994 as the beginning of Stage Two.

'We need a European Central Bank', the Chancellor said, 'which is completely independent and whose sole concern is the quality of the currency'.[57]

At the European Council meeting in Rome on October 27–28, 1990, the Bundesbank won acceptance of its preconditions. The independence of the new monetary institute to be set up in January 1994 would result from 'a process (that) has been set in train designed to ensure the independence of the members of the new monetary institution at the latest when monetary powers have been transferred'. In 1997, the EU Commission and Council would report on the progress achieved, and advise on the move to Stage Three.

The draft treaty, drawn up by the Central Bank Governors' Committee, was presented to the intergovernmental conference held in Rome on December 15, 1990. The first multilateral surveillance exercise by EU Finance Ministers was held in January 1991. The Council of Ministers would make recommendations every six months, with responsibility for implementing macroeconomic policy left in the hands of each government. The declared aim was to bring policy and performance into line, in preparation for the beginning of Stage Two. Two basic rules had been agreed: (1) there should be no central bank financing of government deficits; and (2) errant governments should not be bailed out, but be held liable for their debts.

From France's perspective, the ECB was designed to end the DM's supremacy in Europe, but there was to be no immediate counterpart in the form of a common security policy, which would involve a modification of France's nuclear strategy. 'The mission of France', Mitterrand declared in October 1988, 'is not to assure the protection of other European countries'.[58] The creation of a European pillar within the Atlantic alliance would have to wait until 1992–93, and the completion of the internal market. Mitterrand had sketched his vision of France's place in the new Europe in a major policy statement of May 1989.[59] France's role, he stated, was to preserve its status as a permanent member of the Security Council and as a leading economic, military, cultural and (he could have added) diplomatic power.[60] Paris shared London's concern at Germany's denuclearisation, but at the Franco-German summit of May 1989, Mitterand had picked up on Bonn's initiative to reassert the common objectives of a 'social Europe' and a European monetary union, in contrast to Prime Minister Thatcher's known hostility to both projects

Still, France's nuclear posture towards uniting Germany was scarcely that of a friendly partner. France's nuclear doctrine of massive retaliation was confirmed in the defence programme presented to the National Assembly in September 1989. Nine regiments, posted on France's eastern frontier, were to be equipped from 1992 on with the Hades nuclear missile system, with a range of 450 kilometres covering mostly German territory. Bonn was not consulted.[61]

The manner of Germany's move to unity prompted a sharp deterioration in Franco-German relations. Paris, along with London and Rome, had been by-passed in Bonn's dealings with Washington and Moscow. So Kohl and Mitterrand, in a bid to repair relations, launched a Franco-German proposal to accelerate the EU's political construction on April 19, 1990. The differences between the two on security policy were papered over at a Franco-German summit immediately prior to the April 28 EU summit at Dublin, where the member states agreed to hold a second intergovernmental conference on political union. Mitterrand then disassociated France from the July NATO summit statement on 'last resort' use of nuclear weapons, and the French Council of Ministers agreed to Strasburg as the seat for a new military command, tied into the tactical nuclear-strike force located at Metz and stretching from Belgium to Switzerland. Still, French concerns over Germany were compounded by the German–Soviet Friendship and Cooperation Treaty, and a Franco-German Munich summit of 17–18 September 1990 was reported as a disaster.[62] On 22 September 1990 the French Council of Ministers decided to start withdrawal of the French army corps in Germany starting in 1991, although the Franco-German brigade would stay in Germany at the request of Bonn.

The Gulf war, the USSR's disintegration and the collapse of Yugoslavia subsequently revealed Germany's domestic sensitivity and geopolitical vulnerability to the momentous changes in world politics. A poll on German public opinion showed 75 per cent of respondents opposed to Germany's engagement in international conflicts, and wanting good relations primarily with the Soviet Union (59 per cent), the United States (44 per cent) and France in third place (38 per cent).[63] For France, Germany's changed position in a new Europe meant moving closer to its Atlantic allies, redefining national security policy, and repairing relations with Germany. In June 1992, France followed NATO's example and announced the halt of production and deployment of battlefield nuclear weapons.

The alternative to France's seeking to accommodate a united Germany on security policy, while developing a more federalist strand of policies within the EU, was for Germany to consolidate its own internal structures and networks, thereby installing a hierarchy in Europe that had been absent for forty-five years. It was fear of this Germany that drove Mitterrand towards an intergovernmental conference designed to put the accompanying measures – security, money, social affairs – more firmly into the EU's domain.

The United Kingdom and the liberal camp

Prime Minister Thatcher was a notable proponent of the internal-market policy outlined in Lord Cockfield's White Book, presented to the EU Council in June 1985. Opening up markets would strike at the heart of the continental states' mercantilisms. 'No one', the Prime Minister stated in an interview of November 1987, 'is entitled to have a balance of payments surplus entrenched in the way in which they [the Federal Republic and Japan] run both their economy and also their society'.[64] A liberal-market policy in the EU would also place British foreign policy in line with domestic practice in that financial services and labour-market freedoms could be sold abroad. Not least, market liberalisation could be presented as being in the EU's best interest in that it would address the sources of the Continent's persistently high rates of unemployment. These were generally recognised as due to high-cost welfare systems,[65] the emergence of dual labour markets, with insiders enjoying the panoply of social security and legal protection and outsiders unemployed, working part-time or in the unofficial markets,[66] and inappropriate training systems. By 1988, there were 17 million unemployed in the EU, high underemployment relative to both the United States and Japan, 40–45 million people living in poverty,[67] a weakening of the trade unions[68] and an ageing population.

The liberal offensive was launched during the 1986 British EU Presidency. London's 'Big Bang' in October of that year accelerated reforms under way in the major EC financial markets, while the government proposal for an Action Programme for Employment and Growth was presented for the EU's reflection.[69] The Programme, with Irish and Italian backing, championed the freeing of labour markets. It was promptly scotched by an alliance between the Commission and the early 1987 Belgian EU Presidency. After a hard-fought February 1988 budget settlement, the continental alliance in favour of social protection took shape, even as the internal market programme, notably in financial services, gathered pace.

Britain's free-market EU crusade held a number of weaknesses. One was the fragility of the British economy. Since 1979, Tory government policy was to achieve non-inflationary growth, reduce the role of the state, and enhance individual responsibilities. This was to be achieved by control over the money supply, reduced government spending, free wage bargaining and a floating exchange rate. Foreign-exchange controls were freed. But the initial tight monetary policy, combined with a soaring pound sterling, saw a collapse of UK manufacturing output by 18 per cent by 1983. Unemployment rates rose to over 3 million. The subsequent upturn was facilitated by the continued high oil prices, disguising the shift to trade deficit on manufacturing trade. When oil prices collapsed in 1986, the manufacturing sector (only 20 per cent of GDP) proved inadequate to claw the country back into the red. Productivity improvements had been achieved by shedding labour, not investing in new plant and equipment.

With foreign exchange controls freed, corporate Britain's overseas investments soared: between 1985 and 1988, the outflow of foreign direct investment from Britain was over 18 per cent of gross fixed capital formation, compared to 4.5 per cent and 4.1 per cent respectively in Germany and France.[70] Given Britain's precarious manufacturing base, the government promoted Britain's attraction as an offshore production base for United States and Japanese multinational corporations. 'They use us', Thatcher declared, 'as a springboard into Europe. They come here because of our traditions and because we are British'.[71] This meant making inward investment to Britain relatively more attractive than alternative locations in the EU. Britain had a low strike record in the 1980s, a pro-multinational business government, and labour costs and tax burdens more in line with Spain and Ireland than with Germany or France. Thatcher's arguments against the Social Charter were therefore that it would raise labour costs, create unemployment, and scare away foreign investment. Its thrust was incompatible with the Tory government's domestic labour-market policies.[72]

Another weakness was the government's internal confusion over exchange-rate policy. Fearful of the social effects of continued high unemployment levels, the government had engineered a boom and allowed the exchange rate to slide. High growth facilitated the Tory election victory of June 1987. Further stimulus to domestic demand was provided in the government's budget of March 1988, with corporate tax rates lowered from 52 to 35 per cent. The next two years saw the trade deficit widen to 4 per cent of GDP, interest rates rise to double digits, inflation rates back up to over 8 per cent, and the government dependent on the confidence of the overseas holders of $35 billion of short-term funds invested in London. Under these conditions, Mrs Thatcher argued on free-market grounds that Britain was better off outside the ERM, while Chancellor of the Exchequer Lawson favoured ERM entry of sterling, both to stabilise the exchange rate and to enhance Britain's position in the internal market negotiations. As Jacques Delors stated, it was difficult 'to imagine a common financial zone with eight countries in 1990 freeing capital movements, without the UK taking a clear position on participating in the EMS'.[73] Lawson resigned in autumn 1989, followed a year later by the Prime Minister, who reluctantly conceded on sterling's entry to ERM but opposed any British commitment to monetary union.

German leadership of a continental alliance in favour of social protection pointed to a showdown with Britain. The leitmotif of the campaign was that social rights were for 'workers', rather than for citizens.[74] The main difference with Britain was hidden in the argument on labour-market 'rigidities'. For Thatcher, they had to be removed. For Germany, they were built in to the social-market economy. The Social Charter thus became a battleground for the two positions. Germany had the upper hand. Spain, Portugal, Ireland and Greece were now major recipients of EU funds. France was on board. The Labour party grasped the opportunity to join the continental alliance against Thatcher, and to seek to counter Tory labour-market policies by coming out in support of the Community's 'social dimension'. German business stopped harping on about high domestic costs and joined Kohl and the trade unions in a national pact to preserve Germany's social-market economy. 'Integration among the twelve economies', the employer–union pact stated, 'would be incomplete without an approximation in the longer term of progressive social standards towards a high level'.[75] As Kohl argued, the German model should serve as an example for the EU as a whole.[76]

British and German government and business interests nonetheless coincided on the Commission's draft proposal for a European Company Statute. Both Britain and Germany were eager to participate in the European merger market, involving inevitable corporate restructurings. But Britain questioned the Commission's assumption that business needed European incorporation, and was positively hostile – as it had been in the past[77] – to any inclusion of worker participation rights in the draft. The British government also objected to the Commission's idea of submitting the Charter to a qualified majority vote on the grounds that it fell under internal-market measures. German government, business, and unions agreed, but for opposite reasons. There was the fear that German corporations could avoid national laws by opting for a looser European statute, decided on by majority vote,[78] while German corporations realised that the presence of trade unionists on supervisory boards provided an additional defence against hostile takeovers. And the Ministry of Economics was concerned that Mittelstand (medium-sized, family-owned) firms would be absorbed by European predators.[79] Hence, Britain's open-market approach and Germany's protectionist corporate networks conspired to keep a key element of social policy firmly within the domain of state prerogatives.[80] Bonn, though, backed legally binding EU rights for employee representation in the governance of multi-national firms.

Monetary union was another battering-ram, as Chancellor Lawson realised, which blunted the thrust toward freeing up the internal market.[81] It required further treaty modifications, and a centralisation of decision-making, for which there was little support in the member states. The British position, as spelled out by Thatcher, was for 'willing and active co-operation between independent sovereign states [as] the best way to build a successful European Community'.[82] This position held a number of far-reaching consequences. Thatcher's negative stance on the accompanying measures enabled her opponents to set her up as a scapegoat, thereby keeping their own differences out of the limelight. It prompted fears in the City of London of Britain's marginalisation in the financial services discussions, as the continental member states implemented legislation favouring universal banks over Anglo-American-style investment houses. It meant that Britain's eventual suggestion for a 'hard ecu', managed by a Monetary Fund, could be dismissed by ECB supporters as a diversionary tactic.[83] And it clearly indicated Germany's growing weight in European affairs, as the US 'partner in leadership' in a new and wider Europe.

German unity in 1990 marked the re-emergence of a Europe of the great powers and demonstrated the centrality of Germany's relationship with the United States. The end of the Cold War opened the prospect for Germany of a European peace system, hinging on a continued US presence and a network of institutions, centring on the EU. This implied keeping defence policy within the domain of the sovereign states, and therefore NATO. The United States was reunited Germany's prime ally in the maintenance of the new European balance. Germany championed the EU's rapid enlargement, while nothing within the EU could be agreed on without Germany's consent. 'Our aim', Chancellor Kohl stated, 'is the European Union as model and keystone of a peace order including the whole of Europe, because – let us not forget: Europe is much more than the European Community'.[84] Such a wider Europe pointed to further areas of discord between France and Germany, over opening to eastern European trade, the pace and method of the EU's enlargement, and the balance to be struck between the demands of the countries of central–eastern Europe, and those of the southern Mediterranean. 'In these circumstances', former Prime Minister Thatcher concluded, 'the Community augments Germany's power rather than constraining it'.[85]

The unfinished business of the Maastricht Treaty

Differences among the EU member states over the 'accompanying measures' were at the heart of the ambiguities and unfinished business embedded in the Maastricht Treaty, agreed to at the European Council on December 9, 1991 and signed on February 7, 1992. The Treaty modified the Rome Treaty, and is seventy-two pages in length, containing forty-eight annexes or protocols. Three pillars were to sustain the European Union: (1) the internal market, to which was added the European System of Central Banks; (2) a common foreign and security policy; and (3) home and legal affairs.

The heart of the Treaty was the member states' 'irreversible' commitment to achieve monetary union by 1997–99. The gap between signing the Treaty and making the leap was necessary for Germany to digest the costs of unification, for implementation of the internal market and its accompanying legislation, and for the member states to address the budgetary and labour-market imbalances that had been built up since the 1960s. As noted earlier, the technical arguments in favour of monetary union included the reduction in transaction costs involved in a multi-currency and highly interdependent trading area. Equally important was the promise that a single currency would provide much greater transparency to customers of pricing differentials across the EU. It would cement the internal market, as producers in member states whose governments were profligate would not be able to seize market shares through competitive devaluations from producers in countries whose governments pursued more virtuous policies. The major arguments in favour of monetary union on its own terms, though, were political: it would be an ECB, not the Bundesbank, which in the future would set monetary policy for the Union. Other member states would gain by participating in monetary decisions. Germany would gain, because the Bank's mandate was a duplicate of its own and because it would not be making policies for others on a national mandate alone.

Stage Two was to begin in 1994, with the creation of a 'European Monetary Institute', with responsibility 'to coordinate monetary policies'. The Institute's powers would be greater than the Central Bank Governors Committee, but less than the ECB, which the French and Italians wanted. Member states would be free to hand over their foreign-exchange reserves, but their central banks would not have to alter their relations with their governments until the end of Stage Two. This hybrid EMI, along with the EU Commission, was to report in 1996 on the degree of 'convergence' achieved. As noted, the convergence criteria were essentially financial: low inflation, stable interest rates, stable currencies in the ERM and moderate government deficits and public debt. If seven member states met the criteria, the finance ministers would advise when Stage Three was to start. The decision was to be taken by unanimous vote in the European Council. The Finance Ministers would then decide by majority vote who was qualified to join. All participants could claim partial victories.

• The French won Kohl's acknowledgement of the 'irreversibility' of the process of monetary union and a single currency but not as early as 1993, as Delors wanted. Mitterrand extracted a concession that if the European Council decided against a move to Stage Three in 1996–97, the passage would be in 1998 for those member states which met the convergence criteria. Those member states not able or willing to join would be excluded from the ECB's 'Governing Council', with full powers over the union's monetary policy. But all would have a seat on the 'General Council'.

• The Germans won agreement for an ECB based on their own design. The member states, it was agreed, would keep control of fiscal policy. But the German negotiators won their point that governments running 'excessive government deficits' would be subject to sanctions. Council and Commission were to supervise the economic policies of member states, and make appropriate recommendations. President Mitterrand chose to interpret this as meaning that the future ECB would be subordinate to member-state governments assembled in Council.

• Britain won an escape clause that would allow it to opt in, but Germany had laid the ground to win member-state support to locate the ECB in Frankfurt.

• Italy won time to reform its public finances on the EU's tough convergence criteria, but that meant fundamental political reform at home.

• Spain won a promise to increase the 'structural' funds flowing to the poorer states. This was facilitated by agreement of the EFTA countries to contribute funds to EC budgetary resources in return for the access they enjoyed to southern markets.

The German government's counter to France's demand for sacrifice of the DM was to request a common foreign and security policy. But this was the area where European governments and public opinion were most divergent. German unity, the Gulf War, the USSR's disintegration and the collapse of Yugoslavia all brought the differences to the fore. The modesty of the Treaty's innovations merely covered the extent of Western European states' differences over security and defence policy. France and Britain, as permanent members of the UN Security Council – without prejudice to their responsibilities in the Charter – were to promote the position and interests of the Union. The Mitterrand–Kohl plan of October 14, 1991, was incorporated into the Treaty, whereby the WEU was to be an 'integral part of the development of the European Union'. But the British and Dutch won agreement that these arrangements would be compatible with NATO. In supporting them, either Kohl wanted to pull the French into the ongoing NATO reforms, or he wanted to go ahead with the French in creating the kernel of a European military power in anticipation of a much-reduced US military presence in Europe. The choice would be postponed until the inter-governmental conference of 1996, in anticipation of 1998 when the WEU Treaty was slated to run out, and it would be possible for the EU to take over its role.

Optimally for Germany, all decisions regarding foreign and security policy would have to be adopted by majority voting. But at the heart of French foreign policy stood France's view of its standing as a great power, with its permanent seat on the Security Council, its *mission universelle* as the country of the Rights of Man, and its nuclear weapons. Germany had renounced its ambition as a great power in the traditional sense, but sought a permanent seat on the Security Council, and equates its eventual role there with implementing the UN Charter. Above all, Germany voluntarily renounced nuclear weapons by signing the Non-Proliferation Treaty in 1968, and lobbied heavily for its extension in 1995. Yet the heart of French military strategy was nuclear weapons. The ultimate exchange in the negotiations over monetary union was thus the price of surrendering the DM for a deal involving Germany's relationship to the French nuclear *force de frappe*. The spectrum of options ran from maintenance of French nuclear inde-pendence through joint planning to disarmament. As the French Ambassador to Australia stated in justifying the renewal of nuclear testing in Mururoa in the South Pacific: 'Certainly, the fact that we wanted to exclude for good the possibil-ity of any further conflict between France and Germany was at the root of our European policy.'[86]

Kohl also pledged in the Maastricht negotiations that the DM would only be handed over if the powers of the European Parliament were augmented. They were in fact enhanced, but far less than desired by supporters of a federal EU. On the insistence of the British government, reference to the whole enterprise as a 'Union with a federal goal' was dropped. The Treaty was defined as 'a stage in the realisation of an ever closer Union between the peoples'. The Union, the Treaty stated, 'is to have due regard to the national identity of its member states' and is to respect their rights and liberties such as they have developed from their constitutional traditions. The Council was confirmed as both executive and leg-islature in the EU, to which the Commission and Parliament were associated through a variety of procedures. This indivisibility of authority in the EU risked bringing the law into disrepute as an instrument of particular state interests, rather than as a body of doctrine applicable equally to all citizens, organisations and governments of the Union.[87] In the opinion delivered on the Treaty by the German Constitutional Court, there could be no automatic surrender of sove-reign powers in the future by Germany unless the EU's development was compat-ible with the principles laid down in the Basic Law. That placed the burden of proof on Europe's national leaders to negotiate a Treaty in 1996–97 which squared the circle between preserving their states' 'identity' and merging them in a federal EU.

Indeed, the loyalties of Europeans remained primarily national throughout, and their concerns mainly economic in nature. The launching of the EU's inter-nal-market programme was designed in part to meet widespread concern about unemployment. Yet promotion of the 'social dimension' as a vital accompany-ing measure was prompted by the prospect of the populist backlash against the EU's liberal-market programme (as mentioned in the previous chapter, the back-lash helped to derail the ERM in 1992 and 1993). Here at least was an area where the distinctive European endorsement of a social net commanded widespread support.[88] But the campaign for social protection against 'Thatcherism' pre-served intact the various national social systems. This meant in effect restricting competition within labour markets while negotiating in the EU over Europe-wide regulations which preserved the *acquis national*. This ambiguity was written into the Maastricht Treaty in a separate protocol where eleven states other than Britain agreed to adopt the EU's Action Programme of 1989 by qual-ified majority voting on social policy. The measures included 'the promotion of employment, improved living and working conditions, proper social protection, dialogue between management and labour, and the development of human resources with a view to lasting high employment'. Unanimous voting was required for matters affecting social security (highly sensitive in France), worker-management negotiations (highly sensitive in Germany), and the conditions of work for immigrants (highly sensitive across all of Western Europe).

Whether the ultimate result was seen as laden with federal intent, or as per-petuating a Europe of the states in an open-ended process, the concessions made by all parties to the Treaty meant that none was satisfied with the result and all could claim a partial victory, while arguing the need to make partial sacrifices. As the concessions had to be balanced by future rewards, and the partial victo-ries opened a prospect of further benefits, none had the incentive to drop out and all had an incentive to stay in 'at the heart of Europe', as Prime Minister Major described Great Britain's position in the EU. The treaty also underwrote a multi-speed, variable-geometry Europe of concentric circles and special relations. It left the inner core of states, led by France and Germany, to set the agenda for the union's future developments in any of the three pillars. *De facto*, the Treaty barely impaired the member states' powers to act alone. If progress towards union was the goal, the Treaty left open the way for an inner core of members to make the first move, and provide an incentive to the laggards to join sooner or later. The Treaty thus incorporated Europe's diversity into its complex pro-cedures, but provided a timetable for commitments and further amendments. It did not escape the reversible incrementalism inherent to negotiations among the states, with their dual membership in the EU and in the world community of states.

The politics of the 'accompanying measures' in Maastricht Europe

The German government, including the Bundesbank, presented a choice for its prospective partners in monetary marriage between acceptance of Germany's unilateral decisions, or multilateralising them on Frankfurt's conditions. This assertion of German interests was etched into the structural requirement for the

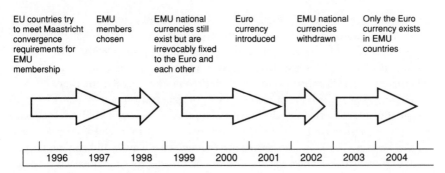

Figure 3.1 Economic and monetary union, 1996–2004

German government to protect domestic arrangements by exporting them as a non-negotiable demand into the EU. It was also inherent to the process of German unity. As the cost of German reunification rose, the rift within the country deepened between those favouring giving priority to reconstruction in the immediate future, and those like Kohl, who anticipated the costs to Germany and Europe of a German go-it-alone policy (*Alleingang*). If the other member states were determined to have Germany abandon the DM, their only course of action was to walk the Bundesbank's path of price stability. The hope was that their moment to call in the political credits accumulated in the Bundesbank's metaphorical vaults would come in 1997–99. Any backsliding then would be tantamount to the Federal Republic breaking a Treaty commitment.

Yet the fate of the ERM in 1992 and 1993 suggested that the German rather than the other member-state governments was best positioned to judge who should join an ECB, and when. Not least, the foreign-exchange turmoil of those years was built on inadequate public support for political union, which the Bundesbank had repeatedly urged as a prerequisite for a successful move to monetary union. Simply, the probability of a stable monetary regime in the EU was low, not only if the institutions of the EU remained partial, but especially if they developed without overwhelming popular support.

After extensive additional political jockeying with respect to the EMU timetable during 1994 – in the wake of the currency crises of 1992 and 1993 – it was not until the Spanish EU presidency at the December 1995 summit in Madrid that the decision was made to name the future currency the 'Euro'. This represented a further blow to the French strategy to promote the ECU, and was accompanied by further German intransigence on the passage to a single currency. Having passed Stage One (ERM) and the initial phases of Stage Two (creation of the EMI (European Monetary Institute)), the day of judgement was approaching as to who would be in and who would be out, a decision to be made at the intergovernmental meeting of heads of state at the end of 1997 under the Luxemburg EU presidency. The date for the launch of the Euro under EMU was set at January 1, 1999 – see Figure 3.1. In the meantime, the EMI was scheduled to be transformed into the ECB early in 1998, to begin running a single monetary policy for the EMU participants following an irrevocable locking-in of exchange rates. No agreement was reached initially on whether the lock-in would involve an administrative decision on rates on the part of the EU or whether the lock-in rates would simply follow market rates at the time.

There was also the issue of critical mass, the suggestion that 90 per cent of all EU financial transactions, including new issues of private and public debt and all secondary-market trading, would have to be covered by the new currency if it was to have credibility. A switch-over to the new currency would come later in a big-bang transition. The Germans were reluctant to commit themselves to the switch-over as far as public accounts were concerned until the new currency proved itself to be sound, while the Commission took the position that delays would undermine irreversibility.

The politics surrounding this historic decision included issues of timing, with the French and Italians suspected of wanting to push the date into 1998 in order to gain more time to meet convergence criteria. Political events scheduled between 1995 and 1999 included the United Kingdom (general election, 1997), France (parliamentary elections, March 1998) and Germany (national elections, October 1998) – see Figure 3.2.

The politics would also include issues of content, most visibly in the negotiations over the EU's institutions and security arrangements. Post-Maastricht Europe was balanced delicately between a very partial programme of liberalisation in factor markets and a state system where German unity installed a hierarchy in Europe that had been absent for forty-five years. At the interface between European market and European hierarchy lay the close identity established between labour markets, nationality and EU policies. The moment that the EU's agenda for the internal market had been freed in February 1988, the forces favouring 'accompanying measures' to stall or channel the anticipated move to liberalisation were mobilised. Paradoxically, they adopted a posture as the champions of European political integration, while in effect acting to preserve national social policies within a Europe of states. The question could well be asked how a monetary union would work between regions, whose labour markets operated in distinct ways and with different structures. Equally, the question could be asked whether different labour-market policies within the states did not imply continuing competition between discrete but connected national financial systems. This was the determinant condition which European policy would have to address in the years ahead.

Notes

1 Commission Européenne, *1992: Le Défi Nouvelles données économiques de l'Europe sans frontières* (Paris: Flammarion, 1988).
2 Economie Européenne, Commission des Communautés Européennes, *1992: La Nouvelle Economie Européenne*, No. 35, March 1988, p. 21.

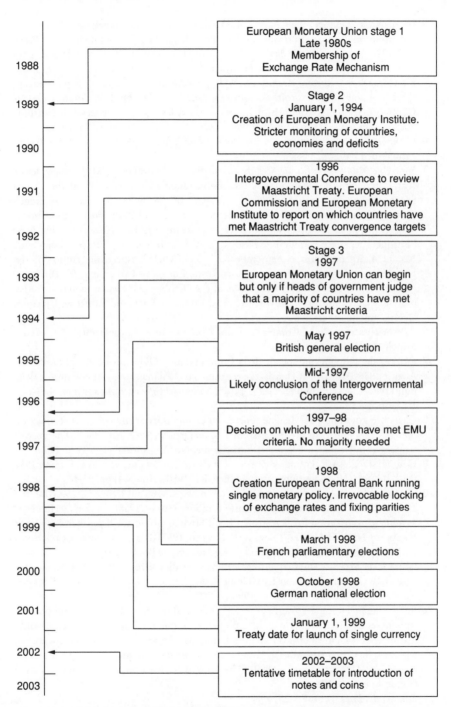

Figure 3.2 The Economic and Monetary Union time-line, 1988–2003

3 See Gaetano Zingone, 'La Charte communautaire des droits sociaux fondamentaux et l'evolution du droit du travail dans les Pays de la C.E.E.', Communication, Paris, 12.2.1990, Journée d'Etude de l'EJA-Formation; Les Relations de Travail dans les pays de la Communauté Européenne; Heinrich Rentmeister, 'Die soziale dimension des Binnenmarktes', *Europa Archiv*, 20, 1989, pp. 627–34; Information, 'Espace Social: Quel Contenu?', *Observatoire Social Européen*, June 1988, pp. 1–3; Commission des CE, Information, 'La Commission Européenne fixe les lignes directrices de la Politique Sociale Communautaire pour les années à venir', Brussels, February 24, 1988.

4 *L'Année Politique, Economique et Sociale en France, 1983* (Paris: Editions du Moniteur, 1984), pp. 35–6.

5 *Pour Une Nouvelle Politique Sociale en Europe*, avant-propos de M. Jacques Delors (Paris: Economica, 1984). This is the compendium of a conference at the French Senate, held October 6–8, 1983. It was part of the wider definition of French Community policy going on at that time. In September 1983, the French government had presented to the other member states a document, 'Une Nouvelle Etape pour l'Europe: un espace commun de l'industrie et de la recherche', Europe Documents, No. 1274, Agence Europe, September 16, 1983. Michel Albert, the author of the popularised version of a parallel report to the European Parliament, *Un Pari pour l'Europe* (Paris: Seuil, 1983), was present at the October 1983 Senate conference. Also present were Commissioner Ivor Richards, Professor Raymond Rifflet and Jacques Delors, among others.

6 'Les orientations de la Commission des Communautés Européennes', *Futuribles*, March 1985, pp. 3–18.

7 Extraits de 'La politique sociale de la Communauté', *Observatoire Social Européen*, August 1986. Also Ivor Richards, 'Le reexamen de la dimension communautaire de la politique sociale à moyen terme s'impose', *Bulletin d'Informations sociales*, ILO, No. 1/85, pp. 11–18.

8 Chris Brewster and Paul Teague, *European Community Social Policy: Its Impact on the UK* (London: Institute of Personnel Management, 1989), pp. 95–9. The growth strategy is published in *Economie Européenne*, No. 30, November 1986, p. 115.

9 Commission des CE, Patrick Venturini, *Un Espace Social Européen A l'Horizon 1992* (Luxemburg: Office des publications officielles, 1988), Annex 4, pp. 93–6.

10 For the general argument as applied to the powers, see Paul Kennedy, *The Rise and Decline of the Great Powers* (New York: Random House, 1988). On high technology as a key consideration for perestroika, see Marshall Goldman, *Economic Reform in the Age of High Technology* (New York: Norton, 1987). For US–Japan trade relations, see Clyde Prestowitz, *Trading Places* (New York: Basic Books, 1989).

11 Franz-Josef Strauss, *Die Errinerungen* (Berlin: Siedler Verlag, 1990), p. 435. See also Joseph Rovan's introduction to Helmut Kohl, *L'Europe est notre destin: Discours actuels* (Paris: Editions de Fallois, 1990), p. 32.

12 Italian financial circles were generally sceptical at the efficacy of supposedly 'spontaneous' mechanisms leading to monetary union. Free capital movements would disrupt the EMS, in view of different inflation rates between European currencies. See Marcello de Cecco and Alberto Giovannini, *A European Central Bank?* (Cambridge: Cambridge University Press, 1989). The book was based on a conference at Castel Gandolfo in June 1988.

13 *Financial Times*, February 25, 1988.

14 Peter Hort, 'Ein Bilanz der deutschen EC-Präsidentschaft', *Europa-Archiv*, 15, 1988,

pp. 421–8. François Puaux, *La politique internationale des années quatre-vingt* (Paris: PVF, 1989), pp. 159–77.

15 'La Commission Européenne fixe les lignes directrices de la Politique Sociale Communautaire pour les années à venir', Information Commission of the European Communities, February 24, 1988.

16 *Financial Times*, May 9, 1988; *Le Monde,* May 8–9, 1988.

17 Economie Européenne, *La création d'un espace financier européen*, No. 36, May 1988, pp. 9–10.

18 'Extracts from the summit communiqué', *Financial Times*, June 28, 1989: 'the role to be played by community standards, national legislation and contractual relations must be clearly established'.

19 Interview with President Mitterrand, *Le Nouvel Observateur*, July 27, 1989.

20 *Europolitique*, No. 1538, November 8, 1989.

21 *Europolitique*, No. 1553, January 10, 1990. These measures dealt with 'atypical work', with a view to limiting labour-market competition, working hours, work contracts, and an EC instrument for information, consultation and participation of workers in multinational corporations.

22 'The wall which divides Berlin', the communiqué read, 'is an unacceptable symbol of the division of Europe. We wish for the establishment of a situation of peace in Europe in which the German people recovers its unity through free self-determination.' *Le Monde*, May 31, 1989.

23 'Nato agrees its approach to German reunification', *Financial Times*, December 5, 1989.

24 'Les Douze acceptent que le peuple allemand retrouve son identité', *Le Monde*, December 10–11, 1989. No date was named for completion of monetary union, reflecting Kohl's misgivings and Thatcher's opposition.

25 *Le Monde*, January 19, 1990.

26 Elizabeth Noelle-Neumann, 'Europa – das unbekannte, ungeliebte Wesen?', *Frankfurter Allgemeine Zeitung*, December 19, 1988; 'Europe: la grande prudence des Allemands face à 1992', *Les Echos*, March 6, 1989.

27 See Helmut Kohl's government statement to the Bundestag, April 27, 1989, in Kohl, *L'Europe est notre destin*, pp. 315–27; and summary of the CDU-CSU Bundestag grouping on the EC social space, April 24–27, 'Soziale Aspekte des Europäischen Binnenmarktes', *Ifo Schell-dienst*, No. 25, September 8, 1989, pp. 8–17.

28 See Presse und Informationsamt der Bundesregierung, Nr. 40/S, 333, Bonn, March 22, 1988; Ansprache des Bundeskanzlers, 'Europas Zukunft-Vollendung des Binnenmarktes 1992', Nr. 172/S, 1525, Bonn, December 9, 1988; Erklärung des Bundeskanzlers zur Eröffnung, Nationale Europa-Konferenz in Bonn. Also 'Europakonferenz: Kohl will Mitbestimmungsmodell offensiv vertreten'. *Handelsblatt*, August 31, 1989.

29 See Arbeitgeber, Bundesvereinigung der Deutschen Arbeitgeberverbände, Jahresbericht (1989), pp. 135–7.

30 *Financial Times*, October 31, 1989.

31 *Financial Times*, June 23, 1988.

32 H.-D. Genscher, 'Die Rolle der Bundesrepublik Deutschland bei der Vollendung des Europäischen Währungssystem Ergebnisse einer Fachsagung, Strategie und Ergebnisse für die Zukunft Europas' (Gütersloh: Bertelsmann Stiftung, 1989), pp. 13–20.

33 *Le Monde*, 18 January, 1990.
34 On the 'coronation' and 'leap in the dark' approaches to the ECB, Dr Köhler, in a speech at the Caisse des Dépôts et Consignations, Paris, October 3, 1988, ECU Banking Association, Newsletter No. 5, November 1988; Dr Kloten to the Austrian National Bank, April 17, 1989; 'Perspektiven der europäischen Währungsintegration', in *Deutsche Bundesbank, Auszüge aus Presseartikeln,* April 27, 1989, pp. 6–11; Pöhl on ending asymmetry, in a speech of October 27, 1988 to the Comité National Luxembourgeois de la Ligue Européenne de Coopération Economique, *Repères*, No. 1, 1989, pp. 6–11.
35 As stated by Hans Tietmeyer, then a key figure in the Finance Ministry: *Financial Times*, May 13, 1988.
36 *Neue Zurcher Zeitung*, September 8, 1990.
37 *Le Monde*, May 23, 1989.
38 *Europe*, November 4, 1989.
39 'Pöhl pocht auf Unabhängigkeit einer Europäischen Notenbank', *Die Welt*, September 4, 1990.
40 *Le Monde*, February 10, 1989.
41 'Das Diktat der Stunde liess längeres warten nicht zu', *Frankfurter Rundschau*, July 4, 1990.
42 Schlesinger outlined his vision of a European monetary union at a speech in Frankfurt on December 17, 1992.
43 *Financial Times*, January 9, 1989. See Niels Thygessen, 'A European Central Banking System – Why and When?', Association Bancaire pour l'Ecu, No. 4, 1988, pp. 6–13; 'Centralisation and Accountability within the Central Bank: Any Lessons from the US Experience for the Potential Organisation of a European Central Banking Institution?' in Paul de Grauwe and Theo Peters, *The ECU and European Monetary Integration* (London: Macmillan, 1989), pp. 91–114.
44 *Financial Times*, July 8–9, 1990.
45 *Financial Times*, July 17, 1990.
46 *Die Welt*, Interview with President von Weizäcker, March 23, 1990. He added: 'it is clear that we do not wish to return to the old continental power system or to alter the policy of the European Community'.
47 *Le Monde*, 18 January, 1990.
48 The Aubry report, requested by Prime Minister Chirac's Social Affairs Minister Philippe Séguin was presented in September 1988 to his centrist successor in the Rocard government, Jean-Pierre Soisson. The document was to serve as a basis for policy during the French Presidency. See Martine Aubry, *Pour Une Europe Sociale* (Paris: La Documentation Française, 1989). The proposals are very similar to those of the Commission.
49 On June 18, 1987, Social Affairs Philippe Séguin, in his speech to the National Assembly on the financing of the social security regime, stated that 'the cathedral' constructed in 1945 had to be preserved. Quoted in *l'Année Politique, 1987* (Paris: Editions du Moniteur, 1988), p. 305.
50 See his 'Lettre à tous les Français', *Le Monde*, April 8, 9, 1988.
51 By February 1989, 58 per cent of French people interviewed declared themselves worried about the internal market: *Le Monde, SOFRES*, March 3, 1989. Only 28 per cent considered that the economic difficulties caused would be limited: *Le Monde, SOFRES*, May 13, 1989.

52 La déclaration de politique générale du premier ministre au Parlement, 'Construire un nouvel espoir', *Le Monde*, July 1, 1988.

53 *Neue Zurcher Zeitung*, December 10–11, 1990.

54 *Le Monde*, September 5, 1992.

55 These were: the EC must have completed the internal market; all member states would have to be in the narrow band; the treaties in monetary union would have to be ratified by all; monetary and compulsory financing of deficits would have to be banned in all member states; laws would have to be changed to ensure that central-bank governors would not be subject to instructions or to recall; anti-inflationary policies would have to have 'progressed substantially'. *Financial Times*, October 8, 1990.

56 *Le Monde*, December 17, 1990.

57 *Die Welt*, October 19, 1990.

58 Fondation pour les Etudes de Défense Nationale, 1989, pp. 316–26.

59 *Le Monde*, May 20, 1989.

60 As the Dutch Foreign Minister van den Broek pointed out in the quarrel about the chairmanship of the European Bank for Reconstruction and Development (EBRD), France was royally served as far as international institutions were concerned. It held the Presidencies, Secretary- or Directorate-Generals of the EC Commission, the OECD, the IMF, the Council of Europe and the EBRD. *Le Monde*, March 17, 1990.

61 *Die Welt*, September 15, 1989.

62 *Le Monde*, October 9, 1990.

63 *Suddeutsche Zeitung*, January 4, 1990.

64 An interview with the Prime Minister, *Financial Times*, November 23, 1987.

65 Murray Seeger, 'Europe Social Programs: endangered species', *International Herald Tribune*, March 12, 1981; 'La Commission Européenne est invité à formuler des propositions pour lutter contre le chomage', *Le Monde*, May 29, 1982. Assessment of the early 1980s by the then Social Affairs Commissioner, Ivor Richards, 'Le réexamen de la dimension communautaire de la politique sociale à moyen terme s'impose'; 'Devant les prélèvements communautaires', *Revue du Marché Commun*, No. 288, June 1985, pp. 301–6.

66 Office des Publications Officielles de la Communauté, 'La Politique Sociale de la Communauté', 8/86, pp. 12–13; 23–4.

67 Parlement Européen, Documents de Séance, Strasburg, 16.8.88, Série A, Doc. A2–177/88.

68 Robert Taylor, 'The workers prepare for 1992', *Financial Times*, May 9, 1988.

69 Brewster and Teague, *European Community Social Policy*, pp. 94–9. 'Résolution du Conseil du 22 décembre 1986 concernant un programme d'action pour la croissance de l'emploi' (86/C 340/02).

70 OECD Economic Surveys, *Germany*, 1988/1989, Annex, p. 122.

71 Service de Presse de l'Ambassade de Grande-Bretagne, Textes et Déclarations, July 29, 1988. Extracts from BBC interview with Prime Minister Thatcher, July 27, 1988.

72 The philosophy is clearly stated in *Removing Barriers to Employment, Proposals for the further reform of industrial relations and trade union law* (Cm. 655, London: HMSO, 1989).

73 *Financial Times*, June 24, 1988.

74 Assemblée Consultative Economique et Sociale, Communiqué de presse, 'M. Jean-Pierre Soisson au CES Européen', October 19, 1989.

75 Arbeitgeber, Jahresbericht, 1989, p. 135.
76 'Kohl will Mitbestimmungsmodell offensive vertreten', *Handelsblatt*, August 31, 1988.
77 Brewster and Teague, *European Community Social Policy*, pp. 91–4; 141; 225–7.
78 *Frankfurter Rundschau*, November 2, 1989; *Handelsblatt*, November 3–4, 1989.
79 *Frankfurter Allgemeine Zeitung*, January 20, 1989. Minister of Economy Haussman, in the Bundestag Europe debate, said that the merger wave must not sweep away Mittelstand firms, on which the vitality of the German economy depended.
80 'Grossbritannien will keine Mitbestimmung', *Frankfurter Allgemeine Zeitung*, November 17, 1989. The Social Charter agreed on by the eleven Social Affairs Ministers stated that worker-participation rights were to be developed in the light of 'prevalent national customs'.
81 Chancellor Lawson speech at Chatham House. 'What European Financial Space?' *Agence Europe*, Documents, No. 1545, February 8, 1989.
82 The harsher version of these views was provided by Secretary of Trade Nicholas Ridley's statement to the *Spectator*, July 12, 1990, to the effect that the Germans were trying to take over Europe with the proposal of a European System of Central Banks, and that the French were behaving like poodles. Polls showed that 66 per cent of those British people interviewed disagreed on the first statement, and 60 per cent disagreed with the second. See *Financial Times*, July 16, 1990. Sixty-four per cent in the summer *Eurobarometer* poll trusted Germans 'a lot', *Independent*, July 13, 1990.
83 'Major sets out a new role for the ecu in Europe', and 'The Bank of England's Statement', *Financial Times*, June 22, 1990.
84 Kohl, *L'Europe est notre destin*.
85 *The Times*, May 18, 1992.
86 *Financial Times*, September 4, 1995.
87 Laurent Cohen-Tanuggi, *L'Europe en Danger* (Paris: Fayard, 1992).
88 *The Pulse of Europe: A Survey of Political and Social Values and Attitudes* (Washington, DC: Times Mirror Center for the People and the Press, September 1991), pp. 43–5.

4

Financial system benchmarks: efficiency, stability and competitive performance

The last three chapters have analysed the politics and diplomacy surrounding the EU's financial services area, exchange-rate regimes, and repeated attempts to make a big leap to monetary union. Whether the EU succeeds or continues in the current hierarchical multi-currency trading area will have dramatic and as yet not fully understood consequences for Europe's financial markets and institutions, whatever the outcome.

Few issues are more important in setting the agenda of economic growth than the structure, conduct and performance of a nation's financial system. Standing at the centre of the transactions and resource-allocation process, high-performance financial systems are increasingly important as determinants of sustainable economic progress and stability. This is as true domestically as it is internationally, where global financial-market developments require an efficient 'window' on sources and uses of capital as well as market developments and technologies that change in substance and form at a rapid pace. Few countries can afford to be de-linked from these developments – especially as they develop mature industrial structures and rapidly evolving services sectors – or fail to create and maintain domestic financial systems that meet world performance standards. Their financial systems are therefore in a constant process of change, as schematically presented below.

This chapter outlines the framework parameters of high-performance financial systems and for financial firms operating in them. We begin with a formal presentation of change in financial systems. We then consider an intuitive structural model of financial intermediation and discuss the various stages of its evolution in terms of static and dynamic efficiency characteristics. We then consider issues facing the participants in, and users of, the financial system, with an emphasis on strategic-positioning alternatives and determinants of competitive performance. Finally, we discuss the role of regulation as a major factor affecting the performance of the financial system itself, both in the context of the economic development process and as a factor in defining the future of various types of financial firms.

Europe houses a mosaic of financial arrangements, embedded in the historical and political fabric of each one of the states, and yet linked to each other through multiple channels. Within any state, or between them, these financial arrangements may be presented in terms of regime, system and process.

- *Regime* is a normative concept, and may be taken as referring to the form of rule or constitutional order with regard to the evolution of financial institutions.
- *System* is used here in the sense that financial institutions effect payments and manage risks, and thereby interact with sufficient regularity to behave as parts of a whole. The emphasis is not so much on the normative aspects governing the regime, as on the permanent interactions between institutions.
- *Process* refers to financial intermediation between the end-users of the system, between those who *save* (abstain from absorbing current income in consumption, investment or government spending) and those who *borrow* (consume, invest or engage in public-sector spending above current fiscal revenue).[1]

Regime, system and process are static only in a theoretical presentation. In such a case, as outlined below, the three elements may be in equilibrium, where the process of financial intermediation evolves within a financial system that is regulated according to a hierarchy of norms, effectively implemented. But equally, the three categories may be in disequilibrium, where the process creates a parallel set of markets to the official system, whose regulatory norms may be ineffectively applied. Two paths can be posited as defining departures from equilibrium.

- From a market perspective, the starting-point for a move away from a stable equilibrium opens with the process of intermediation, whose role evolves with the development of the financial system and the distribution of functions between institutions such as commercial and savings banks, merchant banks, fund managers and other competitors. As roles and functions alter, norms within the regime are called into question or adapted, leading cumulatively to changes in regime. At any point in the process, discretionary policies or actions may be adopted within the financial system, or in ways that impinge upon it, and alter the path taken.
- From a policy or regulatory perspective, the character of change is driven by the regulatory authorities' preferences with regard to system and process. The authorities may guard their autonomy and adhere to a constant set of norms, for which they develop and apply instruments to influence the evolution of the system and the process of saving and borrowing. They may be attacked, intimidated, or captured by special interests, which disregard the norms and skew the system and process to their own advantage. The regulatory authorities may pursue incompatible objectives, allowing intermediation to transgress inherited boundaries within or across the system, or by simple ignorance of what is going on. They may then have to adapt norms to the new and evolving system through a period of learning, while adopting a style which seeks to hide the

gap between their concept of the system and process and what in effect is happening in the markets and in interactions among institutions. Or they may prefer an a priori path, running from the definition of new norms and reform of the system, implying modifications in the process of behaviour by borrowers and savers. Given the speed at which market participants adapt or learn to circumvent the spirit if not the letter of the law, regulators' attempts to impose an a priori path may serve as an ex-post vindication, but rather less so as an *ex-ante* description of the trial-and-error path actually taken.[2]

Regime, system and process evolve within a state and market system. This, too, may be presented theoretically as in equilibrium. Suppose a number of states, whose regimes governing financial institutions are compatible, whose financial systems bear only minor differences, and where the process of saving and borrowing evolves along parallel paths. The states exist in a system in that they regularly interact through numerous political or market channels. Over time, their regimes, systems and processes move into disequilibrium, where the process, too, creates a set of parallel markets to the official systems – whose regulatory norms are increasingly ineffectively applied. The move away from equilibrium may be presented also along two paths.

- From a market perspective, savers and borrowers look for the best opportunities on offer. Assuming some degree of liberalisation of capital movements, they seek to place their assets or to borrow funds in locations which offer higher rewards outside the bounds of their state's regime. The opportunities available modify the financial flows in the state's internal system, and the process of intermediation among savers and borrowers on international markets. This in turn affects the international financial system, and the distribution of roles and functions between institutions on international markets, as well as operating a feedback process into domestic markets. As the pace of change accelerates on both international and national markets, the norms governing the previous international regime are called into question or adapted, leading cumulatively to changes in regime.[3]
- From a policy perspective, the location of change is situated in the regulatory authorities' divergent preferences with regard to system and process, alluded to above. At any point in the story, discretionary policies or actions may be adopted within the financial system – or in ways that impinge upon it – that alter the paths of regulatory authorities in ways that may converge or diverge (or both), but without their paths ever meeting. The elusiveness of agreeing on and then implementing an international regime – or indeed of an even more ambitious regime such as that postulated by the EU, where the member states in effect replace national norms – is all the greater in that the balance of advantages between compliance and non-compliance may have very different implications for individual member states. But it is unlikely to benefit all equally and simultaneously.

This highly restrictive condition for shifting from one point of equilibrium to another in an international regime, system and process becomes more constraining in view of the simultaneous competition that occurs internationally, not only across traditional sectoral lines but also across political frontiers in a heated battle for market share. This battle is played out in Europe's interdependent states, where technological changes play a catalytic role in intensifying competition both within and between strategic groups of financial services firms. Not least, Europe is only one location – or, more accurately, many locations – in a global state and market system.

Stylised process of financial intermediation

The central component of any model of the modern financial system is the nature of the *conduits* through which the financial assets of the ultimate savers flow to the liabilities of the ultimate users of finance, both within and between national economies. This involves alternative and competing modes of financial intermediation, or 'contracting' between counterparties in financial transactions. A convenient model that can be used to guide thinking on financial contracting and the role of financial institutions and markets is summarised in Figure 4.1 – a generic flow-of-funds diagram that can apply equally at the domestic and global levels.[4]

The diagram depicts the financial process among the different sectors of the national and international economy in terms of: (1) the underlying environmental and regulatory determinants, or drivers; (2) the financial infrastructure services that need to be provided – market information, financial research and its dissemination, financial rating services and portfolio diagnostics on the one hand, and trading, payments, transactions clearance and settlement, and custody services on the other; as well as (3) the generic information, interpretation and transactions cost advantages or 'competencies' needed to add value and profit from the three primary intersectoral linkages, namely:

- savings/commercial banking and other traditional forms of intermediated finance;
- investment banking and securitised intermediation;
- various financial direct-connect mechanisms between borrowers and lenders.

Ultimate *sources* of surplus funds tapped by financial intermediaries arise in the household sector (deferred consumption or savings), the corporate sector (retained earnings or business savings) and the government sector (budgetary surpluses and external reserve build-ups).

- Under the first or 'classic' mode of financial intermediation, savings (or funds-sources) are held in the form of deposits or alternative types of claims issued by commercial banks, savings organisations, insurance companies or other forms of financial institutions entitled to finance themselves by placing their

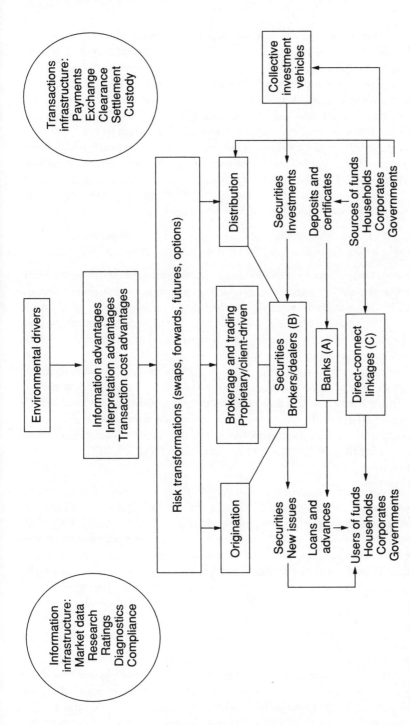

Figure 4.1 Financial intermediation dynamics

liabilities directly with the general public. Financial institutions then use these funds flows (liabilities) to purchase domestic and international assets issued by non-financial institution agents such as firms and governments.

- Under the second mode of funds flows, savings may be allocated directly (or indirectly, via so-called *collective investment vehicles*) to the purchase of securities publicly issued and sold by various governmental and private-sector organisations in the domestic and international financial markets.
- Under the third alternative, savings held in collective investment vehicles may be allocated directly to borrowers through various forms of private placement and other (possibly automated) direct-sale mechanisms to distribute their obligations, or they may be internally deployed within the saving entity (e.g. retained earnings of non-financial corporations).

Ultimate *users* of funds comprise the same three segments of the economy – the household or consumer sector, the business sector and the government sector.

- Consumers may finance purchases by means of personal loans from banks or by loans secured by purchased assets (hire-purchase or instalment loans). These may appear on the asset side of the balance sheets of credit institutions on a revolving basis for the duration of the respective loan contracts, or they may be sold off into the financial market in the form of structured securities backed by various types of receivables.
- Corporations may borrow from banks in the form of unsecured or asset-backed straight or revolving credit facilities and/or they may sell debt obligations (e.g. commercial paper, receivables financing, fixed-income securities of various types) or equities directly into the financial market.
- Governments can likewise borrow from credit institutions (sovereign borrowing) or issue full faith and credit or revenue-backed securities directly into the market.

Unlike consumers, borrowers such as corporations and governments also have the possibility of privately issuing and placing their obligations with institutional investors, thereby circumventing both credit institutions and the public debt and equity markets, and even consumer debt can be repackaged as structured asset-backed securities and sold to private investors.[5] And as noted, internal financial flows within economic entities comprising the end-users of the financial system are an ever-present alternative to external finance.

Alternative modes of financial contracting

In the first mode of external financial contracting (Mode A in Figure 4.1), depositors buy the 'secondary' financial claims or liabilities issued by credit institutions, and benefit from liquidity, convenience and safety through the ability of financial institutions to diversify risk and improve credit quality through professional management and monitoring of their holdings of primary financial claims (debt and equity). Savers can choose from a set of standardised contracts and receive payments/transactions services and interest that may or may nor be subject to varying degrees of government regulation.[6]

In the second mode (Mode B), investors may select their own portfolios of financial assets directly from among the publicly issued debt and equity instruments on offer. This may provide a broader range of options than standardised bank contracts, and permit the larger investors to tailor portfolios more closely to their objectives while still achieving acceptable liquidity through rapid execution of trades – aided by linkages with banks and other financial institutions that are part of the domestic payments mechanism. Investors may also choose to have their portfolios professionally managed, through various types of collective investment vehicles (mutual funds, pension funds, life insurance companies).

In the third mode (Mode C), institutional investors buy large blocks of privately issued securities. In doing so, they may face a liquidity penalty – due to the absence or limited availability of a liquid secondary market – for which they normally are rewarded via a higher yield. On the other hand, directly-placed securities usually involve lower issuing costs and can be specifically 'tailored' to more closely match issuer and investor requirements than can publicly-issued securities. Institutional and regulatory developments, especially in the United States, have added to the liquidity and depth of some direct-placement markets in recent years.

Value to ultimate savers and investors, inherent in the financial processes described here, accrues in the form of a three-way combination of yield, safety and liquidity. Value to ultimate users of funds likewise accrues in the form of a combination of financing cost, transactions cost, flexibility and liquidity. This value can be enhanced through credit backstops, guarantees and derivative instruments such as forward-rate agreements, caps, collars, futures and options provided by financial institutions acting either as banks or as securities firms.

Finally, the three intermediation channels identified in Figure 4.1 can be linked functionally and geographically, both domestically and internationally.

- *Functional* linkages permit bank receivables, for example, to be repackaged and sold to non-bank securities investors. Or bank-credit facilities or insurance-company guarantees can support the issuance of securities. Or privately placed securities may eventually be eligible for sale in public markets.
- *Geographic* linkages make it possible for savers and issuers to access markets in foreign and offshore markets, thereby improving risk, liquidity and yield or reducing transaction costs.

If permitted by financial regulation, various kinds of financial firms emerge to perform one or more of the roles suggested in Figure 4.1 – commercial banks, savings banks, postal savings institutions, savings cooperatives, credit unions, securities firms (full-service firms and various kinds of specialists), mutual funds, insurance companies, finance companies, finance subsidiaries of industrial companies, and others. Members of each *strategic group* compete with each other, as well as with members of other strategic groups. Assuming it is allowed to do

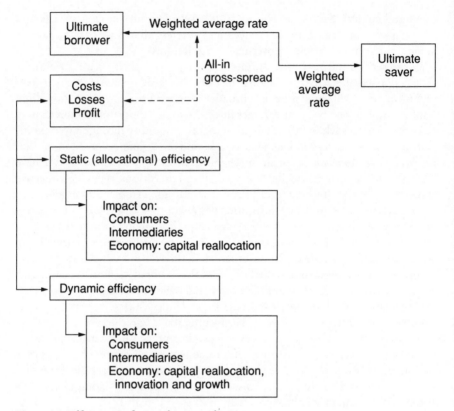

Figure 4.2 Efficiency in financial intermediation

so by the regulators, each firm elects to operate in one or more of the three finan-
cial-process modes identified in Figure 4.1, according to its own competitive
advantages – i.e. its comparative efficiency in the relevant financial production
mode compared to that of other firms. Tables 4.1 and 4.2 provide a dramatic
example of how strategic groups have evolved from 1950 to 1995 in providing
financial services in the United States. If EU financial intermediation develops in
a similar way assuming achievement of EMU, the dramatic change in competitive dynamics facing established vendors of financial services becomes clear.

Static and dynamic efficiency aspects

Issues relating to the static and dynamic efficiency of the three alternative, stylised
financial processes depicted in Figure 4.1 are summarised in Figures 4.2 and 4.3.

Static efficiency is represented as the all-in, weighted average spread (differential) between rates of return provided to ultimate *savers* and the cost of funds to
users. This 'gap' in Figure 4.2 depicts the overall cost of using a particular mode
or type of financial process, and is reflected in the monetary value of resources

Table 4.1 The US financial services sector, 1950

Institution	Payment services	Savings products	Fiduciary services	Lending		Underwriting issuance of		Insurance and risk management products
				Business	Consumer	equity	debt	
Insured depository institutions	•	•	•	•	•			
Insurance companies		•		○				•
Finance companies				○	•			
Securities firms		•	•			•	•	
Pension funds		•						
Mutual funds		•						

Note: ° = Minor involvement.
Source: General Accounting Office.

Table 4.2 The US financial services sector, 1995

Institution	Payment services	Savings products	Fiduciary services	Lending		Underwriting issuance of		Insurance and risk management products
				Business	Consumer	equity	debt	
Insured depository institutions	•	•	•	•	•	○	○	
Insurance companies	•	•	•	•	•	○	○	•
Finance companies	•	•	•	•	•	○	○	•
Securities firms	•	•	•	•	•	•	•	•
Pension funds		•	•					•
Mutual funds	•	•	•					•
Diversified financial firms	•	•	•	•	•	•	•	•
Specialist firms	•	•	•		•	•	•	•

Note: ° = Selective involvement of large firms via affiliates.
Source: General Accounting Office.

used up in the course of financial intermediation. In particular, it reflects the direct costs of production (operating and administrative costs, cost of capital, net regulatory burdens, etc.). It also reflects losses incurred in the financial process, as well as liquidity premiums and any monopoly profits earned. Financial processes that are considered 'statically inefficient' are usually characterised by high spreads due to high overhead costs, high losses and high levels of regulation, including barriers to market access, excess intermediation profits and the like.

Dynamic efficiency is characterised by rates of financial product and process innovation through time.

- *Product innovations* usually involve creation of new financial instruments (e.g. caps, futures, options, swaps) along with the ability to replicate certain instruments by bundling existing ones (synthetic securities) or to highlight a new financial attribute by re-bundling existing instruments. New approaches to contract pricing, passive or index-based portfolio investment techniques also fall under this rubric.
- *Process innovations* include contract design (e.g. cash settlement futures contracts), methods of clearance, payments, custody, securities settlement and trading, and techniques for efficient margin calculation.

Successful product and process innovation broadens the menu of financial services available to ultimate issuers, ultimate savers, or other agents along the various financial channels described in Figure 4.1. Probably the most powerful catalyst affecting the competitive dynamics of the financial services industry has been technological change. However, there may be costs associated with financial innovation as well. Examples include financial instruments and processes that take substantial resources to develop but that ultimately fail to meet a need in the market-place, that are misrepresented to end-users, or that are inadequately managed with respect to the various market or credit risks involved. It is against a background of continuous innovation and pressure for dynamic efficiency that financial markets and institutions have evolved and converged.[7]

Global financial markets for foreign exchange, debt instruments and, to a lesser extent, equity, have developed various degrees of 'seamlessness', as depicted in Figure 4.3. Indeed, it is arguable that the most advanced of the world's financial markets are approaching a theoretical, 'complete' optimum where there are sufficient financial instruments and markets to span the whole spectrum of risk and return outcomes. Financial systems that are deemed *inefficient* or *incomplete* are characterised by a high-cost, limited range of financial services and obsolescent financial processes.[8]

Both static and dynamic efficiency are obviously important from the standpoint of national and global resource allocation, not only within the financial services industry itself but also as it affects *users* of financial services. That is, since financial services can be viewed as 'inputs' to the overall real-sector production process, the level of national output and income – as well as its rate of

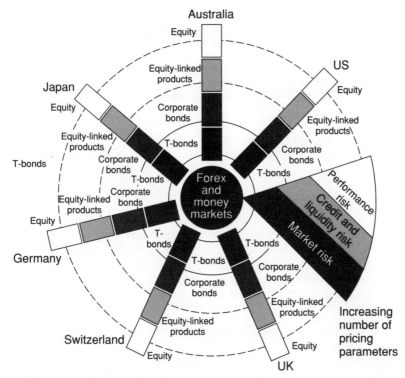

Figure 4.3 Integration of global financial markets
Source: McKinsey & Co., Inc.

economic growth – is directly or indirectly affected by the static and dynamic efficiency attributes of the financial system. A 'retarded' financial services sector can represent an important impediment to a nation's overall real economic performance. As such, inefficiencies distort the patterns of allocation of labour as well as capital. Figure 4.4, using a relatively crude measure of financial-system development, suggests the impact the state of development of national financial systems may have had in seventy-seven countries as of 1960 on the rate of economic growth in the following thirty years. Indeed, one major reason for progressive deregulation in many countries during the 1980s and 1990s has been an attempt to capture, for the countries involved, static and dynamic efficiency gains – and at the same time to maximise the real value-added generated in the financial services industry itself.

Financial system infrastructure and risk management

The efficiency characteristics of the financial intermediation process is significantly affected by various components of financial market infrastructure

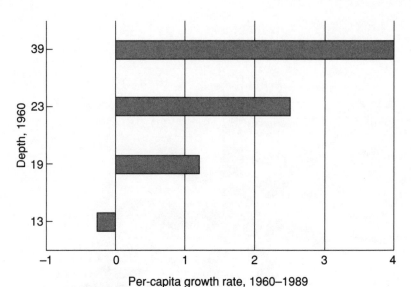

Per-capita growth rate, 1960–1989
Number of observations in each quartile = 11
Growth: per-capita GDP growth, 1960–1989
Depth: liquid liabilities divided by GDP, 1960

Figure 4.4 Initial depth of financial development, 1960, versus future growth, 1960–1989, for selected countries
Source: World Bank.

depicted at the top of Figure 4.1. These include (a) information-gathering and dissemination, (b) provision of analytics and research, (c) establishment and maintenance of efficient physical or electronic trading systems, (d) transactions clearance and settlement, and (e) post-trade custody and safe-keeping of securities and other financial assets. Some of these are businesses which compete vigorously among each other. For example, Reuters competes with Telerate and Bloomberg in information services, Standard & Poors competes with Moody's in credit-rating services, and Morningstar competes with Lipper Analytics in portfolio-performance ratings, even as individual researchers and research units of banks and securities firms are engaged in vigorous competition for accuracy in forecasting. Meanwhile, different payments and exchange systems – unless they are granted monopoly rights – likewise compete with each other in an increasingly contestable 'market for markets', with end-users gravitating towards the most efficient and transparent conduits.

The financial market infrastructure services perform a crucial function in a modern economy, and an efficient and resilient information, trading, settlement and custody system arguably increases the availability, and lowers the cost, of risk capital. This is accomplished by allowing investors a high degree of portfolio diversification and asset-reallocation opportunities as well as significant liquidity, which means that investors will be much more willing to invest in assets that, on their own, would seem risky and illiquid. An efficient system does so promptly at low cost, with a minimum of errors and a maximum degree of certainty that the transaction will be concluded on the precise terms agreed to in the trade. Because friction-free financial transactions can remove major barriers to trading, the clearing and settlement infrastructure can play a key role in the evolution of both domestic and international financial markets.

Many of the benefits from efficient financial markets may be reaped by removing barriers to capital flows and financial services, allowing capital markets to allocate resources more efficiently. Recognising this, many countries are seeking to improve their financial market infrastructure services by aligning them progressively with international standards. In turn, this has a catalytic effect on competition among the intermediation channels depicted in Figure 4.1 and the various types of financial institutions that compete in the system.

Finally, financial intermediation invariably involves the management of risk, mainly market risk and credit risk. Especially in the face of volatile interest rates and exchange-rates, end-users of the financial system, ranging from issuers and borrowers to investors, as well as financial intermediaries themselves, must avail themselves of a broad array of risk-management techniques and instruments. These include swap contracts, financial futures and options, *derivatives* that are often highly complex but that, properly used, play an enormously useful role in calibrating the sourcing of financial services to the needs and risk-preferences of the various market participants.

Internationalising the model

The stylised model of financial intermediation presented here is cast implicitly in the context of domestic financial systems. The discussion can, however, easily be internationalised.

- Sources of funds in national economies can be accessed by users of funds resident abroad. Examples include purchases of foreign securities by institutional investors, and by domestic households, either as individual securities or through collective investment vehicles such as mutual funds. International access to national savings pools is of particular importance in view of the wide differences that exist in savings rates among countries.
- Users of funds ranging from international organisations and government entities to corporations and even households (through asset-backed securities collateralised by consumer credit, mortgages, etc.) can access foreign sources of financing by borrowing or issuing securities outside the home country, either in foreign markets or in the offshore markets. International financings are particularly important in the light of large differences that exist in national levels of consumer, corporate and governmental borrowing requirements.

Financial intermediaries connecting sources and users of funds operate internationally as well as domestically. Cross-border lending and foreign-currency

funding are forms of international banking via the classic financial intermediation mode. New issues of securities undertaken abroad or offshore, or domestic
issues incorporating international tranches, link issuers and investors across
financial markets.

The role of derivatives and other hedging instruments – and portfolio
diversification for investors – is substantially more important as well when the
model is internationalised rather than in the purely domestic version, due to the
existence of different national currencies, macroeconomic environments and
financial market conditions.

Competitors on the playing-field

In terms of Figure 4.1, it is clear that different types of financial intermediaries
occupy the playing-field in competing for financial intermediation, transactions
and payments services, risk management and other activities identified here.
These can be identified as (1) credit institutions, (2) full-service securities firms,
(3) universals and (4) specialists and fund managers.

Credit institutions dominate Mode A of Figure 4.1, and comprise commercial
banks, savings banks, postal savings institutions, building societies and mortgage banks, credit unions, and other types of entities that basically take deposits
from the public and make loans. In continental Europe this type of financial
intermediation has traditionally pervaded national economies.[9] The techniques
involved include straight lending, revolving credit lines, syndicated lending by
groups of banks, trade financing, asset-based lending such as mortgage and
automobile financing, project financing and the like.[10]

Securities firms and the securities activities of universal banks dominate Mode
B of financial intermediation in Figure 4.1.[11]

First, capital-market activities of securities firms comprise underwriting new
issues of securities, dealing in these securities on the firm's own account and on
behalf of clients, providing brokerage services, conducting and disseminating
research on issuers, markets and macroeconomic developments, and supplying
risk-management services to issuers and investors. These can be detailed as
follows

• *Underwriting* new issues of debt and equity securities – both seasoned and
  initial public offerings – for a range of clients including private-sector corporations, government-owned or government-controlled entities, sovereign governments and multilateral agencies. The underwriting function involves
  purchasing the securities from the issuer and on-selling them either in public
  markets or to large institutional investors in the form of private placements.
  Earnings (and exposure of the firm to underwriting risk) typically come from
  the 'spread' between the buying and selling prices.
• Bond (fixed-income) underwriting is usually carried out through domestic and
  international underwriting syndicates of securities firms with access to local

investors, investors in various foreign markets such as Switzerland (foreign bonds) and investors in offshore markets (Eurobonds), using one of several alternative distribution techniques. Placements may also be restricted to selected institutional investors (private placements) rather than the general public. Access to various foreign markets is facilitated by means of interest-rate and currency swaps (swap-driven issues), and some widely-distributed multi-market issues have become known as 'global issues'. In some markets, intense competition and deregulation have narrowed spreads to the point that the number of firms in underwriting syndicates has declined over time, and in some cases a single firm handles an entire issue – the so-called 'bought deal'.

- Stock underwriting is usually heavily concentrated in the home country of the issuing firm, which is normally where the secondary-market trading and liquidity is to be found. New issues of stock may be offered to investors for the first time (initial public offerings, or IPOs), to the general public on a repeat basis (seasoned issues), to existing holders of the stock (rights issues) or only to selected institutional investors (private placements).
- *Secondary market trading* of cash instruments such as stocks, bonds, asset-backed securities, foreign exchange, and sometimes commodities such as cereal grains, pork bellies and gold – as well as derivatives on individual securities or commodities (mainly futures and options) or on indexes. Activities include customer trading (executing client orders), proprietary trading (for the firm's own account) and *market-making* (being prepared to quote both bid and offer prices), and arbitrage – buying and selling simultaneously in at least two markets to capitalise on price discrepancies between different markets for underlying financial instruments or derivatives, or between cash and derivatives markets (e.g. 'program trading' computer-driven arbitrage between the futures and cash markets). Some firms also engage in 'risk arbitrage', usually involving speculative purchases of stock on the basis of public information relating to mergers and acquisitions.
- *Brokerage*, involving executing buy or sell orders for customers without actually taking possession of the security or derivative concerned, sometimes including complex instructions based on various contingencies in the market.
- *Research*, into factors affecting the various markets as well as individual securities and derivatives. Securities research is made available to investor clients by presumably independent analysts within the firm whose opinion can be taken seriously (as opposed to validating vested interests of the firm) by analysts whose careers depend on the quality and objectivity of their work. The value of research provided to clients depends critically on its quality and timeliness, and is often compensated by business channelled though the firm, such as brokerage commissions and underwriting mandates. Closely allied are research activities – often highly technical modelling exercises – involving innovative financial instruments which link market developments and sources of value-added to issuer-clients and/or investor-clients.
- *Hedging and risk management*, mainly involving the use of derivative

instruments to reduce exposure to risk associated with individual transactions or markets affecting corporate, institutional or individual clients. These include interest-rate caps, floors and collars, various kinds of contingent contracts, as well as futures and options on various types of instruments. It may be quicker, easier and cheaper, for example, for an investor to alter the risk profile on an investment portfolio using derivatives than by buying and selling the underlying instruments.

Second, in addition to capital-market activities, securities firms and universal banks are active in advisory work for clients, notably relating to mergers, acquisitions, divestitures, recapitalisations, leveraged buyouts and a variety of other generic and specialised corporate transactions.

- *Mergers and acquisitions (M&A)*, involving fee-based advisory assignments to firms wishing to acquire others (buy-side assignments) or firms wishing to be sold or to sell certain business units to prospective acquirers (sell-side assignments). The M&A business is closely associated with the market for corporate control, and may involve advisories and fund-raising efforts for hostile acquirers or plotting defensive strategies and recapitalisations for firms subject to unwanted takeover bids. It may also involve providing independent valuations and 'fairness opinions' to buyers or sellers of companies to protect against lawsuits from disgruntled investors alleging that the price paid for a company was either too high or too low. Such activities may be domestic, within a single national economy, or cross-border, between a buyer in one country and a seller in another.
- *Recapitalisations*, tending to involve advice to corporations concerning optimum capital structure, increasing or decreasing the proportion of debt to equity in the balance-sheet, types and maturity-structure of liabilities, stock repurchase programmes, and the like. The securities firm may provide financial advice on these matters as well as providing the required execution services through its capital-market activities.
- *Real estate* and other special transactions, including advisory services for energy, transportation or project financings, requiring specialised industry expertise.
- *Merchant banking*, involving securities firms putting their clients' and their own capital on the line in M&A transactions and other equity participations. This could involve buying control of entire firms in order to restructure them and eventually sell them, in whole or in part, to other companies or to the investing public. It may also involve large, essentially permanent stakeholdings in business enterprises, including board-level representation and supervision of management. Or it may involve short-term subordinated lending (bridge loans or mezzanine financing) to assure the success of an M&A transaction, intended to be quickly repaid out of the assets of the surviving entity. Other areas of significant direct investments may include real estate and leveraged lease transactions.

Third, securities firms, commercial banks, trust banks, universal banks and a host of fund managers all offer various types of asset management or fiduciary services for individuals and institutions, denoted as *Collective Investment Vehicles* in Figure 4.1.

- *Investment management* for institutions and individuals. With respect to institutions, major investors such as pension funds and insurance companies may allocate blocks of assets to securities firms to manage against specific performance targets (usually stock or bond indexes), or 'bogeys'. Individuals may also assign discretionary management to securities firms. Those with significant assets (high net-worth clients) may couple asset management with tax planning, estates and trusts, and similar services in a 'private banking' relationship with the securities firm, either directly or with the help of independent financial advisers. Closed-end or open-end mutual funds or unit trusts may also be operated by a securities firm and either marketed to selected institutions and high net-worth individuals or mass-marketed to the general investor community as tax-advantaged pension holdings or to capture general household savings.
- *Investor services.* There is an array of services that lie between buyers and sellers of securities, domestically as well as internationally, which are critical for the effective operation of securities markets. This centres on domestic and international systems for clearing and settling securities transactions via efficient central securities depositories (CSDs), discussed above, which in turn are prerequisites for a 'value-chain' of services, often supplied on the basis of quality and price by competing private-sector vendors of information services, analytical services, trading services and information processing, credit services, custody and safekeeping, and portfolio diagnostic services. Many such infrastructure services, including trading information, securities clearance and settlement and global custody, are supplied internationally by specialised firms or commercial banks and a number of securities firms as well.

Full-service investment banks comprise such firms as Morgan Stanley, Goldman Sachs or Merrill Lynch of the United States or British merchant banks such as Schroders, Rothschilds or Robert Fleming. Some of these also engage in commercial lending. A French *banque d'affaires* such as Banque Indosuez or Paribas would tend to have a greater emphasis on quasi-permanent holdings of securities in non-financial corporations. Japanese securities companies such as Nomura, Nikko, Daiwa and Yamaichi would be similarly structured, traditionally with a relatively greater emphasis on retail brokerage and no commercial lending. All such firms select in various ways from the above 'menu' of services and organise themselves in various strategic configurations. Some securities firms encompass the entire range of activities as 'full-service' vendors, supplying such services to institutional and retail clients, with other full-service firms providing more or less the same range, only to institutional (wholesale) clients. Others specialise in a narrower range of services, including financial 'boutiques' that may limit themselves to a few areas or only one area, such as M&A advisory services or leveraged buyout transactions.[12]

Still others are units of universal banks. As can be seen in Figure 4.5, in the pure universal bank and in the German variant of universal banking, securities and corporate finance activities are carried out by the bank itself. In the British version of universal banking, they tend to be carried out by a separately capitalised securities subsidiary of the bank, competing with similarly structured firms and with free-standing merchant banks. In the US version of universal banking, such as it is, they will be organised as separately capitalised subsidiaries of bank holding companies.[13]

Structural shifts in the intermediation process

As noted, the three alternative channels of financial funds flows identified in Figure 4.1 often compete vigorously with each other for transaction volume in the financial intermediation process. The winners and losers among institutions competing in this process tend to be relatively consistent across national and international financial markets. In the case of the most highly developed financial systems, the securities industry (Mode B in Figure 4.1) has gained at the expense of the banking industry (Mode A) – see Table 4.3 for the United States as an example. The reason for this migration of financial flows from one process to another arguably has much to do with changes in the relative static and dynamic efficiency characteristics and costs (or spreads) of intermediation via traditional financial institutions, as against more direct securities-market processes as a result of superior static and dynamic efficiency properties – and less oppressive regulation.

On the borrower side of Figure 4.1, this has been manifested in the increasing use of the commercial paper markets as a substitute for bank credit lines as well as domestic and international bond issues for longer-term debt financing. Non-bank lending to business by finance companies and insurance companies, as well as private placements of securities with such institutions, have further eroded the market share of banks in a number of national financial environments. Whereas corporate and institutional access to the securities markets is obvious, even households have greatly increased their access to financing via securities issues in a number of countries, via securitised liabilities such as mortgage loans and credit-card debt, i.e. the issuance of traded financial instruments against anticipated cash-flows of interest and principal from various kinds of receivables. Securitisation tends to allow both increased asset portfolio liquidity and a better ability to manage interest-rate risk exposures. Most types of bank loans have become potentially securitisable – a trend that has not necessarily abated, as governments in various countries change bank and securities regulations to allow the process to spread, and as pressure mounts from financial services firms as well as non-financial corporations for access to this technology. Thus, a major integrating factor in financial markets is likely to

(a) Full integration

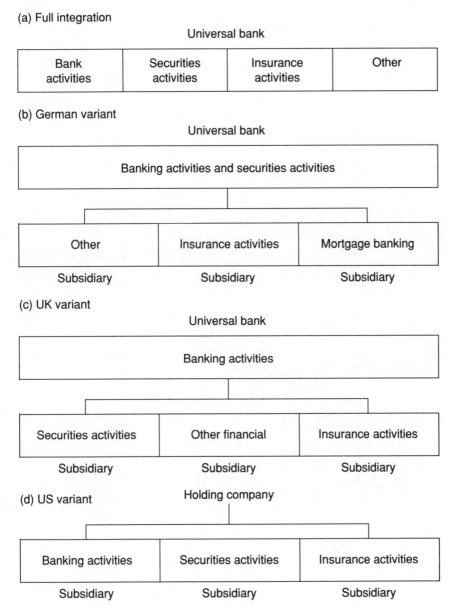

Figure 4.5 Universal bank organisation structures

come from the direct recycling of bank loans through one of the many available securitisation vehicles.

On the investor side of Figure 4.1 the same migration from banks to the securities industry is evident in the growing share of investments as a form of savings,

Table 4.3 Percentage shares of assets of financial institutions in the United States, 1860–1993

	1860	1880	1900	1912	1922	1929	1939	1948	1960	1970	1980	1993
Commercial banks	71.4	60.6	62.9	64.5	63.3	53.7	51.2	55.9	38.2	37.9	34.8	25.4
Thrift institutions	17.8	22.8	18.2	14.8	13.9	14.0	13.6	12.3	19.7	20.4	21.4	9.4
Insurance companies	10.7	13.9	13.8	16.6	16.7	18.6	27.2	24.3	23.8	18.9	16.1	17.4
Investment companies	—	—	—	—	0.0	2.4	1.9	1.3	2.9	3.5	3.6	14.9
Pension funds	—	—	0.0	0.0	0.0	0.7	2.1	3.1	9.7	13.0	17.4	24.4
Finance companies	—	0.0	0.0	0.0	0.0	2.0	2.2	2.0	4.6	4.8	5.1	4.7
Securities brokers and dealers	0.0	0.0	3.8	3.0	5.3	8.1	1.5	1.0	1.1	1.2	1.1	3.3
Mortgage companies	0.0	2.7	1.3	1.2	0.8	0.6	0.3	0.1	a	a	0.4	0.2
Real-estate investment trusts	—	—	—	—	—	—	—	—	0.0	0.3	0.1	0.1
Total (per cent)	100	100	100	100	100	100	100	100	100	100	100	100
Total ($ trillion)	.001	.005	.016	.034	.075	.123	.129	.281	.596	1.328	4.025	13.952

Note: [a] Data not available.

particularly through fiduciaries such as pension funds, insurance companies and mutual funds.

The next set of developments in some of the most innovative financial markets is likely to involve replacement of traditional banking and securities forms of financial intermediation, by direct financial links between sources and users of funds that have the potential for further cutting out traditional financial inter-mediaries – the direct-connect mechanisms identified as Mode C in Figure 4.1. This will include direct inter-company payments clearing such as electronic data interchange (EDI) and automated private placements of securities, for example, as is already done in some European financial markets, using automated Dutch-auction distribution of government securities. Although they are often closely interrelated, the three intermediation modes in Figure 4.1 thus compete with one another in a modern financial system on the basis of static and dynamic efficiency as well as differential regulatory burdens to which they are exposed.

As a consequence of these developments, borrowers in many national finan-cial systems today face a range of alternatives for obtaining financing, and even households and small or medium-size companies which are basically limited to bank credit can subsequently have their loans securitised, and benefit from both access to a much broader pool of funding sources and conversion of illiquid bank loans into liquid securities form. The gains from both activities will tend to be partially passed backward to the borrower. Similarly, today's modern finan-cial systems tend to provide a wide range of opportunities and services to investors which allow them to optimise their asset portfolios by taking advantage of the domestic and international portfolio diversification across the range of financial instruments being offered, as well as improvements in the securities market infrastructure services. Again, even the retail investor can take advantage of these investment alternatives and process-technology improvements by taking advantage of the broad array of mutual funds, unit trusts and other collective investment vehicles being aggressively marketed to households – in many cases using imaginative, high-technology non-stationary distribution techniques backed by extensive macroeconomic, financial market and securities research.

In short, the economic dynamics of financial intermediation appears to have systematically favored the securities industry at the expense of the banking industry, as a result of the process of disintermediation and securitisation based on superior static and dynamic efficiency attributes – but may yet be challenged by various direct-connect and private-placement linkages between issues and investors. However, the pace of change has hardly been uniform around the world, as seen in the differences in household asset composition in the United States, Europe and developing countries, depicted in Figure 4.6. Still, more effi-cient modes of financial contracting will progressively encroach on less efficient ones, and to the extent that the securities industry is in the vanguard of this development a growing demand for its services seems assured – as does the inter-national competitive positioning of securities firms based in countries with financial systems which themselves lead this development.

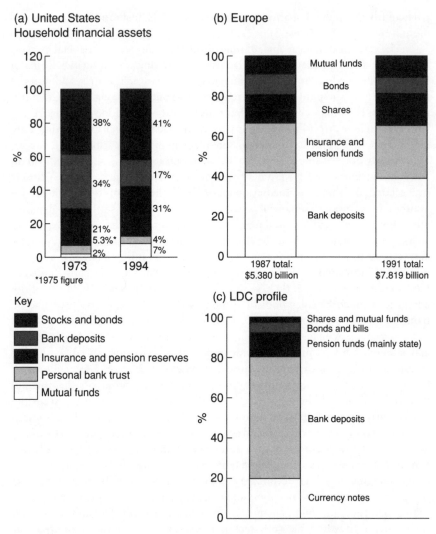

Figure 4.6 Comparative household asset deployment in the USA, Europe and developing countries, 1995
Sources: (a) Federal Reserve Board, Flow of Funds, 3rd Quarter, 1994; (b) McKinsey & Co., Inc. (Belgium, Britain, France, Germany, the Netherlands, Norway, Portugal, Spain, Sweden and Switzerland); (c) Estimates from World Bank data.

Even as intense competition across financial intermediation channels has developed, similar competition has emerged among national financial systems, as well as between them and offshore financial markets. Again, the borrower not only has the choice between bank credits and securities issues in the domestic market, but also has the alternative of borrowing or issuing abroad if foreign or offshore financing alternatives are more attractive. Similarly, savers and their fiduciaries have the option of going abroad to place funds if the returns and portfolio alternatives on offer are superior to those available at home. Securities firms active in the most competitive markets thus have a dual advantage in this bi-directional financial intermediation competition: they can export to others the product and process technologies that they have honed in the most advanced markets, and they can attract lending or underwriting, trading and distribution activities to these markets from less efficient markets. Policies that prevent either of these development largely define the realm of protectionism and barriers to market access in the national and global financial services industry. It is precisely this dimension that will undergo a sea-change as a result of a transition to the single financial market in Europe.

Regulatory determinants of financial structures

The kinds of financial flows that are the basis of the preceding discussion of financial intermediation are dramatically affected by regulatory factors. Financial services comprise an industry that has usually been, and will continue to be, subject to significant public-authority regulation and supervision due to its fiduciary nature and the possibility of social costs associated with institutional failure. Indeed, small changes in financial regulation can bring about truly massive changes in financial activity. In the process, they can affect the competitive viability and performance of different types of financial institutions spreading their activities across the financial spectrum depicted in Figure 4.1.

Regulatory tradeoffs
The right-hand side of Figure 4.7 identifies the policy tradeoffs that invariably confront those charged with designing and implementing a properly structured financial system. On the one hand, they must strive to achieve maximum static and dynamic efficiency, with respect to the financial system as a whole, as well as the competitive viability of financial institutions that are subject to regulation, as discussed above. On the other hand, they must safeguard the stability of institutions and the financial markets as a whole, in addition to encouraging what is considered acceptable market conduct, including the politically sensitive implied social contract between financial institutions and small, unsophisticated customers as well as problems of contagion and systemic risk. The problem of safety-net design is beset with difficulties such as moral hazard and adverse selection, and becomes especially problematic when products and activities shade into one another, when on- and off-balance sheet activities are involved, and

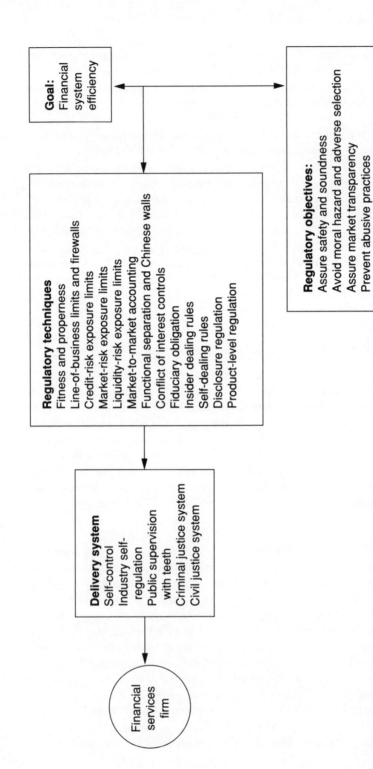

Figure 4.7 Regulatory tradeoffs, techniques and control

when domestic and offshore business is conducted simultaneously. Regulators constantly face the dilemma of *inadequate* regulation, resulting in costly failures, versus *overregulation,* resulting in opportunity costs in the form of efficiencies not achieved.

Some of the principal options that regulators have at their disposal identified in Figure 4.7 range from 'fitness and properness' criteria under which a financial institution may be established, continue to operate or be shut down – including jurisdictional issues – line-of-business regulation as to what specific types of institutions may do, as well as regulations as to liquidity, various types of exposures, capital adequacy, and the like, as well as marked-to-market (or lack thereof) of assets and liabilities. Regulatory initiatives, however, can have their own distortive impact on financial markets, and regulation becomes especially difficult when financial markets evolve rapidly and the regulator can easily get one or two steps behind.

The final element of Figure 4.7 involves the regulatory vehicles that may be used, ranging from reliance on self-control on the part of boards and senior managements of financial firms concerned with protecting their franchises, through industry self-regulation, to public oversight by regulators with teeth – including criminal prosecution.

Just as there are tradeoffs implicit in Figure 4.7 between financial-system performance and stability, so also there are tradeoffs between regulation and supervision, with some regulatory options (e.g. capital adequacy rules) fairly easy to supervise but full of distortive potential due to their broad-gauge nature, and others (e.g. fitness and properness criteria) possibly highly cost-effective but devilishly difficult to supervise. Finally there are tradeoffs between supervision and performance, with some supervisory techniques far more costly to comply with than others. Regulators must try to optimise across this three-dimensional set of tradeoffs under conditions of rapid market and industry change, blurred institutional and activity demarcations, and international regulatory fault-lines.

Net regulatory burden and transactional mobility

It is useful to think of financial regulation and supervision as imposing a set of 'taxes' and 'subsidies' on the operations of financial firms, whether banks or securities firms, exposed to them.[14] On the one hand, the imposition of reserve requirements, capital adequacy rules, interest/usury ceilings and certain forms of financial disclosure requirements can be viewed as imposing additional implicit 'taxes' on a financial firm's activities in the sense that they increase the costs of financial intermediation.[15] On the other hand, regulator-supplied deposit insurance, lender-of-last-resort facilities and institutional bailouts serve to stabilise financial markets and reduce the risk of systemic failure, thereby lowering the costs of financial intermediation. They can therefore be viewed as implicit 'subsidies' by taxpayers.[16]

The difference between these 'tax' and 'subsidy' elements of regulation can be viewed as the *net regulatory burden* (NRB) faced by financial firms in any given jurisdiction. Private, profit-maximising financial firms tend to migrate towards those financial centres where the NRB is lowest – assuming all other economic factors are the same. Thus, at any point in time NRB differences will induce firms to relocate as long as NRB savings exceed the transaction, communication, information and other economic costs of doing so.[17] Since one can argue that, in today's global financial market-place, transaction and other economic costs of relocating are likely to be small, one can expect financial-market participants to be extremely sensitive to changes in current and perceived NRBs among competing regulatory environments. To some extent, the regulators responsible for particular jurisdictions appear to recognise this sensitivity and in their competition for employment and value-added creation, taxes and other revenues have engaged in a form of competition over their levels of NRB.[18]

In an individual economy with a single regulatory body, competition will spark a dynamic interplay between demanders and suppliers of financial services. Banks and securities firms will seek to reduce their NRB and increase their profitability. If they can do so at low cost, they will actively seek product innovations and new avenues that avoid cumbersome and costly regulations. This may be facilitated both in the case of multiple and sometimes overlapping domestic regulatory bodies and in the global case of multiple and often competing regulatory bodies.[19]

A single economy may have multiple national regulatory authorities, complemented by a host of other regulatory groups at the state and local levels – especially in countries organised politically along federal lines. In the case of the United States, for example, at the Federal level financial activities could fall into the regulatory domain of the Federal Reserve Board, the Comptroller of the Currency, the Securities and Exchange Commission, and the Commodity Futures Trading Commission, to name just the major regulatory agencies. Each of the fifty states has its own regulatory bodies to deal with banking and insurance. In Europe, each country has its own work banking and securities regulators, many countries have multiple exchanges, and approaches to regulation vary widely.[20] With many governments and many regulatory authorities, there is fertile ground for banks and securities firms to reduce NRB. National regulatory authorities may compete among each other on the basis of NRB to preserve or reclaim financial activities within their respective regulatory domains, and firms benefit from such international competition, especially if financial innovation and technological change allow them to operate successfully at a distance from their home bases. Users of financial services also benefit to the extent that competition forces financial firms to pass through to them the lower NRB. And in addition, every city and municipality has an agency responsible for local income taxes, real-estate taxes, transfer taxes, stamp duties, and so on, all of which affect the NRB falling on financial institutions. The situation is complicated still further by ambiguity regarding the definition of a 'bank', a 'security', an 'exchange', and so forth – blurring the lines of demarcation between products and institutions, and raising questions about which regulatory agency holds jurisdiction.[21]

The NRB associated with regulations in onshore financial markets creates opportunities to develop a parallel, offshore market for the delivery of similar services. Barriers such as political risk, minimum transaction size, firm size and credit quality help temper the migration of financial activity offshore, although offshore markets can be used to replicate a variety of financial instruments such as long-term forward contracts, short-term commercial paper, long-term bonds, Eurocurrency interest-rate futures, and the like – many of which are exposed to a significant NRB by onshore financial authorities – and pose a general competitive threat to onshore securities or banking activities.

The rise of regulatory competition and the existence of offshore markets thus underscores the fact that market participants face a range of alternatives for executing transactions in any of several financial centres. The development of offshore currency and bond markets in the 1960s represents a case in which borrowers and lenders alike found that they could carry out the requisite market transactions more efficiently and with sufficient safety by operating offshore – in a parallel market. If domestic regulators desire to have the transactions conducted within their respective financial centres – driven by their regulators' desire to maintain an adequate level of prudential regulation, to sustain their revenues from the taxation of financial services, to support employment and output in the financial services industry and linked economic sectors, or simply to maximise their regulatory domain,[22] regulatory requirements cannot be set arbitrarily. Consequently, national financial regulations tend to be determined competitively after taking account of regulations (both present and prospective) in other financial centres. The essence of Kane's analysis is that the market for suppliers of financial regulation is highly competitive. As such, the movement to liberalise regulations tends to be a consequence of national regulators vying for market share, and the market for financial regulation is 'contestable' in the sense that other national regulatory bodies offer (or threaten to offer) rules that may be more favourable than those of the domestic regulator. This actual or threatened competition may serve to constrain the actions of financial regulators and tax authorities from increasing levels of NRB.

This view results in a 'regulatory dialectic' – a dynamic interaction between the regulator and the regulated, in which there is continuous action and reaction by all parties, in which the players may behave aggressively or defensively, and adapt with varying speed and degrees of freedom in line with their 'average adaptive efficiencies' as follows.[23]

- Less-regulated players move faster and more freely than more tightly regulated players.
- Private players move faster and more freely than governmental players.
- Regulated players move faster and more freely than their regulators.

• International regulatory bodies move more slowly and less freely than all of the other players.

Given this ordering of adaptive efficiencies, it is likely that the lag between a regulation and its avoidance is on average shorter than the lag between avoidance and *re-regulation*. The lag in re-regulation may be shorter for industry-based, self-regulatory groups than for governments. It may be longest when international regulatory efforts are involved.

Financial firms constantly monitor their NRB, and transfer activities into another regulatory regime when their NRB can be reduced. Various imperfections exist that permit some variance in NRB across countries. For example, when transaction costs and information costs are significant, firms will need to be located in those regulatory domains where they intend to sell their services. Nevertheless, this dispersion among NRBs cannot be too great, otherwise firms will have an incentive to relocate their activities. Entry and exit costs, currency conversion costs, and distance-related delivery costs, plus uncertainties surrounding these costs and other control measures, act as effective barriers to complete NRB equalisation across countries. However, technological change that has markedly lowered communications and information processing costs, combined with the rapid growth of international financial transactions, has cut the gap in the NRB needed to induce regulatory arbitrage.

The point is simply that, as any factor of production or economic activity gains mobility, it becomes increasingly difficult to subject it to regulation, and in today's world communications costs are low and capital mobility is high, so that it is becoming less feasible for a state or a nation to impose an NRB that stands too far apart from world norms. Still, it is likely that a long-run equilibrium can be maintained with a *positive* NRB. Financial transactions involve uncertainty – about the monetary unit of account, about the creditworthiness of the financial institutions and other counterparties, and about the political stability of the financial centre. Financial institutions ought to value their access to lender-of-last-resort facilities, deposit/liability insurance, the opportunity to be headquartered in a stable political climate, and the like. Indeed, we observe that those markets which are almost totally unregulated, such as the Eurocurrency market (with a NRB approaching zero) have not in fact completely dominated financial transactions subject to location-shifting. If financial institutions find it in their interest to pay some regulatory tax, the economic question then concerns the sustainable magnitude of this NRB.

The NRB in most countries comprises a variety of constraints on financial firms, ranging from capital adequacy standards, exposure limits and liquidity requirements, to fitness and properness criteria and periodic compliance reviews – usually set in place in order to mitigate concerns related to fiduciary responsibilities, market conduct and systemic safety and soundness. Each imposes economic costs, and may therefore erode the static or dynamic efficiency properties of all or parts of the financial intermediation process depicted in

Figure 4.1. Improved stability is rarely cost-free, and the question whether the social gains in terms of improved firm and industry stability and fiduciary performance exceed these costs is a complex and difficult matter for debate. And since any such improvements can only be measured in terms of damage that *did not occur* and costs that were successfully *avoided*, the argumentation is invariably based on 'what if' hypotheticals. There are no definitive answers with respect to optimum regulatory structures. There are only 'better' and 'worse' solutions as perceived by those ultimately responsible for the regulators, and their collective risk-aversion and reaction to past regulatory failures.

The regulatory environments and NRBs associated with national bond and stock markets have certainly changed dramatically over the years. Starting in 1975 with the US introduction of negotiated securities commission rates on 'Mayday', and working through assorted deregulation in the 1986 'Big-Bang' reforms in London, as well as significant reforms in Tokyo, Toronto and Paris, restrictive pricing conventions have been eliminated and business practices liberalised. Regulatory convergence has thus come some distance. Despite this, international equity markets, especially, have remained relatively fragmented. Each country maintains its own securities exchanges. Each exchange operates according to its own regulations, which have been subject in recent years to widespread reforms, and many countries have implemented over-the-counter markets which form a second-level trading structure that is in the process of being institutionalised and integrated. Offshore, the Euromarkets form an integrated self-regulated, over-the-counter market trading in deposits and debt securities – listed, unlisted and derivative.

It seems likely that progressive convergence in regulation of banks and securities firms will continue, with players based in the more heavily regulated countries successfully lobbying for liberalisation, and the emergence among regulators of a consensus on minimum acceptable standards that will eventually be accepted by home countries with substandard regulatory regimes. The objective, once again, is to optimise the balance between market efficiency and regulatory soundness, so that market forces are the main determinants of what investment is carried out, where and by whom in the global capital market. The progression of these developments within the context of the EU is outlined in Chapter 9 of this book.

Summary

Financial integration in the EU follows two distinct currents. Both are related, and both have macro and micro dimensions. But both are played out in distinct regimes, which have evolved over their own historic paths. One current points towards EMU with a single currency, a single central bank and monetary policy, and far-reaching coordination of fiscal policies among EU member states. Its macro stream ends in a single, unified financial market and regime where any number can play. The other current sees the national regimes continuing to evolve within their own internal logic, with their own currencies and financial systems, adapting in their own particular ways to the permanent changes under way in world financial markets. The international regulatory regime would tend to be adaptive to circumstances, due to extensive differences in NRBs imposed on the intermediation process discussed here. In the following chapters we shall examine these differences by focusing on Germany, France and Great Britain, with particular attention to the politics of financial-market development.

Notes

1 Jean Dermine (ed.), *European Banking After 1992*, revised edition (Oxford: Basil Blackwell, 1993).

2 Edwin Neave, *The Economic Organisation of a Financial System* (London: Routledge, 1992).

3 H. C. Reed, *The Preeminence of International Financial Centres* (New York, Praeger, 1981).

4 The underlying model and discussion were first developed in Ingo Walter, *High-Performance Financial Systems* (Singapore: Institute of Southeast Asian Studies, 1994) and developed further in Roy C. Smith and Ingo Walter, *Global Banking* (New York: Oxford University Press, 1996).

5 Ingo Walter, *Global Competition in Financial Services* (Cambridge, MA: Ballinger–Harper & Row, 1988).

6 Robert Z. Aliber, 'International Banking: A Survey', *Journal of Money, Credit and Banking,* November 1984.

7 R. Levich and I. Walter, 'Tax Driven Regulatory Drag: European Financial Centres in the 1990s' in Horst Siebert (ed.), *Reforming Capital Income Taxation* (Tübingen: J. C. B. Mohr (Paul Siebeck), 1990).

8 Bank for International Settlements, *Recent Innovations in International Banking,* (Basle: Bank for International Settlements, 1986).

9 Ingo Walter and Roy C. Smith, *Investment Banking in Europe: Restructuring for the 1990s* (Oxford: Basil Blackwell, 1989).

10 Anthony Saunders, 'The Separation of Banking and Commerce', New York University Salomon Centre, Working Paper, September 1990.

11 Anthony Saunders and Ingo Walter, *Universal Banking in The United States* (New York: Oxford University Press, 1994).

12 Roy C. Smith, *Comeback: The Restoration of American Banking Power in the New World Economy* (Boston, MA: Harvard Business School Press, 1993).

13 Smith and Walter, *Global Banking*.

14 For a discussion, see Levich and Walter, 'Tax Driven Regulatory Drag'.

15 Ingo Walter, *Barriers to Trade in Banking and Financial Services* (London: Trade Policy Research Centre, 1985).

16 Edward J. Kane, 'Competitive Financial Reregulation: An International Perspective' in R. Portes and A. Swoboda (eds), *Threats to International Financial Stability* (Cambridge: Cambridge University Press, 1987).

17 M. Goldberg, R. W. Helseley and M. D. Levi, 'The Location of International Financial Centres', *Annals of Regional Science*, November 1988, pp. 81–94, and M. Goldberg,

R. W. Helseley and M. D. Levi, 'The Location of International Financial Centre Activity', *Regional Studies*, January 1989, pp. 1–7.

18 See Levich and Walter, 'Tax Driven Regulatory Drag'.

19 Samuel Hayes III, A. M. Spence and D. v. P. Marks, *Competition in the Investment Banking Industry* (Cambridge, MA: Harvard University Press, 1983).

20 Ingo Walter (ed.), *Deregulating Wall Street* (New York: John Wiley & Sons, 1985).

21 Kane ('Competitive Financial Reregulation') has argued that regulation itself may be thought of in a 'market' context, with regulatory bodies established along geographic, product or functional lines competing to extend their regulatory domains. Financial firms understand this regulatory competition and try to exploit it to enhance their market share or profitability, even as domestic regulators try to respond with *reregu-lation* in an effort to recover part of their regulatory domain.

22 *Ibid.*

23 *Ibid.*

5

Financial structure and corporate control

A key dimension of financial integration in Europe is the complex relationship between the structure of the financial system, the control of enterprises, and the role of the state. The discussion in the previous chapter identifies the hallmarks of efficiency and innovation in the allocation of financial resources, both nationally and globally. Beyond this, the financial system plays a critical role in corporate governance – in determining to whom management reports and the performance standards to which management is held. If Europe is to have a truly integrated financial market in which capital is continuously allocated to the most productive uses (and, equally important, denied to the *least* competitive), a uniform approach to corporate control will ultimately have to emerge from the highly divergent systems that have traditionally existed in the EU member states.

In this chapter we focus on how the organisation and regulation of the financial system – the role of banks and other types of financial institutions (notably insurance companies and fund-management entities such as pension funds) – influence critical dimensions of domestic and international economic performance through the process of corporate control. That is, how the institutional design of the financial system influences the character of the capital-allocation process, national economic performance, and international economic and financial relationships. Following a discussion of alternative financial–industrial control structures, we provide short, stylised and static comparisons of four quite different approaches that coexist uneasily in Europe – the Anglo-American, German and French approaches, as well as the Japanese system, as one that has certain attributes reflected in Europe. All of the remaining European approaches are variants of these three. Each can be evaluated in terms of how it appears to stand up against a set of performance benchmarks, with the role of financial institutions as the centrepiece of the discussion. Each can be assessed in terms of its implications for structural adjustment, financial integration and market access. All financial systems are tied into political structures and relationships, illustrated in Figure 5.1, which describes a 'financial policy community', incorporating all participants with direct interest – as depositors, investors, shareholders, lobbyists or regulators – in the evolution of the

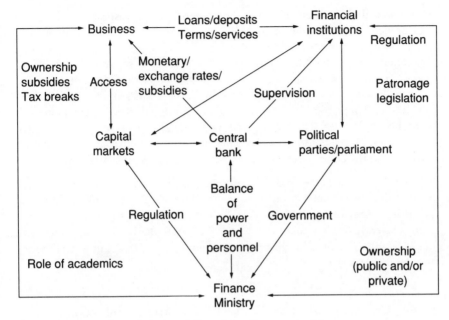

Figure 5.1 National regulations and financial policy communities

financial system. These participants are also subject to multiple forces obliging them to adapt to changing economic and political realities, in a process of transition which too may be stylised.

Structure of the banking system

The role of financial institutions depends importantly on how the banking system is structured, in particular the degree of *universality* it incorporates.[1] Universal banking can be defined as the conduct of an array of financial services comprising credit, trading of financial instruments and foreign exchange (and their derivatives), underwriting of new debt and equity issues, brokerage, corporate advisory services (including mergers and acquisitions advice), investment management and insurance.[2] This can take the four basic forms depicted in Figure 4.5 in the previous chapter.[3]

- The *fully-integrated universal bank*, capable of supplying the complete range of financial services from one institutional entity.
- The *partially-integrated financial conglomerate*, capable of supplying substantially the same set of services but with several (such as mortgage banking, leasing and insurance) provided through wholly-owned or partially-owned subsidiaries.
- The *bank-subsidiary structure*, under which the bank focuses essentially on

commercial banking and all other services, including investment banking and insurance, are carried out through legally separate subsidiaries of the bank.

• The *holding-company structure*, where a holding company owns both banking and non-banking subsidiaries that are legally separate and individually capitalised, in so far as financial activities other than 'banking' are permitted by law. These may be separated by *Chinese walls* and *firewalls* if there are internal or regulatory concerns about institutional safety and soundness or conflicts of interest. The holding company may also be allowed to own industrial firms. Or the holding company may itself be an industrial company. Both cases raise the issue of central-bank bailouts of industrial companies.

The role of government and the structure of the financial system, in turn, may be related. A more interventionist role of the state may be facilitated or hindered by the kind of banking structure that exists.[4] One hypothesis might be that the more universal the banking system and the closer the bank–industry control linkages, the easier it is for government to implement activist industrial policy and the more tempted it will be to apply it.[5]

Financial institutions as a central element in corporate control systems

Corporate control has to do with the management of enterprises. Under classic assumptions underlying market capitalism, management is deemed to consistently act in the interest of shareholders to maximise their long-term wealth as measured by equity values. Agency problems, wherein managers' and owners' interests diverge, are not supposed to arise, and managers strive to meet their fiduciary responsibilities to the shareholders in a firm's purchasing and marketing decisions, in selecting investment projects and making financing decisions, in the use of human resources, and in maximising available economies of scale and scope.[6]

In the real world, of course, agency problems can and do arise, and present some of the greater difficulties in market economies. How these problems are resolved, therefore, is of great importance. Four stylised models for handling them can be described in terms such as those shown in Figure 5.2. All assign central but quite distinct roles to financial institutions. Each model holds a particular structure of bank relations with industrial firms that in turn is related to the comparative importance of earnings retention (self-financing) and disintermediation via capital markets as alternative sources of direct finance. Second, the bank–industry linkages are examined at the level of equity shareholdings between banks and industrial firms, particularly the holding of stakes in industrial companies by banks. Third, the linkages are examined at the level of corporate surveillance and control, drawing distinctions between *outsider* systems – in which control runs directly from shareholders to companies – and *insider* systems, in which industrial companies and banks have interlocking control structures. Finally, each system-profile addresses some of the informal structures

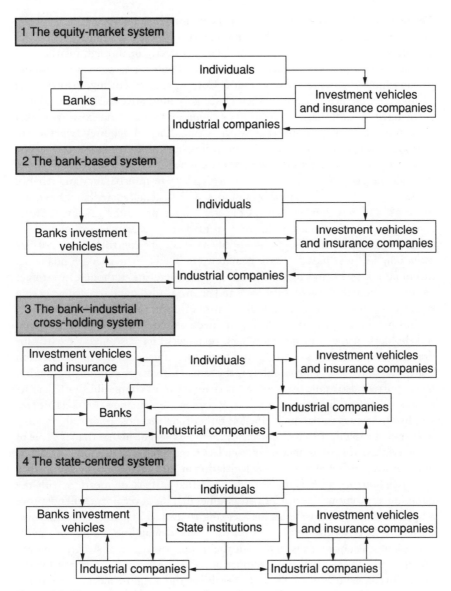

Figure 5.2 Alternative corporate control structures

which, in some countries, play as important a role in binding industry and finance together as do the various formal institutional and legal linkages.

The equity-market system
In this essentially Anglo-American approach, bank functions are split by legislative action between commercial banking and financial market institutions.

The former may provide short-term financing for firms, but the major source of external financing for firms is the capital market. In the capital markets, shares of corporations are held by the public, either directly or through institutional vehicles – like funds managed by insurance companies, mutual funds and pension funds – and are actively traded. Corporate restructuring, involving the shrinking of the firms' assets or their shifting to alternative uses or locations[7] – is triggered by exploitation of a *control premium* between the existing market capitalisation of a firm and that which an unaffiliated acquirer (whether an industrial company or an active financial investor) perceives and acts upon by suggesting or initiating a takeover effort designed to unlock shareholder value through management changes. There is a high level of transparency and reliance on public information provided by auditors, with systemic surveillance by equity investors and research analysts. Concerns about unwanted takeover efforts prompt management to act in the interests of shareholders, many of whom tend to view their shares as put-options – options to sell. The control structure of this essentially *outsider-based system* is mainly confined to arm's-length financing, including takeovers and internal corporate restructuring, although investment banks may be active in giving strategic and financial advice and sometimes taking equity positions in (and occasionally control of) firms of their own accord.[8]

This model, to operate to maximum effect, assumes that the more powerful stakeholders in the firm (shareholders, managers and customers) regard this process as legitimate. Its central claim to that legitimacy resides in an assertion that, everything else being equal, it is the most efficient for maximising wealth. Its supporters also argue that free markets are the most compatible with democracy as a system of limited government. If, for instance, financial markets are free to allocate savings to the most efficient rather than the most politically influential users of capital, then the returns for the savers will be higher than if some of them use their vote to extract rents from less remunerative, but politically-determined investments. Labour-market legislation in particular has to be supportive, so that labour forces may be shrunk or shifted in task or location with the minimum of friction. The model also assumes that the government will not prove a light touch for corporate lobbies seeking to avoid restructuring or takeover through access to the public purse, as a less demanding source of funds. Government's major task is to provide the regulatory and legal structure within which open capital markets may function, and to supply a safety net for the unemployed, the infirm or the old. Not least, this Anglo-American approach assumes that the two kings of the corporate roost are shareholders and customers – if other types of financial systems in world markets have different priorities, benefiting other interests, they will eventually be forced to adapt or to lose market share to rivals focusing firmly on consumer and shareholder interests.

The bank-based system

The bank-based system of corporate control is often associated with Germany, where the rules of the game have traditionally enabled banks to take deposits, extend loans to firms and issue securities on capital markets in a tight relationship to clients. In this system, significant equity stakes in non-financial companies are held by banks and by investment companies run by banks, who act as both commercial and investment bankers to their clients. With significant equity as well as debt exposures to their clients, banks exert a vital monitoring role in the management of corporations, including active boardroom participation and guidance with the benefit of non-public (*inside*) information. Insurance companies may hold significant stakes in banks and non-financial companies, which in turn may also hold shares in insurance companies. The public holds shares in both banks and corporations, but these shares tend to be ceded by individual owners for voting by banks, on the grounds that the banks have superior information about corporate policy and performance as a result of their expertise and of their privileged access to corporate information. However, markets for corporate equity and debt tend to be poorly developed in bank-based systems, with relatively large investor holdings of public-sector bonds as opposed to corporate bonds or stocks. The investing public in such a system tends to be risk-averse, preferring predictability and reliability to lack of transparency and the 'surprises' that come with it. This attitude among the public is reciprocated by the management of firms who invite 'patient' investors to hold their shares in return for capital gains and collateral business in the long run as the firm expands, rather than to higher dividends now that could deprive management of the financial resources needed to invest in the firm later. Financial disclosure tends to be relatively low as accounts are drawn up essentially to meet tax and reporting obligations rather than to inform a shareholding public. The portion of shares which float freely on the market is small, so that stock markets may be thin and volatile as investors (including foreigners) move in and out of shares.

The bank-based system is embedded in a regime which buttresses its legitimacy.[9] Regulatory bodies are supported by framework laws, which provide ample discretion for both regulators and the market operators in the relevant sectors of the financial system to adapt to changing circumstances and market processes. The central bank gives priority to maintaining the value of the currency, in order to secure the adherence of depositors and investors. With its related banking and insurance regulators, the central bank polices the financial system, imposing reserve requirements on banks, requiring financial institutions to maintain provisions and capital reserves, and placing limits on exposures to credit risk. As the bank-based system personalises many of the market functions performed by impersonal capital markets, trust is an essential ingredient of relations among its insider élites. Bankers play a central 'coordinating' function through their positions on corporate supervisory boards,[10] their close relations with the central bank, and management of the bond markets, their administration of delegated shares in annual general meetings and their provision of multiple services to clients.

This role, however, is shared with other bodies, such as labour unions, local or central government officials, and managers in their capacity as stakeholders in corporations. Bankers are not, therefore, left alone to carry the burden of public acclaim or hostility through fluctuating corporate performances over the business cycle. Above all, they are guardians of a stable, property-holding democracy which has co-opted labour unions through their representatives' acquired positions on works councils and on corporate supervisory boards.[11]

The bank–industrial crossholding system

The crossholding system is rooted in close collaboration between government bureaucrats, corporate managers, and party politicians who share a common aim to achieve rapid economic growth. This is achieved initially through a favourable combination of external circumstances and in the abundance of low-cost capital and labour. As corporations develop under this system, they seek stable shareholders who are sufficiently patient to enable managers to recuperate investments in the development of products and processes, and in their stable labour force.[12] Corporations prefer other corporations as shareholders to banks because they share similar concerns, as compared to banks, which are suspect of wanting even a modest flow of income from their lending exposures as market processes start to alter the financial system. The best condition for corporations with high fixed costs is to achieve self-financing by building market share. If bank–industrial crossholdings are pervasive, banks in any event are most comfortable when the corporations in which they hold stakes rely mainly on their own resources. The financial system as a whole must be prepared to deal with the consequences of large trade surpluses, which flow from joint corporate interest in market shares. Domestic inflationary pressures have to be kept down through rapid recycling of funds earned from exports. This entails the building-up of portfolio investments in other markets around the world. Revaluations of the currency from exports and investment income abroad may be delayed by further external portfolio investments, as well as by corporate direct investments abroad, as domestic production costs continue to rise relative to other locations around the world.

The bank–industrial crossholding system is perhaps best embodied in Japan's *keiretsu* (see below), where non-financial corporations as well as banks hold significant stakes in each other and hold reciprocal seats on boards of directors. Both linkages may complement close domestically-based supplier–customer relationships, with dependability and cooperation often dominating price as transactions criteria. The central paradox of such a bank–industrial cross-holding system is that it seeks to exclude foreign ownership and market access, while requiring open markets for corporate assets in other countries alongside open access for exports – including heavy reliance on export finance.

The state-led financial market system

France is the reference-point for the *state-led financial market system*.[13] The Ministry of Finance is the dominant focus for savers and borrowers as it regulates the capital market directly. Deposit-taking institutions with surplus funds place them in the capital markets, and are taken up by public-sector institutions which lend them to specific industries, such as housing, agriculture, nuclear energy or regional investments. Both lending and borrowing institutions fall under the tutelage of the Ministry of Finance, which formally draws up investment priorities through elaborate consultations with trade associations recorded in 'The Plan', through negotiations with the Ministry of Industry or in response to requests filtered through the political parties. Public officials in the Finance Ministry enjoy prestige conveyed by their position in the state hierarchy, and because of the value of their contacts across the extensive state sector to those seeking access to it.

As resources of personnel and time are scarce, such a state-centred administrative mechanism at the heart of the financial system promotes a queue. Organisations with close contacts and claims on the loyalties of public officials, such as state-controlled economic enterprises or large private firms, get served first. Small and medium-size firms are squeezed aside, so their representatives join one or another of the political armies contending for privileged access to the state's resources through elections. The regular cycle of local, regional or national elections are thus also contests between competing producer coalitions for a silver key to public finance.

A state-led financial system also features other characteristics. Financial resources are not alone in flowing through the hands of public officials. Patronage also flows in the form of appointments to the management and boards of state enterprises, or to large private enterprises in receipt of various state benefits. Public officials enter into competition among themselves, through their own organisations and to a lesser extent through their proclamations of party-political fealty. Their legitimacy derives from a claim to act in the public interest. Yet the institutions whose resources they deploy directly or indirectly may expand their stakes in business enterprises, extending further the field open to public patronage in the pursuit of private promotion.

Indeed, a cynic could argue that such a state-led system has a vested interest in nationalising private enterprise in order to expand the reach of public officials, and then in privatising the assets in exchange for comfortable positions in the management or on the boards of companies. Ownership of these corporations is less significant than the fact that they remain on the career circuit, and that they stay within the bounds of what is in effect a political market for economic control. Such a political market extends throughout the multiple levels of government, as local mayors become businessmen and bankers for their local communities through resources obtained through the political process. Ultimately, the state can lose its status as acting in the public interest, and merges into the surrounding maze of non-transparent political markets.

The role of public officials

Note that the roles of public officials in the corporate control process in the four systems described here range from *laissez-faire* to active participation in a political market for resources of all types. At one extreme, public officials enjoy autonomy, set the macroeconomic policy, competition policy and international trade parameters under which enterprises operate, and essentially all other industrial outcomes are left to markets. These outcomes are considered legitimate precisely because impersonal forces are at work. Quite simply, the argument runs, corporate restructuring is called for because the consumers decree it, and the shareholders have heeded their cry. At the other extreme, public officials become fully-fledged participants in the market process. Their involvement on behalf of 'the government' may include full or partial ownership of corporations, public stakes in financial institutions with major influence on investment or lending decisions, influence on credit allocation through the process of bank regulation and supervision, or some combination of these channels. The nature of the corporate control structure and bank–industry linkages may have a significant bearing on the willingness and ability of public officials to affect industrial outcomes.

As indicated, the role of public officials and the structure of the financial system are closely related. Where public officials are located with regard to financial markets affects what they can do. In a centralised state, Finance Ministry officials may have inherited a rigid and compartmentalised national financial system, which obliges them to discharge the functions of a market. In a federal state, regulators and public officials are more likely to be dispersed, with a variety of related, disjointed or competing functions to fulfil. Conversely, the structure of financial markets will tend to pattern the structure of the state, as well as that of bank–industry linkages. A centralised state is likely to have centralised markets to finance its various activities and ambitions. A federal state is likely to find the regions well organised to defend the causes of their local institutions against centralising tendencies from the country's political or financial capital. Appointments, patronage or sources and uses of funds may be either central or local in origin, just as *implicit* state or mutualist guarantees of particular financial institutions – no matter what kind of *explicit* ownership and control structure exists – may originate from the centre or the regions. In the last analysis, the financial system provides the arteries of the state's resource flows. Politics and markets are inseparable.

Benchmarking against Japan

The inseparability of policies and markets is discussed here briefly in the one approach that serves as an additional benchmark for the design of financial structures in Europe, namely Japan. Japan is closer to our stylised presentation of the bank–industrial cross-shareholding system and is significant in the context of an analysis of the European financial area, because any trend towards bank–industrial crossholding in a national context would mark a major step away from an integrated European financial area.

Japan's industrial and financial communities have historically been interlinked more closely than in any other advanced economy. The state exerts a powerful and multi-level influence on both financial and real sectors using the financial sector – through the Ministry of Finance (MoF) – to influence the real sector in the implementation of a centrally-guided industrial policy. The effectiveness of this guidance is amplified by an institutional structure in which banks are normally part of interlinked groups of companies (*keiretsu*), tied together by long-standing supplier relationships, with banks often acting as the leading force in the groups.[14] Leaders in finance, industry and government are closely bound together by a very strong informal network. While it is true that change has occurred in recent years, especially with the reduced dependence of industrial companies on bank financing and the development of Japanese capital markets second only to those of the United States in size and depth, the Japanese approach to corporate control retains a number of unique features.

Historical development of the Japanese model

Japan has rebuilt its economic and financial systems twice since the Meiji Restoration of 1868. Both efforts were extremely successful – first in converting a primitive, feudal economic system into one capable of competing with advanced industrial countries around the world within a generation or two, and second, after the physical devastation of World War II.

In the first restructuring, Japan looked mainly to Europe where large, family-dominated industrial groups with very close banking ties were common. The Japanese *zaibatsu* were not dissimilar to their European models, especially in the period prior to the takeover of political power by the militarists in the early 1930s.

The rapid recovery of the Japanese industrial and financial system from the devastation of World War II had its roots (as did the German experience) in a benign and helpful conqueror able to maintain discipline and political control until local conditions could tolerate democratic self-governance, and in a society of skilled and educated survivors whose motivation for economic recovery was enormous. The requisite human capital and technologies were largely in place not long after the war. The missing ingredient was physical capital. This was mainly provided by the resurrection and modification of Japan's pre-war financial system – one that was accustomed to, and depended upon, the utilisation of the maximum leverage available for the pursuit of growth.

In the Meiji tradition, financial leverage was as simple in concept as it is difficult to visualise in execution. All uses of credit were subject to the meticulous control of the Ministry of Finance. Bank loans were allocated preferentially to carefully researched industrial sectors based on government perceptions of long-term international comparative advantage (industrial targeting). From the outset, banks represented the dominant vehicle for capital allocation and, to do this job efficiently, they were encouraged to maximise their loan-to-deposit ratios.

While systematically high bank leverage (gearing) would be considered extremely risky by regulatory authorities in the United States or Europe,

Japanese banks – although nominally owned by the private sector – for all practical purposes were controlled affiliates of the Bank of Japan and the MoF. All credit was subject to meticulous MoF control. To guard against 'errors' in credit allocation and financial 'accidents', banks were subjected to extremely careful and tight regulation, constant supervision, and strict limitations on the scope of their activities. The regulators could, in principle, have access to the details of every loan to every client, as well as the daily cash flows and, of course, the problem credits of all the banks.

A strong, centralised banking and credit system was thus used right from the outset as an instrument of Japan's post-war recovery policy. The original encouragement of household savings (from a very low base), the marshalling of funds for economic expansion, the arrangement of foreign credits, and the ruthless allocation of capital to targeted sectors of industry were among the vital attributes of the Meiji-era financial system. The approach – dating back to the National Banking Law of 1882 – was important not only in the redevelopment of the currency and credit system after the war, but also in laying the foundation for the modernisation of the Japanese economy and the growth of modern industries.[15]

In time, the system attracted both capital and talent from all types of domestic and foreign sources. Meanwhile, it was fed by extraordinary levels of debt exposure – in stark contrast to so many other countries during the same period – because of the credibility of the intricate, finely-meshed web of mutually supporting mechanisms in the highly organised, centrally controlled Japanese system. The safety net erected by the regulators protected and nourished the prospects of its most promising industrial enterprises.

During most of the post-war period, Japanese companies were encouraged to rely upon their linkages to banks, suppliers, agents and customers to maximise their borrowings, which in the end had to be for the 'right' purposes as defined by the Ministries of International Trade and Industry (MITI) and the MoF. Companies' 'main bank' relationships in Japan were very similar to those of the *Hausbanken* in Germany. However, the banks were so tightly regulated that companies could only finance new facilities and inventories. No credit was made available for unauthorised investments or for speculation.

Specialisation of financial institutions
Several different kinds of banks and bank-like institutions were established in Japan immediately after the war, and each was confined to a prescribed function within the system. These included Japan's very large postal saving system, government-owned development and reconstruction banks (specialising in private-sector infrastructure projects), an export credit bank, agricultural cooperative banks, credit-cooperative banks, trust banks (for managing institutional savings and pension funds), long-term credit banks to finance capital equipment for industry, large urban commercial banks and small (mainly rural) commercial banks.

The Ministry of Finance also regulated the non-bank financial sector, including the insurance and securities industries. Prior to World War II, Japan had no substantive separation between banking and securities activities. Banks monopolised the underwriting of government bonds and corporate securities under a cartel arrangement initially established in 1911. Securities distribution, brokerage and related functions were carried out by independent securities firms, as were equity underwriting and bond trading, mainly because banks were wary of the risks involved. Acceptance of proposals insisted upon by the US General Headquarters of the Occupation to introduce Article 65 of the Securities and Exchange Law of 1947 to separate the banking and securities industries, was based on the view that underwriting (even of bonds) was excessively risky for banks. However, Article 65 did not place limits on bank holdings of either debt or equity securities for investment purposes, which turned out to be an important source of competitive strength for Japanese banks in the 1980s – and a weakness in the 1990s during the dramatic and prolonged decline in the stock market and property values.

Another apparent purpose of Article 65 was to prevent bank monopolisation of the securities industry. This was later reinforced by 'administrative guidance' from the MoF to prevent banks from underwriting local and government-guaranteed bonds, evidently in order to provide the securities firms with a monopoly that would help assure their competitive survival.

Japanese banks were allowed to own shares in their clients, which also owned shares in their main banks. Although the nominal value of these crossholdings was small at the beginning, their practical impact on Japan's corporate control structure was critical. Cross-shareholding (*mochiai*) groups formed the basis for today's *keiretsu*, which in the early post-war years constituted an effective grouping-together of dissimilar companies for mutual support and protection. Banks in Japan today may hold up to 5 per cent of their assets (10 per cent prior to 1987) in the form of equity shares in industrial companies – about equal to the 4.9 per cent limitation for US bank holding companies. They may have additional equity holdings in affiliated insurance companies. About 30 per cent of the equity of Japanese industrial companies is held by banks in this manner within the crossholding structures.[16] The banks act as treasurers to their particular *keiretsu* industrial groupings, and often represent the leading force within them. As much as 60 per cent of Japanese shares in 1990 were held in crossholdings, up from about 50 per cent in 1980.[17]

Financial liberalisation and the development of capital markets
Since the late 1970s, Japan has experienced substantial liberalisation in this highly regulated financial system, although this process has been gradual rather than imposed by sudden legislative change. It may also have been accelerated by foreign pressure for improved access to Japan's financial markets. It is anchored in a number of deregulatory measures, such as greater flexibility in bank certificates of deposit, the introduction of money-market certificates, and relaxation of interest-rate controls. Japan's bond markets have grown rapidly as well,

spurred on by government issuance of large volumes of ten-year debt securities after the 1973 oil crisis.[18] And the country's equity markets have expanded dramatically. In the early 1970s, only about 10 per cent of Japanese external corporate funds came from the equity markets and 80 per cent from bank lending. By 1985, equity accounted for some 45 per cent of funds raised by industrial companies (with convertible bonds adding another 20 per cent), and the share of bank loans had fallen to only 20 per cent. By 1990, bank debt among the major Japanese companies was minimal, with reliance for external financing about equally split between bond and stock issues. It should be noted, however, that a large share of these capital market transactions was executed in London using straight and equity-linked Eurobonds, often sold back to Japanese investors, in order to take advantage of London's superior efficiency as a financial market.

Gradual change has also taken place in bringing down the walls between the various types of financial institutions in Japan. Its securities houses became more powerful with the growth of the capital markets, and banks have been prepared to negotiate away some of their monopoly privileges with the MoF in return for access to growing markets from which they were previously barred. In late 1992 the orderly phasing-out of Article 65 restrictions was implemented by the MoF. As from April 1993, separately capitalised subsidiaries of the ten Japanese trust banks have been allowed to underwrite and deal in government and corporate bonds, underwrite (but not distribute) equity-linked securities, and manage investment trusts such as mutual funds – limited privileges that were extended to Japan's commercial banks in 1994. At the same time, securities firms are allowed to set up trust-banking subsidiaries to deal in investment trusts and currency instruments. Asset management for pension funds was likewise liberalised. Indications are that further deregulation may occur, depending on the results of these initial steps. Liberalisation will shift the Japanese system significantly in the direction of universal banking, and lead to a degree of re-intermediation of finance, a development fiercely resisted by the major securities firms using conflict-of-interest arguments regarding equity underwriting for companies with which a main-bank relationship exists.[19] But deregulation remains the official policy.

Industrial surveillance and control
As noted earlier, a unique form of corporate control has been integral to the Japanese model of industrial development within the context of the *keiretsu* system.[20] Given the Japanese approach to financing enterprises and equity crossholdings, the focus was on continuous surveillance and monitoring of management performance by the managements of affiliated firms and banks as well as, through them, the Ministry of Finance. Non-affiliated corporate equity-holders were (and continue to be) largely passive investors except in cases of corporate emergencies, where the public shareholder was expected to go along with the policies of the group. Efforts to exert control through unwanted shareholder actions have been minimal in *keiretsu* companies. The consequence is a system

remarkable for its stability, continuity and (for the most part) single-minded pursuit of industrial objectives arrived at by management–bank–government consensus, one closely aligned to the national culture and the unique position of Japan in the post-war global economy.

The equity markets have not so far played a large role in corporate monitoring and control in Japan, initially because of their small size and later because the tightly-held nature of many listed companies resulted in very few shares available for purchase in the market. There is little or no opportunity for acquiring influential stakes. Takeovers most frequently take the form of 'rescues' organised by the government. Given the small free-float of shares, stock prices do not necessarily convey accurate information about the value of companies and the potential for market-rigging is great – a fact that has been evidenced on numerous occasions in the Tokyo market.

Informal links

Informal connections play a very important role in Japan in linking the banks to industry. The graduates of a few prestigious universities (notably *Todai*, the University of Tokyo) are highly sought after by the civil service, the top banks and the major industrial groupings, and friendships formed at Todai can tie individuals together from these groups throughout their careers. These links are reinforced by the fact that civil servants close to the top of their profession often move out to industry, banking or politics (in a similar fashion to the French *pantouflage*, discussed in Chapter 6). This 'descent from heaven' is not simply the personal choice of particular civil servants, but is embedded in the system itself. It is understood that when one member of a civil service entry-class reaches the most senior post possible, his classmates must resign. So there is a steady movement of senior civil servants into the private sector, ensuring the tightest of informal networks between government, industry and banking.

Patterns of convergence and divergence

The discussion of the four government – bank – industry models can be summarised as follows.

- The profile of the large UK industrial firm is 'semi-detached' from the banks, and maintains an arm's-length relationship with government. Financing is done to a significant degree through the capital markets, with short-term needs satisfied through commercial paper programmes, longer-term debt through straight or structured bond issues and medium-term note programmes, and equity through public issues or private placements. Bank relationships continue to exist and can be very important indeed, often through backstop credit lines, but the relationship is between arm's-length *buyer and seller*, with closer monitoring and control coming into play only in cases of difficulty. Corporate control is exercised through the takeover market on the basis of outside information, with bank roles limited to financing bids of defensive restructurings. The government role is normally even more arm's-length, with a focus on setting ground-rules considered to be in the public interest, and relations between government, banks and industry are sometimes antagonistic.

- The German approach centres on close bank–industry relationships, with financing needs met by retained earnings and bank financing and bank roles extending beyond credit to stock ownership, share voting and board member-ships.[21] Capital allocation and restructuring of enterprises is undertaken sig-nificantly on the basis of inside information, and unwanted takeovers are rare. Mergers and acquisitions tend to be undertaken by *Hausbanken*, whose importance is amplified by the large role played by Mittelstand firms in the German economy. Capital markets are relatively poorly developed with respect to both corporate debt and equity. Although state (*Länder*) govern-ments play an important role in bank ownership and control, the relations between the federal government and both industrial firms and banks are mainly arm's-length in nature, with some exceptions involving public-sector shareholdings.

- The French approach involves a strong role for government through national ownership of major banks and corporations as well as government central savings institutions such as the *Caisse de Depôts*. Financing of enterprises represents a mixture of bank credits and capital markets issues, domestic as well as international, on the part of both private- and public-sector firms. Formal channels of government influence exercised through the Ministry of Finance are supplemented by informal channels centred on the Grandes Ecoles, and government generally appoints the heads of state-owned compa-nies. The market for corporate control operates on the basis of both public and private information. There have been a number of takeover battles, but the Ministry of Finance has often played a determining role in the outcomes. Privately-owned *Banques d'Affaires* are active in ownership of enterprise and corporate restructuring, although the state actively seeks to shape French industrial structure through patterns of public ownership and influence.

- Under the Japanese *keiretsu approach* inter-firm boundaries themselves become blurred through equity crossholdings and long-term supplier––customer relationships. Banks have traditionally played a central role and pro-vided guidance and coordination, as well as financing, although in recent years the financing role has been somewhat diminished, with the development of active capital-markets access for Japanese companies domestically and inter-nationally. There are strong formal and informal links which run from the government, through the Ministry of Finance and the Ministry of International Trade and Industry to both the financial and the real sectors of the economy. Restructuring tends to be done on the basis of inside informa-tion by drawing on these business–banking–government ties, and the open market for corporate control is virtually non-existent.

Tables 5.1 to 5.3 summarise the legal conditions under which banks, insurance companies and fiduciaries may control shares in the United Kingdom and Germany, benchmarked against the United States and Japan, the comparative pattern of ownership and agency relationships in the four countries, as well as differences in board structures.

Comparative performance issues
Given the dramatically different characteristics of the British, German and French approaches to government–bank–industry linkages, it is not at all surprising that there has been continuing debate about the degree to which these differences have been responsible for the performance of the respective national economies during different chapters of their economic histories. The arguments have been part of the economic policy scene for many years. Not least important is whether the structure of government–bank–industry links has anything to do with international trade and the flow of investment.

Especially during the 1960s and 1970s in the United Kingdom (and in the United States) there was an active debate whether the unguided rule of the market and outsider-based corporate control systems was indeed the key to optimum national economic performance – whether control systems that were perceived (rightly or wrongly) to be significantly more interventionist economically out-performed the market-based system. In the 1990s the pendulum has swung, with both the German and French (and indeed Japanese) approaches coming under increasing scrutiny for lack of transparency, flexibility and creativity.

In order to reach a conclusion on this issue, one would have to define carefully the term 'economic performance' as some multi-dimensional composite of real economic growth – as determined mainly by the quantitative and qualitative development of the labour force, physical capital formation and technological change – as well as long-term unemployment, shifts in the terms of international trade, and other familiar measures. Even if one could agree empirically that one approach has been demonstrably 'superior' to another, one would still have to graft that approach on to the economy in question and determine how things *might have gone* historically if the approach had been different.

In the United Kingdom, admiration of the German economy has often centred on the differences in corporate governance. This usually involves heated discussions of the contribution of (or damage caused by) corporate takeovers, the proper role of pension funds, insurance companies and other institutional investors, management and/or employee holdings of equity stakes in their own firms, the nature of executive compensation schemes, inter-company equity link-ages and strategic alliances, and the appropriate control-function of banks and other financial institutions.[22] The continuing debates on the 'optimum' system of enterprise governance, together with pressure for change in virtually all indus-trial countries, suggests that we are far from a resolution of these matters.

The idea that the German-style *Hausbank* shareholding and proxy-voting systems impart preemptive adjustment and stability to industrial firms is based

Table 5.1 Legal and regulatory restraints on corporate control in the United States, the United Kingdom, Japan and Germany

Institution	US	UK	Japan	Germany
Banks	Stock ownership prohibited or requires prior approval of FRB and must be passive. *Source*: Glass-Steagall and BHC Act.	Bank of England may discourage ownership on prudential grounds. Capital adequacy rules discourage large stakes.	Prior to 1987, banks can hold up to 10% of firm's stock. After 1987, can hold up to 5%. *Source*: Anti-Monopoly Act.	No restrictions, apart from some generous prudential rules.
Life insurance companies	Can hold up to 2% of assets in a single company's securities. Can hold up to 20% of assets in equities. *Source*: NY Insurance Law.	Self-imposed limits on fund assets invested in one company, stemming from fiduciary requirements of liquidity.	Can hold up to 10% of firm's stock. *Source*: Anti-Monopoly Act.	No restrictions.
Other insurers	Control of non-insurance company prohibited. *Source*: NY Insurance Law.		Can hold up to 10% of firm's stock. *Source*: Anti-Monopoly Act.	No restrictions.
Mutual funds	Tax penalties and regulatory restrictions if own 10% of firm's stock. *Source*: Investment Company Act, IRS.	Cannot take large stakes in firms. *Source*: Financial Services Act, 1986.	No restrictions.	No restrictions.
Pension funds	Must diversify. *Source*: ERISA.	Self-imposed limits on fund assets invested in one company, stemming from fiduciary requirement for liquidity.	No restrictions.	No restrictions.
General	SEC filing required for 5% ownership. Anti-trust laws prohibiting vertical restraints. Insider trading laws discouraging active shareholding. Creditor in control of firm liable to subordination of its loans. *Source*: Bankruptcy case law.	Insider trading laws discourage large stakeholders from exerting control. *Source*: Insider Dealing Act.		Regulatory filing required for 25% ownership.

Table 5.2 Estimated comparative pattern of ownership and agency relationships in the United States, the United Kingdom, Japan and Germany (% of total outstanding shares)

	US	UK	Japan	Germany
Individuals	30–35	24	22.4	3.09
Financial institutions – agents	55–62	57.2	12.7	3.0
Financial institutions – owners	2.0	0.7	38.5	33.0
Non-financial corporations	7	3.0	24.9	42.0
Foreign	5.4	5.6	4.0	14.0
Government	0	3.6	0	5.0

on the idea that markets are short-sighted (dynamically inefficient), and that placing a significant degree of corporate governance in the hands of bankers will achieve greater social welfare over the long term. This view is supported to some degree by financial theoreticians, who have argued that a strong benefit may arise in resolving information asymmetries when the bank is both an equity insider and a creditor.

Some observers[23] have argued that the success of the German and Japanese economies is partly attributable to the direct equity links and 'main-bank' relationships. Fama argued that, while lending makes a bank a privileged insider to the firm, the control of ownership stakes makes the bank even more of an insider to the operations of the firm than if it remained just a privileged creditor.[24] As a result, a bank can exercise greater control over the riskiness of projects chosen by the firm. He suggests that full insider status internalises and perfects information flows from the firm to the bank, allowing the bank to make more efficient and timely financing decisions. That is, German-type organisational structures in which banks hold both debt and equity stakes in client firms can be seen as creating an internal (but informal) capital market between bank and firm. In empirical work, Steinherr and Huveneers were unable to reject the hypothesis that universal banks better support the long-term financial strategies of non-financial companies than do financial systems based on capital markets.[25]

On the negative side is the problem of endemic conflicts of interest due to the breadth of the banks' involvement and the absence of internal controls. Especially in the German model, conflicts between the fiduciary responsibilities of a bank and its role as an investment banker, between its interest in completing an M&A transaction and its obligation to a target company that is (or has been) a client, between the profitability of stuffing or churning investment portfolios and its fiduciary responsibilities to the asset-holders, and between its interests as an investor and as a lender to the same firm, are some of the agency issues extensively explored in the literature.[26] Indeed, it may be that conflicts of interest which arise in serving various clients increase with the *breadth* of activities of a financial services firm. Economists generally rely on adverse reputation-effects and on legal sanctions to check the incentives to exploit such conflicts,[27] and

Table 5.3 Differences in the structure of the board of large non-financial firms in the United States, the United Kingdom, Japan and Germany

	US	UK	Japan	Germany
Effective method of board appointment	By invitation of CEO	By invitation of CEO	By invitation of CEO	50% of board elected by shareholders, the rest by employees. CEO may not be a member.
Method of appointment of chairman of the board	Selected by board	Selected by board	Selected by board	Elected by shareholder/employee representatives. Usually a shareholder representative.
CEO and chairman of the board are the same person?	Frequently	Frequently	Frequently	Never
Sources of information	Management	Management	Management, informally, president's club members of stakeholder firms.	Management
Ratio of management directors to total	High	High	High	Zero
Presence of large shareholders on board	Rarely	Rarely	Sometimes	Always
Presence of banks on board	Rarely	Rarely	Sometimes	Always

Note: CEO = Chief Executive Officer.
Source = Theodor Baums, University of Osnabrück.

some observers point out that larger customers will in any case progressively turn away bank relations if they are not as competitive as offerings from non-affiliated banks.[28]

There is also the argument that large universal banks inevitably will not be permitted to fail due to the social costs of such failure – *too-big-to-fail*, or TBTF – and that they therefore have an artificial advantage in competing with institutions that have no such access to implied state support. Even in cases of failure of separately incorporated non-bank affiliates of TBTF banks (possibly including industrial companies), it may be necessary to bring the safety net into play, leading to unfair advantages in funding costs and the possibility of public bail-outs of industrial companies. If the market perceives this to be the case, the safety net effectively stretches under such affiliates as well. Counter-arguments focus on the view that a broader range of activities increases the inherent diversification and stability of the financial institution, and therefore *decreases* the likelihood that the safety net will come into play.[29]

Beyond corporate control issues, German *Hausbank*-type linkages and, to a lesser extent, the French state-centred approach, may have had an adverse bearing on the historical development of each country's financial markets as against the Anglo-American system, with possibly significant opportunity costs due to inefficiencies in the financial intermediation process. The interests of institutions with strong links to their clients rarely create fertile ground for innovations that compete with financial services already being offered, and possibly contribute to an erosion of the bank–client relationship itself. In view of this, market-oriented financial systems are often credited with greater efficiency, greater innovation and dynamism, superior resistance to inherent conflicts of interests among the various stakeholders involved, and (through better transparency) less susceptibility to major uncorrected industrial blunders – as well as politically 'excessive' concentration of economic influence.

In this regard, control of large blocks of stock in industrial companies in the hands of banks, investment companies, insurance companies or other industrial companies are sometimes considered capable of influencing the structure of the national economy in ways that run counter to the public interest. Examples often cited include the role in US economic history of universal banking houses such as J. P. Morgan during the 1920s and the more recent role of the German *Grossbanken* and insurers. Counter-arguments generally refer to the vigour and sophistication of current anti-trust enforcement in many countries and at the level of the EU.

There is also the argument that universal banks, through their dominance of client relationships and presumed degree of economic influence, have the ability to suborn the political process and ram through political action that shifts the balance of risks and returns in their favour. This may include favourable tax legislation, access to government guarantees, anti-trust exemptions, and the like. Counter-arguments focus on the fact that special-interest pressures from other types of financial firms (e.g. savings institutions) or sectors of the real economy (e.g. farmers) are no less capable of co-opting the political process, and that the root of any such problem may therefore lie in the political process itself.

Transition in financial systems

The EU is thus home to several competing types of organisation of corporate governance, three of which we have discussed in this chapter. These very different types of corporate governance are embedded in their specific financial systems, and share a common trait in that they were all structured by a crucial and specific constellation of founding circumstances. Different points of departure imprinted their own shape and their own internal consistency on their later evolution. As mentioned in the case of Japan, for example, the system was rebuilt twice under the Meiji restoration and after 1945 under US guidance. As in the United States, the United Kingdom, France or Germany, Japan's post-war arrangements were never entirely static, nor were they in a state of permanent flux. Interactions between the institutions in the market process or relations between firms and financial institutions were always altering, but at greater or lesser degrees of speed or intensity. There were four broad sources of change, whose relative importance varied with time.

- National societies in all five countries were transformed as their economies developed. Financial systems were crucially affected by the growth in incomes and expanding volumes of savings. An ever-larger fraction of their populations entrusted their assets to financial institutions, which had often been created for specific social groups, such as farm populations, industrial workers or small enterprises. As the occupation structures changed, the original functions and weight of farm, cooperative or mutual banks altered too.
- National 'policy communities' were subject to evolution as well – alongside enduring features such as the role of the bureaucrats in the Japanese Ministry of Finance and the products of the French '*grandes écoles*'. In some countries, the structure of government remained stable whereas in France, for instance, considerable financial autonomy was delegated after 1970, and particularly after 1982, to the regions and departments. Within the 'policy communities', changes in the relative weighting of different types of financial institution were common to all, but the reasons for the rise of some institutions and the decline of others were often idiosyncratic. In the United Kingdom, for instance, commercial banks dominated about 80 per cent of the deposit market in the 1920s, but held a market share of under 30 per cent by the late 1970s. In France, by contrast, the top ten banks have consistently held about 90 per cent of the market as measured by deposits.
- The style of public policy varied considerably, both over time and between the countries. In all countries, the financial disaster of 1929–31 undermined the legitimacy of capitalism, leading to a general sidelining of securities markets and a high degree of formal regulation. After the war, the particular circum-

stances of each country conditioned style and language for nearly four decades. The ideas behind the economic programme of the French National Council of Resistance were predominantly Marxist, for example, favourable to extensive nationalisation and dismissive of a bourgeoisie which was widely blamed for the stagnation of the 1930s. In Germany, by contrast, the language of public policy was consistently expressed in terms of the 'social market economy', whereby government regulators set the legal parameters within which market processes could evolve. In the 1960s, however, the content of Germany's style altered, as elsewhere, to incorporate prevalent ideas on the benefits to economic growth of stimulative fiscal policies. These in turn promoted the expansion of bond markets, with far-reaching implications for financial systems.

- International or global forces impinged more or less simultaneously on all countries, but the content and timing of reactions to them remained specific. All five countries were affected by both flows and structures in the world political economy. The flows included variations in the prevailing climate of diplomatic or military relations between the major powers, the rapid growth of international trade and the operations of multinational corporations, developments on financial markets and relations between the major-currency countries, and global communications. They were also conditioned by the structure of the global political economy whose four components—security, production, finance and knowledge—fashion the constraints within which organisations may exert discretion.[30] 'Structural power', in Susan Strange's words, 'is the power to shape and determine the structures of the global political economy within which other states, their political institutions, their economic enterprises and (not least) their scientists and other professional people have to operate'.

The evolution of different types of corporate governance and financial systems may also be traced over time by reference to the literature on the political dynamics of regime change. Transitions have been defined as the interval between one regime and another.[31] Adapting this scheme to financial systems, the familiar sequence is of a pre-transition or preparatory phase, a decision phase and a phase of habituation or consolidation.[32] Whatever the terminology used, the content of the phases – which themselves may greatly vary in duration – may be adapted to the analysis of financial systems.

- The *pre-transition* phase may be characterised by such factors as inflation, bank overexposure and corporate bankruptcies, inadequate control over monetary aggregates and credit, an intellectual battle of ideas among economists and within the media, and an increasing vulnerability of the currency or the domestic financial system to external sources of disturbance.
- A *decision phase* is shaped by the actions of leaders who seek to regain control over the financial system by altering it. In the period under discussion for the three EU countries, efforts to regain control have focused on the organisation

of securities markets – a clear indication of how significant state financing had become. This phase is characterised by a contest between contending parties over the rules and norms which are to prevail in the new regime, and the appropriate means to be applied. The moderates offer one set of proposals, which are not a priori doomed to failure. If they fail, a reign of the radicals begins, and the transition moves away from mere regime change to a revolution from above.

• The third phase of *consolidation*, or habituation, involves a 'joint learning process' about the procedures of the new regime, where competition in markets and between systems evolves along more pragmatic channels, and the procedures of the new regime gradually acquire the features of an old regime. This phase may last for an indefinite period, depending on whether the regime's norms, procedures or performance are compatible with the ever-changing conditions of its context. If they are compatible, consolidation continues to occur. But if they are not, either consolidation is accelerated to confront a common challenge – or the regime, system and market process moves towards breakdown in a (new) hostile international context.

Evolution along such a political trajectory is not pre-ordained, any more than the weighting of forces driving change remains constant. At any moment, developments may accelerate, stagnate or take unexpected turns. And given the intricacy of financial systems, there may be substantial changes in one component of the system which alter the context for others but to which they may or may not respond promptly. This means that, in theory, movement is possible between any one of the stylised systems to which we have referred in this chapter – or to a mixture of them – as EU financial markets simultaneously converge, compete, cross-penetrate and subvert each other as they simultaneously adapt yet strive to stay distinct. Furthermore, the regulatory authorities responsible for financial markets are always seeking to learn from their own past, and from others' considered failures or successes. The process of selective emulation or rejection is a key feature of policy change, just as defensive measures to protect or offensive measures to project financial market arrangements are key components of the battle between the systems.

Conclusions

The EU is home to several competing types of corporate control, three of which we have discussed in this chapter. They differ in several important and inter-related ways: (1) the sourcing of debt and equity financing for enterprises; (2) the role of financial institutions in the process of corporate control and economic restructuring of business firms; and (3) the role of the state regulator as a source of capital and in the exercise of corporate governance.

As noted, empirical assessment of the comparative performance of different industry–bank–government models is basically impossible, due both to its complexity and to the essentially *political* definition of the dependent variable. There is also the issue of tracking measurable performance attributes under different model assumptions – either longitudinally for a single country or cross-sectionally among countries.

In a 1995 report by the Centre for European Policy Studies (CEPS) a set of draft guidelines was proposed which suggested that, for all European companies:

- Shareholders should determine which rights are attached to their shares, and should in principle be entitled to one vote per share.
- Shareholders' basic rights should include the appointment and removal of board members and auditors, approval of the dividend, approval of by-laws and creation of new shares.
- The board should be responsible for sound management of the company, and should include a sufficient number of outside directors who are highly qualified and experienced.
- All information given to the market should be provided in a way that respects equal treatment of shareholders.
- The board should make sure that an objective and clear relationship is maintained with the auditors. In view of their position on the board, outside directors should take a special responsibility in overseeing the audit.

This is, of course, a policy proposal – along the rhetorical lines of the European financial area – for further liberalisation of financial markets in the EU. It is not yet a factual description of those markets, although signs abound that financial liberalisation and the wider use of securities markets by continental European corporations – including German companies – together with increasingly performance-oriented portfolio management on the part of mutual funds, insurance companies and other institutional investors have led to a shift away from bank finance, and to a weakening of tight industry–bank relationships. There are the beginnings of unwanted takeover attempts in continental Europe through acquisition of shareholdings by unaffiliated (often foreign) investors.[33] Easing of bank activity-limits in the United Kingdom and the United States is allowing them to play a larger role in industrial restructuring transactions, and to exploit some of the information and relationship advantages they have as lenders. Gradual convergence of Anglo-American style capital-market orientation and Euro-Japanese style bank–firm linkages may be expected to test the relative merits of outsider and insider systems – that is, the importance of information asymmetries against the free market's capability of allocating and pricing capital both within and across national frontiers.[34]

The possible outcomes of convergence are many. Germany could move broadly from bank-based to capital market-based. But within that trajectory, the system could modify to remain bank-based for Mittelstand firms, while moving in the direction of the Japanese model for industrial cross-shareholdings for large firms. Equally, some large firms could move rapidly to the capital-market model, thereby diversifying the nature and type of financing and governance within the German corporate community. If the German bank-based system moves towards the Anglo-American approach, that would require the evolution of a large primary and secondary equity market, with major implications for corporate governance and for labour market or fiscal policy. Meanwhile, stylised France could move from a state-led to a capital market-based system, possibly much more dramatically than in Germany, but stay bank-based for the *petites et moyennes* enterprises – it could also move to the Japan-based crossholding structure for big corporate groups, and at the same time remain state-led in its guidance of markets and corporate control. The Anglo-American system may itself move toward a more bank-based or institutional investor-based system.

The following chapters discuss the process of policy change in each one of the three countries, analyse the negotiations and legislative results in the EU on the European Financial Area, and then place the transition in European financial services in the broader context of the 'battle of the systems'.

Notes

1 Anthony Saunders and Ingo Walter (eds), *Universal Banking* (Oak Brook, IL: Irwin Professional, 1996).
2 Edwin Neave, *The Economic Organization of a Financial System* (London: Routledge, 1992).
3 Saunders and Walter (eds), *Universal Banking*.
4 Richard J. Herring and A. M. Santomero, 'The Corporate Structure of Financial Conglomerates', *Journal of Financial Services Research,* December 1990.
5 Jean Dermine (ed.), *European Banking After 1992* (Oxford: Basil Blackwell, 1990).
6 Ingo Walter, *The Battle of the Systems* (Kiel: Institut für Weltwirtschaft, 1993).
7 See Henry Ergas, 'Does Technology Matter?', Brussels, Centre for European Policy Studies, 1986.
8 T. N. Rybczynski, 'Corporate Restructuring', *National Westminster Bank Review,* August 1989.
9 Wolfgang Röller, 'Die Macht der Banken', *Zeitschrift für das Gesamte Kreditwesen,* January 1, 1990.
10 Andrew Schonfield, *Modern Capitalism: The Changing Balance of Public and Private Power* (New York: Oxford University Press, 1965), p. 253.
11 Theodor Baums, 'Universal Banks and Investment Companies in Germany' in Anthony Saunders and Ingo Walter (eds), *Financial System Design* (Oak Brook, IL: Irwin Professional, 1996).
12 S. D. Prowse, 'Institutional Investment Patterns and Corporate Financial Behavior in the US and Japan', Board of Governors of the Federal Reserve System, Working Paper, January 1990.
13 John Zysman, *Governments, Markets and Growth: Financial Systems and Policies of Industrial Change* (Oxford: Martin Robertson, 1983), pp. 99–169.
14 Olivier Pastré, 'International Bank-Industry Relations: An Empirical Assessment', *Journal of Banking and Finance,* March 1981.
15 Roy C. Smith and Ingo Walter, *Global Banking* (New York: Oxford University Press, 1996).

16 Randall J. Pozdena, 'Do Banks Need Securities Powers?', *Federal Reserve Bank of San Francisco Weekly Letter,* December 29, 1989.

17 Richard P. Mattione, 'A Capital Cost Disadvantage for Japan?', *Journal of International Securities Markets,* September 1992.

18 George Kaufman (ed.), *Banking in Major Countries* (New York: Oxford University Press, 1992).

19 A. Gnehm and C. Thalmann, 'Conflicts of Interest in Financial Operations: Problems of Regulation in the National and International Context', paper prepared for the Swiss Bank Corporation, Basle, 1989.

20 T. Hoshi, A. Kayshap and D. Sharfstein, 'The Role of Banks in Reducing the Costs of Financial Distress in Japan', *Journal of Financial Economics,* 1991. See also their 'Corporate Structure, Liquidity and Investment, Evidence from Japanese Industrial Groups', *Quarterly Journal of Economics,* 1991.

21 James Edwards and Klaus Fischer, *Banks, Finance and Investment in Germany* (Cambridge: Cambridge University Press, 1994).

22 J. Cable, 'Capital Market Information and Industrial Performance: The Role of West German Banks', *The Economic Journal,* 1985, pp. 118–32.

23 *Ibid.,* P. Sheard, 'The Main Bank System and Corporate Monitoring and Control in Japan', *Journal of Commercial Banking and Organization,* 1989; S. B. Kim, 'Modus Operandi of Lenders-cum-Shareholder Banks', Federal Reserve Bank of San Francisco, mimeo, September 1990.

24 Ingo, Walter (ed.), *Deregulating Wall Street* (New York: John Wiley & Sons, 1985). See also Roy C. Smith and Ingo Walter, 'Bank – Industry Linkages: Models for Eastern European Restructuring', paper presented at a SUERF conference on *The New Europe: Evolving Economic and Financial Systems in East and West,* Berlin, October 8–10, 1992.

25 Alfred Steinherr and Christian Huveneers, 'On the Performance of Differently Regulated Financial Institutions: Some Empirical Evidence', Université Catholique de Louvain Working Paper, mimeo, February 1992.

26 Anthony Saunders, 'The Separation of Banking and Commerce', New York University Salomon Center Working Paper, mimeo, September 1990.

27 Hans-Jakob Krümmel, 'German Universal Banking Scrutinized', *Journal of Banking and Finance,* March 1980.

28 Roy C. Smith, *Comeback* (Boston, MA: Harvard Business School Press, 1994).

29 Michael Jensen and Richard Ruback, 'The Market for Corporate Control: The Scientific Evidence', *Journal of Financial Economics,* Vol. 11, April 1983.

30 Susan Strange, *States and Markets* (London: Frances Pinter, 1988).

31 G. O'Donnell and P. Schmitter, *Transitions From Authoritarian Rule: Tentative Conclusions about Uncertain Democracies* (Baltimore, MD: Johns Hopkins University Press, 1986).

32 D. Rustow, 'Transitions to Democracy: Towards a Dynamic Model', *Comparative Politics,* Vol. 22, No. 3.

33 Ingo Walter and Roy C. Smith, *Investment Banking in Europe: Restructuring for the 1990s* (Oxford: Basil Blackwell, 1989).

34 Ingo Walter (ed.), *Reforming Japan's Securities Markets* (Homewood, IL: Business One/Irwin, 1994).

6

The politics and markets of German financial services

With the switch in Bonn in winter 1982–83 from a liberal–social democrat to a liberal–Christian democrat coalition, Chancellor Kohl's new government embarked on a pro-business platform to shift financial resources back from the government sector to the private sector. But little had been achieved in the way of financial market reform by the end of the decade, when the EU's internal-market programme was in full swing and the Berlin Wall was dismantled, ending Germany's division. The government was content to preside over incremental changes, and remained averse to any 'Big-Bang' experiment along British lines. Essential to this hesitancy was the long shadow cast over financial arrangements under the Federal Republic by Germany's turbulent history between 1870 and 1945.

Several features of German banking survived the two world wars.

- One was the determination, born of war and defeat, to avoid the mistakes of the past. For that, an essential condition for an effective financial system was a stable monetary environment.
- Another was the reluctance of the Bundesbank, at the pinnacle of the German regulatory structure, to engage in intemperate experiments. The universal banking principle, where banks provide both commercial and investment services, applied to all. Legislation was concerned with general regulations involving the granting of licences, solvency ratios and ensuring liquidity for the system as a whole.
- A third feature – outlined in Chapter 5 and elaborated in Chapter 10 in connection with the political legitimacy of Germany's financial system – is the recurrent debate on 'bank power' usually served up as a political vent against the private commercial banks, originally set up in Berlin by German industrialists in 1870–72 with a view to promoting industrial growth.[1] The banks dominate the stock exchanges, hold shares, maintain privileged *Hausbank* relations with German corporations, and have seats on a range of corporate supervisory boards. But they accounted for only a fraction of banking activity, which was largely controlled or directly influenced by state and local governments. The

broad spirit of German banking remained servicing the industrial and export activities of the economy.[2]

Banks, too, were closely associated with state policy to promote growth and fund government spending. They and insurance companies were organised in hierarchically-structured trade associations.[3] State regulation was general in scope – extensive powers of self-governance were delegated to the associations and their leading members, and complexity was built into the financial system of the Federal Republic.

The post-1945 regulatory system

The central principle permeating the style of public policy in the Federal Republic is the 'social market economy'. The concept derives from the Freiburg school of liberal economists, whose ideas found favour in the Economics Ministry of the 1950s.[4] The doctrine delineates the boundaries between public authority and private interests, linking the respective roles of competition in markets, state supervision and the law.

- Public authority sets the broad regulatory framework, within which competitive markets operate.
- Competitive markets provide an essential ingredient of a liberal market order.
- Statutory law is required to broadly define and delimit the competences of the public powers and the banking profession.

In practice, this 'organised liberalism' yields a dense field of regulatory institutions, where public authorities enjoy specific powers which are restricted in operation to a specialised area, and are often at variance with other functions of the state. This dispersion of public authority is reinforced by the workings of federalism, as supervision of stock exchanges and savings banks is in the hands of the German state government rather than of the federal authorities. The federal government also owns a plethora of specialised institutions. Detailed supervision of markets is by financial institutions, with the public authorities playing a limited and distant role.

Financial markets are broadly regulated by legislation on banking, insurance and competition policy, drawn up by the ministries in close cooperation with sectoral representatives and discussed in parliamentary committee. The ultimate court of appeal regarding parliamentary legislation in Germany is the Constitutional Court. Its exclusive competence – in parallel to that of the Bundesbank to guard the value of the currency – is to define the spirit and letter of the Basic Law, the Constitution of 1949. The Court, established in Karlsruhe in 1951, has the power to nullify legislative acts of parliament, and thereby not only interprets but makes law. It is the custodian of basic rights, the umpire on disputes between the federal authorities and the states, and the guardian of the social market. Law prevails over politics. Disputes tend to be referred to judicial review, making constitutionality the benchmark against which public policies are assessed. Banking and insurance do not escape its purview. The Court regularly pronounces on a range of issues, from competition policy, to consumer interests, to bank secrecy and taxation.

At the heart of the regulatory complex lies the Bundesbank,[5] set up in its present form in 1957, and located in Frankfurt, the capital of the state of Hesse. Its statutory task, in cooperation with the federal government, is maintenance of price stability. Daily business is the responsibility of the Directorate, whose members are appointed *ex officio* by the government to the Council, which sets policy guidelines at its fortnightly meetings. Each state is represented on the Council through the president of its own central bank (*Landeszentralbank*), which operates on the Bank's behalf and as a regulator of local financial institutions. Regional concerns are thus incorporated into national policy, while central decisions are implemented locally. The Bundesbank's regulatory powers extend over all credit institutions. Control of money and credit is centred on the Bank's manipulation of key interest rates, and in particular of reserve requirements. These oblige banks to keep non-remunerated assets with the Bundesbank, thereby restricting their loan activities. The Bank also keeps tight control over the money market. This ensures that banks remain dependent on its refinancing facilities. Not least, a range of tax and spending decisions by federal and state governments affect liquidity and investment prospects in the economy. Bank announcements of money-supply targets since 1974 also serve to place a cap on wage negotiations in the economy, and tend to be taken by the banks as a target for price stability.

Another state regulator is the Finance Ministry, located in Bonn. State regulation of the financial system was introduced in a major way in 1931, following the financial crash. The Bank Credit Law, introduced by the National Socialists in December 1934, provides the modern framework, governing rules on admission, large exposure, capital and liquidity, as well as restrictions on the number of supervisory board seats occupied by any single banker.[6] The Law was modified in 1961, when bank supervision was centralised in the Federal Bank Supervisory Office, based in Berlin. It exercises tutelage as an autonomous federal authority over the banking system, and is placed under the authority of the Finance Ministry. The Office is supported by the Bundesbank, which is not directly charged with supervising banks. The law was tightened by two modifications to the Credit Law in 1976 and 1984, regarding large exposures and own funds. Banks make monthly reports to the Bundesbank, which are then transmitted to the Supervisory Office. Annual bank accounts are supervised by an auditor, appointed by the Bundesbank, with the Supervisory Office's accord. The Supervisory Office has powers to discipline banks, sack their directors or withdraw licences. But it shares supervision of the state savings banks with the supervisory authorities in each state; and its mandate is to ensure the system's overall stability. The Supervisory Office consistently champions bank exemptions from competition law in the interests of consumers.[7]

Insurance also falls into the Finance Ministry's domain. State regulation is based on the law of 1901, as modified by the National Socialists in the 1930s. The powers of the Federal Supervisory Office for Insurance, located in Berlin, were subsequently redefined in the law of 1961. The least that can be said is that relations between the insurance industry and its supervisors are intimate. The Berlin office, with 300 employees, has nine-tenths of its finances met by contributions from the insurance sector.[8] It is flanked by an insurance supervisory council, composed of up to sixty members. Any alterations to existing regulations on the issue of licences, pricing, product content or own funds are closely discussed between the federal supervisor and trade associations.[9] Both supervisor and trade associations concur that their prime task is to ensure consumer safety, and that the insurance companies are adequately funded through stable, high prices in order to be able to meet their obligations over the longer term. Competition is restricted as being incompatible with the interests of the insured. The Office exercises regular and detailed supervision over insurance products and premiums. As in banking, product innovation is discouraged. Insurance companies are prohibited from entering new markets. They may not become members of the stock exchanges, and there is an upper limit, raised over the 1980s from 10 per cent to 30 per cent of financial assets from life insurance that may be placed in shares.

Competition law, introduced in 1958, comes within the province of the Ministry of Economics and the Berlin-based Federal Cartel Office. Banks and insurance companies were granted exemptions from the full force of the law, although they were subject to restrictions under the 'abuse of power' principle. The official explanation for perpetuating these exemptions was the need to protect depositors' confidence in the stability of the banking system, and the special role played by the two sectors in monetary and credit policies.[10] The insurance sector was seen as particularly sensitive to price competition, and to major uncertainties over the likely costs of past or future business. The coalition in favour of cartel privileges held a more mixed bag of motives. In the course of negotiations, the state governments battled to keep as many of their local supervisory powers as possible from slipping into the hands of the federal authorities.[11] The bank associations had a vested interest in perpetuating the powers of the 1939 Bank Credit Law, whereby the Reichskommissar could declare the majority decisions of the trade associations as binding on all,[12] a provision that was eventually ended in the 1984 Bank Credit Law. The competition law was amended in 1973 in order to extend state regulation over corporate mergers.[13] A further amendment in 1990 brought banks and insurance under EU competition law.

State supervision for banks and insurance companies is complemented by sectoral self-governance. The three associations representing the private, savings and cooperative banks, as well as the insurance association, play a dominant role in defending sector-wide interests. Their representatives articulate policy at federal or state levels, and the largest members provide the bulk of their financing, personnel and administrative support. Their leaders' public pronouncements receive wide coverage in the media. They manage their own deposit guarantee and settlement systems, pool resources to ensure the solvency of their borrowers, provide liquidity for banks in difficulty, and run the Federal Bond Consortium, all under the direct authority of the Bundesbank. They maintain intimate relations with their regulators, whose budgets they also help finance. The pinnacle of prestige for the bank associations is the joint Central Credit Committee, where common positions are worked out and discussed. The Insurance Federation plays a similar role. It helps restrain competition, permits nation-wide wage negotiations with bank employers and unions, and maintains discipline among members. The sectoral union – the *Gewerkschaft Handel, Banken und Versicherungen* – represents 600,000 employees in the public, private and mutual financial services sectors. Bank staff costs have risen steadily, and employment contracts are geared to those of the public-sector employees.

Public power: state ownership and self-regulation

The most prominent of Germany's banks are the 'big three' – Deutsche, Dresdner Bank and Commerzbank – all founded in the years 1870–72 to finance Germany's industrial expansion. They operated from the start as industrial banks, taking deposits, extending loans, underwriting new issues on the stock market and engaging in trade finance. As described in 1900 by the speaker of Deutscher Bank, Georg von Siemens, the banks function 'as a kind of leader of the entrepreneurial spirit of the nation'.[14] In the initial years after 1945, the Western allies divided the 'big three' among the states on the grounds of their association with the German war effort. But Deutsche and Dresdner soon regained control over their branch networks. The 1952 Law on the Regional Scope of Credit Institutions acknowledged the fact, and the process was completed in 1957 with full reconstitution of the traditional banking system. The big banks played a central role in Germany's export drive in the 1950s, financing four-fifths of German trade transactions. In the 1960s, they expanded their branch networks, and consolidated their hold over Germany's local stock exchanges. They raised capital for their clients, enjoyed privileged access to corporate information, and managed corporate equities. Yet the big three found that their overall market share dropped from over 11 per cent in 1960 to below 10 per cent by 1990 (Table 6.1). The 'big three' are flanked by sizeable regional private banks and smaller financial houses.

Not only do the 'big three' have a rather small market share. Banking in the Federal Republic is divided formally into the three sectors: private commercial, savings and cooperative banks. Representatives from all three sectors have been active in public policy, and prominent commercial bankers have advised successive Chancellors. Savings banks help finance state governments or operate as instruments of industrial development policies. Appointments to senior posts in

Table 6.1 Market shares of bank groups in percentage of all bank turnover,* 1960–1989

	–1960	1970	1980	1989
1 Large banks	11.4	10.2	9.6	9.6
2 Regional, other banks	10.6	10.7	10.6	11.8
Total banks	22.0	20.9	20.2	21.4
3 Savings banks	22.2	22.9	22.1	22.4
4 Girobanks	13.5	15.8	16.3	15.5
Total savings bank sector	35.7	38.7	38.4	37.9
5 Credit cooperatives	5.6	7.7	10.9	12.2
6 Central banks	2.8	3.8	4.3	4.3
Total cooperative sector	8.4	11.5	15.2	16.5

Note: *Excluding foreign subsidiaries.
Source: Bundesbank Monthly Reports.

such institutions are a matter of state policy. Cooperative banks stand in similar relation to local and municipal governments. Both types of banks have small and medium-size enterprises as their clients, and conceive of their function mainly in terms of serving local communities. With one bank to every 1,500 citizens, the retail financial services market in Germany is densely populated, and scarcely a village is without its cooperative bank. Bank and insurance associations have made clear their preferences for political parties' positions. But the bank associations' interests – or those of their members – are often disparate and divergent. They are only one of many producer-group constituencies which the federal or state governments attend to. This relative positioning in the changing hierarchy of successive government concerns has meant that bank or insurance interests have had to constantly cultivate constituencies favourable to their interests.

German banking and insurance has become highly competitive. In the early 1990s, there were 4,000-odd banks and 745 insurance companies under federal regulation. Interest rates were set in a competitive market, and customer options were many. The German banking system today also encompasses building societies, mortgage banks and specialised institutions. The mortgage banks are practically wholly dependent for funds on bond-issues, and are dominated by the 'big three' private banks. The nineteen specialised institutions are engaged essentially in medium- and long-term lending, and obtain their funds from government endowments or from other banks. The most important is the European Recovery Programme Special Fund, a public institution set up in 1948 to administer Marshall Aid. The Kreditanstalt für Wiederaufbau, later owned 80 per cent by the federation and 20 per cent by the states, was created as the Fund's financing instrument. Initially used to help in German reconstruction, it was later deployed to promote exports, smaller businesses or investments in developing countries. Without a branch network of its own, it relies for information on other banks. Finally, the German postal service operates a large retail banking operation through its post offices, which compete with other sectors in retail deposit-taking.

Government policy has helped dismantle the older divisions between the three sectors of private commercial, savings and cooperative banks. By the 1970s, three-fourths of them functioned as industrial banks, providing both commercial and investment banking services. Capital movements were freed in 1961, and the thirty-five-year regime of interest-bonding was ended in 1967. All types of banks were allowed to expand their field of operations into providing universal financial services. This enabled them to offer a range of investments close to money market rates, and to maintain their control over the intermediation of savings.

Still, banks and insurers remained exempt from competition law, and bank associations continued to coordinate policies on interest rates. This practice came under attack from the Bundesbank, which sought greater flexibility from banks. The Constitutional Court decided against the banks in the case of a client whose deposit had been credited one day late.[15] The Cartel Office's criticisms of the insurance cartel were given teeth with the passage of the EU directives liberalising the market. But the main factor impinging on banks and insurers, as the sectors' representatives regularly recalled, was sharpening competition.[16] The combined market share of the big German banks had been less than 4 per cent of the EU's internal market as measured by deposits.

The savings banks had held their domestic market share at around 37 per cent since the early 1960s, but now saw their numbers fall sharply. As noted earlier, German savings banks are local banks, subject to strict prudential rules, and the municipalities stand as guarantors of their deposits. Their statute is defined by each state according to general principles laid down in the federal law of 1969. This structure has proved to be a serious barrier to their merging in order to preserve market positions. Their main loan business is to local firms and households. In the 1970s, their important status helped the savings banks gain market share from the private banks, which had become deeply involved in the restructuring of large swathes of German industry. In the 1980s, the private banks, led by Deutsche Bank, responded by aggressively building the loan business for smaller firms. As the savings banks found credits to firms shrinking, they shifted to financing the states. They also placed deposits with the Landesbanken, accounting for 15 per cent of German bank turnover. The Landesbanken, owned by the state governments and the savings banks, were therefore well placed to operate as house banks for the various state and local governments, underwriting their bonds and lending to them. But their statute enabled them also to expand into activities from which savings banks were excluded. The Landesbanken thus entered into direct competition with the private banks on trade financing and investment services, as well as money and capital market activities.

Once the way was open for Landesbanken to provide universal banking services, they rapidly emerged as a new pole of countervailing bank power to the private banks in Germany. They came to enjoy the backing of their governments, the trade unions, their clients, and EU and national law. In the 1970s, they spearheaded the expansion of the state governments into industrial policy, attracting criticism among competitors. With the introduction of uniform capital ratios across all banking sectors, pressure rapidly built for them to merge. One proposal advanced in July 1987 was for the twelve Landesbanken to consolidate into five or six, and for the savings banks to seek out whichever provided the appropriate services for their needs. But the plan was vetoed by most regional governments, concerned to preserve their local financial services. The other proposal to privatise the Landesbanken, advanced by the Monopoly Commission,[17] was categorically rejected by state governments,[18] which typically pushed their banks to acquire industrial stakes.[19] WestLB, the Landesbank of North-Rhine Westphalia, took the lead. The EU's internal market provided a further spur to achieve size. Three groups subsequently emerged, structured around WestLB, Hanover's NordLB, and the Bayerische Landesbank. WestLB in addition set up an abortive joint venture with Standard Chartered, with its presence in over seventy countries, later taking over its investment banking activities.

The cooperative banks represented the one sector that expanded its market share, from 8 per cent in 1971 to about 20 per cent by 1990. Rooted in the nineteenth century, the cooperative movement was helped by the post-war merger between the urban and rural branches. Over 23,000 cooperatives joined the new association in 1948. Their number was down to 3,000 by 1990. Several factors prompted this process. The two rural and urban branches were eventually merged in 1972. The banks pool their joint expertise and have a dense branch network with over 11 million members who pledge a formal guarantee for new capital up to a certain limit. They enjoy tax and refinancing advantages. They are supervised by their own trade association, not by the Federal Bank Supervisory Office. The cooperative banks receive their funds from personal depositors, and lend on to their regional institutions. The latter have the status of universal banks, and own the Deutsche Genossenschaftbank (DG Bank), the system's central bank. The DG Bank is located in Frankfurt, also with the status of a universal bank. The cooperatives thus enjoy central liquidity and settlement services and have access to the stock exchanges. Through the DG Bank, they participate in the Federal Bond Consortium, and are present on the international markets. In the reorganisation of December 1989, each regional bank was allowed to merge with the DG Bank, making it the fourth largest bank in Germany.

The German insurance sector is dominated by the five giants – Allianz, Munich Re, Colonia, Aachener und Münchner Beteiligungs Gesellschaft (AMB) and Gerling. The German insurance market is the third largest in the world, growing rapidly from 3 per cent of GDP in 1960 to over 6 per cent in 1990. Most of this growth came in the form of premiums on life and pension policies, which amounted to three-quarters of the total. This growth rate was facilitated by regulation requiring premiums to be priced at a generously high level, thereby ensuring that the stock of the major insurance companies listed on the stock exchange retained their attraction to investors. Generous premiums also underpinned the growth of the multi-purpose insurers, notably the Munich giant

Allianz. Indeed, Allianz lies at the hub of the cross-shareholding typical of German capitalism. Allianz and Munich Re hold 25 per cent of each others' stock. Dresdner Bank and Deutsche Bank hold 30 per cent of Allianz, and Bayerische Hypo has 25 per cent. Both Munich Re and Allianz hold 76 per cent between them of the stock in Hermes, the agency used by the federal government for export credit reinsurance. They also have extensive stakes in real estate, banks and industrial corporations, and as mentioned, provide technical advice, financial support and personnel for the Supervisory Office in Berlin.

The bank federations have cooperated to keep foreigners out of domestic markets. German banks for years slammed the door on international credit-card purveyors, such as Citibank or American Express, in favour of their own Eurocard, managed by the Gesellschaft für Zahlungssysteme (GZS), an organisation set up by all the domestic banks in 1982. The aim was to keep the business 'in the family', prevent foreign incursions into the domestic payments system, and avoid an uncontrollable explosion of credit. Both the Bank Supervisory Office and the Cartel Office gave the go-ahead for the GZS, which effectively monopolised the business on behalf of the three bank federations. When the retailers launched their own card, the banks squeezed their challengers by joining forces with the oil companies and petrol stations for the market in electronic payments. Similarly, the banks pushed Visa to one side, and launched Eurocard as a mass-market credit and payments card in 1988. Foreign competitors sought to exploit rivalries between the federations, particularly in the area of travellers' cheques, or to forge alliances with retailers and the German Automobile Association. Citibank eventually concluded a joint venture with Deutsche Bahn, the state-owned railway, to link its railcard into Citibank's world-wide network. GZS made a counter-offer, but withdrew when the Cartel Office began an investigation.[20] Citibank and American Express together have under one-third of the German card market.

Internationalisation of German finance and state unity

Lower growth in Europe's leading economy in the early 1990s set the context for an internationalisation of German savings habits, and the internationalisation of Germany's financial regulatory framework. One factor pushing Germany towards slower growth was its wealthy and ageing population, with household savings up by a factor of five in real terms over 1950. By the year 2030, nearly 40 per cent of the population will be over sixty, against 20 per cent in the 1990s. This transformation in German society had a profound impact on business and banking. German savers became more demanding, asking for higher returns on their investments in addition to the stability which they cherished. At home, they sought more sophisticated assets to invest in, driving up the cost of funds to financial institutions just as competition in loan business sharpened. Commercial banks entered the market for life insurance in competition with the insurers. Brokers sought to by-pass strict regulations protecting the domestic market from foreign competition. Consumer organisations pressed their demands to reduce the cost of insurance and greater transparency in German accounting. And an ageing population looked to the higher return outlets available abroad to place their savings.

A further trend diluting the internal cohesion of German financing was globalisation. Domestic business has been a declining proportion of German banking and insurance activities since the early 1970s. As international monetary conditions became more turbulent and lucrative, the German banks ventured into Luxemburg, then joined international groups with other European banks, and by the 1970s were actively participating on the Eurocredit markets. In the 1980s, they entered investment banking. By the end of the decade, they were buying subsidiaries in the United States, the United Kingdom, Italy and Spain, and negotiating cross-shareholdings with their major French counterparts.

This evolution was driven by the relative decline in domestic growth, compared to the attractions and risks of doing business in global markets. Already by the late 1970s, seven out of ten of Germany's largest banks owed 25 to 40 per cent of their profits and balance-sheet assets to international operations.[21] The trend was accentuated with the development of off-balance-sheet activities on world securities markets. Off-balance-sheet activities meant that banks faced an accumulation of risks on loan commitments, swaps, interest-rate and exchange-rate contracts. They would have to be covered by considerable increases in banks' provisions, greater attention to risk management, and possibly full-blooded penetration of international wholesale banking markets.

This extroversion of German financial interests was accompanied by a further centralisation of regulatory powers, and attempts to export regulations tailored to German requirements into the international arena. Within Germany, all banks converged on the provision of universal services. Preserving the sectoral definitions for capital in the Credit Law would have meant allowing one sector to extend its loan business at the expense of another. Negotiations during 1982–84 on the Credit Law amendment were heated. The commercial banks feared high capital standards would victimise them alone. The cooperatives lobbied to keep their members' guarantee for new capital. The savings banks proposed to count the own funds of the local governments which controlled them in their definition of capital. After the change in government in 1982, the Bundesbank won its demands for a uniform increase in capital.[22]

Another factor was EU negotiations on the internal market, which enveloped German financial mercantilism within EU law. Banks' and insurers' exemptions under national anti-cartel law were pulled into EU competition law. The Commission in January 1988 enthroned the German universal bank as the model for the EU, but the German banks had to scramble to defend their interests in the more fluid legislative environment opened up by the introduction of majority voting to internal market matters. The public tone that was adopted suggested a stable and proven German financial system under siege from abroad. The banks defended their industrial shareholdings, and galvanised parliamentary support in Bonn against Brussels' determination to harmonise legislation on insider trading.[23]

German unity came in a rush, interrupting the flush of excitement in 1988 and early 1989 over EU integration. The Berlin Wall was breached in November 1989. The State Treaty, laying down the terms for economic, social and monetary union between the two Germanies, was ratified by the two parliaments in June 1990. The Bundesbank took over full monetary powers on July 2. East Germany's conglomerates were to be privatised and market institutions introduced. The Federal Republic's tax and social security system would be adopted. All contractual obligations with COMECON trade partners would be met. Conversion from Ostmarks to DM was set at 1:1 for current payments and 2:1 for savings. A German Unity Fund, initially capitalised at DM115 billion, was set up by Bonn and the states. It was to issue Federal bonds, which the Finance Ministry initially reckoned could be financed easily out of German savings, DM120 billion of which was exported yearly.

But total public transfers from West to East Germany swelled to about 4–5 per cent of western German GDP annually over the next five years. As the coalition government, returned in the October 1990 elections, was reluctant to raise taxes to fund the additional expenditures, it turned to the bond markets. The Bundesbank introduced new issue procedures, which improved the market's efficiency but also preserved the existing bond underwriting consortium.[24] Market participants could only be banks or non-banks registered in Germany, and fully subject to Bundesbank reserve requirements. Attractive yields on German bonds ensured that East German reconstruction would be heavily financed by borrowing on international capital markets.[25]

Finanzplatz Deutschland: the impossibility of being cosmopolitan

A central feature of German stock exchanges is their diminutive size. There are two main legal forms of corporate ownership: (1) joint-stock companies, which separate management and ownership (AG); and (2) private limited-liability companies (GmbH). Between the signing of the Rome Treaty in 1957 and 1982, the number of joint stock firms declined through a process of market attrition from 2,545 to 2,140. Many remained under family ownership, with the families reluctant to go public. The number of listed firms declined from 600 to 450.[26] Between 1983 and 1991, about 165 companies, mainly from the Mittelstand, were persuaded by the banks to go public. The main change came in the surge in private limited companies, from about 70,000 in 1970 to 300,000 in 1983,[27] and a further 70,000 by the end of the decade. Over the whole period, equities were an unpopular form of holding wealth in Germany, compared to bank deposits, insurance and fixed-rate securities – see Figure 6.1. Furthermore, the structure of share-ownership shifted. The proportion held by private households declined, to the benefit of insurance companies and foreigners. Enterprises and banks saw their

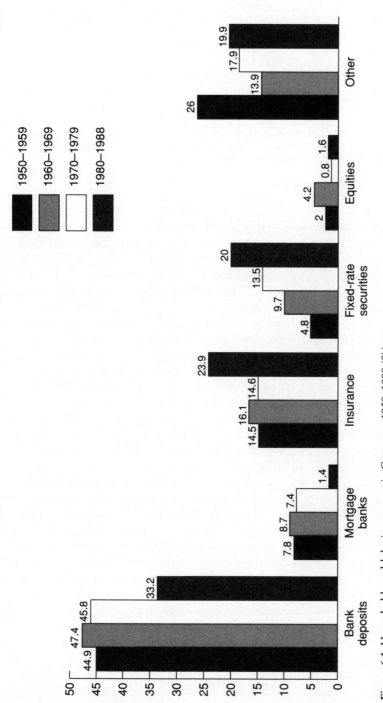

Figure 6.1 Household wealth by investment in Germany, 1950–1988 (%)
Source: Bundesbank Monthly Reports.

Table 6.2 Structure of share ownership in Germany, 1960–1990 (shares in %)

	1960	1970	1980	1990
Private households	27	28	19	17
Enterprises	44	41	45	42
Public sector	14	11	10	5
Foreigners	6	8	11	14
Banks	6	7	9	10
Insurance companies	3	4	6	12

Source: Bundesbank Monthly Report, October 1991.

holdings remain at about 42 per cent and 10 per cent respectively – see Figure 6.1 and Table 6.2. These figures suggest a narrow and illiquid market in corporate paper. They indicate that most AGs have stable corporate, as well as bank, participations, and they show both that the great majority of companies dislike going public, and that German savers and firms prefer bonds.

One reason for the restricted size of the official German equities market is the existence of an extensive shadow market alongside it. The overwhelming proportion of German corporate investment between 1950 and 1989 came from internally generated funds, 61 per cent of the total. Bank borrowing accounted for 18 per cent, and new issues of shares for 2.4 per cent only.[28] Legislation has helped companies build up their own reserves. High corporate tax, and allowances for accelerated depreciation, encourage firms to retain their funds and allow them to offset the cost of borrowing. By contrast, a stiff capital gains tax discourages the sale of shares by long-term holders, and prompts cross-shareholding among corporations, banks and institutions. Companies turn for new funds to their own employees' pension assets, which can be retained on the company books as capital. In similar fashion, banks have been able to stash away funds into hidden reserves, enabling them to ride out turbulent market conditions. Institutional and legal incentives thus give priority to corporate accumulation. Institutional shareholders have played a minor part in providing corporate finance. Germany's state pension scheme has no surplus available for investment. It is a pay-as-you-go service for an ageing population, with any asset accumulations attracted by tax incentives into life insurance. These assets have grown rapidly, but only 5 per cent are placed in shares. German contractual savings barely find their way to equity markets.

Another reason for narrow equity markets in Germany is the broad aversion to them. Germany is not a nation of shareholders. It is an industrial state run by managers and owners. Only a fraction of total savings reach the equity market. Most privately owned shares are held by the banks, which advise their owners on how to vote at annual general meetings. Share turnover is limited, and dividend payouts are low. Shareholders in effect are invited to observe their investment gain in value in the longer term, rather than to take their profit and then decide what to do with them. Everything in the German institutional and legal environment for shares promotes shareholder patience. Management performance is assessed more in terms of growth, capital outlays or good citizenship than in terms of profits. At the same time, the Equity Law of 1966 provides owners and managers with powers to protect their companies from takeover by active minorities. The principle of one shareholder, one vote cedes pride of place to preference voting for privacy. The great majority of larger firms are GmbHs because their owner-managers dislike going public, want to keep control over corporate policy, and prefer ploughing profits back into the firm to paying dividends. The AG is not popular as a legal form, because it entails making results public and because it is subject to the two-tier board system under Germany's 1976 codetermination law.

An international financial centre requires two things: a liquid securities market, and a strong foreign institutional presence. Frankfurt's bond market, the fourth largest in the world, supplied the first. An Association of Foreign Banks was created in 1982 to secure the second.[29] The Association has lobbied for market-opening measures, in line with international trends and EU legislation. At its origin, there were 230 foreign banks in Germany with only a 2 per cent market share. Loans were costly as subsidiaries had to have their own capital base, and access to corporate business was tightly sealed. Their main presence was in the interbank market. Escape came in April 1984, when the Bundesbank sought to halt the drain of German savings to the United States by allowing foreign subsidiaries to lead-manage DM bond issues for foreign borrowers. In October, the coupon which foreigners had to pay to buy bonds was abolished. By 1990, 272 foreign banks[30] accounted for 5 per cent of total German bank assets. American and Japanese institutions led the pack, with the French in third place. Foreign banks accounted for one-half of Frankfurt stock exchange members, with over half of new issues ending up in the hands of foreign investors. They also began to enter investment banking business, but were kept on the sidelines by Germany's cross-shareholding structure.[31] New share issues were restricted,[32] and the authorities remained vigilant against the introduction of new financial products.[33]

As already discussed, the Bundesbank's method of managing the trade surplus was to encourage the recycling of surplus funds to Luxemburg, London or elsewhere. This approach ran into difficulties whenever the Bundesbank was not able to have the DM's value set by market forces, prompting it to intervene. One alternative was to make Frankfurt a cosmopolitan financial centre, in the manner of London. A starting-point would be for the Bundesbank to meet the commercial banks' demands and repatriate the Euro–DM bond market by ending the tax disadvantages weighing on domestic bond business. The Bundesbank could then promote a liquid secondary market, flanked by a short-term money market. The latter would, however, encourage a flight from bank deposits, and create a constituency of savers with a vested interest in higher returns. The market's liquidity would have to be supplied from mutual funds, including money market funds.

Institutions on the market would lobby the Bundesbank to allow them to deal in all instruments traded on international markets. Foreign institutions would demand a slice of the action, and an end to the German bank bond consortium. The Bundesbank would be prompted to shift fundamentally its control of monetary aggregates. Dearer credit would encourage firms to move away from bank borrowing as the primary source of external funding, to the new issue of debt securities and equities. An enlarged primary-issue market for corporate securities would in turn foster a demand for secondary markets along Anglo-American lines. National ownership would be diluted. Germany would become a major source of international capital, and possibly move to a regular deficit on trade account. European integration would be accelerated.

The founding legislation on German stock exchanges dates from 1896, and provides a framework law, predicated on the principles of limited state intervention in the market and self-regulation by banks operating as issuing houses and brokers. The 1934 Credit Law strengthened the regional exchanges at the expense of Berlin, and charged the states with the supervision of markets. After 1945, the reconstitution of the states entrenched this regional organisation within the structure of the Federal Republic. But rivalry proved endemic, with relations between them governed by a web of inter-state treaties. In 1952, the *Arbeitsgemeinschaft der deutschen Wertpapierbörsen* was created to provide some minimum of cooperation between the exchanges. But the states refused to accept majority voting and provided the *Arbeitsgemeinschaft* with no full-time staff.

This arrangement lasted until the 1979–82 recession, when Frankfurt's deficiencies became glaringly evident as an external provider of funds for companies. Frankfurt was home to the big three commercial banks, the leading regional banks, and the DG Bank – the cooperative's central bank. But the Frankfurt exchange accounted for only 44 per cent of the turnover in German securities. There was no coordinated clearance and settlement system, little investment in data processing and information technology and no markets for new instruments, such as options and futures. There was no formal legislation to outlaw insider trading. The ownership of Mittelstand firms remained almost exclusively in private hands. Overall responsibility for supervision of the stock exchanges lay with the Economy Ministries of the states. The eight stock exchanges were regulated by their own executive staffs, and by their own supervisory bodies, but in practice these were dominated by the banks. The states appointed their official brokers, each specialising in a number of securities on the official market, which was only open for two hours a day. The more active market was the non-regulated free market, run by the banks in off-hours and by telephone. Trade in both markets was restricted to government and corporate securities.

The Bundesbank became convinced that German corporate financing was in urgent need of reform in the course of the recession of 1979–82. A Bundesbank study of about 70,000 non-financial enterprises[34] pointed out that companies, which funded investments out of own funds or by bank loans, were highly vulnerable to union wage demands and to interest-rate changes. Wage demands between 1968 and 1975 had seriously eroded corporate profitability, but stabilised in the years 1975–79. Another trend in the 1970s was the sharp rise in public indebtedness as federal government outlays rose. During that period, banks borrowed cheaply and extended fixed interest loans, helping to finance a revival in manufacturing investment. In 1981, the Bundesbank raised interest rates in response to an unprecedented current account deficit, caused by a combination of government spending and the world-wide rise in oil prices of the previous year. Inflationary pressures were amplified by the weak DM. Corporate profits fell abruptly, and in 1982 12,000 bankruptcies were recorded. A lowering of interest rates became imperative.

For the Bundesbank, three policy decisions were necessary: the first was that Germany had to return promptly to trade surplus,[35] and thereby enable the Bundesbank to lower interest rates. Germany's return to surplus in the years 1981–90 saw a remarkable transformation in German corporate finances – see Figure 6.2. Flush with cash, large corporations decoupled from their dependence on bank financing, and Germany moved to become a major net creditor with respect to the rest of the world. Germany's external assets were invested more in foreign securities than in Bundesbank foreign-exchange reserves.[36] Along with OPEC until the fall of the world oil price in January 1986, and in the company of Japan, Germany fed the growth of the world financial markets.

The second policy decision was to have the bond market switched from funding the public to financing the private sector.[37] The change of government from a social–liberal to a conservative–liberal coalition in the winter of 1982–83 revolved around this structural debate on the German economy. The Bundesbank and the commercial banks gave unanimous support to the tax and expenditure-cutting strategy outlined by the Finance Ministry. The subsequent seven years until German unity saw slow growth and a continuation of the government deficits that began in 1973, despite a public policy aimed at budget reduction.

The lifting of restrictions on German capital markets was initiated in 1984 with a view to stemming the outflow of capital to the United States, influenced by the deficit spending of President Reagan's first administration. In April 1984, the withholding tax on securities was dropped as a counter to a similar move by the United States Treasury, hungry for an increased share of world savings. In October, the Bundesbank agreed to open the bond consortium for lead-managing bond issues to the subsidiaries of foreign banks as part of the wider negotiations under way in Western capital markets on reciprocal access. But the Bundesbank rejected the banks' demands to repatriate the offshore secondary markets in German securities.[38] It was clear that nothing would be done to endanger the stability on which German capital markets depended.[39] Germany would not be a testing ground for Thatcher-type policies.[40]

The Bundesbank's writ did not run to tax policy. The Ministry of Finance, in

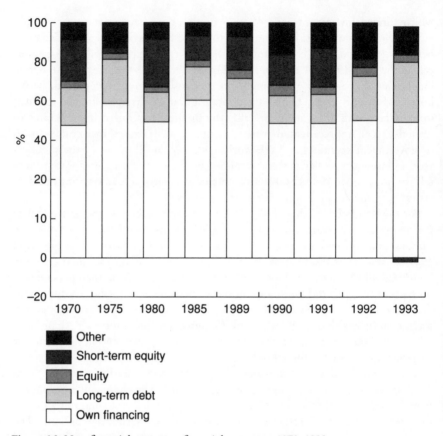

Figure 6.2 Non-financial corporate financial structure, 1970–1993
Source: Bundesbank Monthly Reports; supplementary statistics.

negotiations with the states and the coalition parties, in 1988 announced a reintroduction of the withholding tax for 1989, accelerating an outflow of funds and further weakening a fragile bond market. The measure was taken as part of the ongoing negotiations in the EU on harmonisation of tax on capital. But the measure weakened the DM, and revived Bundesbank fears of imported inflation. Both Bundesbank and German banks welcomed Chancellor Kohl's government reshuffle in April 1989, and the appointment of the conservative Theo Waigel to the Finance Ministry. Waigel immediately had the tax revoked, as part of his determined support for Finanzplatz Deutschland.[41] But the tax was reintroduced in 1993, after a Constitutional Court judgement that the tax should not have been withdrawn in the first place.

The third policy decision was to have stock markets play a larger part in German corporate financing.[42] The champions of this reform were the big banks.[43] But their only vehicle for negotiation among the stock exchanges was the moribund working-group created in 1952. It enabled local interests to delay or to veto legislation so as not to be sidelined by reformers. Talks among its members opened in 1986. A relatively non-controversial measure was chosen to lighten the stock-listing procedures, while reassuring the Mittelstand that their equity would not have to be widely dispersed. A third market was introduced in May 1987, alongside the official market for the AGs and the over-the-counter telephone market for shares run by the banks. In July 1986, it was agreed to convert the working-group into a Federation of German Stock Exchanges, with a full-time staff, and headed by Rudiger von Rosen, a Bundesbank official.[44] But the staff had a limited mandate.[45] All major decisions had to be reached on a collective basis. Their expenses were covered by the eight stock exchanges. An expert group, dominated by the banks, provided advice.

Frankfurt remained a relatively unattractive market. Over 100 companies listed within the first year, but many came from the telephone market, and they were only a fraction of the 400,000 eligible firms. Germany's principal new equity market was in London, when Deutsche Bank set the pace by moving its investment services operations there in 1984. The move signified Deutsche Bank's recognition of 'the preeminence of the London market in the domain of corporate finance and money management'.[46] The London markets offered the liquidity that was lacking in Frankfurt. British regulators also allowed German banks to float new issues with restricted voting rights – a privilege denied British companies.

The big banks were much less sanguine about Frankfurt losing the market for DM futures to London or Paris. One requirement was reform of the law. Futures trading had been outlawed in 1931 and legalised anew in 1971. This market was run by the banks under complex regulations, and the Bundesbank was divided over reform. Its main concern was that new financial instruments might escape regulation. Yet the cost of not having a futures market enabling financial institutions in Frankfurt to hedge their risks became evident in the equity market crash of October 1987. The Bundesbank's change of heart was hastened when London and Paris in October 1988 launched their own markets in DM futures. A draft bill, presented to parliament by the Finance Ministry that November, was endorsed by the cabinet, and passed on for examination to the two houses of the legislature. Resistance by the states was only overcome after the banks had appealed to the Chancellor's office, and because both Hesse and North-Rhine Westphalia – as the home states to Frankfurt and Düsseldorf – had much to gain by the measures.

Another requirement for making Frankfurt into a viable financial centre was to computerise trading. Here, too, the reformers ran up against a host of vested interests. The state supervisors anticipated that a more centralised market would not be dominated by them. The brokers, organised in their own association, feared that reforms would lead to a two-tiered market structure, one for small trades during market hours and the other for large trades in computerised over-the-counter operations. The Frankfurt banks therefore opted for non-controversial initiatives, such as the joint production of statistics, and a joint annual report. Even these moves aroused latent suspicion that the whole exercise was designed to siphon business to Frankfurt. It was only in July 1989[47] that the Federation agreed on a plan to run computer trading on thirty securities in parallel to the official two-hour limit. The computer exchange was to be based on the market-maker principle. But the brokers insisted on preserving the floor-trading system, and the state supervisors opposed giving overall supervisory powers to the Hesse government.[48] These political inhibitions precluded any UK-style 'Big Bang', led by computer technology, as all the interested parties had a say in the policy process. The Frankfurt banks eventually had to settle in October 1992 for a second-best solution, and accept the continuation of floor trading while restricting electronic trading to thirty securities.[49]

The Law to Promote Financial Markets passed parliament in June 1989 and came into effect in August. It widened market participation beyond professional traders on condition that all participants were fully informed of the risks. It implemented existing EU measures on listing, and allowed quotations to be made on the exchanges in foreign currencies. It allowed for the establishment of a computer exchange. The law ended the stock exchange turnover tax, which had restricted the growth of new financial instruments. But supervision remained a prerogative of the states. The EU directive on unit trusts that came into effect in October 1989 (UCITS) was implemented so as to channel funds into Germany's new futures markets.[50] In other words, EU measures combined with competition between financial centres prompted reforms fostering Germany's national securities market integration.

The Bundesbank's campaign against the development of money markets received a serious blow with German unity. The Ministry of Finance needed readier and cheaper access to savings in order to finance reconstruction. Furthermore, the Maastricht Treaty severely limited the use of central-bank credits to finance government deficits – a practice in which both the Bank and the Ministry had indulged during the 1980s. Not least, the Bank's Direktorium favoured the development of short-term instruments that would help it manage the markets.[51] In January 1992, Finance Minister Waigel proposed that investment trusts be allowed to operate in the money markets. The Bundesbank objected: 'The possible shift of funds from bank deposits covered by the reserve requirements to a money market fund not covered by the requirement would lead to a reduction in the minimum reserve base and weaken the efficiency of minimum reserves.'[52] The Ministry promptly withdrew its proposal. Government funding, though, remained urgent and in February 1993, the Bundesbank announced a reduction in reserve requirements, thereby releasing funds. In July 1994, further legislation was introduced allowing money market mutual funds. Deutsche Bank calculated that up to 50 per cent of deposits and saving accounts would end up in money-market funds.[53] This posed a serious potential threat to German cross-shareholding, and to national managerial-cum-union control over German corporate assets.

'Standort' competition: the national solution

The national solution to retain control over the German corporate equity market required a determined bid to centralise direction in Frankfurt. A Finance Ministry round table in January 1990 was the first of a series on how to consolidate Germany's position as a financial centre in international competition. The comprehensive package of reforms was presented by Finance Minister Waigel in January 1992.[54] The endorsement provided partial sanction for the big banks' efforts to create a German stock exchange, and entailed an incorporation of EU directives into German financial law. It gave political support for the introduction of new technology. It proposed the supervision of securities markets by a national regulatory authority. It suggested improvements in investor protection, with a law on insider trading and measures to improve the transparency of markets. And it was accompanied by Finance Ministry proposals for sweeping reforms of money markets. Chancellor Kohl sanctioned the proceedings with his presence, and a promise to ensure that Frankfurt would be the home for the European Central Bank.

A major step to creating a German stock exchange had been taken in July 1990, when the banks announced privatisation of the Frankfurt Stock Exchange, and the transfer of its ownership from the Frankfurt chamber of commerce to the new shareholders – composed of all bank groups – and the brokers. A holding structure was to be created in which all eight exchanges would have a stake. The Frankfurt Stock Exchange came into operation as a private AG in January 1991. The next step was to win acceptance from the states for Frankfurt as the hub of the German Stock Exchange. But this required two years of negotiation with the state supervisors, brokers and governments, as well as strong support from the Finance Ministry and Chancellor Kohl. The Frankfurt banks had to water down their maximum demands for a controlling say in the new organisation.[55] The Frankfurt exchange, accounting for 70 per cent of German securities business, was to be transformed into a holding company, with the local stock exchanges and brokers owning 10 per cent each in the capital. The Deutsche Börse AG came into effect in January 1993, under the chairmanship of Rolf E. Breuer, head of Deutsche Bank's capital markets activities.

Technology had all along been a priority for the Frankfurt banks. Electronic trading was seen as the only way to overcome the disadvantages of fragmentation among the eight stock exchanges. The Deutsche Termin Börse (DTB) was launched in January 1990, and operated from the start as a fully computerised futures market dealing mainly in Bund bonds. It linked market participants electronically, and connected into the supportive networks created in the previous three years by the banks. Its price information system, KISS, came to be flanked by an order-routing system, BOSS. Both fed into the DWZ – the Deutsche Wertpapierdatenzentrale GmbH – developed by the banks to function as the exchange's single centre for stock-exchange information in the interbank market. This effectively squeezed the role of the official brokers in the price-setting process. The German share index, DAX, fielded financial futures alongside information on equities. It was flanked by REX, which provided instant information on ten-year government securities. A crucial aspect of the whole package was the share-settlement system, formed out of a painful merger negotiated between six operators in 1989 – the Deutscher Kassenverein – and boasted a settlement delay of only two days. The heart of the computerised equity market was IBIS – the Inter-bank Information System – which was supposed to operate alongside the old trading floor up to 1995. But technology proved costly, and ambitious plans were shelved following the Transfer and Automated Registration of Uncertified Stock (TAURUS) disaster in London (see Chapter 8).[56]

The Frankfurt banks had not grasped the potential of electronic trading as an aid to market supervision. They were satisfied with their 'code of conduct', and had opposed the EU insider-trading directive. That directive required Germany to have a state supervisory office, but banks and states had agreed in the 1989 Law to Promote Financial Markets to keep supervision in local hands. The banks feared handing powers to a federal authority – such as the United States SEC – and were reluctant to strengthen in-house rules against insider trading, a significant detail in view of the multiple opportunities in Germany's universal banks for a sharing of information about clients' affairs and performance.

None of these inhibitions were compatible with the banks' ambitions for Frankfurt. There was not much comfort for investors in German exchanges that the state supervisors had caught only one insider between 1975 and 1990.[57] But confidence was shaken in summer 1991, when forty-five stock exchange members were accused of insider trading. Those under a cloud of suspicion included senior bankers active in promoting Finanzplatz Deutschland. The scandals coincided with the BCCI affair, and others in Japan, the United Kingdom, France and the United States.

It took until 1993, the completion of EU negotiations on investment services, and a further spate of scandals, for the Finance Ministry to present a bill.[58] Long under preparation, the draft proposed revision to a number of existing laws on securities, as well as incorporating EU legislation into German law. It went to the two legislative houses for examination, and was ratified as the Second Law on Promotion of Financial Markets in November 1994. The Law introduced three major innovations.

• A Supervisory Office for Securities was created to operate as an independent body, based in Frankfurt and with 100 employees. It opened in January 1995. It reports to the Finance Ministry and represents Germany in international negotiations on securities, thereby ending the banks' representative role. The Office incorporates all three securities markets in its scope, and it is armed with powers of investigation and search. But the detailed structure of supervision was the result of a federal compromise – (1) each of the local stock exchanges retained an 'independent trade supervisory authority'; (2) the states were to ensure orderly trading conditions; and (3) the Supervisory Office was to use its powers to prevent and to pre-empt insider dealing. This was far from the centralised authority which Pöhl had in mind when thinking of 'the French model' (see p. 297). Nor was the law explicit about the position of the Office in relation to the Economics Ministry of Hesse, which had built up a considerable capability to regulate securities markets. The Supervisory Office represented one more authority in an already crowded field.

- The Second Law criminalised insider trading, with a punishment of either five years in prison or DM500,000, or both. The definition of insider trading codified the EU directive into German law, with the distinction between primary and secondary trading. The measures came into effect three years after the EU deadline. The banks had taken their own in-house measures earlier.
- The Second Law also aligned German corporate law on practice in the EU. It introduced new rules of disclosure – shareholdings were to be disclosed when they reached or exceeded 5 per cent, 10 per cent, 25 per cent and 75 per cent successively. This replaced previous requirements of disclosure obligations above 25 per cent or 50 per cent. The law also modified the Stock Corporation Act, allowing companies to lower the threshold of shares from DM50 to DM5, opening up the market for small investors. Money-market funds, too, were permitted.

But the Law had a number of important deficiencies. The three-tiered structure for supervising the securities industry was cumbrous and complex. The Supervisory Office was untried. The federal structure of the markets fragmented their liquidity, while the open-outcry trading system was an anachronism. There was no takeover code. Under existing practice, takeovers were negotiated with the German corporate nexus, and involved acquisition of a majority of shares or a blocking minority. There was not the obligation, as in the United Kingdom or the United States, for an offer to be extended to all shareholders.

Political support for an open market in corporate assets was minimal. The most ambiguous of all political parties was the SPD. Its representatives called for disclosure above 3 per cent, but the party was not ready to cut back on the secretive activities of Landesbanken. The SPD, said the Liberal leader Lambsdorff, were like directors of a schnapps factory who preach abstinence.[59]

Furthermore, the practice of multiple voting rights was not ended, nor were the *de-facto* barriers to foreign takeovers, which had been stiffened in the 1970s. A German 'equity culture' could not be conjured into existence by a wave of the legislative wand – note the cross-shareholdings depicted in Figure 6.3. But it was already present in London. That is where the Deutsche Bank – the Finanzplatz's leading champion – and the other major banks continued to place much of their business.

Conclusion

The spirit underlying the creation of Finanzplatz Deutschland was captured by two statements, one on the urgency of preserving national ownership and business

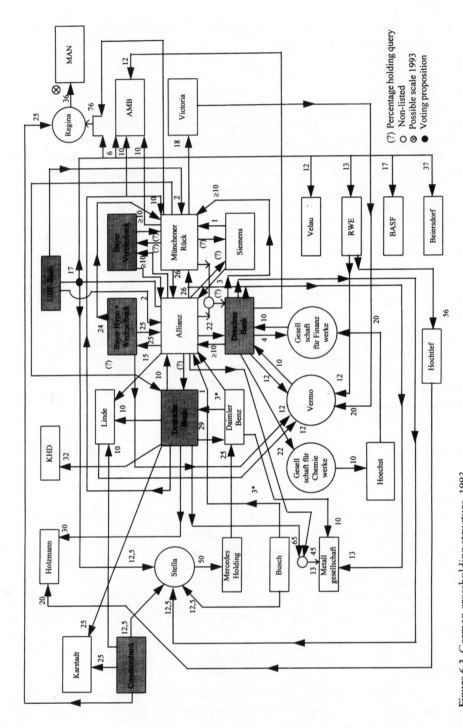

Figure 6.3 German crossholding structure, 1993

Source: Professor E. Wenger, University of Würzburg, reproduced in M. Adams, *Anhörung Macht von Banken und Versicherungen –
Wettbewerb im Finanzdienstleistungssektor 8.12.1993 Deutscher Bundestag*, Ausschuss für Wirtschaft.

practices, and the other on the threat to politics in modern states posed by world financial markets. In Bundestag hearings of May 1990 on the theme of 'bank power', the representative of German industry stated that there was a need, in the light of internationalisation, 'for a strong domestic anchoring of capital and investors'.[60] After the widening of the bands in the exchange-rate mechanism in August 1993, Wilhelm Nölling, member of the Bundesbank Council and president of the Hamburg Landeszentralbank from 1982 to 1992, said, 'It is no exaggeration to speak of an abdication of the democracies in the face of anonymous, uncontrolled market forces'.[61]

The firm intention of German political, business or labour leaders was to ensure that capitalism in Germany would remain a *national* brand of its European variant. Continuity along the beaten path of proven practice was the thread around which policy was woven. The regulatory institutions and laws set up in the 1930s, or earlier, were adapted by the authoritative institutions set up under the Federal Republic to police the markets. Liberal social-market doctrine and practice juxtaposed competitive markets with systemic stability. Custodianship, whether private or managerial, was secured by preserving narrow equity markets, encouraging the development of a shadow capital market, providing state support for cross-shareholding, and extending membership in supervisory boards as symbols of the stakeholder culture. Inclusiveness was a feature both of corporate governance of the corporate sector and of federal and state politics, where interested parties had multiple points of access to policy. It ensured that change came slowly, and as a function of the multiple interests to be reconciled in negotiations, rather than by any national or technological imperatives. Conservatism was the inevitable product. Reforms were partial, and always incomplete. The consequence for German policy was to grasp for the familiar methods that had succeeded in the past, rather than to jeopardise a functioning financial system by experimentation. These characteristics of continuity, custodianship, inclusiveness and conservatism had already been coming under strain in the 1980s as the international system ground towards the great transformation of the years 1989–91. In the early 1990s, Germany faced a double threat to established practice from the shock of German unity and implementation of the EU's new financial services regime. There was no assurance that the ongoing process of German adaptation to the changing context of world financial markets would not end in a victory for the latter.

Notes

1 Richard Tilly, 'An Overview on the Role of the Banks Up to 1914' in Youssef Cassis (ed.), *Finance and Finances in European History: 1880–1960* (Cambridge: Cambridge University Press, 1966).
2 J. Riesser, *Die Deutsche Grossbanken und ihre Konzentration*, 1905; translated into English (Washington, DC: Government Printing Office, 1911); Barrett Whale, *Joint Stock Banking in Germany* (London: Macmillan, 1930).

3 Klaus Schubert, *Interessenvermittlung und staatliche Regulation* (Opladen: Westdeutsche Verlag, 1989).

4 Marcello Clarich, *The German Banking System: Legal Foundations and Recent Trends* Working Paper 7–269, (Florence: EUI, 1987).

5 David Marsh, *The Bundesbank: The Bank That Rules Europe* (London: Heinemann, 1992); 'Monetary Stability and Industrial Adaptation in West Germany' in *Monetary Policy, Selective Credit and Industrial Policy in France, Britain, West Germany and Sweden* (Washington, DC: Joint Economic Committee, Congress of the United States, 97th Congress, 1st Session, 1981), pp. 92–131.

6 Henry James, 'Banks and Bankers in the German Interwar Depression', in Cassis (ed.), *Finance and Financiers in European History, 1880–1960*.

7 Deutscher Bundestag, *Anhörung: Macht von Banken und Versicherungen*, December 8, 1993 (Bundesaufsichtsamt für das Kreditwesen, November 26, 1993).

8 'Die Älteste Verbraucherschutzbehörde Deutschlands', *Handelsblatt*, April 26, 1991.

9 M. Krakowski (ed.), *Regulierung in der Bundesrepublik Deutschland* (Hamburg: Verlag Weltarchiv, 1988).

10 *Bericht der Bundesregierung über die Ausnahmebereiche*, BT Druck, 7/3206, February 4, 1975.

11 Deutscher Bundestag, *Anhörung: Macht von Banken und Versicherungen*, December 8, 1993.

12 *Ibid.*

13 'Crackdown on Cartels', *Financial Times*, October 14, 1974.

14 Quoted in Yao-Su Hu, *National Attitudes and The Financing of Industry* (London: PEP, Broadsheet No. 559, Vol. XLI, December 1975).

15 'Sous la tutelle des banques', *Le Monde*, January 31, 1989.

16 For instance, 'Wir Müssen in Globalen Dimensionen Denken', *Der Spiegel*, July 14, 1986. 'Der Scharfe Wettbewerb in der Kreditwirtschaft Verhindert das Entstehen von Macht', *Handelsblatt*, July 12, 1989. Also in the hearings on banking power in 1990 and 1993.

17 'Der Staat als Unternehmer Ungeeignet', *Neue Zurcher Zeitung*, July 4, 1992.

18 'Die Sparkassen und Landesbanken Sind für Fast Alle Bundesländer Unverzichtbar', *Handelsblatt*, July 23, 1992.

19 Deutscher Bundestag, *Öffentliche Anhörung: Macht von Banken und Versicherungen*, Helmut Geiger, President of the Savings Bank Association, Protokoll Nr. 74.

20 'Germans Flexible at Last on Credit Cards', *Financial Times*, November 11, 1994.

21 'The German Banks' Reluctant Rise to World Power', *Financial Times*, February 20, 1979.

22 'Banken Müssen Eigenkapital Erhohen', *Frankfurter Allgemeine Zeitung*, December 8, 1984.

23 'Les Délits d'Initiés au Régime de l'Honneur', *Journal de Genève*, January 28, 1989.

24 'Bundesbank in the First Move to Update Issue Practices', *Financial Times*, July 10, 1990; 'Reality Dispels Euphoria', *Financial Times*, July 17, 1991; 'Liberalisierung des Deutschen Finanzplatzes', *Neue Zurcher Zeitung*, July 5, 1992.

25 Net transfers from 1991–93 to eastern Germany totalled DM352 billion, according to the Ministry of Finance, compared to DM 437 billion invested by foreigners in domestic securities. See OECD Economic Surveys, *Germany*, 1994.

26 Ellen R. Schneider Lenné, 'Corporate Control in Germany', *Oxford Review of Economic Policy*, Vol. 8, No. 3, 1992.

27 'Moving Towards Graduation from the Kindergarten', *Financial Times*, July 4, 1984.
28 Jeremy Edwards and Klaus Fischer, *Banks, Finance and Investment in Germany* (Cambridge: Cambridge University Press, 1993).
29 'Foreign Banking: Nation Provides a Complex Market', *International Herald Tribune*, April 12, 1983.
30 'Mehr Marktorientierung der Bankenaufsicht Gefordert', *Handelsblatt*, January 24, 1991.
31 'Nur der Verband der Auslandsbanken ist für einen Beteiligungsabbau per Gesetz', *Handelsblatt*, December 8, 1993.
32 Deutscher Bundestag, *Öffentliche Anhörung.*
33 'Im Vergleich Schneidet Frankfurt Nicht Günstig Ab', *Handelsblatt,* August 30, 1990.
34 Deutsche Bundesbank, 'Jahresabschlüsse der Unternehmen in der Bundesrepublik Deutschland, 1965–1981', *Sonderdrücke der Deutschen Bundesbank*, Nr. 5, Frankfurt, 1982.
35 Otmar Emminger, 'La République Fédérale d'Allemagne: Cheval de Trait de l'Europe?' in Ralf Dahrendorf, *La Crise en Europe* (Paris: Fayard, 1981).
36 'Germany as a World Financier', *Financial Times* May 15, 1989.
37 'The Dangers of Bank Finance', *Financial Times*, November 24, 1981.
38 'Banken für Verzicht auf Spätförderung', *Frankfurter Allgemeine Zeitung*, March 27, 1985.
39 'Surge of New Issues', *Financial Times*, November 11, 1986.
40 Interview with State Secretary Tietmeyer, 'Enlightened Orthodoxist', *Financial Times*, July 6, 1987.
41 Norbert Hellman, 'Les Habits Neufs des Bourses Allemandes', *Eurépargne*, June 1989.
42 'Stock Markets Need to Play Bigger Role in Equity Finance', *Financial Times*, June 9, 1982.
43 Michael Moran, 'A State of Inaction: The State and Stock Exchange Reform in the Federal Republic of Germany' in Simon Bulmer (ed.), *Changing Agenda of West German Public Policy* (Gower: Aldershot, 1989).
44 'The Wallflower Takes Third Place', *Financial Times*, July 7, 1986.
45 'In Frankfurt, dem Zentrum des Finanzplatzes Deutschland, Hat die Arbeitsgemeinschaft der Deutschen Wertpapierbörsen Ihren Sitz', *Frankfurter Allgemeine Zeitung*, September 20, 1988.
46 Alfred Herrhausen, spokesperson for Deutsche Bank, quoted in *Financial Times*, November 28, 1984.
47 'Grossbanken Einigen Sich auf Computerbörse', *Frankfurter Allgemeine Zeitung*, July 21, 1989.
48 'Widerstand Gegen Hessen als Landkontrolleur', *Handelsblatt*, November 13, 1989.
49 'German Bourses Combine to Take on Europe', *Financial Times*, October 8, 1992.
50 'Les Allemands dans l'Attente d'Une Plus Grande Liberté', *Les Echos*, February 20, 1990.
51 *Frankfurter Allgemeine Zeitung*, January 7, 1992.
52 'The Bundesbank Opposes Money Market Funds', *Financial Times*, March 19, 1992.
53 'Fund Raising', *The Economist*, August 27, 1994.
54 'Waigel-Konzept Sieht eine Zentrale Börsenaufsicht Vor', *Handelsblatt*, January 17, 1992; 'Germany Plans Shake-up of Stock Markets', *Financial Times*, January 17, 1992; 'Politics Comes to Finanzplatz', *Financial Times*, January 24, 1992.

55 'German Bourses Combine to Take on Europe', *Financial Times*, October 8, 1992.
56 *Financial Times*, February 18, 1994; *Handelsblatt*, February 18, 1994.
57 'Himmlische Zustände', *Die Zeit*, April 13, 1990.
58 'Cabinet Drafts Draft Financial Law', *Financial Times*, November 4, 1993.
59 'Begrenzung des Individuellen Beteiligungsbesitzes der Banken', *Handelsblatt*, May 30, 1994.
60 Deutscher Bundestag, 'Wortprotokoll der Öffentlichen Anhörung zur Macht von Banken und Versicherungen', December 8, 1993.
61 Quoted in 'The Dangers of Capital Mobility', *Financial Times*, October 22, 1993.

7

The politics and markets of French financial services

President Mitterrand's *grand tournant* of March 1983 ended his short-lived experiment to harness the inherited state-led credit system to a policy of economic expansion, and opened the way to extensive financial market reforms. The bulk of these reforms were implemented in the years 1984–88, enabling French negotiators to play a decisive role in the EU internal market discussions. They were enacted by a determined group of modernisers in the Trésor, within the Finance Ministry. Although many of the concepts applied were of Anglo-American origin, the measures were enacted within the context of a financial system where the state retained a visible hand.

As with Germany, the years prior to 1945 cast a long shadow over post-war financial arrangements in France. The defeat of 1940 was blamed by both Vichy and the Resistance on the failings of a liberal economy. The state–corporatist mechanisms, rooted in legislation of 1941 and 1945, were designed to overcome the hesitancy of bourgeois France to invest in the nation's industrial regeneration. Central to the inflationary growth policies pursued under the aegis of the Finance Ministry in the four decades following the end of the war was the idea that state influence alone could transform short-term savings into long-term investments. Equity markets were sidelined on quasi-Marxist grounds that the interests of a narrow class of shareholders were not compatible with those of the nation as a whole, in a vibrant economy based on high levels of employment, the near-equal of Germany. This 'overdraft economy'[1] was constantly modified by shifts in public policy and by the economic and social forces which its successes generated.

France's financial system had never been free of political controversy. Reforms had been introduced in 1966 to ease the budgetary burden of financing the state-influenced corporate sector, and to create French universal banks on the 'German model'. But it was in the early 1970s that the system ran into serious difficulties as inflation rates rose, followed by world oil prices. In 1972, the left-wing parties under Mitterrand's leadership signed the Common Programme of the Left. This programme proposed extensive state ownership as well as control over the financial system, and launched France into two decades of partisan and electoral struggle where control of banks, insurance companies and capital markets were among the major stakes. In the 1980s, the politics of French finance was a fitting battleground for special interests and the ideas of statist, Marxist, corporatist, or social market pedigree. This chapter considers the politics of the French financial system, and the reform of French securities markets. A later chapter examines its evolution towards cross-shareholdings centred on parastatal organisations.

French state corporatism: capitalism without capital

The public discourse of French economic policy after 1945 had two objectives: industrial expansion, and (from 1957 on) the promotion of exports in world markets. Jean Monnet's first plan of 1947 set the tone for the coming decades by defining the choice confronting the country as one between 'modernisation or decadence'. Economic growth was the key measure. Already high under the Fourth Republic, French growth rates were surpassed between 1960 and 1973 only by Japan. The rule of thumb for French state planners was to create large enterprises where 20 per cent of firms would account for 80 per cent of national manufacturing output.[2] 'Expansion, production, competition, concentration', de Gaulle declared, 'these, evidently, are the rules which henceforth the French economy, traditionally circumspect, conservative, protected and dispersed must impose on itself'.[3] Per-capita incomes came to equal those of Germany. Growth rates slowed after 1974 to about 3.5 per cent per annum, but continued to exceed Germany's. In the first half of the 1980s, France for the first time since 1945 grew below the average rate of its main OECD partners. The economy picked up from 1987 on, but in the early 1990s sank back again, achieving negative growth in 1994 and lacklustre performance in 1995 and 1996. Unemployment rates rose from half a million in 1974 to over 3 million in the 1990s. In the early 1990s, 2 per cent of firms accounted for 74 per cent of exports, 67 per cent of investment and 93 per cent of research and development expenditure.[4]

France's post-1945 state-led capitalism has been the reverse of France's pre-war 'stalemate society',[5] where the influence of the 200 families who elected delegates to the Regency Council of the Bank of France, created by Napoleon in 1800,[6] had become a symbolic 'wall of money' standing in the way of national reconstruction. The Council was abolished by the left-wing government of 1936. Marshal Pétain's Vichy regime in 1940 then launched its own national revolution, creating professional associations to organise and modernise the economy under state direction.[7] It was guided in part by Catholic social doctrine, which condemned both free-market liberalism and the class struggle of Marxist doctrine. The regime sidelined 'apatride [cosmopolitan] bank capitalism', associated with the older Protestant and Jewish banks, and provided the opportunity to restrict competition in favour of the large Catholic banks.[8]

On December 2, 1945 General de Gaulle's first post-war government proceeded to nationalise the Banque de France along with the four major commercial banks and the largest insurance firms. It also constituted a Conseil National de Crédit (CNC) to act as a corporatist parliament of interests, to make key decisions on the allocation of credit. Financial markets were compartmentalised between registered banks, mutuals and savings banks, each with their own specific arrangements, but ruled by the state. Private financial institutions were assumed to put profits before nation.[9] French growth was to be based on government-directed credit.

Both the Fourth and Fifth Republics have been served by an élitist and hierarchical administration, their recruitment into the *grand corps de l'Etat* running through the competitive examinations for entry to the Ecole Nationale d'Administration (ENA) or the Ecole Polytechnique. Their distinctive instrument has been the financial system,[10] for which the Banque de France was co-responsible with the Trésor in the Finance Ministry. The formal powers of the CNC merely masked the real powers of this formidable duo. Subordination to political authority was initiated in the law of July 1936,[11] confirmed with the nationalisation of December 1945 and modified by the law of August 1993.[12] Until the mid-1980s, the Banque de France provided generous rediscounting facilities to insure banks against the risk of deposit withdrawals and to encourage lending. But the price of cheap credit was inflation. The franc depreciated by 90 per cent against the dollar between 1945 and 1958, and then by 71 per cent against the dollar between 1958 and 1987, and even more against the DM between 1958 and 1983. Periodically, efforts were made to adopt a hard franc policy, as in the years 1965–68 under Finance Minister Debré. Prime Minister Barre's governments of 1976–81 aimed to achieve 'disinflation without deflation'.[13] Monetary targets were introduced to strengthen the Banque de France in internal negotiations with the Trésor on the budget.[14] But budgetary caution was thrown to the winds in 1981 with the election of President Mitterrand, and expansionary policies were resumed accompanied by three further devaluations of the franc by March 1983.

At the core of the French financial system was the 'Treasury circuit', where institutions with surplus funds were obliged to deposit their resources.[15] The Trésor set the lead rate on this market through the sale and purchase of government paper. The calendar of new bond issues was managed by a committee of underwriting banks, chaired by the Trésor. The funds were distributed through three channels.

- Deposits from local governments, the post office and savings banks were returned into circulation through government expenditures. This direct aid through public funds was allocated through the *Fond de Développement Economique et Social* (FDES), an interministerial committee chaired by the Trésor.
- Commercial banks whose loan portfolios exceeded their deposit base borrowed on the money market, so that bank credits were tied to the lead rate.
- The Trésor distributed funds raised on the bond market to specified sectors

through the public and para-public institutions, chief of which was the Caisse des Dépots et Consignations (CdC). Between 1945 and 1958, this circuit provided 80 per cent of investment credits to the French economy.[16] In the 1960s, the Trésor moved to de-budgetise corporate financing. Nationalised industries' share in new investment declined from 37 per cent in 1956 to 24 per cent in 1972.[17] The motive was to promote French industrial corporations,[18] and the means was to have French banks take the German universal banks as their model.

The 1945 model of state tutelage and corporatist networks inherited from Vichy underpinned the segmentation of the French financial system.[19] The Association Française des Banques (AFB) and the Fédération Française des Sociétés d'Assurance (FFSA) were both compulsory and monopolistic organisations, whose statutes were subject to approval by their respective state authorities. The old model aimed to create an equilibrium between distinct social groups or organised interests conducting their financial affairs through one or other of the state-influenced financial institutions. The relevant competences in the Ministry of Finance were distributed between the Trésor, the Insurance Directorate or the Banque de France, each specifically responsible for the CdC, Post Office, insurance companies and registered (AFB) banks, respectively. The Crédit Agricole was an institution unto itself, with a mandate to distribute state subsidies to the farm sector stemming from the Ministry of Agriculture and the Budget Directorate within the Trésor. This maze of state–corporatist networks became increasingly unwieldy as the economy expanded, and opened to international exchanges. The balance between the various types of banks altered as their deposit bases changed, as regulations imposed on commercial banks were not applied to investment banks, and as insurance companies ate into the resources of the social security system.

Finance Minister Debré, assisted by his cabinet director Jean-Yves Haberer, launched the first major bank reform in January 1966. Unlike Germany, French banking was – and remains – one of the most highly concentrated in the Western world. The top ten banks account for about 90 per cent of the deposit base. Debré's decree allowed commercial and investment banks to compete, in that the former could own up to 20 per cent of equities in companies, and investment banks could raise deposits. Bank lending-rates were freed and bank branching was liberalised. A system of reserve requirements was imposed.

These reforms proved decisive. They helped to create a managerial 'osmosis between the private and public sectors'.[20] The investment banks – Paribas and Suez – came to own important shareholdings in the 100 large family firms included in France's top 200 corporations.[21] The number of individuals holding bank accounts rose from 35 per cent of the adult population in the 1960s to nearly 90 per cent by the 1980s.[22] The banks, assured of refinancing by the Banque de France, rushed into lending, and their branch network grew. In 1972, the Finance Ministry clamped quantitative controls on commercial bank credits, but not on savings or mutual banks. As commercial banks were not allowed to offer interest on deposit accounts, their market share began to shrink rapidly. Commercial banks consequently turned to the bond market for funds, and their debt grew.[23] Haberer, now Director of the Trésor, launched the process for further bank reforms in 1980.[24]

Insurance firms bathed in more secluded waters, under the supervision of the Ministry of Finance. Insurance business in France was small and fragmented, dwarfed by commercial banks and the social security system. State control was pervasive. The Insurance Directorate in the Ministry held the power to grant and withdraw licences, and submitted firms to regular inspection on matters of administration, taxation and accounting. One-third of the highly protected market was in the hands of the five nationalised insurance groups. The General Code of Insurance stipulated strict rules on investment, whereby insurers were to invest their funds in shares and bonds according to a ratio of 25:75. The trade insurance association – the FFSA – was licenced by the Ministry as the sector's certifying agent.

In the 1970s, this cosy environment was disturbed by new entrants into the lucrative motor insurance, life insurance and savings markets. International business expanded. Governments turned to the insurance sector as a new source of untapped funds. In 1982, the Finance Ministry ordered the sector to invest 30 per cent of reserves in 'participative loans' to state corporations. And the January 1984 Banking Act enabled insurers to conduct all types of banking activity as well. EC law on the internal market was incorporated into the December 1989 Insurance Act.

The Crédit Agricole, for its part, had become a key instrument of French farm policy and a conduit for farm influence in Paris. The Crédit Agricole, like the agricultural cooperatives in Germany, originated in the farm mutuals of the 1840s. The Caisse Nationale du Crédit Agricole (CA) was created in 1920 to represent the regional and local member banks to the government. Through to the 1970s, the bank accumulated various privileges: the Vichy government allowed it to issue long-term bonds. The Fourth Republic granted it the right to finance the agricultural cooperatives. The Fifth Republic used it to channel subsidies. In 1971, it was granted the privilege of extending its loan business throughout France ('la ruralité'). As France became the world's second farm exporter, CA became international. By the late 1970s, it was eating rapidly into the deposit-base of the commercial banks and had become the main provider, along with the CdC, of funds to the money market. In 1978, the Finance Ministry began to claw back some of the privileges so readily conceded. For the first time, CA had to pay corporate tax. The Finance Ministry, faced with scarce resources, had grown impatient over subsidising the bank's profits. In January 1988, CA was 'privatised' as an unquoted joint stock company owned by farmers, businesses and employees. Under its new status, the bank regrouped, and negotiated a further extension of its business activities in return for a surrender of its agricultural monopoly rights.

There was also much continuity over export financing, which remained under the tutelage of the Ministry of Finance. Between 1947 and 1985, the Banque Française de Commerce Extérieure (BFCE) held the monopoly on export credits. The Compagnie Française pour le Commerce Extérieur (COFACE) administered, on the Trésor's behalf, the insurance of large export contracts as against various risks. These channels had been mobilised anew in the 1970s,[25] but pushed France into increasing the state's debt as exports rose. The main change in the 1985 Banking Act was an end to the BFCE's monopoly and a withdrawal of the automatic refinancing facility at the Banque de France. But the BFCE remained a subsidiary of the central bank, with shares held by the CdC, the Crédit Agricole, the Crédit National and the major commercial banks. These owners kept the BFCE low on capital, not least because it was a competitor for the profitable export-credit business. Funding for the BFCE came from the Trésor, and the priority to large foreign contracts – which accounted for 10 per cent of French exports – remained intact. COFACE insurance facilities were opened to EU companies in 1991, in conformity with EU law, but its insurance facilities were still covered ultimately by the French budget. As a critical report summarised the situation on export credits and foreign-aid policy, ' an inextricable interpenetration of financial circuits' remained in place, fostering questions about how 'certain investments are decided or certain markets are allocated'.[26]

Towards reform of the financial system

By the late 1970s, multiple strains had become visible in the inherited French financial system. For an oil import-dependent country such as France, the shocks of 1973 and 1979 proved a major setback. Earnings from tourist income and from engineering projects abroad were not enough to compensate for a weakening trade position in the main markets of Western Europe. The Federal Republic's surplus with France accounted for two-thirds of its trade deficit. As French firms bought in German capital goods in order to modernise their plant and equipment, the current account worsened and French governments had to restrain the rate of growth relative to that of Germany. French exports, which benefited from heavy state subsidy, overemphasised on developing-country or Soviet-bloc markets. The overall balance of payments was weakened also by the growth in French corporate investments abroad, which expanded rapidly in the 1980s as capital controls were lifted. As the outflow exceeded inward investment, government policy had to compensate for the imbalance by attracting portfolio inflows. Even so, a French government study claimed that in 1988 industrial enterprises under foreign control in France represented 28 per cent of national turnover and 22 per cent of employment, as against 21 per cent of turnover and 16 per cent of employment for foreign companies in Germany and an estimated 21 per cent and 13 per cent in the United Kingdom.[27]

Mitterrand's accession to power in 1981 also coincided with a collapse in French savings. Conservative governments in the 1970s had chosen, for electoral reasons, to sustain consumption and household savings at the expense of corporate finances. In 1981, household savings dropped from 18 per cent of GDP to 12 per cent, where they remained. The socialists had hoped to provide state financing for lame ducks as well as for 'sunrise' industries. But they met stiff resistance from the nationalised banks when asking them in February 1982 to inject capital into the state enterprises, on the grounds that there was a distinction between a bank as lender of other people's money and a shareholder who takes risks. In November, a FDES meeting decided that the state enterprises' calls on their shareholder had to be restricted.[28] The Trésor, meanwhile, authorised additional savings products on favourable terms in order to attract households, but controversy was fuelled over whether the funds should help small firms or state corporations, foster industrial development, build up pension funds, or feed the money market. Furthermore, the state's demand for funds helped to ratchet up tax rates and constrained outlays. Mitterrand's March 1983 decision thus meant adopting policies to foster corporate profits and to discourage the state corporations' recourse to debt. If France was to avoid overdependence on foreign funds, the gap between national savings and outlays would have to be closed. By 1993, non-residents held one-third of the negotiable Trésor debt.[29]

Mitterrand came to office as the country's debts were sharply on the rise. His policies only made matters worse. The export-credit regime was no longer feasible in light of the debt crisis of sovereign borrowers that began in 1982. Paris Club meetings between debtor and creditor countries, held under Trésor auspices, increased to eighteen per annum after 1982.[30] French exports declined to the African franc (CFA) zone and to Eastern Europe. Paris Club lending conditions were tightened, and eventually the CFA franc was devalued in 1994.

The French state's credit was also undermined by the deterioration in public finances from 1974 on. From a decade of budget surpluses, the state moved to two decades of deficits. The state's borrowing requirements rose to peaks of 3 per cent of GDP 1975–76, and again in 1983–86, and fell back to troughs of 1 per cent in 1980 and 1990, to resume growth to 5 per cent of GDP by 1993. That year, the annual burden of the debt exceeded the deficit. The state's long-term financing requirements rose from FF30 billion in 1978 to FF100 billion in 1985.[31] The stock of long-term debt was composed of a jumble of loans, issued on varied conditions. State borrowings multiplied, stimulating a rapid growth in bond trading. The external debt rose from $34 billion in 1979 to $80 billion by 1984.

France's greater trade interdependence had brought its incorporation into a tightening web of international markets and regulation. Its extensive overseas banking network was redeployed out of Africa into Europe, the United States and Asia Pacific.[32] Between 1974 to 1982, the Trésor had encouraged state enterprises to borrow in London. Foreign loans helped overcome the narrowness of the French domestic market, sustain investment, and cover the current account deficit.[33] The subsequent explosion in debt charges payable in hard currencies was a prime reason for Mitterrand's decision in March 1983 not to devalue[34] and to stay in the ERM. At the same time as French financial management was thus being brought within the EU's exchange-rate constraints, the BIS requirement on banks to raise own funds as a precaution against exposures meant French banks having to move away from their old overdraft habits. To raise own funds from 3.6 per cent in 1978 to the required BIS 8 per cent by the early 1990s,[35] French banks adopted two strategies. In the shorter term, the Trésor and the banks used various devices to raise capital, but at the expense of their international ratings. They aggressively internationalised and expanded their off-balance-sheet activities. Measured in terms of overall foreign business conducted from home or abroad, French banks' share rose from 42.8 per cent of total revenues in 1984 to 67.7 per cent in 1993.[36]

The crescendo to the French political battle over nationalisation and privatisation, and over protection or freer trade within a national or wider European context, was reached in 1981 with the election to the Presidency of Mitterrand. In the radical early months of his administration, prime policy objectives were the extension of state-ownership and the 'reconquest of the domestic market'. This threatened to further sap the EU of substance and evoked allied efforts to prevent France from 'breaking with capitalism' – as Mitterrand had announced was his intent. The programme for an internal market was thus the completion of a movement begun in the early 1980s. The Trésor's reforms of the French financial system were launched in 1983–84, prior to Jacques Delors taking up his new post as President of the European Commission, and provided the national counterpart to French support for an integrated market for financial services, without which the proposal for the single market would not have got off the ground.[37] Yet the internal market programme impinged upon politically charged matters, such as state-ownership, insurance, or mutual funds. State-owned corporations fell under closer Commission scrutiny and were encouraged to behave more like private-sector firms, providing an additional reason for privatisation. EU jurisprudence and legislation on insurance demanded major changes to adapt French practices. French law was adapted to accommodate mutual fund techniques developed by 'Anglo-Saxons'.

France followed the moves in Belgium, Italy and Spain to decentralise state functions. Successive governments had inched towards devolving political powers to regions in order to foster local financial communities supportive of local business.[38] In the 1982 reforms, running in parallel to President Mitterrand's ambitious scheme for nationalisation, France's twenty-two regions were given real powers to duplicate the subsidy of business characteristics of the French financial system as a whole. Regional committees of banks, linked to the AFB, were formed. The Sociétés de Développement Regionale, set up in the main after 1960s, raised their support for local firms and the six local stock exchanges. Central government transfers to the regions exploded, followed by a growth in loans from the CdC. With resources in limited supply, the Trésor consequently sought to re-establish central control, promoted local courts of account, and in 1988 merged the six regional stock exchanges with the Paris Bourse. Paris also fostered inward direct investment, and ensured a growing flow of EU 'structural funds' to the regions, as well as investments by the European Investment Bank (EIB). These funds flowed through central government hands. In 1993, regional and local administrations had a combined budget of 10 per cent of GDP, or half the size of the central state budget.

Incorporating EU legislation challenged French statecraft to move away from the 'Colbertisme' of the Fifth Republic towards state–corporatist regulation of the market. The FBCD in 1977 had laid down initial terms for an EU banking regime, and stimulated the French debate over bank reform. Trésor Director Haberer's study was presented to Finance Minister Delors in 1981. The draft bill came before the National Assembly in April 1983, and the Banking Act entered into effect in July 1984. The Banking Act formally introduced universal banking to France, and provided a uniform set of prudential rules for all financial institutions, and all registered banks, mutuals and cooperatives were incorporated under the Act.

This modernised state–corporatism reinforced the position of the Trésor and the Banque de France. The 1984 Banking Act centralised regulatory powers for all bank sectors in a Comité de la Réglementation Bancaire (CRB), presided over by the Governor of the Banque de France, and the Director of the Trésor. The Governor also chaired a Comité des Etablissements de Crédit (CET), which operated as registrar for rules and regulations. The sole authority to implement the rules was the Commission Bancaire (CB), whose personnel came from the Banque de France. The Act stipulated that all banks would join a common umbrella organisation – the Association Française des Etablissements de Crédit (AFEC) – answerable to the Competition Commission, established in 1977.

The 1984 Act initiated a revolution for banking in France. Banks could no longer count on automatic rediscounting at the Banque de France. Tighter regulations forced banks to raise their own capital, and to pay more attention to profits. On the resource side, AFB banks faced disintermediation as customers moved out of zero-interest deposits. So the banks moved to corner the fast-developing markets in life insurance or unit trusts, where their subsidiaries held up to 50 per cent of the market. Their off-balance-sheet activities surged as well, and their role in bond issues rose.

Similarly, the ending in 1986 of quantitative credit restrictions brought competition to the loan business. Corporate demand for credits fell away, as their self-financing rose from 68 per cent in 1984 to over 100 per cent in the 1990s.[39] The banks rushed into household loans, developed advisory services, and adopted different corporate strategies in response to the prospect of the EU's internal market. In the early 1990s, the boom ended, and bank margins fell. Individually, the recession of the 1990s revealed the stark differences in corporate strategies adopted by the major banks: the Societé Générale, the only commercial bank privatised in 1986–87, registered record profits. The Banque Nationale de Paris's (BNP) results were mediocre. Crédit Lyonnais, driven by the ambitions of its chairman, Jean-Yves Haberer, to imitate what he considered the 'German model' of close 'bank–industry' partnerships, in effect went bankrupt.

The role of the state at its zenith: the Crédit Lyonnais saga

In late 1992 Jean-Yves Haberer, Chairman of Crédit Lyonnais (CL), reaffirmed at every opportunity his aim to turn his institution from a staid, state-controlled French bank into a high-performance pan-European universal bank – a consummate player in both commercial and investment banking and a veritable cornerstone of European finance – by the turn of the century.[40]

According to Haberer, the banks likely to be the future leaders in Europe were the Deutsche Bank of Germany, Barclays Bank of Great Britain, Instituto Bancaria San Paolo di Torino of Italy, and Crédit Lyonnais – i.e. the leading banks located in the leading European countries. Few others, he believed, had much of a chance. Only the leaders would, he believed, have the capital strength, the domestic market share, and the intra-European networks to intimidate rivals and repel all competitive threats from all sources, European or otherwise.

Haberer had chosen the grandest strategy of all. It was a strategy that would have enormous appeal to CL's owner, the French state, in its vision that a few Euro-champions needed to be nurtured in each important industry through an aggressive 'industrial policy' of protection, subsidy, ministerial guidance and selective capital infusions. Each Euro-champion – as many as possible French – must be capable of prevailing in commercial warfare on the global battlefield against all comers. In financial services, according to Haberer, Crédit Lyonnais would be the chosen instrument. Four daring ideas outlined Haberer's plan for achieving his objective.

- Crédit Lyonnais had to grow to be large, very large. The size goal was to capture between one and two per cent of all bank deposits in the twelve EC countries. This meant capturing a significant market share in multiple areas of banking and securities activities at once, and doing so quickly. Given the competitive dynamics of the financial services sector, urgency was of the essence. The only viable solution required acquisitions of existing businesses in various countries on several fronts simultaneously.
- Crédit Lyonnais had to become very European. That meant going up against entrenched domestic competition in most of the national EC markets simultaneously, either via aggressive expansion, strategic alliances and networks, or acquisitions. The strategy was clear, but no one tactic would suffice. Opportunism and flexibility were key.
- Crédit Lyonnais had to exert significant control over its corporate banking customers via both deep-lending and investment-banking relationships with major non-financial firms and via large ownership stakes in many of these same firms. Only in this way, he felt, could CL exert sufficient influence over their financial and business affairs to direct large and profitable business his way.
- Crédit Lyonnais had to retain the confidence of the French government. It owned the bank. It would have to inject a great deal of capital. It would have

to clear the way for acquisitions and ownership stakes. It would have to look beyond the inevitable 'accidents' that would occur on the road to greater glory. Crédit Lyonnais would have to become an indispensable instrument of French and European industrial policy. And the special relationship would have to survive political changes in France, even changes leading to CL's own privatisation.

Crédit Lyonnais first opened for business in Lyon in 1863 as a *banque de dépôts*.[41] CL began its international operations in London during the Franco-Prussian war, and expanded throughout France and in many of the major foreign business centres in the 1870s. By 1900, it was the largest French bank in terms of assets.

With World War I, many large-bank personnel were conscripted, and competition in French banking increased. Smaller banks took advantage of the larger banks' staffing difficulties and expanded rapidly. Beginning in 1917, *Crédits Populaires*, a new form of banking establishment, were allowed to be established and added to the domestic competition in France. With the Revolution in 1918, sizeable Russian deposits were withdrawn as their owners demanded that CL restitute assets confiscated by the Bolsheviks. Although profitable, CL was not making nearly the kinds of profits during the 1920s that it had enjoyed before the war.

During the Great Depression CL adopted a cautious approach, closing about 100 offices in France and abroad. With the onset of World War II, CL remained essentially apolitical, maintaining the majority of its banking activities – although some foreign offices were not under the control of the main office during the German occupation. With the restoration of peace in 1945, a number of events were of signal importance in determining CL's future course.

- 1945: the French government nationalised the *Banques de Dépôts* – Crédit Lyonnais, the Société Générale, the Comptoir National d'Escomptes de Paris (CNEP), and the Banque Nationale de Commerce et d'Industrie (BNCI).
- 1966: the Ministry of Finance merged the two smaller banks, CNEP and BNCI into BNP (Banque Nationale de Paris).
- 1970: the president of CL, François Bloch-Lainé, Inspecteur des Finances, adopted a strategy of partnerships with other banks in the form of Union des Banques Arabes et Françaises (UBAF), and Europartners (see below).
- 1973: a law was passed that allowed the distribution of shares to the employees of nationalised banks and insurance companies such as Crédit Lyonnais.
- 1974: election victory of the conservative parties, led by Valéry Giscard d'Estaing, and the appointment of Jacques Chaine (Inspecteur des Finances) to replace François Bloch-Lainé as chief executive of CL.
- 1981: election victory of the leftist parties and François Mitterand. Appointment of Jean Deflassieux, financial adviser to the Socialist Party to replace Jacques Chaine at CL.
- 1982: nationalisation by the Socialists of all major French banks. The

government's declared objective was to influence the functioning of the banks in a direction more favourable to small and medium-sized business, as well as to help define and implement a new and more interventionist industrial and monetary policy. For CL, the only immediate implication was the re-nationalisation of the shares the bank had sold to employees in 1973.

- 1986: the Gaullists once again regained power in the legislative assembly, with the appointment of Jacques Chirac as Prime Minister. This ushered in a period of 'cohabitation' with a Socialist president, François Mitterand. Jean Deflassieux was replaced as CL chief executive by an ardent privatisation advocate, Jean-Maxime Lévêque. A privatisation law authorised the public sale of sixty-five large industrial companies, although CL was not targeted for the first round of privatisation. The Groupe Financière de Paribas and the Société Générale were both successfully privatised.

- 1988: the Socialists regained power. Privatisations were immediately suspended, and Jean-Yves Haberer replaced Jean-Maxime Lévêque as president of CL.

- 1992: the Socialists were locked in an election battle with a conservative coalition led by Edouard Balladur and Jacques Chirac, which could lead to another period of cohabitation, since things looked bleak for the Socialists and the French presidential elections were not due until 1995. A plank in the conservative-party platform promised a resumption of privatisations to include a broad array of state-owned enterprises. Names such as Thomson, Bull, Péchiney, Rhône-Poulenc, Elf-Aquitaine, Aerospatiale, Air France, Cie Générale Maritime, SNECMA, Usinor-Sacilor, GAN, UAP, BNP and CL were all thought to be on the list.

The successive changes of chief executives at Crédit Lyonnais with incoming governments illustrated the persistent intervention of the State in the running of companies, commonly known in France as *dirigisme*. From relative independence after nationalisation in 1945, when most of the original CL board remained intact, the government had been playing an increasingly important role in defining the bank's strategic direction and the structure of its leadership. In effect, the government used the nationalised banks as an industrial policy tool.

Regardless of the political ebb and flow, the French financial system – traditionally highly concentrated and compartmentalised – underwent substantial structural change, resulting in the reforms of 1984–86 and the rapid development of the domestic capital market. In part, this reflected government efforts to promote Paris as a viable financial-centre competitor to London, and in part, changing political fashion. The financial market reforms undertaken with special vigour by the Chirac administration helped shift French corporate finance towards open capital markets.

Jean-Yves Haberer was a paragon of the French system. He graduated first in his class at the elite École Nationale d'Administration, and joined the French Treasury as an Inspecteur Général des Finances. As mentioned, he had served as

Finance Minister Debré's Chef de Cabinet, playing the leading part in the 1966 bank reforms. And then, in the capacity of Directeur du Trésor, he launched the process of further financial reform which led to the Banking Act of 1984. His consistent intent was to create a French style of universal banking capable of competing on an even footing with its German counterpart. Paradoxically, the opportunity to put the idea into practice coincided with the German universal banks' efforts to disengage from both expansionary retail banking abroad and excessively intimate bank–industry relationships, as recorded in the previous chapter.

Haberer's career illustrated the French élite's ability to serve governments of both Right and Left. Thus, in 1982, he was pulled by François Mitterand from the Trésor where he had served under President Giscard d'Estaing, to run the newly nationalised Paribas (Compagnie Financière de Paris et des Pay-Bas). Haberer was widely resented within Paribas, and was seen as the instrument of its nationalisation. During his leadership, Paribas suffered its worst fiasco, with the acquisition of the stockbroker A. G. Becker in New York, which it sold a few years later at a $70 million loss. When Paribas was re-privatised in 1986, Haberer was removed from office.

Widely described as authoritarian, brilliant, intimidating and driven, Haberer's endorsement of Mitterand's nationalisations led to his being soundly disliked by the Right for serving as a tool of the Left at Paribas in 1982. Without important political friends on the Right, his personal career came to depend on the political fortunes of the Socialists, particularly Jacques Delors in his capacity of Minister of Finance and later President of the EU Commission, and Pierre Bérégovoy, Minister of Finance in 1984–86 and again in 1988–92, at which point Bérégovoy was appointed Prime Minister. Bérégovoy appointed Haberer to the position of chief executive at CL despite his record at Paribas, with a clear mandate to deploy the bank as an arm of French state policy in the EU's internal financial market. There, he was repeatedly criticised for grand schemes that might never have survived board scrutiny or shareholder reactions in privately-owned financial institutions.

By the early 1990s, CL had become a highly diversified bank that offered a complete spectrum of financial services to most client segments across much of Europe. Elsewhere, CL had holdings in Asia and in North America under its own name. In South America and Africa it generally operated under the name of either partially or wholly-owned subsidiaries.

In its drive to be a functionally 'universal' bank CL offered a very broad spectrum of financial services. At the end of 1992, CL had 2,639 retail banking outlets in France, as well as an array of specialised affiliates such as the Paris broker Cholet-Dupont Michaux, money-management affiliates, and niche-type businesses such as leasing. It also offered a range of insurance services (particularly life insurance) and maintained a major portfolio of holdings in different French and European companies.

Operationally, CL was structured into five more or less distinct units.

- The *banque des entreprises* (business bank) catered to the financial requirements of a broad spectrum of business and industry. The core function was
  commercial lending. For small and medium businesses, CL also offered risk-
  management products, including financial and foreign-exchange options and
  other derivatives, asset-management services covering a broad range of investments, and international development assistance such as helping to initiate
  cross-border partnerships and alliances. For large companies, CL services
  extended from fund-raising through syndicated lending, Euronote and Euro-
  commercial paper distribution to large and complex financing arrangements,
  such as project and acquisitions financing, M&A advisory activities, and property financing. It also maintained leasing subsidiaries – Slibail, Slificom and
  Slifergie in France, Woodchester in Ireland and the United Kingdom, and
  Leasimpresa in Italy.
- The *banque des particuliers et des professionels* (retail bank) serviced private
  individuals and professional clients, and carried out basic banking services
  such as deposits, payments services and personal loans. There had been a significant decline in demand for deposit-account balances in favour of interest-
  bearing accounts in recent years. Traditionally, French retail clients maintained
  non-interest-bearing checking accounts, but with intensified competition and
  changes in legislation, clients were increasingly opting for *SICAVs* – open-
  ended unit trusts – and specifically *SICAVs monétaires*, or money-market
  mutual funds. To attract and maintain retail clients (and achieve cost-
  economies, especially in payments transactions for retail clients), CL was
  forced to innovate and enhance the retail banking services available. These
  included debit cards and ATMs, and home banking through Minitel (the
  French interactive telephone information system). In addition to life insurance,
  CL provided cover for personal lines (e.g. motor insurance) through its Lion
  Assurances subsidiary. And for large individual and professional clients it also
  provided private banking services and tailored insurance plans as well as
  special financing arrangements – such as Inter-Fimo or Crédit Médical de
  France, which financed the purchase and installation of medical equipment.
- The *banque des marchés de capitaux* (investment bank) was responsible for
  underwriting and distributing bonds and equity new issues. In global markets,
  CL Capital Markets International's units – such as CL Securities in London –
  assured the bank's presence in foreign financial centres, while the French
  markets were covered by affiliates such as Cholet-Dupont. In 1991, CL was
  ranked first in placing domestic and Euro-franc bonds. In the derivatives
  sector, it accounted for about 10 per cent of volume on the MATIF, France's
  futures and options exchange.
- A finance company, *Altus Finance*, was the former finance subsidiary of
  Thomson, in which CL acquired a 66 per cent interest in 1991. During that year
  Altus increased its portfolio of high-yield (junk) bonds from the failed
  American insurance company Executive Life – an amount equivalent to one-
  third of CL's Tier-1 capital.

- The *gestionnaire pour compte de tiers* (fund-management group) was responsible for the management of private portfolios as well as SICAVs in which private individuals held shares. CL had enhanced its offerings to include those guaranteeing capital (CAC-40 Sécurité), revenue (Performance Olympique), and global funds (CL Growth Fund).

As *actionnaire des entreprises*, CL had been increasing its shareholdings in other companies to further the concept of a universal bank. The notion was that, by holding substantial shares especially in non-financial companies, CL would be able to develop a much better understanding of those companies' financial needs. Its holding structures included:

- Clinvest, CL's *banque d'affaires*, with a diversified holding of French companies, which had been a highly profitable part of the bank.
- Euro-Clinvest, a Clinvest subsidiary, with a portfolio of shares of companies in eight European countries.
- Clindus, established in 1991, had strategic and statutory holdings, principally in Rhône-Poulenc and Usinor-Sacilor, that were added to CL's balance sheet with the 'assistance' of the government.
- Innolion, a high-tech, start-up venture-capital fund operating in France.
- Compagnie Financière d'Investissement Rhône-Alpes, which invested in the Rhône-Alpes region of France.
- Lion Expansion, a development capital fund for small and medium-sized businesses and industries.

The pan-European launching-pad

Haberer considered CL's existing structure to be an ideal basis upon which to build his *banque industrie* concept of a pan-European universal financial institution, with enough capacity to launch a simultaneous multi-pronged attack on an array of national markets, financial services and client segments, and to do so rapidly.

By late 1992 Jean-Yves Haberer had already developed the beginnings of a pan-European bank in the retail sector via an extensive cross-border branch network. This was needed to meet his target of capturing between one and two per cent of total retail deposits in Europe, which in turn was intended to provide the 'bulk' the bank needed and the basis for all of the other growth initiatives. He had in fact moved systematically in this direction since 1988. Several acquisitions and purchases of strategic stakes in other banks had been undertaken in quick succession as CL bought local medium-sized financial institutions in Belgium, Spain, Italy and Germany. Consequently, between 1987 and 1992 the number of branches in Europe had increased threefold, and in 1991 47 per cent of the bank's profits came from outside France (compared with 30 per cent in 1987).

- In Belgium, CL had rapidly expanded its local presence via aggressive branching. It tripled the number of retail and private banking clients in eighteen months with a new higher-yield account called *Rendement Plus*. It offered 9 per cent on savings deposits, compared to 3–4 per cent offered by local banks. These rates were possible mainly because CL did not have the cumbersome and expensive infrastructure of the Belgian banks. It had only 960 employees for 32 branches in that country, three per branch; the three big Belgian banks each had at least 10 employees per branch in over 1,000 branches.

- In the Netherlands, CL had raised from 78 per cent to 100 per cent its stake in the Slavenburgs Bank (renamed Crédit Lyonnais Bank Nederland NV) and in 1987 had acquired Nederlandse Credietbank, a former subsidiary of Chase Manhattan Bank of the United States.
- In Ireland, CL held a 48 per cent stake in Woodchester (renamed Woodchester Crédit Lyonnais Bank), a leasing and financing company which intended to acquire a total of forty to fifty retail banking outlets.
- CL had reinforced its position in the London market by buying the firm of Alexanders Laing & Cruickshank after the 'Big Bang' in 1986, subsequently renamed Crédit Lyonnais Capital Markets in 1989.
- In Spain CL's branches had been merged with Banco Commercial Español (renamed Crédit Lyonnais España SA), complemented by the acquisition of the medium-sized Banco Jover in 1991.
- In Germany, it completed a deal to purchase 50.1 per cent of the Bank für Gemeinwirtschaft (BfG) for DM1.42 billion, thereby ending a five-year search for a viable presence in the most important European market outside France.

The acquisition of BfG was a key achievement, in Haberer's view. Not only was Germany the largest European banking market, but it was also the most difficult to penetrate. Others had tried, and many had failed. Those who succeeded had done so by building or buying niche-type businesses, often with indifferent results. None were taken especially seriously as major contenders alongside the three *Großbanken*, the large regionals and state-affiliated banks, and the cooperative and savings-bank networks. With the acquisition of BfG, CL promised to break the mould.

In 1990, the third largest German insurer AMB (Aachener und Münchener Beteiligungs GmbH), had negotiated with the state-owned French insurer AGF (Assurances Générales de France) about a partnership arrangement. Besides the attractiveness of the German market, AGF was watching strategic moves by its arch-rival, the state-owned insurer UAP, whose expansion into Germany had come by way of the acquisition from Banque Indosuez of a 34 per cent stake in Groupe Victoire, a major French insurer which had earlier purchased a German insurer, Colonia Versicherungs AG.

AGF had bought 25 per cent of AMB stock, yet was limited to only 9 per cent of the voting rights by the AMB board, clearly concerned that the French company, twice its size, was out to control and eventually swallow it. Alongside the AGF acquisition of AMB stock, CL bought a 1.8 per cent stake in AMB as well. As part of its defensive tactics, AMB arranged for an Italian insurer, La

Fondaria, to acquire a 'friendly' stake amounting to 20 per cent of AMB shares. AGF then fought an historic shareholder-rights battle in the German courts against the AGF board and a German industrial 'establishment' instinctively distrustful of hostile changes in corporate control. The defence was further bolstered by the fact that 11 per cent of AMB stock was held by Dresdner Bank, 6 per cent by Munich Re – and Allianz, the largest German insurer, was a major shareholder in both Dresdner Bank and Munich Re. It was a sign of the times, Haberer thought, that AGF prevailed in the German courts and, with the help of CL's AMB shares, was able to obtain AGF recognition of its voting rights – no doubt the basis for further share acquisitions, possibly the La Fondaria stake.

The AGF–AMB battle provided Haberer with the opening he was looking for – appearing on his radar-screen when AGF proposed that CL buy AMB's bank, the BfG, which AMB was keen to dispose of and which had been for sale for some time. BfG had been the bank of the German labour movement, plagued by poor management, periodic large losses and scandals, and a down-market client-base. AMB had already made great strides in turning BfG around. Still, a loss of DM 400 million in 1990 and a profit of DM120 million in 1991 indicated that a major capital infusion would be required in 1993. AMB was hardly interested in supplying it, and a takeover by CL was seen as a welcome opportunity to divest itself of an albatross.

Of course, acquisition battles like BfG were only the first, and perhaps the easiest, part of the building process. Certainly not all of CL's acquisitions had been easy to digest. Its purchase of the Slavenburgs Bank in the Netherlands, for example, had been the source of many headaches. Beyond the corporate culture issue, there had been a serious problem in maintaining supervision. It was CL Nederland that was responsible for the large loans to Giancarlo Parretti in California – loans which CL head office in Paris indicated it was not aware of until it was too late.

Besides outright acquisitions and aggressive expansion in the important European markets, CL employed another strategy as well – strategic alliances and networks. One of the older of these, *Europartners*, was set up as a loose association between CL, Commerzbank, Banco di Roma and Banco Hispano Americano (BHA), based on the idea of extending banking networks into neighbouring countries and setting up new conjoint operations. Its goals were to provide a cheap mechanism to allow each of the partners' customers access to basic banking service in the other countries.

But it was not long before strains began to appear in the partnership. Over the years, Commerzbank had tightened its relations with its Spanish partner, and in 1989 BHA agreed to swap a 11 per cent interest in its shares for a 5 per cent stake in Commerzbank – the 1991 merger of BHA and Banco Central into Banco Central-Hispano diluted Commerzbank's share in the merged bank to 4.5 per cent. At the same time there was a dispute over CL's expansion into Spain with the purchase of Banco Jover in the summer of 1991. A year earlier, CL had tried to purchase a 20 per cent stake in Banco Hispano Americano and was flatly rejected. BHA perceived the new action as a threat of direct competition in its home market, and suspended the relationship with CL.

Rebuffed in Spain, CL had also been thwarted in its attempt to deepen the Franco-German part of the Europartners agreement. In 1991, CL discussed swapping shares with Commerzbank, the smallest of the three German *Großbanken* – thought to have involved 10 per cent of Commerzbank's equity for 7 per cent of CL's equity. Discussions broke down over German fears that the French bank had more in mind than cementing an Europartners alliance. Commerzbank clearly did not want to be the German arm of a French bank. And there was the matter of price: based on comparative profit figures, Commerzbank wanted a 10 per cent for 10 per cent swap – even though the French bank was twice its size – because it considered itself to have a much better future in terms of earnings and margins.

By the end of 1991 Europartners was effectively dead, although this hardly precluded strategic alliances as a further option for Crédit Lyonnais. Other partnerships have been more stable. An example was the Banco de Santander–Royal Bank of Scotland agreement, cemented by a share-swap, to create a link-up through which clients could conduct cross-border transactions at terminals located at either bank's branches. Crédit Commerciale de France had signed up to join this alliance. And there was the BNP–Dresdner deal, a cooperative agreement that involved cross-shareholdings, with each bank continuing to run its existing operations but opening joint offices elsewhere, such as Switzerland, Turkey, Japan and Hungary. Joint board meetings were being held twice yearly, each bank contributed a member to the other's board, and there was considerable discussion about an eventual merger.

The government link
The French economic and financial policy environment over the years had been rather unstable. When President Mitterrand acceded to power in 1981, his approach to reflating the economy by increasing the size of the public sector, cutting the work week and nationalising forty-nine key industrial and financial firms had rapidly increased imports and led to a deterioration of both the trade balance and international capital flows. Under those conditions, the possible solutions were to either devalue the franc and take it out of the ERM or seriously reduce monetary expansion, reduce the fiscal deficit (including cuts in spending) and stimulate the private sector.

The latter route was chosen. Taxes were cut, the capital markets were deregulated, and the economy boomed through most of the 1980s. Finance Minister Pierre Bérégovoy, the driving force of fiscal prudence, maintained a *franc fort,* low-inflation policy throughout the period and committed the country to partial privatisation, starting with the sale of minority stakes in Elf-Aquitaine, Total and Crédit Locale de France in 1991.

On the other hand, the Socialists had not only nationalised the big banks when they came to power in 1981, but had continually influenced their activities since then. For example, in 1992 the BNP had been asked to acquire an equity stake in Air France, and CL itself had been 'encouraged' to buy into Usinor-Sacilor – both of them inefficient state-owned firms making large losses. By linking together the state-owned equity portfolio and the equity holdings of state-owned banks, these deals could allow the government to maintain control, despite partial privatisation of non-financial companies. There was considerable debate whether any new government that might take office in 1993 would couple a pro-gramme of aggressive privatisation with non-intervention in the strategic direc-tion or the operations of banks and industry – that is, whether the micro-intervention of the past was a 'Socialist' or a 'French' attribute.

In addition to its direct and indirect equity holdings, the French government had a strong control lever through 'moral suasion' – a tradition of political med-dling by bureaucrats who considered themselves able to come up with better eco-nomic solutions to national needs than the interplay of market forces. On a European level, beyond the blatant tampering with free competition of the past and a highly protectionist stance within the EU decision process in matters of industrial and trade policy, there was concern that the French government would continue its *dirigiste* role and even try to extend it to the cross-border relation-ships of French firms and banks.

Haberer considered the role of the state in France as a two-edged sword. It could at times make life difficult in doing what needed to be done in carrying out the vision, but the backing of the state could provide the deep pockets and polit-ical support to overcome obstacles and setbacks that would stop ordinary banks in their tracks. Maximising the advantages and minimising the drawbacks meant that strong backing by the mandarins who mattered was critical.

The value of the government link became obvious in several 'accidents' that befell CL in its drive for growth. Specifically in wholesale lending, where balance-sheet growth could be most rapidly achieved, growth meant narrower lending margins. Moreover, as the European recession began to set in during 1990 and 1991, most banks retrenched to weather the storm. CL, on the other hand, announced that it would maintain its set course and 'buy' its way out of the recession. The bank had thus taken on much riskier projects than many of its competitors, and the list of CL's lending problems in the early 1990s included (a) the Robert Maxwell affair, involving significant credit losses; (b) Hachette, the French publisher, whose television channel *La Cinq* went bankrupt; (c) Olympia & York, the failed Canadian property developer, where CL was the second largest European creditor of the firm's Canary Wharf project in London; and (d) loans of over $1 billion by CL's Dutch subsidiary to Giancarlo Parretti, an Italian financier (later accused of fraud), for his purchase of the Hollywood film studio MGM/UA Communications.

Rapid expansion during 1991 and 1992 did indeed provide a significant increase in CL's net banking income. In 1990 CL achieved a net profit of FF3.7 billion, a 20 per cent increase over 1989, although a major portion of this increase was attributable to Altus Finance. But a long list of bad debts and investments produced an equally large increase in provisions. By the end of 1991, CL was suffering serious growth pains as profits fell to FF3.16 billion and provisions were increased from FF4.2 billion to FF9.6 billion. At 1.6 per cent of total loans, CL's level of provisions was precarious when compared to those of other French banks. They were three times those of its main French competitors – but still better than most UK banks, for example. Nevertheless, the MGM/UA Communications controversy and CL's increasing exposure to risky loans resulted in Moody's Investor Services downgrading CL's bond rating from Aa1 to Aa2, despite the French government's continuing ownership of the bank and its own Aaa rating.

Also worrisome was the fact that CL's interest margins continued to decline as competition for deposits increased. At the same time, costs were rising as investment in technologies became increasingly necessary to keep pace with the competition, and difficulties were encountered in curbing rising personnel costs. Assuming that margins were unlikely to improve and cost pressures would be difficult to reverse, CL would have to rely more heavily on commission income in the future than it had in the past.

In September 1992 CL announced its group profits had plunged 92 per cent, to FF119 million for the first half, compared to FF1.6 billion for the same period the year before. The precipitous drop was again due to an increase in provisions against bad debts, from FF3.4 billion for the first half of 1991 to FF6.3 billion for the first half of 1992 – even as net banking income grew by 16 per cent and gross operating profit before provisions increased by 33 per cent in the same period. Forty per cent of the bad-debt provisions were attributed to CL Bank Nederland, the Dutch subsidiary, in connection with the MGM/UA Communications loans. In December 1992 Moody's once again downgraded CL's debt to Aa3, citing 'higher risk in both the loan portfolio and the bank strategy'.[42]

All of these problems notwithstanding, CL's performance was considered acceptable by its owner, the French Republic, with growth evidently deemed more important than profits. Still, the issue of capital adequacy could not be avoided – under either the BIS capital standards or the EC Capital Adequacy and Own Funds Directives – both to absorb the various credit losses and to support Haberer's grand design. As a state-owned bank, CL had not been allowed to raise equity capital independently. Only 5 per cent of CL's capital was owned by shareholders, in the form of non-voting *Certificats d'Investissement*. The rest belonged either to the government or to government-controlled companies. As such, new capital infusions would have to come from the state. Infusions from private sources had been blocked by the Socialist government's 'no-no' policy: 'no privatisation, no nationalisation'.

Complicated arrangements were made under French government sponsorship with five state-controlled companies during 1989–91 in order to bolster CL's capital base and at the same time solve certain industrial problems. In November 1989, CL raised FF1.5 billion by selling shares to the Caisse de Dépôts et Consignations. In February and December 1990, share-swaps with Thomson brought in FF6.4 billion. A deal with Rhône-Poulenc raised another FF1.7 billion in 1990 as well. In 1991, at the request of Prime Minister Edith Cresson, CL invested FF2.5 billion in the state-owned steelworks, Usinor-Sacilor, and gained a 10 per cent stake. The bank also swapped 10 per cent of Usinor's shares for 10 per cent of new CL shares, thereby boosting CL's shareholder equity by about FF3 billion. This allowed CL to consolidate its share of Usinor-Sacilor's profits and losses, which had the effect of diluting CL's earnings, but provided a neat (if temporary) solution for the steelmaker's problems.

Altogether, by late 1992 about 28 per cent of CL's total capital base thus consisted of shares in state-owned firms. In all of the share-swaps, both parties paid much higher than book values. These agreements had the effect of linking the fate of the bank to the success of the companies concerned, and also represented a powerful incentive to support these same companies in the future in the face of uncertain profitability. In any case, the resulting capital infusions were insufficient to meet the bank's future needs, and the question remained what implications these crossholding arrangements would have if and when especially Thomson and Rhône-Poulenc were privatised. The rest of the badly-needed equity would have to be injected by the government.

The grand design

Haberer's mosaic seemed to be coming together much faster than anyone could have predicted when he took control in 1988.

- The bank's balance-sheet had grown enormously under his leadership.
- The bank had penetrated all of the important European markets in significant ways, including the most difficult of all, Germany.
- The bank had maintained its close relationship to its shareholder, the French state, which had shown its willingness to inject capital and to tolerate even serious setbacks on the road to greater glory. The bank's rapid growth and European cross-border market penetration was well suited to the French government's industrial policy objective of having one large French firm as a leader in every major sector of the European economy, notably CL in banking, Thomson in electronics, Rhône-Poulenc in chemicals, Aérospatiale in aerospace, SNECMA in aircraft engines, and so forth.
- The bank's shareholdings in industrial companies had grown from FF10 billion in September 1988 to FF45 billion in early 1992, and it had accumulated significant equity stakes in key French industrial companies, whose strategies and financing activities it was in a position to influence. At the same time, it had provided the government with industrial influence even if the affected firms were to be privatised.

According to Jean-Yves Haberer,

Our strategy considers that Western Europe will be increasingly the domestic market of major European banks for the coming decade. What we are preparing for is no longer the EC market of 1993, but the market of the years 1995 to 2000. For our corporate clients, which are large multinational groups, the location of our teams, mainly in big financial centres, is relatively unimportant. On the other hand, to offer our services to small and medium size corporations and individuals requires vicinity and local intimacy. We intend to build a large and profitable European banking group.[43]

Commentators, on the other hand, pointed to various alleged weaknesses in the strategy, which was considered highly controversial.

• France's EC partners could object to French export of blatant tampering with free competition in the market economy via the acquisition of local banks, and refuse to permit it to continue.
• Haberer had not adequately addressed the problem of how to expand rapidly without buying excessive quantities of low-grade paper. He could therefore eventually create such an awful mess in CL's loan portfolio that the government would blow the whistle.
• Haberer and his strategy were on everyone's casualty list for the political infighting that surely would follow the next French presidential election in 1995. Time was running very short indeed to accomplish all he hoped for.
• Haberer had neglected the investment-banking and capital-markets side of the business. Indeed, even companies in which the bank had holdings, assuming sufficiently high credit standing, would prefer to use the capital markets rather than bank borrowing for their financing requirements.

Indeed, some critics combined all of these points to form a gloomy picture of CL in the late 1990s as a bank with plenty of impotent industrial shareholdings in companies focusing their financing on the capital markets, plenty of acquisitions and alliances with foreign banks whose major clients were likewise using the capital markets, and plenty of bad loans acquired along the way to amassing gigantic size that was of no use. This view turned out to be correct, with the subsequent massive bailout and capital injection by the state to the consternation of its competitors, and a tough slog to fundamental restructuring of the bank, heavily financed by the taxpayer. Jean-Yves Haberer was fired and disgraced by the same system that produced him, with criminal investigations launched into his own conduct, as well as that of the CL board, in July 1996.[44]

Structural reforms

The 1984 French Banking Act did not include the savings network or the postal services[45] – the savings banks' status was redefined in 1983, and more fully in 1991, when they were restructured to become one of the country's nine major retail networks.[46] They were too valuable to the Trésor, and continued to supply the Trésor's circuit – its continued role as market participant, shareholder and regulator. The Commission des Opérations du Bourse (COB), set up in 1967 as watchdog for the securities markets, remained in relative obscurity until the aftermath of the October 1987 crash, when the fall in share prices prompted an outburst of takeover bids. In late 1988, the socialist government used the CdC and state corporations to buy back the shares of privatised companies, and to fill socialist party coffers. The US Securities and Exchange Commission alerted the COB to suspicious share movements, prompting an investigation which revealed that close associates of President Mitterrand and Prime Minister Bérégovoy were involved. Mitterrand sought to head off public criticism by announcing forthcoming legislation to protect French corporations against 'roving, predatory money'.[47] In effect the August 1989 law on 'security and market transparency' implemented the EU directive on insider trading and obliged investors who built up a stake of over 33 per cent of a listed company's capital to make a full bid for at least 66 per cent of shares. The law strengthened the COB to protect companies against hostile takeovers *by other companies*. It did not address the central problem facing the French state of how to police itself.

The French state had other ways of resisting external penetration of its financial system. Greater competition among French banks did not preclude cooperation, notably where it promised to increase the productivity of the banks' highly unionised workforces. Given the state's continued tutelage, cutting back on branches or employment proved difficult.[48] Common technology projects also held the additional attraction of combining the advantages of a banking oligopoly with the monopoly position of the Ministry of Telecommunications and France Télécom. The practice of 'interbancarité' is defined as 'a major characteristic of the French banking and financial system in the service of the clientele which benefits by and aspires to maintain it – it finds expression in technical systems realised and managed together'.[49] This was expressed in two key initiatives: the mutual banks, tied in to the German-centred Eurocard payments system, reached an agreement with the registered and savings banks, affiliated to the Visa international network, to create an electronic 'banking card' system, which allowed for a rapid rise in the use of plastic money in France. The Ministry and France Télécom developed a videotext terminal (Minitel) which was handed out free to French telephone subscribers. The Minitel provided information about financial markets, individual accounts and savings facilities. The technology opened the home banking market to all French banks.

In similar fashion, as insurance moved into the orbit of EU legislation, the domestic-policy thicket in insurance became more dense. The December 1989 Insurance Act incorporated EU legislation, but created a corporatist regulatory framework.[50] The Act established a Control Commission modelled on the CB, and a Conseil National des Assureurs (CNA), presided over by the Finance Ministry and supervising three different committees for licensing, client relations and regulation. This was the one area where the corporatist dimension of rule-making and rule-enforcement gained while the Finance Ministry's Insurance Directorate lost responsibilities. A deal was cut between firms and insurance agents whereby contestants to a territorial market had to offer compensation.[51] The nationalised insurers – AGF, GAN and UAP – were regrouped into holding companies and took advantage of the new legislation to buy participations in banks and industrial companies. But as market pressures revealed the limits of 'bancassurance', direct marketing gained ground, property prices tumbled and bad loans appeared on the books of banks in which they held participations. In 1992, their capital was opened to the private sector. Even the Post Office won permission to sell insurance, prompting the insurers in despair to appeal to the European Commission to end the special privileges of their mutual and savings bank competitors.

Internationalisation of the French banking markets required a strengthening of prudential supervision. In the retail markets, the public was little concerned by the prospect of bankruptcy. Article 52 of the 1984 Banking Act gave official recognition to such inter-bank solidarity, and provided for the Governor of the Banque de France to call on shareholders to protect the interests of depositors and third parties. The state stood behind the deposits of both the CdC and the large banks, whether nationalised or not. The bank cartel ensured that depositors faced nearly identical interest rates. The various categories of banks, whether registered or mutuals, had their own not-so-voluntary deposit-insurance mechanisms. The Commission Bancaire wielded authority in the Compensation Chamber of Financial Instruments of Paris, which was wholly owned by MATIF, the futures market. This mechanism was brought into play first in July 1988, when the stockbrokers lost FF614 million on the MATIF following the 1987 crash. The newly reorganised Stock Exchange was required to cover the losses.[52] On wholesale markets, the Banque de France took a consistent line that AFB banks should indemnify depositors and clients of failed institutions. In November 1988, it ordered banks to help bail out the Al Saudi bank, followed by four other Arab banks. It took a similar hard line on the AFB banks paying indemnities in 1991 for the clients of BCCI.[53]

Reform of the Paris securities markets

The Stock Exchange – the symbol of 'le grand capital' – remained a backwater after 1945, under the tutelage of the Ministry of Finance, which named the 'agents de change' and regulated their operations. The agents had been granted a monopoly to trade in stock by Napoleon in 1807, and their firms had become hereditary. They were too small to trade significantly on their own account, and were undercapitalised. Market regulations required them to assemble all orders to buy and sell, and then clear them during the midday opening hours in order to establish an equilibrium price. A security could be quoted only on one central market-place.

The Bourse had experienced a modest revival in the 1950s, but had stagnated under the Fifth Republic's state-led credit system. Firms had little incentive to list, as their owners or managers could borrow cheaply and feared losing control through a dilution of ownership. About 59 per cent of French equities were not even listed.[54] Market regulations allowed cross-shareholdings and gave priority to existing shareholders in the purchase of new shares. Total bank credits in the

1970s were more than double the value of quoted securities, and bonds on average amounted to only 25 per cent of bank credit – although the value of bonds outstanding exceeded equities market capitalisation by 50 per cent.[55]

The revival of the Stock Exchange began in the 1970s, in the midst of the party-political battle over the direction of change to be taken by the overdraft economy. France's smaller firms were badly hit by the combination of lower growth and higher taxation. Their troubles were not alleviated by the conservative government's response to their complaints – it simply multiplied complex administrative channels to distribute credit, and also had a law passed in July 1976 which introduced a capital gains tax designed to woo centre-left voters from being drawn into the socialist–communist camp. The measure prompted the resignation of Prime Minister Chirac, widened the fissures among the conservative parties, and deepened the gloom enveloping the exchange. But the Bourse perked up after the 'divine surprise' of a conservative victory in the general elections in March 1978. The capital gains tax was shelved in favour of a measure to reduce taxes on savings invested in equities. The number of shareholders rose from one to 1.5 million by 1981.

Paradoxically, it was François Mitterrand's election that launched the Exchange's revival. On the one hand, the recession of the early 1980s saw bankruptcies rise to a rate of 20,000 per annum. On the other hand, Mitterrand's nationalisations had temporarily deprived the main listed market of its blue chips, and the *agents de change* saw an opportunity to champion the cause of France's capital-starved small and medium-sized companies.

The brokers found allies abroad and in Finance Minister Jacques Delors. In September 1981, the International Federation of Stock Exchanges ostentatiously held their meeting in Paris. In January 1983, Delors introduced into the Banking Act (for the savings-bank sector) an offer of tax reduction calculated as a function of the savings invested in French shares. A second market was opened in February alongside the official stock market. London's Unlisted Securities Market – and especially Nasdaq in the United States – served as an example. Listing conditions were made relatively undemanding, as firms were only asked to sell up to 10 per cent of the capital, compared to the 25 per cent required for a listing on an unsuccessful over-the-counter market launched in 1977. That market had only attracted twenty-two companies, but the new market was reckoned as capable of attracting between 300 and 600 firms. The initiative achieved its major successes at Paris and in Lyons between 1983 and 1987, as a mood of confidence gripped investors. But they were discouraged by the 1987 market crash, and turned away.[56] Small family firms, too, remained hostile to public listing. By 1990, only half of one per cent of French small and medium-sized companies had turned to the market for external financing.[57] Of the 287 firms listed, about 100 were subsidiaries of large firms. French investors' conservatism was reflected in their preference for the CAC-40, whose shares attracted 55 per cent of the Stock Exchange capitalisation, and 90 per cent of transactions volume.[58]

France's financial market reforms were also designed to serve the financing interests of the state. They were launched in September 1984 by the new Finance Minister Pierre Bérégovoy and pushed through by a determined team within the Trésor, against opposition from colleagues and bankers.[59] Bérégovoy visited the Stock Exchange in November in a bid to focus public attention on the new direction of policy, the first such visit by a Finance Minister since 1962.[60] His prime objective was the constitution of a 'unified capital market, covering short to long term instruments and all economic agents'.[61] Paris was to develop as an international financial centre, and French corporate financing moved towards the model of Anglo-American financial markets.[62] The reforms entailed wholesale importation of US methods to French conditions.

- The number of instruments, such as certificates of deposit and short-term commercial paper, was increased, standardised and open to all market participants. The money market thus enabled large firms to reduce dependence on bank loans, while bank loans linked to the money-market rate rose from 1.4 per cent of the total in 1984 to 44 per cent in 1993.[63] The banks entered the market actively, so that by 1993, the money market accounted for half their profits.[64] The success of the money market made long-term corporate funds difficult to come by.[65]
- Special provisions were made for specific sectors. Mortgage institutions were provided with their own refinancing arrangements. Specialised financial institutions were allowed to issue bonds to replenish their resources.
- Major changes were introduced in the functioning of the market. In January 1986, the Trésor adopted the auction method for the sale of bonds through a system of primary dealers and on a monthly basis. This ended the placement of non-negotiable bonds with bank syndicates, which continued to prevail in Germany. The issue of state bonds greatly increased market liquidity, although further measures were taken in 1989.[66]
- In January 1985, the French authorities moved away from quantitative controls on the money supply towards more reliance on interest rates and on bank reserve requirements. But the quotas were retained in the form of reserve requirements, indicating reluctance in the Banque de France to abandon residual control over the bank cartel. A full departure from quantitative controls would have meant applying monetary control to a banking system in which all banks competed amongst themselves.[67] To ensure against this, the Banque de France in December 1985 modified the definition of the money supply in order to keep pace with financial innovation, and tied the franc's exchange rate more tightly to the DM. 'France', the Governor declared, 'now accepts the exchange rate constraint'.[68]

Another key element of the Trésor's reforms was the opening in February 1986 of the MATIF, the Paris futures market. The MATIF served many purposes. It provided a market enabling institutional investors to hedge against the risks of volatile interest or exchange rates. It represented France's response to London's creation of LIFFE in 1982. It brought the Paris market into the world web of futures markets. Above all, MATIF was a central element in modernising issuing of state paper. All its major derivative products originated with the Trésor, starting with the state-bond contract launched in January 1986, the less successful Euro-DM contract launched in May 1989, and the long-term ECU contract floated in October 1990 to develop Paris as the centre for trade in ECUs.

Paris rapidly became the second market for futures in Europe, after London. This was consolidated by the Trésor's creation of *spécialistes en valeurs du Trésor* with the task – like primary dealers in the United States – of ensuring the placement and liquidity of state paper on the secondary market. The specialists were selected in 1987, initially numbering eighteen, and included the CdC as well as six foreign firms. They joined the Conseil du Marché à Terme (CMT), set up to approve regulatory measures under the law covering futures markets. These specialists accounted for nearly all transactions on the market, and helped the MATIF to become the central core of the French bond market.

Establishing Paris as a major financial centre meant modernisation of its infrastructure as well. An efficient market which ensured minimal delays for delivery and settlement was essential. The government and Stock Exchange therefore cooperated closely to update facilities for both bond and equity transactions. All operations on state bonds were dealt with through the Saturn network, under the direction of the Banque de France, and tied into the international clearance and settlement houses, Cedel and Euroclear. In July 1986, a system of continuous computerised quotation (CAC), modelled on the Toronto system, was substituted for the open-outcry floor. The floor had been unable to deal with the growth in business and back-office costs had become exorbitant. The introduction of CAC in effect condemned the traditional role of brokers. The CAC was complemented by a system to channel orders automatically (RONA). In 1990, the Exchange started the new automatic-settlement system, RELIT, which covered most actively-traded shares and was based on a standard settlement time, set initially at five days and brought down to two days in 1992. This was seven times faster than settlement operations in London, and five days faster than Cedel or Euroclear.

France's financial market reforms spelled a freeing-up of commissions, entailing an end to the Napoleonic status of brokers. London's 'Big Bang' in October 1986, and the prospect of its capturing business from Paris, added to the Trésor's sense of urgency. The registered banks were anxious to move into the securities business to compensate for losses in their traditional activities. Insurance companies and corporate treasurers joined the lobbying. The end of the brokers' monopoly on the stock exchange was finally agreed in March 1987, following discussions between Finance Minister Balladur and Xavier Dupont, the *syndic* of the brokers. The reform, put into effect in January 1988, was presented as necessary to fend off London's challenge.[69] It was predicated on three principles.

- Substitution of the brokers for Sociétés de Bourse (SDB), with the sole right to negotiate securities. The brokers' monopoly was to be phased out between

1988 and 1992. French and foreign credit institutions were allowed to buy into their capital until 1991, and then set up their own operations.
• Preservation of the principle of centralisation, whereby transactions occurred on an organised market. The Trésor resigned its direct tutelage of the market in favour of two bodies: (1) the Sociétés des Bourses Françaises (SBF), owned by the firms, and which worked with COB in supervising the market; and (2) the Conseil des Bourses de Valeurs (CBV), composed of the firms and a stock-exchange representative to make the rules regarding licences and discipline.
• Establishment of a transparency rule, whereby traders of securities had to disclose the price at which they did deals. This measure was designed to secure the public's funds invested in the Trésor's long-term savings instruments. Such a regulation had the advantage of treating small savers' orders equitably. But its inconvenience was that the market lacked liquidity, and block trades migrated to London.

Inexorably, internationalisation pulled the French economy into the slipstream of the Anglo-American financial markets. France's extensive overseas banking network was redeployed out of Africa into Europe, the United States and Asia Pacific.[70] In the EU, London and Luxemburg proved most attractive to French institutions, accounting respectively for 28 per cent and 20 per cent of total turnover, compared to only 6 per cent for German markets.[71] Of the fifty-five brokerage firms, thirteen were owned by US, Japanese or UK houses. These accounted for 30 per cent of trading in French equities.[72] Turnover in French shares was heavily located in London.[73] Little could be done, since the COB insisted on preserving the centralisation and transparency principles. The SBF then launched a fruitless campaign to create a Europe-wide network of 'organised markets' to counter London's leadership,[74] on the grounds that the EU's investment services directive was drafted to serve London's interest.[75] But once Mitterrand had ceded the principle in early 1991 that state enterprises should semi-privatise, the professionals became convinced that their problem was not just stock-exchange turnover taxes and the regulations on concentration and transparency.[76] Without funded pensions, as in the United Kingdom, France lacked the raw material to make Paris a major financial centre.[77]

Opinion in the Finance Ministry had not been unanimous that investors needed the protection imposed by the COB.[78] The reformers of 1984–88 had recognised the urgency of developing funded pensions. Reforms, though, had been tentative and controversial. Funded pension institutions would be exigent with regard to shareholder rights. This challenged managerial prerogatives. Trade unions were opposed to losing their position as co-managers of social spending. Banks, insurers or brokers were in competition as to who administered the funds. Political parties disagreed over their end-use. It was the coincidence in 1993 of a conservative government with an ambitious FF360 billion privatisation programme, and the awareness that the social security system had to be reformed in depth, that prompted a near-unanimous conservative consensus that the move was essential

- to provide the liquidity required to preserve Paris's position as an international centre;
- to sell French state enterprises into mainly French ownership;
- to provide in the medium term for the ageing French population;
- to repatriate the wholesale market from London.

The stamp duty on securities transactions, which had provided an additional disincentive to block trades in Paris, was abolished in December 1994, and French law was brought into line with US and UK practice on 'netting' of transactions in futures markets.

France's sui-generis 'German model'

As noted in Chapter 2, Paris adopted the hard-franc policy in 1986–87, alongside the negotiations in the EU on liberalisation of capital movements. At the root of this policy was the requirement to ensure that French savings stayed home, rather than move abroad in response to higher real returns. The hard-franc policy was a precondition to maintaining Paris's credibility. But French refusal to have the DM realigned upwards in late 1989 ensured that, as German long-term interest rates rose to attract world savings into government debt to finance reconstruction in the new Bundesländer, French rates were pulled up in their wake. France thus entered into intensified competition with Germany on the international markets for the sale of its securities. Short-term rates rose in sympathy. As only 30 per cent of corporate loans were long-term, havoc was wreaked on the French corporate sector. World financial markets, dominated by institutional investors, scented blood once President Mitterrand in June 1992 decided to hold a referendum on the Maastricht Treaty on September 20. Mounting pressure on the franc presented the Bundesbank with a renewed opportunity to realign parities. But Chancellor Kohl could not afford to see Mitterrand defeated in a crucial referendum by a *de-facto* alliance of the Bundesbank with international speculators. Bonn therefore pressured the Bundesbank to intervene with the Banque de France in a massive support operation of the franc. As French banks were ordered to keep lending rates unchanged, while money-market rates soared, the franc was salvaged, and foreign investors' faith in French securities was preserved.

This expensive victory for France was followed by a further step to implementing 'the German model'. For France to be a viable partner with Bonn in a Maastricht Europe, there was never any doubt that the apparatus of monetary control practised in Germany would have to be imported wholesale. Growth targets were adopted for monetary aggregates.[79] The Banque de France provided the banks with liquidity through open-market operations, the counterpart of which was reserve requirements. The Banque thus acquired great flexibility in manipulating banks' non-interest-bearing reserves. Overall, the aim was price and exchange-rate stability. This hard-franc policy was consecrated by the May 1993 law 'on the status of the Banque de France and the activity and control of credit establishments'. The Banque de France was 'to define and implement monetary policy' in the 'framework of the government's general economic policy'. A Monetary Policy Council was created to supervise the money supply. Appointments of the governor and the two deputies were made by the government, which, however, was not to give the Banque de France orders, and fiscal deficits were not to be financed by money creation. The Banque de France was given control of the banking system. The government, however, was to determine exchange-rate policy. The Banque de France thus reverted in modern guise to its independence lost in 1936, and to splendid isolation from public opinion.

There was nevertheless a major muddle at the heart of the French 'German model' – applied to France, the model failed to separate powers and functions of the state in the workings of the economy. The French democracy had truly become an oligarchy.[80] At its centre was the *grands corps* whose members held the levers of economic policy and of corporate governance in the boardrooms of the major corporations.[81] As in Germany, corporations owned each other's shares and shared each other's membership boards. But unlike Germany, the French political market-place straddled the pinnacles of state and corporate positions. It operated as an exclusive spoils system, where appointments were parcelled out in part by partisan considerations but, more importantly, through membership in the élite. Entry to this inner circle required placing a premium on personal contacts.[82] Privatisations made no difference, as the denationalised corporations formed the cores of the *keiretsu*-type groups which emerged from the battles over private or state ownership. No external control was exercised over this club, as the case of Crédit Lyonnais illustrated. The bank's difficulties had first become evident in spring 1991, but it was only in November 1993 that Haberer was dismissed. Bérégovy, Balladur and Trichet – as Director of the Trésor – shared his aspirations to create 'German-style' bank–industry relationships and pan-European presence. That did not prevent the French financial élites from distancing themselves from the bank's discomfiture, once the true dimensions of its plight had become public.

This bias to insiders was clearly at odds with proclaimed aspirations to develop Paris as a major international financial centre. It penalised outsiders, whether foreign or national, and favoured privileged institutional shareholding over minority shareholders. With the market professionals clamouring for changes, the CBV in two cases in 1991 criticised bidders for not offering to buy all outstanding shares at the same price. This was eventually translated into law in December 1993, whereby majority shareholders should hold no less than 95 per cent of capital and voting shares. The law allowed shareholders to band together and obliged managements to answer questions. A number of dramatic cases ensued, where directors were sacked by irate shareholders, or harassed for not having satisfied minority shareholders' rights. Foreign shareholders, too, held about one-third of equities and bonds, and actively sought out allies. But the insider institutions continued to predominate. Shareholders mostly held bearer shares, so managers or outside investors could not readily contact them. This enabled boards to hold annual or extraordinary general meetings within two weeks and without a quorum. Also, the privatisation clusters enabled French managers to muster sufficient votes to fend off attacks. The one hope of maintaining such autonomy was to ensure self-financing levels remained very high.

Policing of the financial market by the French state was, in a broad perspective, none too different from that of Germany. The Banque de France was independent, and the Constitutional Court was regularly called to judge upon the constitutionality of legislation. The National Assembly vigorously used its investigative powers. The COB tightened its cooperation with the various market regulators, and struck up working relations with counterparts in the United States, the United Kingdom and Germany. Magistrates became much more active in bringing corrupt officials and politicians to trial. A significant number of policy areas slipped into the realm of joint policy within the EU's formal and informal networks. The Finance Ministry determined exchange-rate policy. The boundaries of political authority and constitutional law were unclear, as indicated in the Constitutional Court's objections to the extension of the COB's penal powers. A Council of Competition existed to supplement the powers of the European Commission. But competition policy was reached consensually, together with the Ministry of Finance. Investigations by the National Assembly inevitably were partisan. The COB's powers were hobbled by the fact that the state was the major insider in the French financial system, both before and after the 1984–86 reforms. The aroma of corruption contributed to the steep slide in standing of elected officials.

Conclusions

At the root of the French problem of financial reconfiguration lay the continuity in the French financial system from the legislation of 1941 and 1945, a potent mixture of corporatism, nationalism, Marxism and liberalism. The mixture changed in kaleidoscopic ways, but the ingredients remained the same. In the mid-1980s, the French government made long-debated banking reforms and introduced profound changes in the securities markets. Banking reforms were in the line of Debré's 1966 'German model'. Securities-market reforms drew in particular on US experience. The reforms aimed to reduce the cost of financing state requirements, which included the funding of state-influenced enterprises. But they also required a hard-franc policy to ensure that savings stayed home in a more integrated and more competitive EU market characterised by the free movement of capital.

Mitterrand saw salvation for France in a close link with Germany. As the French banker Henri Ardant had stated in expressing his hope for a united Europe in 1940 under German leadership, after the war, Germany should act 'to eliminate the tariff barriers within the great economic space and move as soon as possible to a single European currency'.[83] A similar programme was now being filtered through the EU. The cost of this prolonged struggle for hegemony between France and Germany in Europe was ascribable to either the mutual lack of internal liberalisation in either of their economies, or to French élites' determination to use the EU as the vehicle for cracking open the German financial system, while keeping as much control and ownership over their own. Cracking open the German financial system also required the support of the 'Anglo-Saxons', support that clearly was conditional.

Meanwhile, French policy had widened the numbers of 'outsiders' among its own citizenry. In the early 1990s, 11.7 million of the 25 million people in the workforce lived in poverty.[84] Financial wealth remained highly concentrated.[85] Around 70,000 firms declared bankruptcy in 1993 under the hammer of the hard-franc policy.[86] Anxiety about the social provision of welfare equalled concern about the lack of funded pensions, slow growth, and Paris's shortage of liquidity. The legitimacy of France's oligarchy became more, not less difficult to defend.

Notes

1 Michael Loriaux, *France After Hegemony: International Change and Financial Reform* (Ithaca, NY: Cornell University Press, 1991).
2 Charles-Albert Michalet, 'France' in Raymond Vernon (ed.), *Big Business and the State: Changing Relations in Western Europe* (Cambridge, MA: Harvard University Press, 1974).
3 Charles de Gaulle, *Mémoires d'Espoir: Le Renouveau, 1958–62* (Paris: Librairie Plon, 1966).
4 OECD Economic Surveys, *France*, 1991.
5 Stanley Hoffman, 'Paradoxes of the French Political Community' in his *In Search of France* (New York: Harper, 1963).
6 Hubert Bonin, *L'Argent en France Depuis 1880: Banquiers Financiers Epargnants* (Paris: Masson, 1989); John B. Goodman, *Monetary Sovereignty: The Politics of Central Banking in Western Europe* (Ithaca, NY: Cornell University Press, 1992).
7 Philippe Burrin, *La France à l'Heure Allemande, 1940–1944* (Paris: Seuil, 1995); Zeev Sternhell, *La Droite Révolutionnaire: 1885–1914. Les Origines Françaises du fascisme* (Paris: Seuil, 1978).
8 Quoted in Burrin, *La France à l'Heure Allemande*, p. 271.
9 As an eminent Director of the Trésor declared, 'The financial market could not be relied upon for financing these investments, so it was the state that took on the responsibility'. Francois Bloch Lainé, *Profession Fonctionnaire* (Paris: Seuil, 1977), p. 115.
10 John Zysman, *Governments, Markets and Growth: Financial Systems and the Politics of Industrial Change* (Ithaca, NY: Cornell University Press, 1983).
11 *Les Notes Bleues de Bercy*, No. 16, 1993.
12 The law was intended to align the Banque's statute on the requirements of the Maastricht Treaty. In effect, the government had to draw up the draft bill mindful of Article 20 of the French Constitution, which gives it the sole responsibility for deciding and implementing the policy of the nation.

13 Raymond Barre, 'L'économie française quatre ans après 1976–1980', *Revue des Deux Mondes*, September 1980.

14 *Selective Credit Policy and Industrial Policy in France, Britain, West Germany and Sweden*, Joint Economic Committee, Congress of the United States, 97th Congress, 1st Session, 1981.

15 For an analysis of the 'Treasury Circuit', see Goodman, *Monetary Sovereignty*; Loriaux, *France After Hegemony*.

16 OECD, Economic Surveys, France, 1987.

17 Rapport Bloch Lainé, *Les Grands Equilibres économiques* (Paris: Documentation Française, 1981), p. 229.

18 'Les Rapports de l'Industrie: Politique Economique et Structure des Interventions de l'Etat', in *Restructuration de l'Appareil Productif Français* (Paris: Documentation Française, 1976).

19 William Coleman, 'Reforming Corporatism: The French Banking Policy Community, 1941–1990', *West European Politics*, Vol. 16, April 1993.

20 Erhard Friedberg, *Administration et Entreprises: Ou Va l'Administration Française?* (Paris: Editions d'Organisations, 1974).

21 See François Morin, *La Structure Financière du Capitalisme Français*, (Paris: Calmann-Lévy, 1974) and *La Banque et les Groupes Industriels à l'Heure des Nationalisations* (Paris: Calmann-Lévy, 1977). Also Bertrand Bellon, *Le Pouvoir Financier et l'Industrie en France* (Paris: Seuil, 1980).

22 Commission Bancaire, *Rapport 1994*, 'Dix Ans d'Activité et de Résultats des Banques Françaises'.

23 Jacques Mélitz, 'Financial Deregulation in France', *European Economic Review*, Vol. 34, 1990.

24 Coleman, 'Reforming Corporatism'.

25 Bonin, *L'argent en France Depuis 1880*.

26 'La Douteuse Efficacité de la Politique Française de Coopération', *Le Monde*, June 30, 1993.

27 'La France est l'un des Pays les Plus Ouverts à l'Investissement Etranger', *Le Monde*, April 22, 1992.

28 *L'Année Politique, Economique, Sociale et Diplomatique, 1982* (Paris: Editeur du Moniteur, 1983).

29 'Comment les Non-résidents Financent la Dette Française', *La Tribune Desfossés*, March 3, 1993.

30 Dov Zerah, *Economie Financière Internationale: Les Interventions du Trésor* (Paris: Documentation Française, 1992).

31 *Ibid.*

32 Bonin, *L'Argent en France Depuis 1880*, p. 126.

33 Commissariat Général du Plan, *Crédit, Change et Inflation, Tome 11* (Paris: Documentation Française, 1979).

34 'Le Poids du Service de la Dette Extérieure Interdit pour Longtemps à la France une Politique de Relance', *Le Monde*, November 15, 1983.

35 The Cooke committee on capital adequacy, held under BIS auspices, in part accepted French arguments on the definition of own funds. The committee included general loan loss reserves in its definition of secondary capital. Second tier includes reserves or preference shares. French banks were able to raise subordinated debt which fitted into two-tier capital. Primary capital, defined as shareholders' equity and disclosed

reserves, had to amount to 50 per cent of the total by 1992. This was a problem to the major banks, as they could not expect capital injections from the state, and non-voting stock held little credit with the markets. 'Many will have to boost their capital base', *Financial Times*, November 10, 1988.

36 Commission Bancaire, *Rapport 1994*, pp. 115–56.

37 Mélitz, 'Financial Deregulation in France'.

38 *Rapport du Groupe de Réflexion sur le Développement des Initiatives Financières, Locales et Régionales* (Paris: Documentation Française, 1979)

39 Commission Bancaire, *Rapport 1994*.

40 This section is based on a teaching case by Roy C. Smith and Ingo Walter, with the assistance of Serge Platonow.

41 A *banque de dépôts* had two functions: (a) a banking function – to collect and distribute deposits and make loans; and (b) a financial function – to assist issuers and underwriters of equity. The first function implied an active role in making the market, whereas the second role was to be an intermediary.

42 *Euromoney*, March 1993.

43 *Euromoney Supplement*, March 1991.

44 'Paris to Probe Former Crédit Lyonnais Chiefs', *Financial Times*, July 9, 1996.

45 This had been excluded from the list of credit establishments covered by the EU First Banking Directive of 1977.

46 Daniel Duet, *Les Caisses d'Epargne* (Paris: PUF, 1991).

47 'Taste for Regulation Revived', *Financial Times*, November 2, 1989.

48 Yves Ullmo, the Secretary-General of the National Council of Credit, as quoted in 'Banques Françaises: le Client Fait les Frais de la Crise', *La Tribune Desfossés*, December 2, 1992. The net job losses of AFB banks during 1978–91 amounted to 1,000 out of a total of over 240,000.

49 'Banques: l'Impératif Informatique', *Le Monde*, October 22, 1992.

50 The Act reorganised the profession. The Conseil National des Assurances was reduced to a consultative role; a Comité Consultatif was created to assess regulations pertaining to relations between insurers and insured. A Commission de Contrôle was given significant disciplinary powers.

51 'Agents Généraux: Un Nouveau Statut', *Le Figaro*, November 16, 1990.

52 'Les Ex-agents de Change ont Perdu 613.7 million', *Le Monde*, July 21, 1988.

53 'Paris Demande à Abu Dhabi d'Indemniser les Déposants', *Libération*, August 3, 1991.

54 Antoine Coutiére *et al.*, 'La Concentration du Patrimoine des Foyers', *Economie et Statistique*, No. 137, October 1981.

55 Jacques Mélitz, 'The French Financial System: Mechanisms and Proposition of Reform', *INSEE*, 1980.

56 French savers remained ambivalent about equities – 78 per cent of those polled about their attitudes to the 1993 privatisations expressed no interest in subscribing. 'Sell-off Generates FF360 billion Shares', *Financial Times*, June 30, 1993.

57 'Un Second Marché Trop Elitiste', *Le Monde*, October 5, 1990.

58 'L'Inquiétante Panne du Financement de l'Industrie', *La Nouvelle Usine*, November 18, 1993.

59 'Crédit Lyonnais: Le Scandale Bancaire du Siècle', *Le Point*, April 7, 1994.

60 Philip C. Cerny, 'The 'Little Big Bang' in Paris: Financial Market Deregulation in a Dirigiste System', *European Journal of Political Research*, Vol. 17, 1989.

61 Ministère de l'Economie, des Finances et du Budget, *Le Livre Blanc sur la Réforme du Financement de l'Economie*, March 1986.

62 Zerah, *Economie Financière Internationale*.

63 Commission Bancaire, *Rapport 1994*.

64 *Ibid.*, p. 132.

65 *Ibid.*, p. 142.

66 Commission Bancaire, *Rapport 1990*, 'La Surveillances des Operations Interbancaires', pp. 309–32.

67 Christian de Boissieu, 'La Suppression de l'Encadrement du Crédit', *Le Monde*, December 18, 1984.

68 *Le Monde*, December 7, 1985.

69 'Paris Riposte', *Le Monde*, October 20, 1987.

70 Bonin, *L'Argent en France Depuis 1880*.

71 Commission Bancaire, *Rapport 1991*, 'L'Implantation des Principaux Etablissements de Crédit Français à Vocation Internationale dans les Autres Pays de la Communauté Economique Européenne'.

72 'Small Bang Fall Out', *Financial Times*, December 12, 1991.

73 'France Presses on with Liberalisation', *Financial Times*, September 26, 1991.

74 'If I were the London Stock Exchange', the chairman of the French exchange was reported as saying, 'I would have made the same proposal that they did. But London frightens the other eleven countries of Europe.' 'In Year of Quiet Change', *Financial Times*, November 2, 1989.

75 'Doubts About Tax Burden', *Financial Times*, October 22, 1990.

76 'The Battle of the Bourses', *The Economist*, February 1, 1992.

77 'France Presses Ahead with Liberalisation', *Financial Times*, September 26, 1991.

78 'London's Irresistible Lure', *Financial Times*, October 22, 1990.

79 Mélitz, 'Financial Deregulation in France'.

80 'Un Entretien avec François Furet', *Le Monde*, May 19, 1992.

81 Michel Bauer and Bénédicte Bertin-Mourot, *Les '200' en France et en Allemagne: Deux Modèles Contrastés de Détection-sélection-formation de Dirigeants des Grandes Entreprises* (Paris: CNRS/Heidrich & Struggles, 1992).

82 'En France, les contacts personnels ont primordiaux', Mr von der Burg, chairman of Allianz Europe was reported as saying, in 'Navigation Mixte: Retour au Calme Relatif après les Grandes Manoeuvres', *Les Echos*, October 18, 1989.

83 Quoted in Burrin, *La France à l'Heure Allemande*.

84 *L'Année Politique, Economique, Sociale et Diplomatique* (Paris: Editeur du Moniteur, 1994).

85 OECD Economic Surveys, France, 1994. At the end of 1987 only 1.1 per cent of all individual securities accounts held 35.5 per cent of total asset value, according to a Banque de France study.

86 'L'Année Terrible des PME', *Le Monde*, July 6, 1993.

8

The politics and markets of UK financial services

With the Conservative victory in the 1983 elections, Prime Minister Thatcher's government embarked on a policy of far-reaching changes to accentuate the dominance of the capital markets in the United Kingdom through a determined exertion of state authority.[1] One outcome was to bind the UK deeper into the EU than ever before, and move the debate on financial policy close to matters of constitutional reform.

In retrospect, a number of political and market considerations had been pointing in the direction of 'the City revolution'.[2] Successive governments after World War II had given priority to re-establishing London as a prime centre for international finance under the aegis of the Bank of England, which had been nationalised in 1946. Partly as a consequence, the various cartels composing the British financial system[3] came under pressure from the development of parallel markets, which escaped the Bank of England's control. The most important of these was the growth in the Eurodollar market, which brought London into close relationship with New York. This interdependence posed a challenge in the longer run to the Bank's inherited style of regulation, predicated on an informal code relayed by the frown on the Governor's brow, and the 'nods and winks' he dispensed to the varied quarters of his financial universe. The fiction held that, assuming that politics and economics were separate, so politicians left the Bank to run the nation's financial capital in its own discrete way. This mask fell away as financial markets – combined with political parties, the press and parliament – brought financial policy into the heart of UK politics.

The post-war UK financial system

Until the late 1960s, the main features of the UK financial system were much the same as in 1945. The City's style of self-regulation, often derived from statutory law, prospered as long as the cartel structure of the financial system remained in place. Decisions could take effect rapidly because they were relayed through the City élite, which dominated the Bank of England's court of part-time directors. The Bank was responsible for the non-statutory supervision of the clearing banks, and the Registrar of Friendly Societies looked after the mutual sector. Other banks and deposit-takers, as well as insurance, were either subject to minimal regulation by the Department of Trade and Industry (DTI), or escaped regulation altogether. The Stock Exchange and Lloyd's were both self-regulated, with their own distinct constitutions.

Two measures had laid the foundations for this UK aura of financial permanence – a set of informal agreements in 1934 concluded among the discount houses, clearing banks and the Bank of England in the wake of the global depression. This arrangement was further strengthened during the war, when the Treasury controlled capital market issues and provided instructions to the clearers to guide their lending according to public-interest criteria.

The Labour government nationalised the Bank of England in 1946. Founded in 1694 under Royal Charter, the Bank acted as the government's banker, managed the public debt, and operated as lender of last resort to other banks. Its post-war status derived from the Bank of England Act of 1946. Its court of directors, including the Governor and Deputy Governor, are appointed by the government. The Bank has all the main functions of a central bank: (1) the exclusive right of currency issue in England and Wales; (2) the operation of the government bond market (gilts) on the Treasury's behalf; (3) responsibility, as the government's adviser, for control of the monetary system; and (4) supervision of financial institutions. The 1946 Act stipulated the Bank's formal subordination to the Treasury. In practice, Bank and Treasury have consulted each other and the Prime Minister on key decisions.

At the heart of the financial structure was the clearing bank cartel, whose share of total UK deposits fell from over two-thirds in the 1920s to under one-third by the late 1960s, when the mergers of 1968 reduced their number to six. The mergers left the United Kingdom with four major banks: Barclays, National Westminster, the Midland and Lloyds. These London-based banks operated as instruments of government monetary and credit policies, in return for which their cartel arrangements curtailed competition for deposits, and set charges on loans and services provided. The cartel extended to abstaining from entry to new markets or services, such as offering higher-rate deposit accounts, access to Eurocurrency markets, or medium- and long-term loans. The banks stayed out of the burgeoning short-term money markets, and stuck to lending to or to drawing on the discount houses in the national money market, operated under the aegis of the Bank of England. Loan rates for borrowers were pegged, in essence, to the rate set by the Bank of England in its capacity as a source of funds to the discount houses. Not least, the London-based clearing banks controlled the interbank clearing mechanism for the settlement of loans and deposits in the system. Other financial institutions were granted access to the London Clearing House on negotiated terms, providing the clearing banks with a major advantage in the market for current and checking accounts.

A notably different category of institutions were the building societies and trustee savings banks, founded in the eighteenth and early nineteenth centuries with the express purpose of providing housing finance and a secure outlet for the savings of working-class people. They were concerned primarily with longer-term savings and investments.

The building societies[4] enjoyed a special status as non-profit organisations, and offered attractive rates on deposit, opened at convenient hours, and provided up to three-quarters of funds necessary for home purchases. They, too, operated a cartel under the authority of the Chief Registrar of Friendly Societies – an official responsible to Treasury and parliament – to ensure that they met their legal commitments to place 95 per cent of their assets in mortgages.

The trustee savings banks were also non-profit organisations – or 'mutuals' organised for the benefit of staff and depositors – that spanned the whole country, assembled by the 1970s into nineteen regional groupings. With 6 million customers, the trustee savings banks could lay claim to being the popular banks of the country, with strong representation in the traditional manufacturing regions of the north.

In addition, the state owned the National Savings banks, and in 1968 set up the National Girobank, using the services of the Post Office to attract savings.

Finally, retail savings in the decades following the end of World War II poured into the life insurance companies, pension funds and unit trusts.

Another group of institutions dealt primarily in the money and short-term credit markets. These were the institutions which the Bank of England sought to influence in implementing monetary and credit policy. The discount house syndicate, formed in 1934, operated at the heart of the system, acting as a warehouse for liquidity and as an intermediary between the Bank of England and the clearing banks. The Bank supplied or withdrew reserves from the banks by buying and selling bills from the discount houses. These manipulations in turn set the rate of interest for the banks in need of funds on the short-term money markets. Prior to 1914, the discount houses had served to discount bills on London, issued by merchant banks in the Accepting Houses Committee to finance international trade. With the collapse of trade in the 1930s, the accepting houses turned to financing sterling business in the markets of the British Commonwealth, and voluntarily excluded themselves from the deposit and loan business of the clearing banks. They had no major deposit base of their own, and had limited capital at their disposal. Their business in the post-war years therefore developed in the direction of corporate financing, the management of institutional funds and dealing in the international interbank market that developed after 1958 in London. In similar fashion, the overseas banks established to finance trade mainly across the British Empire were absorbed by merger into the clearing banks, diversified into the Eurocurrency markets or redeployed into the principal markets of western Europe, the United States and Asia. Standard Chartered, Hong Kong and Shanghai and Grindlays remained well represented in their traditional markets of Asia, Africa and the Indian subcontinent.

The Stock Exchange of the United Kingdom and Ireland was formed in 1973 out of the UK regional and Irish stock exchanges. Regional exchanges had provided external funds for industrial enterprises in the nineteenth century, but the bulk of business in the main London markets was in the quotation of international securities. The link between industrial companies and banks, promoted by the state in Germany from 1871 on, was largely absent in Britain, where the stock market developed in a unique manner. The sources of funds to the markets came not from the banks, as in Germany, but from private shareholders. Rules governing the market, introduced in the early twentieth century, complemented these conditions. Brokers represented their private clients for a commission and recommended the purchase of bonds or equities. Jobbers kept an inventory of stock, for which they held a monopoly on trading. This privilege derived from the 1920 Finance Act, whereby jobbers paid stamp duty on purchases of stock. Separation of function between brokers and jobbers provided an incentive for the broker to serve the client's interest rather than to unload stock, which was in the hands of the jobber. The stamp duty underpinned the jobber's monopoly. A compensation fund existed to protect the investor from the failure of a firm, and fixed commissions were charged on services rendered in order to preserve this single-capacity grouping of functions and to feed the compensation fund. The price of the cartel reflected in higher transaction costs of gilts and equities. But the arrangement proved relatively free of scandals, and served to protect the shareholders from fraud.

Historically, uses of funds on the London Stock Exchange went into government debt and railway bonds, with about 20 per cent going to meet corporate needs for finance beyond those supplied by commercial bank loans and retained earnings. The market was transformed by the expansion of government debt during World War II. In the immediate post-war years, the Treasury's authority was ensured through the Capital Issues Committee and strict foreign-exchange controls. Both were phased out in 1959, following the general move to currency convertibility. This left the Bank of England with the task of managing the maturity structure of gilts in a more open financial environment.

A primary objective of successive governments was to ensure the marketability of long-dated bonds with maturities of fifteen to thirty years. Policy therefore aimed to limit speculation on gilts in order to preserve confidence of gilt-holders. This prompted the extension of quantitative controls over ever-wider swathes of the financial system. Simultaneously, however, governments provided for exemptions for particular categories of loans, continued the upward drive in public expenditure, sought to keep interest rates low through interventions in the short-term money markets and the markets for foreign exchange, and – as inflation rates crept up – moved to control commodity prices and wages. The brunt of restrictions on loans was borne by commercial banks, even as inflation spurred speculation between financial assets.

Finally, the market for insurance at Lloyd's was ruled under the constitution set by Acts of Parliament of 1871 and 1911. The first Act vested the powers of Lloyd's committee in the general meeting of members and made it a criminal offence for non-members to sign a Lloyd's policy. Only wealthy individuals were eligible. The second Act extended the scope of business to 'insurance of every description'. By the late 1960s, no more than 6,000 people were members of Lloyd's. Membership was then opened to non-British Commonwealth members. Market rules were designed to protect the interests of members, called 'names' – individuals who pledged their personal wealth on conditions of unlimited liability in the event that claims had to be paid. The 'single capacity' rule prevailed here as well. Brokers acted as middlemen between the names and the underwriters, organised into syndicates by managing agents. Syndicates and agents were regulated by Lloyds. The market's revival after World War II was encouraged by heavy income tax – up to 98 per cent for the wealthy – and tax rebates provided by the Treasury in the event of losses incurred. Successive governments thereby acted as reinsurance to the names. Even so, a series of major losses incurred in 1965–67 frightened away existing and prospecting members, and prompted Lloyd's to reduce minimum wealth limits in order to attract new names.

Decartelisation of the UK financial system

Market forces and liberal economic policies were the two factors that led to dismantling the various cartel practices that restrained competition. The climate of opinion in the UK in the late 1960s became more favourable to greater competition in the financial sector.[5] The Treasury was won over gradually to ideas circulating in the IMF and elsewhere in favour of a looser exchange-rate regime.[6] Competition and credit control, launched under the Conservatives in September 1971 to free up financial markets as a vehicle for re-establishing regulatory control, was withdrawn by the same government.[7] Two strands of policy fought for the allegiance of the Labour Party in the governments of 1974–79. One emphasised the desirability of introducing more competition through stricter regulation of restrictive practices. The other favoured nationalisation of the clearing banks, and the creation of a National Investment Bank to channel savings into manufacturing.[8] More competition through stricter regulation of market practices was implemented, but not until the radical conservative government of 1983–87.

The clearing bank cartel dissolved slowly. To reverse their long-term decline in the share of total deposits, the clearers first entered the market for wholesale funds and then began to compete more aggressively to win back market-share on the retail side. With the easing of restraints on competition in 1971–73, the commercial banks rushed into bidding for deposits and loans. The explosion of credit, and the series of bank failures which ensued, prompted the government to again impose quantitative restrictions on lending. In the mid-1970s the banks entered the fray to extend loans to developing countries. With the election of the Conservatives in 1979, the cartel restrictions were eased, and the banks again expanded into the domestic retail markets.[9] In this they were encouraged by the heavy losses incurred on their loans to Latin America in the early 1980s.

Domestic competition was further promoted by government policy to equal-ise tax treatment across the various types of financial institutions, and to end the Stock Exchange cartel, prompting clearing banks to form their own merchant banks. By the 1990s, clearing banks had expanded the scope of business from retail to corporate services, with National Westminster and Barclays recording assets twice that of their nearest rivals, Lloyd's and the Midland.

This more competitive environment also helped to break up the building soci-eties' cartel, which had facilitated regulation of the mortgage markets, and taken the societies to a market share of over 50 per cent of UK savings. Alongside this, institutional investors came to control over two-thirds of UK equities by the early 1980s, compared to 58 per cent in private shareholders' hands in 1963.[10] Private investors were net sellers of equities, while pension funds and life insurance com-panies bought up financial assets as household wealth expanded, and as hedges against inflation.

The Conservative government further stimulated the pace of change by turning the Trustee Savings Bank, traditionally close to the Labour movement, into a limited liability company in 1986, and privatised the much smaller Girobank in 1988. Both building societies and clearing banks in the 1980s converged on to the housing market,[11] beating down loan conditions and fuelling the bubble which burst in 1989–90 as interest rates edged up in response to the rise in inflationary pressures. The institutions were poorly prepared for the conditions of the late 1980s, and the threat of competition on domestic markets from the continent as market access to Britain was eased in the light of legisla-tion on the EU's internal single market. Continental institutions faced lower tax rates than those prevailing in the United Kingdom. Competition pared profits, as compared to the major competitors in France and Germany. The institutions were hurt by the October 1987 crash, and the reduction in the value of their assets.

Merchant banks in the UK circumvented the clearing bank cartel – and their exclusion from the Stock Exchange monopoly – by developing a range of cor-porate services in the burgeoning Euromarkets. They also earned income from institutional management of the flow of savings.[12] With the agreement between the government and Stock Exchange to end single-capacity brokerage and jobbing in 1986, the merchant banks moved, with Bank of England support, to create financial conglomerates. There were three main motivations: (1) to compete with the US and Japanese securities houses in world markets by build-ing up a larger capital base; (2) to develop a presence in North America, Asia and the principal continental European markets; and (3) to keep as much central market control as possible of British equities. But, following the October 1987 stock-market crash, financial conglomerates came into disfavour as commission rates fell in highly competitive securities markets, and managerial problems of creating all-purpose universal banks became more evident. A number of US houses withdrew from the British market as it became clearer that established relations between UK banks and corporations counted as much, if not more, than capital. By the early 1990s, the shape of British merchant banking had polarised between a handful of large securities houses, such as S. G. Warburg, Kleinwort Benson, Barclays de Zoete Wedd and County NatWest, and specialist houses with a more narrow focus like Shroders, Rothschilds, Hoare Govett and Flemings. Global ambitions were scaled down, with British and London-based merchant banks concentrating more on cross-border alliances in Europe, only to be re-ignited by a new focus on 'emerging markets' and 'transition economies' following the collapse of the Communist state system.

The biggest changes came in the structure of the UK Stock Exchange. Trading in gilts and equities came to be dominated by institutions which lobbied the government successfully to end the single-capacity rule. Brokers and jobbers were swept into the rush to form financial conglomerates. Buoyant equity markets were fed by the growth in corporate profits, by the government policy to sell off nationalised industries, and the takeover wave of the 1980s. Meanwhile, both government and the London Stock Exchange promoted separate markets with less strict listing requirements. The Unlisted Securities Market, launched in 1978, paved the way for the Third Market, both dealing in the shares of small and medium-size businesses. Licenced securities dealers developed the over-the-counter markets, and formed the National Association of Securities Dealers and Investment Managers (NASDIM). The net effect of this series of market- and policy-driven changes was to extend share ownership in the United Kingdom, provide a highly liquid market for corporate finance, and make London the prime financial capital in the European time-zone.

Internationalisation of UK financial markets

Decartelisation of British financial markets was also driven by the determination of successive British governments, Conservative and Labour, to preserve the City of London as a world financial centre. In the immediate post-war years, this took the form of promoting the use of sterling as an international currency in the role of junior partner to the US dollar. In retrospect, devaluation of the pound sterling in November 1967 marked the end of that road. The new orientation evolved slowly along two not readily compatible tracks. One was to convert the City of London into a world financial centre turning on the dollar. The other was UK entry to the EU, along with Ireland and Denmark, in 1973. As public support was either hostile or cool on the EU, domestic divisions on 'Europe' came back regularly to haunt British public policy. These developments parallelled the collapse in 1971 of the Bretton Woods system. Private financial markets, generated in large part by the expansion of government securities growth in oil money, took over from central bankers the crucial task of setting currency relationships. The process towards privatisation of world money markets created much greater instability and unpredictability, prompting a surge in new financial products designed to hedge against as many risks as possible.

The internalisation of financial markets hinging on the dollar turned London into an offshore financial centre. There was nothing ineluctable about this choice. Despite arguments by British 'declinists' that the sacrifice of the industrial base on the altar of financial gains began some time in the 1880s, Britain emerged from World War II as the United States' junior partner, but one with considerable means. Paul Kennedy writes that Britain's rapid growth of new industries already in 1940 had a 50 per cent greater output than Germany in aircraft as well as in tanks.[13] Only with the boost in German arms production in 1943 did Festland Europa overtake Britain in arms output. This massive German industrial machine was shorn of one-quarter of its productive capacity by war or dismantlement, leaving the remainder to fuel the Federal Republic's trade-based economic revival in the 1950s. The central point of Britain's position was not economic decline, but a conscious act of policy to merge Britain's future security in alliance with the United States.

During the war, new industries had been adopted on a grand scale. The new Keynesian economics provided a theoretical framework for expansionary fiscal policy, while the banking cartel provided the institutional structure for state manipulation of interest rates. All parties were committed to social reforms. Financial aid was forthcoming from the United States. Lend-lease enabled Britain to be supplied without immediate payment. Many dominions had achieved self-government and India was well on the way there prior to the war. Following the war successive British governments had overstretched the country's resources by opting for extensive overseas military commitments, trade liberalisation, active promotion of capital exports, a reserve currency status for sterling and the restoration of London as an international financial centre. Both main parties sought to maintain the wartime consensus on welfare and full employment. Above all, they failed to establish effective labour-market laws and institutions. And they alternated between periodic doses of deflation and reflation until they abandoned attempts to defend sterling's parity with the dollar and the role of sterling as a reserve currency. Britain entered the EU on terms that de Gaulle had insisted should involve the sacrifice of the Commonwealth agricultural system to the EU's common agricultural programme.

Anxieties about Britain's future had come to a head in the late 1950s, with the formation of the EU's customs union and the tightening of exchange controls in 1957 after a run on sterling. Banks began to substitute dollars for sterling in their international transactions. This laid the foundations for the growth of the Eurodollar markets in the subsequent decade, and for London's restoration as a financial centre dealing in dollars rather than in sterling. The number of foreign banks in London rose from 113 in 1967 to 280 in 1973, and 349 in 1974.[14] American banks entered the UK domestic loan business, and helped to fund North Sea oil and gas exploration and development. London financial markets became integrated more closely with those of the United States, increasing the British economy's vulnerability to the twists and turns of US monetary and exchange-rate policy.

Britain entered the EU on an inflationary boom, more than ever integrated into the dollar area and with a widening trade deficit, two-thirds of which was continental Europe. Stagnant investment and falling profits in the subsequent years discouraged any major renewal of plant and equipment. One estimate suggested that the average life of total UK plant and machinery was thirty-five years, or twice the level of that in France or Germany.[15]

While the domestic economy stagnated, corporate Britain expanded overseas. If there was one consistent thread in British economic policy since 1945, it lay in the strategy of British corporations and financial institutions to recover as much as possible the losses incurred by the prosecution of the war. Profits, too, were higher abroad.[16] By 1973, a UN study suggested that the value of British production abroad was twice that of visible export trade.[17] Furthermore, the City of London's earnings on 'invisibles' rose threefold between 1973 and 1979, as financial and bank operations abroad expanded alongside a booming reinsurance market. By the end of the decade, there were 400 foreign banks in London, while the British 'big four' clearing banks expanded their international business on the back of the Eurocurrency boom. Meanwhile, the rise in popular savings had stimulated the growth of unit trusts, pension funds and insurance companies, and had invigorated the London Stock Exchange. The ending of foreign-exchange controls in 1979, forty years after the outbreak of World War II, led to a surge of outward investment into the equity markets of South-East Asia and North America.

The years between 1974 and 1979 witnessed a sea-change in UK economic policy. Initially, the Labour government had responded to the inheritance of the Conservatives' inflationary boom and the rise in oil prices by promoting the development of the world's recycling of OPEC funds in London, and public-sector borrowing to sustain demand. This placed it in the awkward position of borrowing on the world's capital markets at a time when the Labour left was most vociferous in calling for bank nationalisations, price controls and dividend controls, a state-led 'industrial strategy' and withdrawal from the EU. The corporate sector faced a severe liquidity squeeze. When, on March 4, 1976, the markets suspected the government of trying to engineer sterling's devaluation in order to promote exports, OPEC withdrawals of sterling balances and short-term capital outflows turned into an avalanche. Over the coming months, the government edged towards a stabilisation policy, following further runs on sterling and massive sales of government securities by investors.[18] A Letter of Intent was signed with the IMF in December, announcing budgetary restrictions, monetary targets set by the Bank of England, and an 'incomes policy' comprising price and wage controls.

The fall of the dollar against the DM in the course of 1977 enabled the Bank of England to intervene on the exchange markets and to keep sterling down. But that led to an expansion of external reserves and the domestic money supply. On October 31, 1977, the Bank of England announced that sterling would be allowed to float free, since any further attempt to hold down the exchange rate would have inflationary consequences. The flood of dollars then turned on the

DM, driving it upwards and prompting Chancellor Schmidt to propose a 'zone of currency stability' with France in the EU. This move to exchange-rate stability on the Continent left the Labour government with little option other than to follow the priorities laid down in the IMF Letter of Intent. Any expansionary policy would trigger a renewed run to sterling. So the onus of policy fell on incomes restraint. That crumbled in the winter of 1978. A wave of strikes ensued, causing widespread disruption to public services, the calling of a general election, and nearly two decades of Tory government following their sweeping victory in May 1979.

Conservative economic policy, presented in the June 1979 budget, represented an 'experiment akin to those always available in the natural sciences', the BIS commented laconically.[19] The central decision was the freeing of foreign-exchange controls. British corporations were free to invest abroad, while North Sea oil income irrigated the London financial markets. Tight control was exerted over monetary aggregates, and the currency was allowed to soar. Manufacturing output plummeted. The economy began to turn up again in 1981, and the subsequent GDP expansion at 3–4 per cent over the decade was accompanied by a decline in government debt and a major drive to privatise state-owned assets. Government finances moved to surplus from 1985 on. Equity ownership became much more widely diffused. Labour-market legislation was liberalised. Corporate profits improved, and non-residential investment took off. Expansion was facilitated by the high oil prices, disguising the shift to deficit in manufacturing trade. Mrs Thatcher's impact on the UK economy, in short, had been astounding.

When oil prices fell in 1986, the trade accounts plummeted into deficit. Inflation was at 2–3 per cent. Why did Britain's inflation rates rise again, leading to the drama of sterling in the ERM in the years 1990–92? As mentioned, the Tory government eased fiscal policy and encouraged home-ownership on the back of a credit boom. Following the Louvre Accords of February 1987, UK monetary policy was relaxed, as the Bank of England's reserves rose by £20 billion to sustain the dollar. Financial market deregulation restricted the government's ability to control monetary aggregates. As the former Chancellor, Nigel Lawson, pointed out, 'Today, when financial deregulation (which is particularly advanced in the UK) and the globalisation of financial markets have made the domestic monetary aggregates an especially unreliable guide, an external discipline, should there be one readily available, is clearly preferable'.[20] In other words, the financial market reforms in the UK, to which we shall now turn, raised the question of whether the UK should join the ERM and accept the Bundesbank as central bank, or establish its own independent central bank. The Treasury and Foreign Office wanted sterling in the ERM, as 'an anchor against inflation'.[21] The Prime Minister was opposed, on the grounds that 'the DM is slightly deflationary'.[22]

Britain's experience invited comparison with the Federal Republic. The notable feature by the early 1990s was how divergent their structures had become. Germany was the Continent's dominant economy, with tightly-knit insider business and policy networks. All political parties supported the high cost and corporatist institutions of the social market economy. British manufacturing productivity had nearly caught up with Germany's. But manufacturing in Germany made up 31 per cent of GDP, against only 20 per cent for Britain. The DM's undervaluation in the ERM had swollen German surpluses, whereas sterling moved up or down outside it. London was an *international* financial centre, unlike Frankfurt, which was a *national* one. London had an open market for equities, and the UK was a champion of open equities markets in the EU. As the Bundesbank stated with uncharacteristic forthrightness, Germany's universal banks must not be forced 'by virtue of the EU regulations to switch over to a system of functional operation in the financial services sector, such as predominates in the Anglo-Saxon countries'.[23] The British stock of foreign direct investment was 22 per cent of GDP in 1987, probably rising to 50 per cent by 1995, compared to Germany's 8 per cent and 15 per cent respectively.[24] Britain was also the EU's prime recipient of inward foreign direct investment, accounting for 38 per cent of US and Japanese cumulative foreign direct investment in the EU.[25] The promise included an emerging Japanese–British industrial alliance that would help to regenerate British-based manufacturing through the expansion of Japanese-owned plants.[26]

Regulation and the Bank of England

The manner and tempo at which UK financial markets were transformed was driven by the Bank's preference for an informal style of regulation over banks. But as stated by the so-called Wilson Committee, convened under Prime Minister Callaghan to head off a Labour Party proposal for nationalisation of the banks, 'the secondary banking crisis showed that the larger a market becomes and the less homogeneous those operating within it, the more difficult it is to rely on informal non-statutory methods of regulation'.[27] Yet a constant fear of the Bank of England was that more formality would weaken the ability of the authorities to match the inventiveness of markets. And there was the concern that the laws governing depositor protection, particularly popular among politicians of all parties, might take the risk out of banking and allow depositors to contemplate compensation by the state rather than face the discipline of the market. Much intellectual effort was spent on defining the right balance between law and markets. Too much law raised costs for market participants, and inhibited regulators in adapting to market conditions. Too much emphasis on market efficiency overlooked matters of elementary justice and systemic risk.

Statutory amendments to the Bank's supervisory powers were preceded by a series of major regulatory failures. The first was occasioned by the introduction of Competition and Credit Controls in September 1971, intended 'to permit the price mechanism to function efficiently in the allocation of credit and to free the banks from the rigidities and restraints which have for too long inhibited them'.[28]

The unexpected result of this measure to end the cartelisation of financial markets, and simultaneously to strengthen the Bank's control over the financial system, was an explosion of credit. So-called 'fringe' banks sought deposits on the wholesale money markets in London to lend to the property sector. In the dramatic climate of late 1973, the wholesale markets called in their funds from the fringe banks, who suffered a dramatic loss of confidence by depositors. The Bank of England responded by setting up a Control Committee, composed of the clearing banks, who were persuaded to extend emergency facilities to the troubled banks.[29] Its supervisory powers were thereby strengthened, but the Bank continued to rely on outside auditors, responsible to their clients, rather than on its own inspectorate.

Ten years later, in 1984, Johnson Matthey Bankers (JMB), dealing on the gold bullion market, were bailed out by a syndicate of 200 UK and foreign financial institutions, under the aegis of the Bank of England, which was accused of procrastination since it was well aware of JMB's risky loan portfolio. Its supervisory powers were again altered. Then in 1991, the Bank of England led a multinational action to seize the assets of Bank of Credit and Commerce International (BCCI) – based in Luxemburg – with business in over sixty-six countries. The Bank had known of the BCCI's dubious practices as early as the 1970s, but had failed to take action. In both the JMB and BCCI cases, information about the true state of the banks' books was divulged too little and too late.

New statutory powers were grafted on to the Bank's older habits of informality,[30] and with equal regularity proved inadequate to the task. In the aftermath of the secondary banking crisis, City institutions were confirmed in their belief that their interests could only be secured under the aegis of the Bank of England, as the champion to the government of continued self-regulation.[31] This was reflected in the 1979 Banking Act, which established a two-tier definition of banks that rested, in effect, on the Bank's view of their reputation in the markets. A special compensation fund was set up to support depositors in the event of a bank failure.

The Bank assumed that it was the second-tier banks which needed close supervision, rather than the first tier of banks, defined as those 'with a high reputation and standing in the financial community'. But JMB was in the first tier. The Bank's supervisory failure was not appreciated in Whitehall[32] nor in the City. Not least of the government's embarrassments was the gulf between its free-market approach to the non-banking sector and the Bank's rescue of JMB, at City institutions' expense. The 1987 Act, steered by a firm Treasury hand,[33] established a special supervisory board in the Bank, including non-Bank appointments, and provided for closer links between bank auditors and Bank supervisors. After the BCCI affair, the Bank was given positive powers of intervention to close a bank on the suspicion of difficulties and to set up a special investigative unit in the Bank itself.[34]

The 1987 Act also sought to tidy up government thinking about foreign takeovers of financial institutions. The Bank of England's strategy to make London the 'third leg' of world financial markets along with New York and Tokyo required, as the Governor indicated, that London must be a place where 'people other than the home team can play'.[35] But Whitehall preferred domestic ownership of banks, with the Bank exercising a watchful eye. In a 1972 memorandum, the Bank of England had 'understood' that banks would consult with it on all proposals for participations in UK banks exceeding 15 per cent of equity. This was ignored by the Hong Kong and Shanghai Bank in its 1981 bid for the Royal Bank of Scotland (in competition with Standard Chartered). The bid was turned down on grounds of nationality of the Hong Kong and Shanghai Bank (HSBC), that the Royal Bank was judged vital to Edinburgh's future, and that the acquired bank in the hands of an overseas owner would have to respond to the policy requirements of the home government.[36]

This latter point only underlined Whitehall's strong preference for host-country control. It was the nationality issue which needed clarification. This came in two forms. First, the Banking Act of 1987 stipulated that the Bank of England was to have control over mergers and acquisition in the banking sector. All bids were to be preceded by a notification to the Bank. Secondly, a tough reciprocity clause was inserted into the Financial Services Act of 1986, whereby the government had the power to block a foreign takeover if equivalent opportunities were not available to British firms in the acquiring bank's home country. It was this clause which the European Commission transposed directly into its draft for the Second Banking Directive, presented in January 1988.

If there was one area where the Bank asserted its powers, it was in reform of the gilts market. Difficulties in funding the government deficits of the 1970s – in the face of institutions ready to hold more government paper only at a high price – convinced officials in the Bank of England of the need for greater liquidity in the markets for gilts. Two discount houses accounted for up to 90 per cent of the short-term money market, and the level of commissions charged by Stock Exchange member firms in gilt-edged transactions was regarded as excessive.

Bank officials' prime concern was to meet the Bank's statutory obligation to raise money for the government as cheaply as possible. The Treasury was brought around to the view that more competitive and liquid markets in government securities would reduce funding costs, and spill over on to equities to help absorb the size of flotations required in the government privatisation campaign. The Treasury and Bank therefore leaned on the Stock Exchange to relax rules restricting the stakes of non-members and encouraged City institutions to form conglomerates, merging commercial and investment banking.[37] In 1984–85, the Bank organised a new primary-dealer network, much along the lines followed by the New York Federal Reserve.[38] Equity markets were also organised on dual-capacity broker–dealer lines. The main criteria for the selection of participating institutions was that they be well capitalised and that they be members of the Stock Exchange. By October 27, 1986 – the date widely labelled 'Big Bang' – twenty-seven market-makers, ten of which were linked to US groups, had replaced the two discount houses.

Development of the interbank market in London and the new significance of wholesale banking in world markets made the Bank of England particularly sensitive to the need to foster a greater degree of international cooperation among central banks and supervisory authorities. The Bank of International Settlements in Basle provided the main multilateral forum, for discussions both in the EU and with the United States or Japan. Initial steps were taken on the initiative of the Governor of the Bank of England in July 1974, at a regular meeting of the central bankers at Basle in the BIS.[39] The Herstatt Bank in Germany had closed the month previously after heavy losses incurred on the foreign-exchange markets. The central bankers nodded in the direction of home-country responsibility for subsidiaries of banks operating in other countries. In September, the central bankers agreed to establish a Committee on Banking Regulation and Supervisory Practices, headed by the supervisor recently appointed to the position in the Bank. British and foreign banks in London then rushed into the business of borrowing Eurodollars at very low interest rates on the London interbank market and re-lending to developing countries. Once the bubble burst in 1982, an EU directive on consolidated accounting was rushed through Brussels procedures. The Bank of England then became involved with the clearing banks in the 1980s negotiations on developing country debt restructuring, led by the US Treasury. Meanwhile, the Eurobond market had taken off.

Under the 1987 Banking Act, the Bank of England took over as lead regulator for securities firms involved in both securities and banking. This affirmation of the Bank's authority was helped by its success in establishing a settlements system for the gilt market and the money markets, and stood in strong contrast to the failure of the London Stock Exchange to update its own settlements system. Indeed, after 'Big Bang', the Exchange found its varied functions either moving up to the Bank, down to the self-regulatory organisations, or being lost to competitors. Its monopoly on market information services was ended as a restraint on trade. And the Exchange had to close its floor within months of 'Big Bang'. The screen-based SEAQ International operated along the lines of NASDAQ, the US over-the-counter market, and provided a quote-driven system where shares are fixed by competition between market-makers. That left the Exchange in charge of the settlements system, run on 1970s technology. Institutional investors backed a new design, TAURUS (Transfer and Automated Registration of Uncertified Stock), in 1982 but voted to abandon it in 1993. One reason was the technological complexity of meeting the requirement under UK law that shareholder names appear on companies' share registry. The other was that smaller share registrars and companies were opposed to any modification in the law. The Bank therefore moved to squeeze the smaller registrars out of the market by speeding up the settlement cycle.[40] The clearers, with their large registrars, could offer a shorter settlement cycle under more centralised control and economies of scale. The new system, CREST (the British securities clearance and settlement system), was scheduled for introduction in 1996.

Regulation and investor protection

From the viewpoint of City practitioners, there were two features of the US regulatory scene that were anathema: (1) the concentration of investigative, policing and legal powers in the hands of the SEC; and (2) the US method of plea-bargaining, offering discounts from sentences if the accused pleaded guilty in cases such as insider trading. Yet the US experience was the one to which British administrators, politicians and market operators turned for inspiration. The process of introducing US policy experience into the UK market context proved slow, with the City aware that its *de-facto* status as a private club hampered effective policing of the markets.

The process started with concern over insider dealings associated with the takeover spree in the 1960s, and the 1965–67 market losses at Lloyd's. There were then a string of corporate failures in insurance, and the 1973–75 secondary banking crisis. A bill was introduced in 1973 to make insider dealing a criminal offence, and the Fair Trading Act of 1973 made a provision for the registration of restrictive practices in services, which the Labour government expressly extended to the financial sector. The Policyholder's Protection Act of 1974 required that the insurance sector set up a board in order to administer a levy to guard against future collapses. A more stringent monitoring system was introduced under the DTI, which strengthened the British Insurance Brokers Association, formed in 1976, as the sector's umbrella organisation. It was to administer the Insurance Brokers Act of 1977, which provided for registration, a code of conduct and an indemnity fund.

The Labour government was prepared to challenge the self-regulatory traditions of the Stock Exchange and Lloyd's on a platform of statutory powers in a competitive-market framework. In 1978, the insider trading bill was revived, with the Conservatives in opposition less keen on introducing the criminal law and the Stock Exchange expressing reservations. The Office of Fair Trade (OFT) insisted that the Stock Exchange register its rule-book so that, under the Act, the Exchange became guilty until proven innocent. The OFT listed seventeen restrictive practices.[41]

Meanwhile, the Bank of England had the Exchange create a Council for the Securities Industries, as a pre-emptive measure against the threat of statutory law. A similar step was taken by the Lloyd's committee. In response to concerns expressed in the House of Commons and the press about its procedures, the committee in 1978 appointed a working party, led by Sir Henry Fisher, a High Court judge. Lloyd's had become dependent for two-thirds of its income and reinsurance business on the United States, and over two-thirds of its business had come to be controlled by eight publicly quoted brokers which owned underwriters. This undermined the 'single capacity' rule. As noted earlier, membership had been opened to people of more modest wealth, growing from 6,000 in 1969 to about 17,000 names in 1978. As insurance rates were bid down, competition sharpened, with the market plagued by a series of scandals. Names organised to sue Lloyd's, challenging the principle of unlimited liability.

Much the same prevarication between statutory law and non-intervention in City affairs was evident in the Conservative government of 1979–83. Taxes were cut in May and then all foreign exchange controls abolished in October 1979. As the currency rose on foreign-exchange markets, and interest rates remained high to squeeze out inflation, the clearing banks were helpless to prevent the government imposing a profits tax. The OFT continued its investigations into restrictive practices on the Stock Exchange. Insider dealing, defined as the abuse of specific information likely to have a 'material effect' on the price of shares, became a criminal offence in the 1980 Companies Act. In July 1981, the DTI commissioned a study of statutory regulation of the securities markets, the initial proposal of which was to set up four large self-regulatory authorities. Yet City preferences demanded accommodation. The 1980 Companies Act was policed by the Stock Exchange and the Takeover Panel – another self-regulatory organisation composed of the City's great and good. Only three convictions had been recorded by 1985,[42] despite substantial evidence of a surge in securities fraud.[43] The proposals were duly modified. The Bank of England was to supervise commodity and financial markets, while the DTI was to be vested with powers to ensure investors' rights, with responsibility for fraud, registration and drawing up rules of conduct, confirming its role as the main regulatory agency. Alongside this was to be a network of statutorily-based self-regulating bodies, coordinated through the voluntary Council for the Securities Industry (CSI), supervised by the DTI.[44]

The Conservatives made two notable concessions to their City supporters. Conservative members of Lloyd's steered a private member's bill through parliament, with only modest opposition from Labour.[45] Sir Henry Fisher had declared the powers of Lloyd's committee 'inadequate for self-regulation in modern conditions'. He suggested the creation of a new Council, to be elected by working members and to abolish the direct democracy which had prevailed hitherto in Lloyd's governance, whereby authority was vested in the General Meeting of members. The 1982 Lloyd's Act confirmed the working members' position as privileged insiders: the new Council was formed with a chairman drawn from Lloyd's and a chief executive appointed by the Bank of England. An immunity clause made it impossible for any member to sue the Council. Insurance brokers were to direct underwriters, which helped consolidate the position of the underwriters.[46]

After the 1983 Conservative election victory, the Trade Secretary, Cecil Parkinson, struck a deal with the chairman of the Stock Exchange, Sir Nicholas Goodison, to drop the restrictive practices case in return for reforms. A deadline was set for October 27, 1986, the date familiarly associated with the City's 'Big Bang'. The Stock Exchange argued that the adversarial proceedings of the court made any alteration in its rule-book a sign of weakness. There were also the members' fears that a court ban on Stock Exchange rules could have led to the establishment of a statutory body such as the US SEC to regulate securities activities.[47]

The Financial Services Act

In a speech of March 1984, the Governor of the Bank of England announced that reform of the financial markets was to be his prime objective. If the goal was to secure London as the 'third leg' of world financial markets alongside New York and Tokyo, the method was to be along lines combining statutory law with 'practitioner-based regulation'.[48] The government then announced in October 1984 the setting-up of a Securities Investment Board (SIB) to register firms, draw up rules of conduct and enforce them. These suggestions found their way into the White Paper, presented in January 1985,[49] and then in December 1984 into the Financial Services Bill. The bill passed through parliament, at one time facing up to 400 amendments, and received the Royal Assent in November 1986.

The principal feature in the Financial Services Act was for investment services to be subject to regulation under statutory supervision. All persons engaged in the securities business had to be registered as 'fit and proper'. The DTI was to hold statutory powers, and devolve them upon the SIB. The SIB was the key to the system. It received its delegated authority from the state, but operated as a private institution. Senior SIB appointments were to be made by the Bank of England and the DTI. All organisations offering financial services were to receive its authorisation before opening procedures for membership in one or more of the self-regulatory organisations (SROs). These were originally to be seven in number, to be structured along familiar demarcation lines. In effect, they segmented into two broad groups, dealing in wholesale or retail markets. The SROs were to have their own rule-books, equivalent in content to the SIB's Conduct of Rules Book. They were to have their own staff for the process of authorisation and implementation. The SIB was to serve as a court of appeal, with the DTI as ultimate arbiter. The Bank of England, subject to the Treasury, was a *de-facto* partner for the DTI in its capacity as supervisor of the banks and hence the securities markets. Complexity across the 212 articles of the Act was in part due to this hierarchy of cross-cutting competences. The Act came into effect in April 1988, providing the United Kingdom with a statutory regulatory structure, which arguably imposed stricter standards than any in the EU.[50]

Supervision of retail investment services

Inserting the SIB into the UK context was bound to be controversial in view of the City's aversion to statutory law. That did not discourage the SIB's first chairman, Sir Kenneth Berrill – a Whitehall mandarin – from adopting the position, similar to that of the SEC, that strong regulation was good for markets. The SIB's Rules of Conduct reflected this concern to establish the best, rather than minimal, standards. Chancellor of the Exchequer Nigel Lawson had hinted that he was not averse to a more centralised and uniform regulation of financial markets,[51] and the Bank had been weakened by his criticism of its competence, notably in the JMB affair. With the DTI in support, there was little resistance from government departments to the SIB's testing how far to extend its statutory domain.

Nor was there anything to fear from Labour. The call from the left of the party for nationalisation of the clearing banks, and the creation of a National Investment Bank to channel savings into manufacturing, had failed to win electoral support. And the conservative victory in the 1983 general elections left the way clear for the government to stage the flotation of the Trustee Savings Bank and the building societies, both traditionally allied to the Labour Party. It was noticeable that Labour's policy document for the 1987 election – 'Making the City Safe' – concentrated on the weaknesses in the FSA. The new Labour line clearly favoured a SEC-type approach.

Reform of retail investment services on the domestic market proved arduous. In October 1984, the government set up a Marketing Investments Board (MIB) to supervise this disparate sector. But the initiative was dropped in favour of a single authority in the form of the SIB. A galaxy of acronymic organisations emerged to represent retailers – NASDIM, FIMBRA, IMRO, LAUTRO and LUTIRO. None was predominant enough to act as a federator and bring them into one umbrella self-regulatory retail organisation. The most organised group were the insurers, which had associated under pressure from the 1970s Acts. They stacked the SIB committee charged with drawing up regulations for the sector.[52] The main effect of the new rules was to end the independence of intermediaries in life insurance and to encourage them to become tied agents, while banks, insurance houses and building societies entered the insurance field. In 1990, the SIB launched a full review of the rules and organisation of this sprawling sector. Its records showed that one in four life policies lapsed in the first two years.[53] SIB's new policy package for the sector carried two key components: (1) retail salesmen would have to reveal much more about the pricing of commission; and (2) a Personal Investment Authority (PIA) was set up to incorporate the warring factions. The PIA was told to slim down its board, stuffed with the warring factions, and to increase representatives of the public interest.[54]

Supervision of wholesale capital markets

As long as the City remained solidly pro-Tory out of fear of Labour in the 1979, 1983 and 1987 general elections, the government had the upper hand over its City supporters. With nowhere else to go, they could do little other than fight rearguard actions as radical reforms were thrust upon them. The government's attention went to the large institutional investors and security houses, rather than to the smaller stockbrokers and jobbers. Simply, the 'third-leg' wholesale-market strategy meant incorporating foreign institutions in the SROs.

Financial futures was the first market to organise as an SRO. Membership of LIFFE was opened to foreign participation, both US and continental European. The Association of Future Brokers and Dealers (AFBD) was incorporated in 1984.

Next to form an SRO were the international bond traders. A Committee of the International Securities Regulatory Organisation (ISRO) was set up with a view to forming a Recognised Investment Exchange (RIE), together with the Association of International Bond Dealers (AIBD) to supervise the vast Eurobond market. A merger with the London Stock Exchange was announced in September 1986. The merged exchange became the International Stock Exchange (ISE) of the United Kingdom and the Republic of Ireland. Its Council was restricted to thirty-one members, drawn equally from the ISRO and the Exchange. The main Securities Association had a governing body of twenty-five, drawn from either exchange and including six independent members, and the Securities and Futures Securities Association Authority (SFA) took over as the central regulatory authority to police the markets.

As a fractious body of competing members, the Securities Association found a degree of unity in opposition to the SIB, which had won government agreement to impose its own rules on SROs. The ISRO then lobbied successfully for legal immunity of SROs for damage claims arising from action 'taken in good faith'.[55] The SIB furthermore insisted that SROs seeking recognition had to submit rule-books to provide equivalent protection to that offered to investors by the SIB. The Securities Association drew the lesson that its rule-book be spelled out in arcane legal detail, and its publication in July 1987 occasioned a summer of discontent in the City, leading to a new version in December. Acrimonious haggling ensued, resulting in delay in the process of registration and authorisation for investment houses beyond the deadline of April 1988. There was talk of the Bank reasserting its traditional authority over financial markets, and hopes expressed of a more sympathetic ear at the SIB to heed City concerns that complex rule-books for wholesale markets might compromise London's competitive position. SIB duly introduced a Bank distinction pointing to different regulatory approaches for wholesale and retail markets, and defined ten core principles guiding policy, insisting that these be 'entrenched' in SRO rule-books, along with forty basic rules governing market practices.[56]

The period from February 1988 to June 1992 spanned negotiations in the EU on financial services. The 1987 Banking Securities Act provided the statutory basis for the reassertion over the DTI of the Bank's traditional role as ultimate arbiter in financial markets. In July 1987, the Securities Association published its capital adequacy requirements for members, after discussions with the Bank. These were predicated on 'base capital', counted as 25 per cent of annual operating costs, and 'position capital', to ensure against market risks. The downturn came with a vengeance on October 19, 1987, unleashing a price war between market-makers. The Bank slapped on a third category of capital adequacy, termed 'counterparty' funds, to cover credit risks. This was followed by central bank agreement in June 1988 at Basle on capital adequacy ratios for banks.

In late 1988, negotiations on financial services in the EU picked up momentum. This was the moment chosen by an ISE committee, dominated by the 'home team', to push for a change in market rules whereby details of a trade were to be revealed the day after. US investment houses voted against this rule on the grounds that only British firms had the contacts to unwind the deals.[57] In March 1990, four major US securities houses lobbied the EU Commission independently on proposals for capital adequacy in the draft directive on investment services.[58] British firms, however, registered similar complaints through the Bank of England.

This period also spanned negotiations in the BIS on capital adequacy for banks and investment houses. The Securities Association's fractious members needed Treasury, Bank, SIB and DTI support in international negotiations. The SEC had concluded a series of bilateral accords with Switzerland, Japan and the Cayman Islands on securities practices. A 'memorandum of understanding' was signed in September 1986 between the DTI and the two main regulatory authorities covering securities and futures markets, the SEC and the Commodity Futures Trading Commission (CFTC). The agreement set out the conditions for a confidential exchange of information between the US and UK authorities to serve as the basis for world-wide policing of markets.[59] With the launch of the EU internal-market programme in early 1988, the picture was complicated further. The supervisors' meeting in the Basle Committee urged securities houses to hold additional capital against market risks. ISRO members complained that the central bankers had failed to appreciate the difference between bank loans, requiring capital reserves to cover credit risks, and the securities business, where risk was spread across a diversity of assets. The struggle between securities firms and regulators was then projected into the negotiations between the Basle Committee and IOSCO, the International Organisation of Securities Commissions. The investment houses' two foes proved to be the SEC in alliance with the Bundesbank, lined up against the Bank of England and the French authorities. It was a Franco-British alliance in June 1992 which put through the light capital adequacy requirements for security houses in the EU.

Unsurprisingly, neither Mr Justice Bingham, in his report on the Bank's handling of the BCCI collapse, nor the SIB, called for any major change of the United Kingdom's regulatory framework, despite rumours of forthcoming radical revisions. Bingham suggested the Bank strengthen its supervisory methods.[60] The SIB described itself as a regulator of regulators in a two-tier system with the SROs.[61]

A more open question remained the Bank's own status. The Treasury wanted the Bank and the SIB to be answerable to it.[62] The Bank looked forward to greater autonomy in the conduct of monetary policy, but favoured retaining control over bank supervision.[63] In the end, London's mixture of statutory control and self-regulation provided a friendly environment for securities business. Improvements were required in implementation of the 1986 legislation and were undertaken. Overhaul of the 1986 legislation along the lines of a SEC with a clear regulatory mandate could have reduced London's comparative advantage in wholesale trading relative to competing financial centres.[64]

Learning by doing

Here lay the paradox at the heart of the United Kingdom's incremental move to statutory regulation of financial markets. The SIB's main weakness lay in implementation. But SEC-like powers, to be effective, had to have the support of the City. Whether conceived as a strategy or discovered as part of the prolonged policy process, successive governments in effect allowed market participants to discover the limits of self-regulation before taking the next step. There was no confrontation comparable to that between government and coalminers in 1984–85. The government's emphasis was first to create the two-tier structure of SIB and SROs, then to establish rules, and finally to address the central matter of implementation. The procedure adopted over the longer term was to introduce measures which symbolised intent, but had inadequate means to achieve stated objectives. The benefit was to ensure that the learning process was widely shared as the markets stumbled from one scandal to another. The cost was recorded in the various disasters which might have been avoided had supervisory authority been asserted earlier.

The demise of Lloyd's served as one painful lesson of the limits to the Bank's preference for 'practitioner-based regulation'. Lloyd's was not included in the Financial Services Act of 1986, on the grounds that the Lloyd's 1982 Securities Act sufficed. The DTI ordered an inquiry instead,[65] rather than burden the FSA with another sensitive issue.[66] But all was not well. The mid-1980s were years of frenetic boom in the market, despite the Tory government's lowering of top tax rates, providing Lloyd's names with an incentive to place their personal wealth in less risky undertakings. Agents recruited names with modest means in a scramble to expand its capital. Cheap reinsurance meant primary insurers took on poor risks in the rush for market share, while catastrophe risks were shuffled around the syndicates. The DTI set up its own inquiry into the market, and suggested reducing the power of insiders, but fell short of proposing statutory control. Even the US Internal Revenue Service held a joint review with the United Kingdom's Inland Revenue about the goings-on in Lloyd's. Membership reached its peak at 32,000 in 1988. That year the bills began to roll in with a series of natural disasters, huge court claims for damages awarded in the United States and the onset of recession. By 1991, Lloyd's losses amounted to $7 billion.

Another lesson hard learned was the cost of leaving the task of policing the market to private agents, who also participated in it. As a general statement, it was no doubt true that all agents in the market would benefit from high standards, jointly kept. But the incentives in competitive markets stimulate on individual organisations to prosper and perhaps cut corners, involving a calculus of the costs and benefits. Evidently, many individuals or firms felt that the cost of providing evidence against competitors engaged in insider trading outweighed any benefits, in view of the difficulties experienced by the DTI in providing sufficient evidence to meet the rigorous standards of criminal justice required to bring cases of insider trading under the 1980 Act. The Company Securities

(Insider Trading) Act of 1985 failed to modify this weakness, despite the fact that government support at the time to create financial conglomerates made insider dealing more rather than less likely.[67] In part, this was remedied under the 1987 Criminal Justice Act, which gave new powers to a strengthened Serious Fraud Office to compel witnesses to give evidence. But the measure was controversial since it infringed an ancient right to silence in criminal proceedings. Powers to investigate and police were in any case dispersed across a variety of bodies, including the DTI, the SFA, the Director of Public Prosecutions and the Serious Fraud Office. Not least, the Bank of England relied, as did financial markets, on evidence from the auditors about the state of their clients' accounts. The 1987 Banking Securities Act, following the failure of auditors to alert the Bank about the true condition of JMB's finances, suggested that the auditor keep an open line of communication to the Bank. But there was no obligation to do so. The figurative chickens soon came home to roost, with the demise of the Lloyd's market, the Polly Peck and Guinness scandals, the Maxwell affair and the BCCI mess.

It was only when disaster struck in the form of the massive losses of 1988–91 that deep changes began to be implemented in Lloyd's. Revelations of shoddy standards and sharp practices undermined the trust of the names on which self-regulation relied. The only way to attract back capital was to open the doors to corporate money. But that spelled formal abandonment of the principle of unlimited liability and submitting to the rigorous requirements of corporations, themselves subject to the discipline of the equity markets. It also meant a fundamental revision of Lloyd's rule-book, and a new Act.

In retail investment services, the SIB's more assertive posture came after FIMBRA had gone bust and Robert Maxwell – in the summer of 1991, months before his death – had walked away with £400 million from his group pension fund to ward off the banks.

In wholesale markets, the Bank's handling of the BCCI case justified Mr Justice Bingham's critique that its responsibilities to police markets could not be delegated to auditors. Revision in 1992 of the law on insider trading saw a new emphasis placed on the option for civil action to be taken before a special court.[68] The City, in short, was edging towards acceptance of statutory law, involving the clear allocation of responsibilities between accountable authorities.

Summary

Transformation, absorption, autonomy and reform are the four characteristics of the British financial system of the 1990s.

- The system has been *transformed* from a figurative archipelago of cartelised islands to a competitive market for wholesale and retail investment or banking services.
- It has *absorbed* policies and initiatives emanating from the United States, with whose markets interdependence is close, and has become at the same time –

and in its own specific way – Europe's prime financial centre. What has emerged is a particular form of British capitalism, derived from inherited institutions and attitudes, from the US example and (with the creation of multi-purpose banks) comparable but still distinct from German universal banks. The system has been shaped by a state which has sought to sustain its autonomy over markets through a dual process of liberal economic policies and the slow but accretive concentration of powers in a two-tier regulatory framework.

• *Autonomy* has been maintained despite the massive presence of foreign institutions in the United Kingdom, through the medium of international negotiations with other regulators and by the *de-facto* preferential alliance between the Bank of England and the banks, evident in the privileges of the clearing banks and the position of the British merchant banks in securities markets (now mainly subsidiaries of British and continental commercial banks).

• Reforms have been implemented by serendipity in a costly process of learning by doing as accretive changes became open to further modifications through experience. This process won the City to accept some new and as yet undefined balance between authority, informality, law and markets, where powers are more clearly allocated between Treasury and Bank, and between the Bank, the DTI and the Securities Association and the PIA.

With clearer allocation of tasks comes the matter of accountability to parliament, and the broader constitutional issue of reform in the inherited constitution of the United Kingdom.

At the same time, the rhythm of reforms in the United Kingdom has been driven by domestic politics and markets, and the context of the world political economy. Membership of the EU played a marginal role in this process, although the UK representation in Brussels spent much time and energy from 1973 to 1986 – and the launch of the internal-market package – in pressing for greater liberalisation of financial services. By the time that negotiations on financial services were under way, in 1986–92, the broad design of UK regulation was already in place. Given the centrality of investment services for London, and the convergence of institutions from banking, insurance or unit trusts and pension funds on the markets, the central battles for the United Kingdom in the EU were fought over the content and timing of the investment services directives.

The Treasury, the Bank of England, the DTI and the SIB shared responsibility for UK policy towards the EU, supported by a City advisory committee. British negotiators were confronted by two major challenges relating to capital markets. One was the concern among security houses in the ISRO that EU legislation would be less rigorous than the new regulatory framework in the UK.[69] There was also concern that the central banks would impose capital ratios on securities firms that would benefit capital-rich banks. The other was the Commission's inclusion – with French support – of the reciprocity clause in the Second Banking

Directive. But it was not this internal market legislation or procedures which split the City and the Conservative Party so much as French, German and Commission support – with the backing of most other member states – for the project of the Social Chapter, and of monetary and political union. It was not over style so much as over substance, that British differences with the other member states waxed, rather than waned.

Notes

1 For a different slant, arguing from the perspective of 1983 that British governments had limited discretion in the face of Britain's dominant capital markets, see John Zysman, *Governments, Markets and Growth: Financial Systems and the Politics of Industrial Change* (Oxford: Martin Robertson, 1983).
2 Maximilian Hall, *The City Revolution: Causes and Consequences* (London: Macmillan Press, 1987); W. A. Thomas, *The Securities Market* (London: Philip Allan, 1989).
3 Jack Revell, *The British Financial System* (London: Macmillan, 1973).
4 J. S. Fforde, 'Competition, Innovation and Regulation in British Banking', *Bank of England Quarterly Bulletin*, Vol. 23, No. 3, 1983.
5 *Ibid.;* Michael Moran, *The Politics of Banking* (London: Macmillan, 1984) and K. K. Zawadzki, *Competition and Credit Control* (Oxford: Basil Blackwell, 1981).
6 Samuel Brittan, *Steering the Economy: The Role of the Treasury* (London: Penguin, 1971).
7 On the secondary banking crisis, see Moran, *Politics of Banking;* Margaret Reid, *The Secondary Banking Crisis, 1973–75* (London: Macmillan, 1982) and Zawadzki, *Competition and Credit Control.*
8 See the Trades Union Congress submission, 'The Institutions and the Industrial Challenge of the Eighties: The Need for a New Investment Strategy', to the 'Wilson Committee', *Committee to Review the Functioning of Financial Institutions* (Cmnd 7937, London: HMSO).
9 See John Grady and Martin Weale, *British Banking, 1960–85* (New York: St. Martin's Press, 1986) and Fforde, 'Competition, Innovation and Regulation in British Banking'.
10 *The Economist*, July 14, 1988.
11 J. S. Fforde, 'Competition, Innovation and Regulation in British Banking', p. 371.
12 *Financial Times*, June 29, 1985.
13 Paul Kennedy, *The Rise and Decline of the Great Powers: Economic Change and Conflict from 1500 to 2000* (London: Fontana, 1989).
14 William Clarke, *Inside the City* (London: George Allen & Unwin, 1979).
15 OECD Economic Surveys, *United Kingdom*, 1979.
16 W. B. Reddaway, S. J. Potter and C. T. Taylor, *Effects of UK Direct Investment Overseas* (Cambridge: Cambridge University Press, 1968).
17 United Nations, *Multinational Corporations in World Development* (New York: UN, 1973).
18 Barry Riley, 'Gilt Edged: A System Under Strain', *Financial Times*, October 30, 1976.
19 BIS, *Cinquantième Rapport Annuel*, Basle, June 9, 1980.
20 Nigel Lawson, 'No Quick-fix Solutions to Economic Problems', *Financial Times*, October 8, 1990.

21 Chancellor Lawson's words, quoted in the *Financial Times*, January 4, 1988.
22 Interview with the Prime Minister, *Independent*, November 23, 1987.
23 *Report of the Deutche Bundesbank for the Year 1989* (Frankfurt, 1989).
24 See DeAnne Julius, *Global Companies and Public Policy* (London: Frances Pinter, 1990), Table 2.4, p. 38. If these relations are converted into purchasing power parity GDP the global German and British stock of capital are about equal.
25 *Ibid.*, Table 3.3, p. 51. By comparison, in 1987, Britain attracted only 10 per cent of German outward foreign direct investment (FDI), *Financial Times*, April 20, 1989.
26 Chris Dillow, *A Return to Trade Surplus? The Impact of Japanese Investment on the UK* (London: Nomura Research Institute, 1989).
27 *Committee to Review the Functioning of Financial Institutions* (Cmnd 7937, London: HMSO), para. 1102.
28 Quoted by Moran, *Politics of Banking,* p. 30.
29 The Bank of England's submission to the Wilson Committee, 'The Secondary Banking Crisis and the Bank of England's Support Operations', *Bank of England Quarterly Bulletin*, Vol. 18. No. 2, 1978, pp. 230–6.
30 Moran, *Politics of Banking.*
31 Frank Welsh, *Uneasy City: An Insider's View of the City of London* (London: Weidenfeld & Nicolson, 1986).
32 Nigel Lawson, *The View From No.11, Memoirs of a Tory Radical* (London: Bantam Press, 1992).
33 *Report of the Committee Set up to Consider the System of Banking Supervision* (Cmnd 9550, London: HMSO).
34 *Financial Times*, October 23, 1992.
35 Robin Leigh Pemberton, quoted in the *Financial Times*, March 2, 1984.
36 *Financial Times*, January 16, 1982.
37 *Financial Times*, December 28, 1983.
38 'The Future Structure of the Gilt-Edged Market', *Bank of England Quarterly Bulletin*, Vol. 27, No. 2, 1984, pp. 513–17.
39 'Developments in Cooperation Among Banking Supervisory Authorities', *Bank of England Quarterly Bulletin,* Vol. 21, No. 2, 1981.
40 *Financial Times*, November 27, 1993.
41 *Financial Times*, October 9, 1978.
42 *The Economist*, June 15, 1985.
43 *Financial Times*, January 19, 1983.
44 L. C. B. Gower, Review of Investor Protection Report, Part I (Cmnd 9125, London: HMSO).
45 Labour members in the House of Commons Committee voted for legal immunities, in the hope of blocking government legislation to deprive the trade unions of their legal immunities.
46 Godfrey Hodgson, *Lloyd's of London* (Hardmondsworth: Penguin, 1986), pp. 307–24.
47 Hall, *The City Revolution.*
48 'Responsibilities of the private and public sectors', speech by the Deputy Governor of the Manchester Chamber of Commerce and Industry, *Bank of England Quarterly Bulletin*, Vol. 24, No. 4, 1984, pp. 500–2.
49 *Financial Services in the United Kingdom: A New Framework for Investor Protection* (Cmnd 9432, London: HMSO).

50 *The Economist*, June 25, 1988.
51 'As the institutions in the market', Nigel Lawson was quoted as saying in the House of Commons, 'see themselves as providers of financial services across the board, compartmentalised regulation of their separate activities makes less sense', quoted in *Financial Times*, July 4, 1984.
52 *Financial Times*, September 26, 1986.
53 *Financial Times*, March 14, 1992.
54 *Financial Times*, January 14, 1993.
55 *Financial Times*, February 7, 25, 1986.
56 *Financial Times*, March 29, 1989.
57 *Financial Times*, March 20, 1989; *Wall Street Journal*, March 9, 1989.
58 *Wall Street Journal*, March 5, 1990.
59 *Financial Times*, October 11, 1986.
60 *Financial Times*, October 23, 1992.
61 *Financial Times*, May 29, 1993.
62 *Financial Times*, October 12, 1992.
63 Interview with Robin Leigh Pemberton, *Financial Times*, June 23, 1993.
64 *International Herald Tribune*, September 19, 1984. The attraction for members of the Association of Futures Brokers and Dealers (AFBD) was a market for professionals where delinquents, it was argued, would be punished 'in the privacy of the City'.
65 *Report of the Committee of Inquiry, Regulatory Arrangements at Lloyd's* (Cm. 59, London: HMSO, 1987).
66 *Financial Times*, January 11, 1986.
67 Maximilian Hall, 'Reform of the London Stock Exchange: The Prudential Issues', *Banca Nazionale del Lavoro Quarterly Review*, No. 161, June 1987.
68 Lord Alexander, Chairman of NatWest, quoted in *Financial Times*, November 27, 1992.
69 The Chairman of Hambros, 'Chips' Keswick, at the IMF/IBRD meetings in Berlin in 1988, talked of the SIB's 'stifling and excessive bureaucracy'. *The Banker*, November 1988.

9

Building the European Financial Area

A major purpose of the EU programme to complete the internal market was the creation of a European Financial Area, which focused on eliminating restrictions on the movement of capital among the member states and establishing a legal framework for an EU-wide market for financial services. It was introduced at a time of rapid internationalisation of financial services, promoted in part by technological changes and innovations in products and markets.

The rhetoric of the EU Commission suggested a move to an internal market – by applying the device of mutual recognition – to introduce non-discrimination in practice among vendors of financial services, and predicated on liberal principles in broad conformity with the GATT. Yet the single market was legislated and implemented by member states with very different public policy communities, traditions, regulations and administrative practices. Each was bound in a specific way into European and world markets, and each had its cluster of financial and corporate institutions to protect or to promote. Negotiations therefore incorporated very different preferences, which gave rise to a spectrum of complementary, overlapping and contradictory political deals.

Negotiators wove multiple strands between distinct policy domains, once the internal-market process had gained momentum in the course of 1986. But because the stakes in the negotiations were so high – and the trust among negotiating states so low – the process contributed to the revival of competition between the states rather than to a common platform of financial services liberalisation. The Secretary-General of the European Banking Federation, Umberto Burani, was reported as saying that the home-country principle, supposedly the centrepiece of the financial services programme, 'has been introduced in no legislation'.[1]

The ambiguities of EU law bearing on financial services

In effect, the legal principles on which Commission policy for financial services came to be based were not as clear-cut as they may have appeared on the surface. The June 1985 White Paper, *Completing the Internal Market*, put forward a new strategy with regard to harmonisation of laws and procedures. Rather than continue to rely on previous attempts to force harmonisation of EU standards, the Commission adopted a new approach, involving harmonisation of only essential laws and regulations for goods and services. According to this approach, the harmonisation of essential standards was to provide the basis for member states' mutual recognition of equivalence of each other's laws, regulations and administrative practices that were not harmonised at the level of the EU. A corollary to mutual recognition was home-country control, whereby the regulations, laws and practices of the home country must be accepted as applying both to operations of branches and to cross-border provision of services.

The term 'mutual recognition' had already been deployed in Article 57.1 of the Rome Treaty, with reference to professional qualifications. Its elaboration into a serviceable policy doctrine followed from the failure to agree on harmonised standards in the draft directive on credit institutions in 1972. Under British influence, subsequent drafts concentrated 'on basic principles rather than details', and aimed 'to secure acceptance of the equivalence of national legislations rather than their replacement by European law'.[2]

The landmark case, which enabled the Commission to elaborate the concept on the basis of a European Court of Justice decision, was Cassis de Dijon.[3] The principle was formalised in the EU Second Banking Directive, which laid the groundwork for a European banking law. 'The basic approach', the Commission stated on introducing the draft,[4] 'is to realise the essential, necessary and sufficient harmonisation to achieve mutual recognition of systems of control by the country of origin and the granting of a single licence in the Community'.

Cassis de Dijon, the French liqueur manufacturer, had been excluded from the German market on the grounds that its alcoholic content was too low to classify as a liqueur under German law. The Court ruled that a member state may not apply national law to imported products which were lawfully produced and sold in other member states. The Court's judgement was, in fact, cautious and subject to much legal debate.[5] A further judgement in June 1980 prompted the Commission to issue a statement to the member states in October, whereby a product may be freely exported to another member state when it has been produced and commercialised in accordance with the principles and regulations of the exporting country. The principle found its way into the Single European Act (SEA), which stipulates that the Council 'may decide that the provisions in force in a member state must be recognised as being equivalent to those applied by another member state'.

In December 1986, the Court addressed similar issues in four insurance cases of central importance to the financial services area.[6] The Court elaborated on the essential harmonisation required for mutual recognition and home-country control in insurance, and established criteria for indicating permissible host-country restrictions on the cross-border provision of services.

A central issue in the four cases decided by the Court was the extent to which a member state was allowed to impose authorisation and regulatory requirements on firms operating in other states, which wished to provide cross-border services. The Court found that 'the insurance sector is a particularly sensitive area from the point of view of the protection of the consumer both as a policy-holder and as an insured person'. Consequently, the Court considered that there existed in the field of insurance 'imperative reasons relating to the public interest' that might justify restrictions on the provisions of services. The Court added that such restrictions had to apply to domestic and foreign firms alike, and that they could not be justified if they duplicated the rules of the home country.

The Court also distinguished between customers' need for protection, and the legitimate use of the public-interest clause to restrict the cross-border provision of services. In the case of small insurance policy-holders, protective measures, such as the introduction of thresholds by the member states in the taking of mutual coinsurance risks, were justified in cases where EU legislation did not provide sufficient harmonisation to ensure that the public interest was already protected by the home state. As Lord Cockfield stated,[7] the judgements allowed 'all those who want to insure industrial and commercial risks, to seek mutual insurance services installed in different states and to negotiate conditions, in the light of commercial considerations and on conditions of minimum restrictions'.

The Court also dealt with the claim of EU member states that Articles 59 and 60 on the free provision of services could not be introduced (directly applied) until the harmonisation requirements of Article 57 had been met. Referring to earlier cases, the Court found against such an interpretation. Insurance was deemed to fall within the domain of the internal market. Requirements for an insurance company to have an established presence in the member state in which it wanted to sell its services was 'the very negation' of the freedom to provide cross-border services. This was a direct repudiation of German insurance law, which ruled that it was a criminal act to place insurance with companies not licenced to operate in the country.

These insurance cases found their way in turn into EU legislation, but did not bury controversy[8] as to the distinction between 'large' and 'mass' risks and the definition of the public interest. Indeed, the judgements targeted the *public interest* as the key criterion for determining the legality of barriers to cross-border trade. They therefore touched on another principle which underpinned the Rome Treaty, namely that of non-discrimination on the basis of nationality. What this principle suggested is that firms from another member state would have the same opportunities as domestic counterparts with respect to host-country laws and regulations.

The EU had sought to implement non-discrimination by legislating comprehensive standards, but without success. Another approach was for member states to extend national treatment to firms such that they would face 'laws, regulations and administrative practices . . . no less favourable than that accorded in the situation to domestic enterprises'.[9] But such a definition of non-discrimination would have left twelve separate national markets with different rules and regulations. The principle, which lay at the root of the internal market strategy, was mutual recognition, whereby member states recognise each other's laws and practices as equivalent to their own, and thereby preclude the claim that doing things differently provides a legitimate reason for protection.

Negotiations about minimum standards and the need to harmonise them were bedevilled by disputes. Commission drafts suggested the adoption of home-country control for licensing and for prudential supervision. They also covered concerns related to the public interest. The implicit distinction between freedom of access to wholesale markets and consumer protection for retail markets begged the question regarding the relationship between the two. The boundaries were generously drawn around retail markets. An early draft of the Second Banking Directive, for instance, allowed host states to suspend activities of financial institutions providing services in its territory on public-interest grounds; in the final version, the institution wishing to set up shop had to notify the host authorities, provide a programme of activities, and wait for two months for the host country's permission. But the host country reserved the right of suspension if the institution was found not to be complying with its legal provisions.[10]

Another novelty in the Second Banking Directive was the distinction between the provision of services through subsidiaries and branches. Prior to its introduction, the cross-border provision of services had been viewed as falling within the category of liberalising capital movements. But a Court judgement of 1981 held that Article 67 for complete liberalisation of capital movements was not inherent to the Treaty (i.e. directly applicable), and therefore had to be implemented by directive.[11] This meant that the member states' preferences could be woven into the legislation. The liberal principle of *erga omnes* was applied to capital movements. The distinction between subsidiaries and branches in the Second Banking Directive became a central element in the struggle between member states to define an EU regime with regard to the United States and Japan. In conformity with Article 58 of the Treaty, subsidiaries would receive EU-wide licences. Branches of non-EU firms would receive only national treatment.

Indeed, conventional wisdom held that the principle of mutual recognition and market forces would interact to yield a convergence of regulations on a European norm.[12] Individual decisions on the part of financial institutions and consumers seeking to arbitrage different regulatory systems would substitute for the elusive search for harmonisation, and provide an incentive for governments to align the relevant public policies. This held in particular for the banking sector in that regulators had agreed on the list of activities which all banks could pursue across the EU markets. Given the uncertainties engendered by markets and regulatory redefinitions, it was not unreasonable to argue that, as banking stands on reputation and confidence, banks were better served by operating out of 'hard' rather than 'soft' regulatory environments.[13]

Negotiations, however, were permeated by fears that a combination of mutual recognition and market forces could lead to a 'competition in laxity'[14] among supervisory authorities. Such competition could arise out of government's reluctance to maintain prudential and supervisory standards stricter than the minimum required. It could arise from the limits to agreement between the member states as to the scope and content of EU regulation covering financial services. Competition between national interests, mediated through markets, could be expressed in divergent macroeconomic policies and performances – or through a generalised trend to prefer the safety and soundness of national arrangements, rather than to venture into a new and unknown common regime. Not least, there was no evident reason to suspect that market-oriented policies and regulatory convergence were necessarily complementary. Market-oriented policies would point towards equal access of all suppliers to markets, while regulatory convergence pointed to a negotiated compromise between different and competing policy communities – a compromise yielding special exemptions, escape clauses or defence privileges that were far from producing equal market access.

This was evident in the Commission's feeble attempts to extend the competence of competition policy into the financial services sector. EU-wide lobbying by credit institutions in late 1988 prompted the Commission to withdraw its proposals to extend the use of bank cards as substitutes for cheques. The German regulatory authorities had wording written into the Second Banking Directive that the role of banks as instruments of monetary policy fell under the public interest. The Second Banking Directive also contained Article 12.3, which stipulated that the limits on bank holdings of shares in non-financial firms need not be applied to holdings in insurance companies. In 1993, the Commission followed this up by agreeing to a bloc exemption of insurance from competition rules.[15] The politics of mutual recognition thus opened the door to oligopoly in the name of the public interest. That was defined primarily in national terms.

The European Financial Area as a tandem process

The Commission's proposal for a European financial area advanced in the course of 1985–86 represented a significant shift towards integration. As in preceding EU moves in that direction, the dual effort to confirm the customs union and to liberalise EU markets was accompanied by steps to liberalise capital movements, to stabilise exchange rates and to propose moves to monetary union.

Liberalisation of capital movements
For Jacques Delors, liberalisation of capital movements was a first step to legislating the rules for an internal EU market, distinct from ongoing global-market integration. His prime concern after the signing of the SEA in early 1986 was to implement Article 67 of the Rome Treaty. Without an end to capital controls, Bonn and London had made clear there would be no internal market and little prospect for further cooperation in the monetary field. The Commission duly presented its programme for a gradual end to capital controls on May 23, 1986.[16] In the first phase, France, Ireland and Italy were to conform by 1987 to existing rules, as defined in the May 1960 directive. Long-term commercial credits, secur-

ities transactions and collective investments were to be completely liberalised.[17] The second stage – ending all restrictions on short-term capital movements – was voted by the Council on June 24, 1988, enabling EU nationals to open a bank account in another member state, and to trade in stocks and shares. The measure was to come into effect on June 1, 1990.

Putting an end to capital controls clearly made currencies more susceptible to the collective judgements of financial markets. Not surprisingly, negotiations in early 1988 on ending capital controls betrayed EU member states' reservations. Safeguards became the main bone of contention. A number of governments were struggling with large public-sector deficits and feared the political consequences of having to cut back on budgetary outlays. This was particularly true in the case of Italy, Spain, Ireland, Greece and Portugal, which demanded transition periods. Bonn and London preferred no safeguards as a signal to the financial markets of the member states' seriousness of purpose. But the Commission, with the support of the reticent members, secured the insertion of Article 3.1 in the directive, which allowed for the reintroduction of safeguards for a period of six months, under the supervision of the Central Bank Governors and the Monetary Committees. This in turn prompted a certain degree of scepticism about member states' commitments.[18]

The negotiations on freedom of capital flows immediately revived old feuds in the EU between free traders and protagonists of a single internal market distinguishable from world markets. A prevalent concern held that without convergence on rigorous standards of supervision in financial markets, initial disparities would generate competition between systems and evasive behaviour by market participants.[19] As the May 1986 Commission paper on capital movements indicated, the objective *beyond* the establishment of a financial free-trade zone was to establish an EU-wide integrated financial space. This was to be achieved through minimum common rules to protect users of financial services. Indeed, in a speech in December 1986, Jacques Delors clearly distinguished between free trade in financial services and a 'European economic and financial space'.[20] The first entailed the elimination of remaining restrictions on capital flows, while the second required agreement on the new rules in the EU game along the lines of the White Book and the SEA.

An end to capital controls also exposed major differences among national tax regimes. This was a particularly awkward area for the Commission to address, since taxation lay within the domain of the member states' veto rights. Not only did tax levels and structures differ, but collection techniques also diverged widely between member states. French tax authorities, for instance, relied on banks for tax information. Liberalisation therefore entailed, from the French perspective, an alignment of national fiscal regimes and a transmission of information among EU financial institutions to prevent evasion, and France, with Italy in support, was the main champion of this view. But there was little backing for the idea in the Monetary[21] and Central Governors[22] Committees. EU taxation on capital income would prompt an outflow to offshore centres.[23] Luxemburg refused to tamper with its bank secrecy laws, another major cause of tax evasion in other member states. But France persisted, and won a commitment for the Commission to propose by June 1989 measures to align withholding and corporate taxation.

Another concern was that the opening of financial markets could unleash currency turbulence by sending volatile fund flows across frontiers. A constant refrain of the Commission, referred to in the May 1986 proposal, was for a consolidation of the EMS. But this could only be achieved by further convergence in economic policies, and a package deal between the three major member states, France, the United Kingdom and Germany. Repeatedly, Commission officials appealed to the British government to bring the pound sterling into the exchange-rate mechanism. But Prime Minister Thatcher remained adamantly opposed. Frequent references were also made to developing the ECU as a medium of exchange in the EU. But the Bundesbank, charged with management of Europe's key currency, had outlawed the ECU's use in Germany and used only dollars to intervene on foreign-exchange markets. France agreed to end all capital controls, and linked the move in June 1988 to 'the prospect', in Delors' words, 'of a common money and a common central bank'.[24]

Liberalisation of capital movements entailed a compromise between the German and British positions of markets open to the world, and the French aspiration to create a more exclusive internal financial space, subject to EC law and policy and clearly distinct from world markets. Whereas the French position referenced the 'specificity' of the EU financial space, German and British support for the internal market was only to be won by full acceptance of the principle of capital liberalisation *erga omnes*.[25] The text was less assertive. The June 1988 directive stipulated that the condition of *erga omnes* did not prejudice 'the application, towards third countries, of national rules and Community law with respect to conditions of reciprocity' regarding access to financial markets. Equally, member states were only beholden to consult on measures taken to deal with disruptive capital flows. Repeal of the 1972 directive, introduced at Germany's behest to take unilateral defensive measures against financial inflows, did not abrogate *de-facto* national powers of self-defence in the event of financial crisis.

The June 1988 directive also confirmed two principles – one of complete, unconditional and free movement of capital, and the other of non-discrimination based on nationality. But here too, due allowance was made for national susceptibilities. For reasons of monetary policy, the German government was determined to preserve a firewall between the domestic monetary base and short-term capital flows. 'In certain cases', the Central Bank Governors opined, 'limitations on access to the national market should be allowed to be maintained for legitimate motivations of monetary regulation'.[26] In other words, where legitimate national interests were at stake, they took precedence over EU cooperation. Similarly, the directive stipulated that all legislation designed to encourage national savings that afforded privileges to domestic over foreign securities had to be ended. This did not however prevent governments from encouraging domestic investors to buy national securities.

France and collective investment instruments

Nowhere was the French concern to regulate markets more evident than in securities. Coordination, interconnection and stability were the maxims of French policy in promoting an EU-wide capital market. The ground was laid in the July 1977 recommendation for a code of conduct designed to lay the basis for future legislation.[27] The Council of Ministers subsequently adopted directives in 1979,[28] 1980[29] and 1982[30] dealing with the coordination of terms of admission, the listing of particulars, and the periodic publication of information for access to capital markets. None of these measures were to apply to collective investment instruments, which the French government was carefully promoting at home with a view to attracting popular savings to the stock markets. Paris also backed Commission efforts to foster the 'interconnection' of national capital markets.[31] This led in 1984 to the launch of IDIS – the Inter-Bourse Data Information System – designed to transmit officially-quoted equity prices around the EU stock exchanges.

Only in 1985 was the French government prepared to vote with other Council members for a directive on provisions governing collective investment funds, initially advanced in 1976.[32] The directive borrowed heavily from the French 1979 law on unit trusts, notably in Article 19.1, which enumerated the different securities to be counted as assets of collective instruments. These happened to be the markets supervised by the COB,[33] the stock-market watchdog. The rules, which were to come into force in October 1989, promoted official quotations and referred only to instruments that were redeemable at the request of policy-holders. Licences were to be issued by the home-country authority, but host-country clearance was required for a fee and the authorised funds were to comply with host-country laws. Only firms headquartered in the EU and benefiting from mutual recognition could operate as fund managers. Furthermore, Article 1.7 enabled member states to submit funds to stricter rules in the name of consumer protection. Not least, the rules were not comprehensive but were sufficiently imprecise to provide ample room for discretion by member states in their interpretation.[34]

Not surprisingly, October 1, 1989 proved to be a great non-event. True, France accounted for 50 per cent of total EU unit trust assets. Since 1983 and the change in government policy, the funds had grown sixfold and accounted for one-tenth of stock-exchange capitalisation for equities and one-third for bonds. The funds were the most important institutional investors in the French market, ahead of insurance companies and pension funds.[35] But the directive was too timid to open EU markets to French banks, which – like their German counterparts – controlled four-fifths of the funds market, thereby sealing off the domestic client-base to penetration from abroad. Definitions of funds varied from country to country, as did legal status and regulatory provisions. Door-to-door selling was forbidden in Belgium and Luxemburg, and strictly regulated in Germany. Yet in Britain, direct marketing was the norm. Market access therefore varied between the extremes of impenetrability and virtually complete openness. Not least, only Britain, France, Luxemburg and Ireland had adopted the required implementing legislation by the October 1 deadline.

Nonetheless, the mutual funds directive, allied to the move towards EU liberalisation of capital movements, had considerable effects on domestic policies. The most prominent of these was the attractiveness of fund management embodied in the low tax provisions of Luxemburg, prompting the French, Belgian and Italian governments in June 1988 to elicit an agreement from member states to examine common tax measures on interest and dividend income. There ensued a fierce debate across the EU, whose member states' tax systems varied greatly one from another. The Commission, with French backing, proposed that a 15 per cent withholding tax on interest income be applied across the EU.[36] But Britain, the Netherlands and Luxemburg were opposed, while the German Finance Ministry launched its own experiment in autumn 1988 with a 10 per cent interest-withholding tax. DM funds flooded into Luxemburg, until the measure was reversed in April 1989 following a cabinet reshuffle in Bonn. The idea of harmonising taxes was quietly shelved, with the Finance Ministers agreeing in June 1989 to seek alternative ways of cooperation and more effective measures against money laundering.

France's failure to get agreement on an upward realignment of taxation across the EU pointed to a downward realignment of national tax rates. Luxemburg remained the centre of attention. After the 1982 global debt crisis put paid to its previous success as a centre for syndicated loans, the Eurobond market drifted off to London and Luxemburg refocused on private banking and fund management. Funds registered in the country were exempted from taxation. Investors paid no withholding tax on dividends and a 1983 law recognised the French-type Société d'Investissements à Capital Variable (SICAVs). In March 1988, Luxemburg became the first EU member state to ratify the directive on collective investments, opening the prospect for Luxemburg to become the centre for marketing funds throughout the EU. By this time Luxemburg had attracted 132 foreign banks, of which 37 were German and 16 were Scandinavian. Alongside this, Luxemburg was home to 506 mutual funds, up from 76 registered in 1980.[37] Luxemburg licenced 130 new funds in 1988, and another 115 by October 1989.[38] As Luxemburg's then prime minister, Jacques Santer, pointed out,[39] competition in Europe's financial space would determine which financial centre won out. There were no provisions, he said, in EU law for cooperation between tax authorities.[40] Evasion and avoidance of its EU partners' taxes was clearly Luxemburg's source of competitive advantage.

The months leading up to October 1989 therefore witnessed a spate of reforms to galvanise French mutual funds and to keep them at home. Even the prospect of free movement of capital led individuals in all higher-tax EU countries to focus on Luxemburg as the least demanding country for capital income taxes. French collective investment instruments in France were no longer obliged to hold 30 per cent of their assets in Treasury bonds, but were allowed to place them all in equities.[41] The 1989 budget also abolished tax payment on coupons by French UCITs, encouraging banks to convert them into capital-appreciation funds which did not distribute interest as current income. Instead, the interest could be paid in the form of capital gains subject to 17 per cent rather than 27 per cent income tax. This reduced the incentive to move to Luxemburg. On September 7, 1989 a decree had each UCIT limited to a 1.5 per cent gap between its liquidating value and its market price. The measure reduced the risk related to purchase, and resale of UCITs on the stock exchange – an option that was very attractive to conservative investors. The Ministry of Finance had done every-thing to keep capital in France through a policy of the hard franc, lower taxation and an attractive savings policy.

The Second Banking Directive

The Second Banking Directive presented by Lord Cockfield in January 1988 was the centrepiece of the EU's legislation on financial markets. The Directive's key feature was the abandonment of any prior requirement to harmonise existing laws, and substitution of the principles of mutual recognition and home-country control. The principle of mutual recognition held that once agreement had been reached on essential rules, each member state would have to recognise the valid-ity of rules applying in other countries. Member states would not apply all aspects of their own laws to subsidiaries or branches of banks based in other member states operating on their own territory. The corollary was mutual recognition of home-country authorities, who would supervise operations of firms doing business in the territories of other member states, either through their local representations or by exercising their right to provide freedom of ser-vices. The key to implementing this provision was the issuance of a licence (single passport) which would be valid for banking business throughout the EU.

One of the most controversial matters in the negotiations was the scope of the Directive. In the preliminary discussions, the Commission's position was that the Directive should provide comprehensive and uniform legislation for universal banks, which reflected the banking practice of a majority of member states. The final list annexed to the Directive ensured that universal banks could pursue securities business in their own name. But it fell short of being the single, definitive banking law for the internal market. Britain and Italy, where specialised institutions played a key role, feared their inclusion in a law designed for universal banks. The French and German authorities wanted to exclude their state-controlled development and housing banks. The directive's definition of 'credit institutions', lifted from the First Banking Directive of 1977, excluded central banks, postal savings banks and state and mortgage banks in Germany, as well as the CdC, Crédit Foncier and Crédit National in

France[42] – in other words, whole swathes of the French and German financial system.

The battle over the scope of the Directive ignited another over the treatment of investment houses, for which the Commission created an *ad-hoc* directive for investment services (ISD).[43] The working definition of financial institutions as opposed to credit institutions was included – important for implementing the conditions under which mutual recognition would apply. Both Commission and member states were concerned that a simple extension of the right to mutual recognition would have advantaged banks from London or Luxemburg, where regulation was lighter. The Directive therefore stipulated that a bank could enjoy mutual recognition for the activities enumerated in an agreed list, and through its subsidiaries on certain conditions. These included: (1) the legality of the activity in the host-country; (2) the inclusion of the subsidiary in the parents' consolidated accounts; and (3) the way in which the activities would be exercised.

A major innovation was the Second Banking Directive's provision for a 'single banking licence'. The First Banking Directive had already enabled host states to demand minimum capital adequacy as a precondition for granting licences for branches of credit establishments in other member states. The provision perpetuated the status quo, leaving member states the discretion to open or close their financial markets to outsiders. The Second Directive stipulated that a credit institution's activities throughout the EU could be licenced, regulated and supervised by the home country. This immediately triggered a struggle – discussed below under reciprocity and market access – over whether non-EU banks should benefit. It was eventually agreed that only *subsidiaries* of non-member state banks could be armed with a single licence and fall under home-country control. Branches of third-country banks would continue to fall under host-country law.[44]

The member states' determination to retain discretionary powers was evident in the prolonged wrangles over minimum regulatory standards. National authorities were concerned that banks might base their activities in the country with the lowest standards of supervision. The outcome was a significant modification of the home-country principle with respect to five crucial areas of prudential supervision.

• One disincentive for EU-wide branching by banks had been the First Directive's requirement for branches to maintain a minimum level of primary capital. This was abolished in the Second Banking Directive. But home-country control of branches was not enthroned without restrictions. Host countries could still deny licences to institutions with capital under 5 million ECUs, although the United Kingdom insisted that 'particular categories of credit establishments' with minimal capital over that amount could be licenced. The principle of home-country control was established, but host-country powers were preserved. Article 19 spelled out in some detail the procedures to open business in other member states, subject to a general-interest clause which the host state could invoke in defining a given area of activity. The host state could require the provision of extensive information from the bank operating on its territory, and in particular retained the power to close the credit institution's operations if these were deemed to be contrary to the general interest.

- The Directive on Own Funds, introduced in 1986, was modified by the Commission to increase its powers of discretionary supervision, in line with its reading of the SEA.[45] Its content did not differ materially from the measures introduced by the regulatory authorities under the aegis of the Bank for International Settlements (BIS). Not surprisingly, the member states insisted on keeping powers of implementation in the hands of the Bank Advisory Committee.[46] The French government also pushed for a softer EU definition of own funds – softer than that agreed in June 1988 in the BIS – in order to ease the constraints on lending by its undercapitalised banks.[47] The Federal Republic, the United Kingdom, the Netherlands and Luxemburg were allied in favour of a stricter definition.[48] Nonetheless, a compromise was reached, allowing for a unanimous vote in Council.[49] Each member state was free to apply stricter criteria.

- A separate directive on solvency requirements for banks was proposed in April 1988, and finally agreed on in December 1989.[50] It ran parallel to similar negotiations in the BIS. The solvency directive required all EU banks to maintain own funds equal to 8 per cent of risk-weighted assets as a prerequisite to receiving a licence as the basis for home-country control. Germany, Greece and Denmark won temporary derogations on the solvency ratios for mortgage-backed loans. More significantly, host-countries remained responsible for controlling market risk for all financial institutions in their territory.[51] This meant that specialised credit institutions operating in the interbank and public debt markets – and facing mainly foreign-exchange and interest-rate risks – were excluded from the directive. The Bundesbank could thereby retain discretion over participation in the DM bond market, while the UK and French Treasuries retained discretion over which institutions acquired primary dealerships.

- One of the most delicate issues on the Second Banking Directive agenda involved limits on bank equity holdings in financial and non-financial firms. Germany, backed by Spain, Greece and the Netherlands,[52] won a victory favouring bank–insurance links and extensive equity participations in non-financial firms. During the Spanish EU presidency of early 1989, agreement was finally reached on ceilings of 15 per cent (Article 12.1) and 60 per cent (Article 12.2). Credit institutions with excess holdings were granted a ten-year grace period. Furthermore, the thresholds could be exceeded as long as the excess was 100 per cent covered by own funds, which were not included in the solvency ratio. Indeed, Article 12.3 exempted bank holdings in insurance companies from the thresholds. This meant that a bank could raise the capital of an insurance subsidiary by allocating excess stakes in commercial companies, and that the increase in its capital holding in the insurance company would be exempt from threshold requirements. The way was thus open to the formation of national financial conglomerates.

• The last of the accompanying directives to the Second Banking Directive involved large exposures, which illustrated the increasingly complex overlaps between banks, insurance and investment houses. Given the passage of the Second Banking Directive, the Commission decided that the recommendation on large exposures as from 1987[53] required redefinition. The Commission initially sought to tilt the draft in favour of greater competition in the internal market, reducing the definition of large exposure for reporting purposes from 15 per cent to 10 per cent own funds, any single exposure reduced from 40 per cent to 25 per cent, and the cumulative amount of loans limited to no more than 800 per cent own funds. The British defended the competition corner on the grounds of prudential considerations. The French and Germans defended the 'bancassurance' corner on the grounds that sudden changes would adversely affect the loan portfolios of banks.[54] The compromise placed limits on loans to clients after 1994 at 40 per cent, coming down to 25 per cent in 1999, with further delays stretching to 2007.[55]

The Second Banking Directive, together with the own-funds and solvency directives, were all adopted by the Council of Ministers in December 1989 under the French Presidency. They were presented as heralding a new EU world in banking, where the home-country principle held sway. In fact, the negotiations revealed the determination of member states to preserve as much as possible of their host-country powers, as evidenced in the large exposures discussions. The Second Banking Directive's reference to the general interest signalled a consensus on host-country responsibility for monetary policy and for banking solvency, including its linkage to the securities business. The host country retained the power to sanction an offending institution by not granting a licence or by suspending its activities. A bank could do business which was not recorded in the Directive's approved list only with the permission of the host country. The list could also be extended. Legislation did not alter the preconditions for joint supervision of markets by national authorities. These included a degree of trust and a readiness to share information among regulatory authorities.

The insurance directives

The European Court's jurisprudence in December 1986 revived the EU legislative process on insurance. The Commission presented a first draft for annual consolidated accounts. Progress towards more open markets required investors to be able to assess insurance company accounts. Requests for extensive revisions[56] led to an amended version in October 1989, with the Council of Ministers finally reaching a common position in June 1991.[57] Germany and Britain were granted a transition period until 1997 to adapt. German insurers wanted to continue basing accounts on historical costs of assets, which enabled them to build up huge hidden reserves, estimated as a notional difference between historic acquisition price and current market price. The compromise was to allow a choice between historic and market-value accounting. A similar transition was granted to Lloyd's syndicates, whose competitors were well aware of the risks incurred by Lloyd's in changing from a system of global accounts published every three years to annual reporting.[58]

The December 1986 judgements on insurance also enabled the Commission to review the second non-life insurance directive, which had languished since its first presentation in draft in 1975. Its legislative passage proved surprisingly rapid. A compromise was reached by the Council of Ministers in December 1987 and February 1988 on interpreting the Court's verdicts on the four insurance cases. The German Presidency then steered the directive through the new procedures introduced under the SEA. Bonn linked the non-life directive to the liberalisation of capital movements. Large firms were free to guarantee industrial risks with the insurance company of their choice. Both insurers and insured would be allowed to choose the governing law of their contract. Debts set aside for future payments, known as technical provisions, would be constituted according to the rules for country of origin. The tax regime of the country where the risk occurred would apply. The revised draft was adopted by the Internal Market Council on June 22, 1988.[59]

Despite its title, the directive did not secure the free EU-wide provision of insurance services.[60] Rather the text encapsulated a set of political compromises. A coalition centred around Germany and the United Kingdom sought to lower the threshold separating 'large' from 'mass' risks, but had to compromise with a southern coalition, led by France, on a definition of a 'large company' as employing 500 workers with a turnover of 24 million ECUs. Both qualifying levels for the category of 'large' were to be halved in January 1993. Spain was granted exemptions until 1997, and Greece, Ireland and Portugal until 1999.[61]

Article 13 of the Insurance Directive sought to conciliate the right of headquarters to provide complex services beyond the reach of its local branch, and the assurance given to Italy that all business would have to pass through branches.[62] Indeed, the entire text was imbued with the primacy of national law, not least in all risks, whose 'social repercussions' made them inappropriate for EU law – the law applicable to any obligatory insurance was that of the state itself.

Modest reference was paid to the principle of home-country control. The provision of insurance services would not be subordinated to the granting of a licence. Insurers had to provide certificates, delivered by the home-country authorities, attesting to their solvency, the activities to be pursued, and the risks to be insured. Companies could open for business as soon as the documents were handed over. But the host state retained discretionary powers, even the possibility of direct control by host-country authorities. In the area of mass risks, the power to grant licences constituted the legal act which opened the market to the insurer. This was all the more so with regard to non-EU insurers – subsidiaries or agencies of firms based outside the EU fell under host-country control. Only EU-registered firms were to benefit by the free provision of services in large risks. Not surprisingly, in view of this evidence of minimal trust between member states, many states had not implemented the necessary legislation by July 1, 1990, when the second non-life insurance directive came into effect.[63]

The motor-insurance directive,[64] incorporated in the White Book, also ended up favouring host-country controls. The first[65] and second[66] directives had introduced personal, then physical cover across all member states, suppression of green-card checks at frontiers, and cooperation between national insurance bureaux. The draft third motor-insurance directive aimed to define a minimum standard insurance premium for the EU as a whole.[67] The United Kingdom and the Netherlands insisted on the right for insurers to prospect for business across the EU. France, Germany and their allies in the European Parliament[68] emphasised host-country control and maximum coverage for accidents. The final compromise entailed a single premium for the EU, with host-country discretion over 'large' and control for 'mass' risks. Greece, Spain, Portugal and Ireland were granted transition periods until 1996 and 1998, respectively. As the consumer's associations pointed out,[69] the directive would have little effect on the motor insurance market, which was mainly one of mass risks.

Negotiations on the second life insurance directive,[70] presented in December 1988 and adopted by the Internal Market Council in November 1990, illustrated even more clearly the legislative dimension of a broader struggle for market share between EU firms, backed by their respective states. The domain impinged on the politically sensitive terrain of members' social policies. Treatment of insurers based in third countries proved particularly controversial (discussed below). France led a coalition in favour of taxation on insurance premiums in the state where the liability was assumed.[71] The United Kingdom, Italy and the Netherlands failed to avoid continued restrictions on EU-wide activities of multibranch insurance firms which provided life as well as non-life services. Pensions were excluded from the legislation – indeed, discussions on a separate pensions directive ran into the sand of discord, given the political sensitivity of pension policy in the member states. Group insurance contracts were subject to a transitional period until 1995. And provisions were made for insurers from other EU countries to compete on a more or less level playing-field with their German and Danish counterparts, who fell under bank supervision and already benefited from the Second Banking Directive.

The central conflict was over the role of insurance brokers, with the United Kingdom pitted against Germany. Life insurance in the United Kingdom placed a special emphasis on door-to-door selling. In Germany, insurance distribution was tied up by banks and associated life-insurance groups. Legislation effectively cut off the retail markets from foreign salesmen. How was the EU to ensure market access for British or Dutch brokers, and to maintain German standards for consumer protection? The Commission proposed two regimes, depending on whether the provision of services was 'passive' or 'active'. In the first case, policy-holders contract with an insurer abroad, subject to the latter's home law. When the insurer actively prospects to sell policies to individuals in other member states, both the firm and the buyer in effect fall under host-country law. As German delegations argued, brokers were interested in the hard sell rather than in offering advice in their client's interest.[72] It was eventually agreed that the Directive would come into effect in 1993, but brokers would be able to offer their services around the EU from 1996 on. 'Passive' rights could only be exercised thereafter, whereas the active provision of services could be exercised – but the technical provisions would be subject to the rules of the state where the service was rendered.

Many of the insurance directives had not been implemented when the Commission in late 1989 launched a new campaign of so-called 'third genera-tion' directives in a further attempt to break down national market-access restrictions. *Ex post facto*, the 'second generation' directives provided for cross-frontier business under host-country control. The principle of home-country control entered into the legislation with regard to 'large' risks, and individuals ready to take out insurance policies abroad. 'Mass' insurance markets and the regulation of branches of foreign companies remained subject to host-country regulation. Markets therefore remained segmented along a spectrum of member states, restricting consumer choice in the name of consumer protection. One factor militating in favour of more liberal EU markets was the fear among insur-ers that banks had their single EU-wide passport first, and could encroach on their markets.[73] Another was the continued backing in the Commission and from the United Kingdom for more complete market access.

The third life insurance directive was adopted in May 1992,[74] under the Portuguese Presidency, with the non-life directive following in June 1992.[75] Both fitted more neatly the design of an open insurance market, predicated on a single licence supplied by the home country. But France retained the power to license branches of insurance companies from non-EU member states. The principle of home-country control was to be extended to include individuals. In both direc-tives, the aspiration for uniform rules on technical reserves was abandoned in favour of mutual recognition of regulations among the member states. Both listed the types of assets which could be held by insurance companies, and the life directive provided that member states might not require a proportion of assets to be invested in state bonds. Consumer choice was confirmed in that com-panies could prospect for business across the entire spectrum of insurance ser-vices, but consumer protection was ensured by the continued weight given to host-country law. The usual transition periods were granted for Spain, Greece and Portugal, as well as for a ban on setting up new branches for multi-branch business until 1999.

Overall, the insurance directives laid the basis for more open insurance markets, requiring closer cooperation between regulatory bodies and institutions of the member states. The latter retained substantial powers, as evidenced in the pervasiveness of host-country law, the public-interest clause and a newly instituted Insurance Committee. But EU legislation and jurisprudence also paved the way for greater opportunities for insurance business beyond the confines of national markets, by associating both consumer choice and consumer protection. The prospect of greater competition was to be balanced by corporate collaboration – by presenting the new bloc exemption from EU competition rules for the insurance sector, the Commission noted that the measures allowing firms to collaborate and to form groups completed the 'third generation' programme.[76]

The investment services directives

The last of the three main EU financial regimes to be agreed covered investment services. The Commission first advanced the idea of legislation in December 1986. Its draft, proposed in December 1988,[77] provided for the unrestricted provision of services and establishment based on the internal market principles. The Commission proposed a draft directive on capital adequacy for securities firms in April 1990,[78] defining minimal amounts of initial capital and a regime for supervising market risks. Germany and the United Kingdom, the two main protagonists, finally struck a deal in the course of 1992–93 concerning primary capital and large exposures. The directives on investment services[79] and capital adequacy[80] were to enter into effect in January 1996.

The Second Banking Directive's narrow definition of a credit establishment had threatened to exclude non-banks from a wide range of cross-border services. Only banks appeared to be authorised to operate freely in all EU stock markets. Non-bank securities firms were not covered. The fourth investment services draft, proposed by the Commission in winter 1988, aimed to overcome this deficiency.[81] Unlike its predecessors, the draft specifically addressed market access. Investment houses, defined as 'any legal or natural person', were to be supervised by the home country with respect to a list of activities, including financial futures, options and money-market instruments. No mention was made of whether the business was to be conducted on-floor or off-floor. Subsequent lobbying in the course of 1989 prompted the Commission to define investment houses so as to ensure that industrial and commercial firms dealing in securities on their own account were not included in the directive. This meant that a large section of cross-frontier business escaped regulation.

Other sources of controversy lay in the balance between home- and host-country powers of supervision. As in previous directives, lack of trust and disagreements over fundamental matters of market regulation meant that the promise of direct access to stock markets would prove less easy to achieve than the directive's supporters had hoped for.[82] Member states ensured that the balance tilted in favour of host-country supervision.

• One area of disagreement was access to equity markets. Germany admitted only banks. The directive required host states to ensure that authorised investment firms enjoy 'the full range of trading privileges' reserved to national members of stock exchanges. The result was a compromise, delaying until 1996 the time when banks from Italy, Belgium or France could operate directly through a broker or a subsidiary on EU stock exchanges. As in other legislation, this transition period brought member states in line to update their financial market arrangements.

- The lack of common agreed standards on supervising investment firms impinged on the compromises required to obtain agreement on home-country control and the issue of securities licences. The United Kingdom had opposed any role for home-country regulators in matters relating to conduct of business.[83] Eventually, investment firms were allowed to obtain their licences from the home country on the basis of adequate financial resources, reputability and competence.[84] The Directive even allowed home-country authorities to conduct on-the spot verification of the information supplied by state authorities. And the 'public interest' clause was there to protect host states.
- The states were also far apart on transparency rules to regulate disclosure of stock trades. France led a majority of member states,[85] which insisted that transparency was only possible if brokers were required to publish information within two hours of their transactions. London, dominant in wholesale stock trading until the early 1990s, when reforms in Paris and Frankfurt led to a repatriation of equity trades,[86] insisted that its market-makers be permitted to delay or to suspend disclosures. The ultimate compromise allowed for both.[87]
- One particularly delicate matter was the organisation of markets. France, Italy and Spain urged on-market regulation of stock-markets, while the United Kingdom, Germany and the Netherlands agreed with the Commission that operators be granted the greatest possible freedom of access to off-floor markets.[88] These were the markets which the northern countries insisted be exempt from strict transparency regulations.

This series of compromises produced a particularly complex regulatory package, which in effect threatened to enthrone competition between public policies. Not surprisingly, the Commission's biggest headache proved to be disputes over the harmonisation of capital adequacy. The draft capital adequacy directive, presented in April 1990, proposed to establish minimum amounts of initial capital and to define a common framework for supervising market risks.[89] The new directive was to apply both to banks and to investment houses. As defined by Commissioner Leon Brittan, the aim was fourfold: (1) to establish common financial conditions to allow investment firms to operate; (2) to ensure that banks and investment houses be subject to equivalent rules of capital adequacy; (3) to preserve the international competitiveness of the EU financial sector; and (4) to guarantee appropriate protection for investors.

As Brittan admitted, the search for common rules to cover the disparate traditions of member states had occasioned 'long, difficult and sometimes bitter discussions'.[90] The most marked differences were between Germany and the United Kingdom. In Germany, banks were subject to high minimum capital requirements along BIS lines, but no separate capital was required for securities dealings or to back equity holdings. Banks insisted that investment houses be subject to similar requirements in order to ensure equal treatment and to reduce risk. In the United Kingdom, firms providing financial services competed with low initial capital, topped up by additional funds to cover position risk (movements in market prices that reduce securities' valuation). British investment houses argued that German conditions would restrict competition in the markets, and there were suspicions that the proposed legislation on capital adequacy was designed to undermine London's international status.

The Bundesbank's view was that banks and security houses had to be subject to the same rules before receiving their EU passport. But this begged the question of whether the rules should reflect the German concern to subordinate non-bank investment houses to the same requirements as banks, or the British propensity to adapt rules to the particular conditions facing investment houses. The Commission came around to the view that the best way to ensure equivalence of treatment for banks and investment houses was to give the regulatory authorities a choice, whether the operations of banks in securities activities should be subject to the solvency rules already elaborated for banks, or to separate portfolio operations and submit them to specific rules for capital adequacy of investment houses. Compromise satisfactory to German and British negotiators was reached on this 'modular' approach in June 1992,[91] covering definitions of large exposures, own funds and negotiable securities.

One of Sir Leon Brittan's central objectives was to preserve the international competitiveness of the EU financial sector. This also meant protecting the City of London from regulations which would endanger the future of its wholesale markets. The major threat came from an alliance between the Bundesbank and the Federal Reserve, which preferred to stick to the BIS capital-adequacy formula of 1988. SEC President Richard Breeden described the EU's 'modular approach' as 'dangerous'.[92] The central bankers tended toward caution, given their concern about the systemic effects of bank collapse. London security regulators had firms without depositors under their supervision, where competition and pricing was a prior concern. There was also the threat from the US securities houses in London that, if the capital-adequacy and large-exposure directives should write rules to prevent securities firms from underwriting major Eurobond new issues, they would take the business elsewhere.[93]

A final objective was to guarantee protection to investors. There were two ways to achieve this.

• One approach was to establish a level playing-field. But the Commission's 'modular approach' offered commercial banks an opportunity to split commercial from securities business. This challenged the principle of consolidated supervision, which allowed the Bundesbank to regulate all subsidiaries in one group. It also opened the door to a split-up of universal banks and the development of a less malleable securities market in Frankfurt. Since the commercial banks provided vital conduits for the Bundesbank in control over monetary aggregates, there was an evident official reluctance to encourage any weakening in the bank cartel which watched over the Frankfurt markets.

• A second way to secure protection for investors was for host countries to take *de-facto* charge over their own markets. The prerequisite to establishing a common language between investment-services regulators was to strengthen supervision over their respective national jurisdictions. In parallel, the regulators would have to exchange information and ideas on the operations and structures of markets. Since they represented mutually interdependent but often competing constituencies, it was reasonable to argue that the final result of the investment services directives was 'a very detailed legislation, an attempt to harmonise diverse interests, that could prove very difficult to implement in the coming years'.[94]

Brokers and cross-border payments

If there was a domain where state policies channelled markets, it was in the domain of transfrontier payments. The programme to liberalise capital movements – linked by the Commission to the creation of a 'Europe of citizens' – pointed the way to an integrated market where financial intermediaries would be free to operate.[95] The major markets were the United Kingdom and the Netherlands, where brokers accounted for over 50 per cent of the insurance markets, as against 16 per cent in Germany, 13 per cent in Spain and 2 per cent in Italy.[96] Insurance in the latter markets passed through the hands of tied agents, with responsibility for a particular territory. Even so, the Rome Treaty and European Court of Justice indicated that discriminatory treatment on the basis of nationality, with regard to the establishment and provision of services, had been prohibited since 1970. But little had been achieved in the way of market-opening for brokers by 1993, when the internal market was supposed to come into effect.

National regulators effectively remained the guardians of established practices. The 1977 brokers' directive, allowing for the right of establishment but maintaining national discretion over professional qualifications,[97] was so modest that many states forget to put it on to the statute book. The distinction between 'active' and 'passive', introduced by the Commission in the difficult negotiations on the second life directive, was in effect a debate about insurance brokers. The German delegation had to be satisfied that all possible precautions had to be taken to protect consumers of insurance against brokers.[98] The conclusion was that the broker had to be a pure intermediary, an adviser, and not representing an insurance company. Germany also insisted on a transition period – before the introduction of the liberal regime in 1996 – during which member states were to legislate for consumer protection. In 1991, the Commission simply recommended

that the brokers be subject to registration and meet national professional requirements.[99]

A similar fate afflicted the Commission's programme, announced in March
1992, to facilitate transfrontier payments. A notable objective was to ensure that
users have access to procedures equivalent to those in a national payments
system.[100] The consumer's associations reacted sceptically, pointing out the programme was not binding. Indeed, their position that national protection still prevailed[101] received confirmation in a report which suggested that the principles of
mutual recognition and minimal harmonisation of standards – on which the
internal-market programme was based – had created a legislative framework
within the EU in which laws for banks and insurance companies continued to
vary considerably.[102] Furthermore, member states had in many instances not
implemented the legislation. Not least, the continued prevalence of legislative
diversity, rooted in separate institutions, indicated that the development of financial markets in Europe would continue to be largely shaped by the diverse policies of the states.

Summary

The EU member states negotiated a broad framework of laws for a European
financial area on the basis of the European Court of Justice's jurisprudence and
the principles of policy incorporated in the Single European Act. A European
legal space for financial agents and consumers of financial services would serve
to thwart the financial mercantilism practised in different forms by the member
states. Some achievements were recorded. In the language of economics, there
were welfare gains to be expected from the liberalisation of capital movements.[103] The Second Banking Directive ended the requirement on branches of
EU subsidiaries to maintain separate endowment capital for their activities. The
third generation of insurance directives secured rather more open markets,
requiring closer cooperation between member-state authorities. The investment
services directives provided for easier access to securities markets by 1996.
Institutions would be able to operate across boundaries and in the same markets,
but under different home member states' regulations and controls. There was to
be a continued diversity of legislative practice, but policies shaped by member
states were to be aligned with reference to EU law.

Bank regulators, from their central position within the fabric of EU bureaucracies, set the pace and tone of the process on the grounds that there was evident
need for joint supervision of markets by member-state authorities. They faced a
fragmented universe of functional lobbies, eager to provide information and
fearful that competing interests might steal a legislative advantage. Negotiations
in the EU incorporated the different preferences of the states, which was mani-
fest in the host of exemptions, the discretionary powers retained, the importance
attached to national ownership, the reluctance to share information, and the
many distinctions written into the texts to nail down the boundaries of EU

legislation. Particularly delicate balances were struck over the limits to cross-frontier trade, and the 'cohesion and specificity' of the European financial area. The principal benefactors of the legislation were corporate investors and wholesale markets. Legislation firmed up London's position as Europe's prime financial centre, but gave Paris and Frankfurt the time to update their facilities. The European financial area legislation was thus a process igniting competition between financial centres embedded in their distinct national financial systems. It fuelled the multi-dimensional 'Battle of the Systems'.

Notes

1 *Europolitique,* No. 1851, April 17, 1993.
2 Statement of Robin Hutton, Director of Banking, Insurance and Financial Institutions in the Commission, quoted in *Financial Times,* December 5, 1977.
3 *Rewe-Zentral AG* v. *Bundesmonopolverwaltung für Branntwein (Cassis de Dijon),* Case 120/78,1979 Eur. Ct Repts, 649, 1979 Common Mkt L. Repts, 494.
4 *Les Echos,* October 22, 1987.
5 Jean Claude Masclet, 'Les Articles 30, 36 et 100 du Traité CEE à la Lumière de l'Arret "Cassis de Dijon". Cour de Justice des CE, 20 Fevrier 1979', *Revue Trimestrielle de Droit Européen,* Paris No. 4, 1980, pp. 611–34; 'L'Arret "Cassis de Dijon". Une Nouvelle Approche Pour la Réalisation et le Bon Fonctionnement du Marché Interieur', *Revue du Marché Commun,* No. 241, 1980.
6 *Re Insurance Services: EC Commission* v. *Germany,* Case 205/84, 1987 Common Mkt L. Repts, 69; *Re Co-insurance Services: EC Commission* v. *France,* Case 220/83, 1987 Common Mkt L. Repts, 113; *Re Co-insurance Services: EC Commission* v. *Ireland,* Case 206/84, 1987 Common Market L. Rpts, 150; *Re Insurance Services: EC Commission* v. *Denmark,* Case 252/83, 1987 Common Mkt L. Rpts, 169.
7 J.O. C23/7, Réponse Donnée par Lord Cockfield au Nom de la Commission, 6.7.1987.
8 *Europolitique,* No. 1355, November 7, 1987.
9 Definition given in the OECD's National Treatment Instrument.
10 J.O. L386, 30.12.1989, Articles 19, 21.
11 See Jean-Pierre Baché, 'La Libération des Mouvements de Capitaux et l'Intégration Financière de la Communauté', *Revue du Marché Commun,* No. 304, 1987.
12 'Financial Markets in Europe: Toward 1992', J. P. Morgan, *World Financial Markets,* Issue 5, September 9, 1988.
13 Alfred Steinherr, 'Stony Road to an Integrated Financial Market', *European Affairs,* Vol. 4, 1989.
14 Sydney J. Key, 'Mutual Recognition: Integration of the Financial Sector in the European Community', *Federal Reserve Bulletin,* September 1989.
15 *Europolitique,* No. 1828, January 20, 1993. The regulation holds that companies will be able to collaborate to fix premiums covering certain risks, the collection of data, standard contracts, and so forth. This went along with a right to constitute coinsurance and reinsurance groups on condition that no member of the group has more than 15 per cent co-reinsurance and 10 per cent co-assurance.
16 COM (86) 292 final, 23.5.1986.
17 J.O. L322/22, 17.11.1986.

18 Vittorio Grilli, 'Financial Markets and 1992', *Brookings Papers on Economic Activity,* Issue 2, 1989.

19 Lamberto Dini, 'Towards a European Integrated Financial Market', *Banca Nazionale del Lavoro Quarterly Review,* Vol. 159, 1986.

20 Banque Bruxelles Lambert, *Bulletin Financier,* I/10/5.

21 *Europolitique,* No. 1379, February 10, 1988.

22 *Europolitique,* No. 1401, April 30, 1988.

23 *Wall Street Journal,* June 14, 1988.

24 *Le Monde,* June 15, 1988.

25 See Vassili Lelakis, 'La Libération Complète des Mouvements de Capitaux au Sein de la Communauté', *Revue du Marché Commun,* No. 320, 1988.

26 *Europolitique,* No. 1401, April 30, 1988.

27 J.O. L212/37, 20.8.1977.

28 J.O. L66, 16.3.1979.

29 J.O. L100, 17.4.1980.

30 J.O. L48, 20.2.1982.

31 CE Informations, 15.1.1980; 8.12.1980.

32 J.O. C171, 26.7.1976.

33 *Les Echos,* April 2, 1987.

34 See *Rapport de M. Maurice Ligot sur la Directive 85/611/CEE des CE relatives aux OPCVM,* 23.11.1988.

35 'OPCVM: La France s'engage dans la compétition européenne', *Le Figaro,* September 15, 1989.

36 J.O. C141/5, 7.6.1989, Article 4.

37 'The Switzerland of the Future', *The Banker,* November 1988.

38 *Financial Times,* October 2, 1989.

39 *Les Echos,* June 19, 1990.

40 The Economic and Social Council expressed concern that capital be invested in tax-free bonds: J.O. C221/29. The European Parliament also regretted that the EU had been able to reach an agreement on an EC system of taxation on interest: J.O. C68/145, 19.3.1990.

41 *Les Echos,* September 15, 1989.

42 J.O. L322/30, 17.12.1977, Article 2.

43 Paolo Clarotti, 'Un Pas Décisif vers le Marché Commun des Banques', *Revue du Marché Commun,* No. 330, 1989.

44 This was a concession made to European Parliament demands, that branches of non-member banks should not benefit by the right of establishment. Lord Croham, 'Reciprocity and the Unification of the European Banking Market', for the Group of Thirty, December 18, 1989.

45 *Europolitique,* No. 1375, January 29, 1988.

46 *Europolitique,* No. 1436, December 14, 1988.

47 *Tribune de l'Expansion,* July 7, 1988. The French government wanted to include sovereign debt, then selling at 50 per cent of face value on the secondary market, in the definition of own funds. Own funds in the EC directive were divided into two categories, 'hard' and 'soft'. France negotiated to have a generous definition of 'hard'.

48 *Europolitique,* No. 1446, November 9, 1988.

49 *Europolitique,* No. 1489, April 19, 1989.

50 J.O. L386, 30.12.1989. Solvency ratios constitute the relation between own funds of

a credit establishment and the total off-balance sheet assets and liabilities, weighted as a function of the different weighted risks. Supervisors use them to assess credit risk of banks, measured as a fixed multiple of their own capital funds.

51 *Europolitique*, No. 1508, June 29, 1989.
52 *Europolitique*, No. 1491, April 26, 1989.
53 J.O. L33/10, 4.2.1987.
54 *Europolitique*, No. 1753, March 16, 1992.
55 J.O. L29/1, 5.2.1993.
56 *Europolitique*, No. 1348, October 14, 1987.
57 *Europolitique*, No. 1687, June 22, 1991.
58 *Europolitique*, No. 1547, April 4, 1990.
59 J.O. L172, 4.7.1988.
60 Claude-J. Berr, 'Droit Européen des Assurances: la Directive du Juin 1988 sur la Libre Prestation des Services', *Revue Trimestrielle de Droit Européen*, Vol. 4, October–December 1988.
61 *Europolitique*, No. 1355, November 7, 1987; 'Europe's Insurance Map Redrawn', *The Economist*, July 9, 1988.
62 *Europolitique*, No. 1378, February 6, 1988.
63 *Europolitique*, No. 1525, November 1, 1990.
64 J.O. L129, 19.5.1990.
65 J.O. L103, 2.5.1972.
66 J.O. L8, 11.1.1984.
67 *Europolitique*, No. 1543, November 25, 1989.
68 *Europolitique*, No. 1535, October 28, 1989; No. 1564, February 17, 1990.
69 *Le Figaro*, 'Assurance: la Lente Ouverture des Frontières', June 11, 1990.
70 J.O. L330, 29.11.1990.
71 *La Tribune de l'Expansion*, July 20, 1989.
72 *Europolitique*, No. 1543, November 25, 1989.
73 'Liberating Capital', *International Management*, February 1990.
74 *Europolitique*, No. 1769, May 16, 1992.
75 *Europolitique*, No. 1778, June 20, 1992.
76 *Europolitique*, No. 1828, January 20, 1993.
77 COM (88) 778 final-doc. C3–47/89.
78 *Information*, 25.11.1990.
79 J.O. L141/27, 11.6.1993.
80 *Ibid.*
81 'The 1992 European Investment Community: An Exclusive Club', *International Financial Law Review*, Vol. 3, 1989.
82 *Europolitique*, No. 1858, May 12, 1993.
83 *The Economist*, November 19, 1988.
84 'Markets Short on Accord', *International Management*, September 1991.
85 *Europolitique*, No. 1781, July 1, 1992.
86 Ben Steil (ed.), *The European Equity Markets* (London: Royal Institute of International Affairs, 1996).
87 'London, Continental Exchanges Square Off', *Pensions and Investments*, September 14, 1992.
88 'Markets Short on Accord'.
89 *Europolitique*, No. 1581, April 25, 1990.

90 *Ibid.*
91 *Europolitique*, No. 1776, June 13, 1992.
92 'Securities Houses Face Clampdown', *Euromoney*, April 1992.
93 *Ibid.*
94 President Knud Sorensen, in the *Annual Report of the European Banking Federation*, quoted in *Europolitique*, No. 1851, April 17, 1993.
95 Commission Draft Proposal for the Liberalisation of Capital Movements. COM (86) 292 final 23.5.1986.
96 *Wall Street Journal*, June 5, 1990.
97 J.O. L26, 31.1.1977.
98 Annalisa Giannella, *La Libre Prestation de Services dans le Domaine des Assurances* (Paris: Dunod, 1994).
99 J.O. L19, 28.1.1992.
100 *Le Monde*, February 28, 1992.
101 *Le Monde*, June 14, 1991.
102 Karel Lanoo and Jorgen Mortensen, *Towards a European Financial Area: Achievements, Implementation and Remaining Hurdles* (Brussels: CEPS, 1993).
103 Grilli, 'Financial Markets and 1992'.

10

The battle of the systems

Negotiations on financial sector reforms within the framework of the EU, the BIS, or the GATT were reflections of broad-gauge competition on world markets. As market interactions between national economies increased, the scope for discretionary actions by firms and individuals widened, altering their relations to government institutions and to regulatory authorities. Savers looked for a broader range of services than those available at home. Banks faced declining profits in saturated markets, and converged with insurers, securities firms, pension funds, finance companies and unit trusts as suppliers to the global markets. The forces making for financial market liberalisation in the 1970s were accentuated by the world credit crunch of 1982, and the shift from loan business to the international bond markets gained momentum. The 'securitisation' of financial markets pulled equities along in its wake, and sparked sequential reforms among emerging-market economies. But it soon became apparent that one of the limits to the 'globalisation' of finance was drawn around the foreign ownership of financial services firms active in national markets. This was particularly the case of France and Germany, whose governments sought to fend off the 'Anglo-Saxons', while negotiating a market-opening programme in the EU and joint regulatory measures with Japan and the United States in the BIS and the GATT.

The 'battle of systems' took shape because of the different responses of governments to the internationalisation of the business of banking: Britain co-opted the increasingly internalised financial markets, and became the leading exponent of the EU's single financial area. The German government sought to extend joint regulatory reach over the London markets through the BIS and the EU, while the French sought to restrict the access of US and Japanese institutions based in London or Luxemburg to the EU's unified markets. The virulence of the inter-state rivalry unleashed in 1988–89 was rooted not in different responses, but rather in the *reasons* for those different responses to the process of internationalisation. The legitimacy of the national financial systems of Germany and France seemed too frail and too centrally linked to the political consensus in their national economies for either country to adapt Britain's method of internalising global financial markets within a wider EU financial area. The diplomacy of the negotiations therefore saw a Franco-German alliance against 'Anglo-Saxon' finance undermined by their *de-facto* inclusion as national and competitive financial systems within world financial markets.

Great Britain as instigator of EU financial market reforms

The major difference between Britain, on the one hand, and France and Germany, on the other, lay in the prolonged process whereby successive British governments had internalised world financial markets as part of the domestic financial system. The process of converting the City of London into a world financial centre turning on the dollar opened with the devaluation of the pound sterling in November 1967, and Britain's entry to the EU along with Ireland and Denmark in 1973. Growing financial interdependence between New York and London had developed in the 1960s with the freeing of current payments in international trade, and the expansion of the dollar as the world's key currency. The markets provided the medium through which ever-more volatile funds flows in dollars and other currencies helped to undermine the post-war system of stable exchange-rates hinged on the convertibility of the dollar into gold. When oil-producing states sought to recoup some of the value of their dollar reserves by raising prices in 1974, surplus revenues from the Gulf states poured into the London interbank markets, where banks borrowed from each other in dollars and lent on to developing countries, notably in Latin America. Deposits in sterling by the international institutions and central banks picked up after the stabilisation imposed on the Labour government in 1976. This petrocurrency status of the pound was confirmed as North Sea oil began to flow, moving Britain into sizeable current account surplus. The raising of capital controls in October 1979 then allowed UK institutions to spread their investments overseas, reviving Britain's traditional role as exporter of capital. The bonanza lasted until January 1986, when world oil prices fell, in part, under pressure from the Saudi and US governments.

The rhythm of British policy came to be driven by crucial initiatives in the area of public and private finance taken in the United States. The US administration's repeal in January 1974 of the Interest Equalisation Tax – introduced in 1963 to restrict access to US capital markets – stimulated bond markets in both New York and London. A year later, the Securities Exchange Commission ended fixed commissions on the New York Stock Exchange with a view to stimulating a nation-wide market and reducing the cost of corporate or government finance. As UK corporate equities found their way to New York, financial institutions pressed for an end to fixed commissions in London as well. Chicago's experience was the point of reference for the UK supporters of a market for financial futures in London. Bank of England approval was not given before consultations were held with the Federal Reserve, the SEC, and the Commodity Futures Trading Commission (CFTC).[1] Then in 1978, the United States opened offshore banking zones, International Banking Facilities (IBFs), with attractive tax advantages for investors, to repatriate some of the funds benefiting from the dollar markets which had blossomed in London. This in turn stimulated a broadly-based campaign in London to expand UK equity markets parallel to those in the US.

London's prosperity as an international financial centre had been based in part on the stiff regulation of other countries. US commercial banks, excluded from inter-state banking and the securities markets by federal statutes, were pulled to London by the much more hospitable regulatory climate provided by the Bank of England. Japanese, Swiss, German or French banks and securities houses came to London for similar reasons. Their presence grew from 114 in 1967 to over 600 in 1988, edging the local financial institutions on to the sidelines. In the 1970s, US banks formed the heart of the interbank Eurocurrency market, with most of the petrofunds passing through their hands. British clearing banks and US commercial banks rushed into the loan business to Latin America, leading to endless rounds of reschedulings for the major developing country debtors through most of the 1980s. With the end to restraints on capital movements in October 1979, the UK institutions channelled the bulk of their overseas investment through the US securities houses in London,[2] providing one of the major incentives for the government to end the Stock Exchange monopoly and promote universal banking. US insurance brokers bought their way into Lloyd's, unloading reinsurance business through their new channels.

The decision to end UK exchange controls became part of a wider strategy of the newly elected Conservative government to unleash market forces as a means to promote competition across the entire spectrum of the British financial system. Introducing foreign financial institutions to British markets became part of a broader policy to shake up the domestic sector and to encourage greater financial efficiency. The measure also stimulated the UK institutions' interest in the Eurosecurities markets – four-fifths of trading being located in London. These became the core growth markets of the 1980s. The Reagan administration's combination in 1981 of tax cuts and boosts in defence spending – followed by a truce between the White House and Congress to sustain welfare outlays – prompted a surge in the US federal deficit. With the crisis in developing-country debt that began in 1982, governments, commercial banks and multinational corporations turned away from Eurocurrency borrowings on the inter-bank market to the market for Eurobonds, which grew by leaps and bounds. Bank loans were supplanted by tradable bonds, new issues proved cheap, not liable to withholding tax, and readily disposable on a liquid secondary market.

In 1984, the Reagan administration tapped these markets in securities by repealing US withholding tax on interest paid to foreign holders of US Treasury bonds. At the same time, the US Treasury demanded that capital restrictions on yen be lifted, triggering a flow of funds into the US from Japan, easing the problems of financing the federal deficit and forging financial interdependence between the United States and Japan. The German government also ended withholding tax on securities to keep DM savings at home, while the French Socialist government embarked on its own set of market reforms.

A major justification for London's 'Big Bang', as expressed by the Governor of the Bank of England, was to consolidate London's status in the global marketplace. 'Early and substantial change is now unavoidable', he declared in March 1984,[3] 'if we are not to lose out in the world market place'. More prosaically, London was to be the 'third leg' in the triad of world financial centres, together with New York and Tokyo.[4] London's advantages were many. The Bank of England's light regulatory touch attracted financial institutions and foreign banks. London was the home of international bank lending, and the prime centre for the global securities markets and foreign-exchange dealing. The City enjoyed the added advantage of a near-universal language, a good infrastructure, an excellent time zone, a reputable legal system, and a broad range of established financial services firms. London occupied a strategic position across the time zones between Europe, the Asian markets and the United States. But London lacked the economic base of Japan or the United States. That element could only be supplied through integration with the EU.

The major alliance was thus forged with Germany. Given the slow pace of change, Deutsche Bank moved its Eurocurrency operations from Luxemburg to London in 1984, and then acquired the UK merchant bank Morgan Grenfell. The move signified early in the game Deutsche Bank's recognition of 'the pre-eminence of the London market in the domain of corporate finance and money management'.[5] The German and British governments joined in support of free-capital movements within the EU, the programme for which was announced during the British EU Presidency in October 1986.

There were at least three further reasons for the Bank of England's promotion of financial market reform.

- The United Kingdom had become a net importer of manufactured goods, heightening the significance of earnings from financial services and other 'invisibles'.
- UK merchant banks were severely undercapitalised relative to their foreign competitors.
- The international securities houses and markets had effectively by-passed the London Stock Exchange.

Its rules discouraged large-scale operations. Commercial banks and investment houses were kept from the floor, where jobbers traded securities for their own account with brokers. Fixed commissions and stamp duty made trading expensive.

The Bank of England was in any case undermining the Stock Exchange's monopoly with its go-ahead in 1978 to open the Unlisted Securities Market, followed by the Third Market for smaller firms. In 1982, the London International Commodities Clearing House, backed by banks and brokers, won Bank of England support to open the London International Financial Futures Exchange (LIFFE), which drained funds away from the more traditional exchanges and prompted the Exchange to float its own market in traded-options markets. The two were later merged. In December 1983, the Bank endorsed an Exchange proposal to allow member firms to set up International Dealerships (Ids) to trade in foreign securities, using dual-capacity status. Limits on outsiders' ownership of member firms were gradually relaxed. In June 1985, the Exchange voted to allow non-member firms to own up to 100 per cent of brokers and jobbers. This effectively ended single-capacity, and came into effect in March 1986. The international securities houses insisted that the Exchange's rules be changed to shift voting rights from individuals to firms, and threatened to set up their own self-regulated market. In March 1986, the Exchange's Council relented, and – as recounted in Chapter 8 – the Stock Exchange merged *de facto* into the international securities market. London became Europe's wholesale centre for bonds and equities in 24-hour-a-day, around-the-world trading. By 1986, the LIFFE had become the largest futures market outside the United States.

Internationalisation of the stock market in London was predicated on Seaq International, the screen-based quotation system for international equities, modelled on the US Nasdaq market. Its installation was followed by the 'Big Bang' of October 1986, when fixed commissions were abolished, two-way market-makers replaced jobbers and financial institutions were allowed to buy into brokerage houses. The result was the creation of the International Stock Exchange (ISE).

London had thus become the EU's prime city for capital.[6] Domestic and foreign reinsurance companies, and Lloyd's syndicates, combined to form a major insurance market. London's facilities attracted continental European banks, which numbered 219 of the total of 521 foreign banks in the City. Nearly 90 per cent of market-makers on Seaq International were foreign-owned – continental European, Americans and Japanese.[7] By 1989, 340 stocks were traded actively, all but 15 per cent of which were European, with Seaq accountable for four-fifths of cross-border traffic in EU equities. By 1988, the non-EU presence in the UK represented 33 per cent of assets of branches of non-EU banks, as compared with 17.4 per cent in Luxemburg.[8] Japanese banks accounted for 36 per cent of international lending out of London by the end of 1988, with the US banks' share down to 13 per cent. Japanese banks with a presence in London numbered 52, as against 75 US bank branches. Overall, 33 US banks operated 149 branches in the EU and 17 banks owned subsidiaries there,[9] accounting for 5 per cent of total bank assets. EU financial institutions had also become formidable international competitors, providing 34 per cent of the world's direct lending in 1990, as against 7 per cent for the United States.

The London markets were notably different from Paris and Frankfurt. They were wholesale markets, servicing businesses from all over the world as opposed to domestic markets, primarily funding national corporations. At the heart of the market was global foreign-exchange trading – 60 per cent of which was located in London, New York and Tokyo – amounting to a turnover nearly forty times the daily average of world exports of goods and services.[10] In 1992, the stock-market capitalisation of London was 44 per cent of the EU equity-markets' combined capitalisation, compared to 15 per cent each for Paris and the German stock exchanges.[11] London accounted for 11 per cent of global equity turnover, with 43 per cent of its own turnover accounted by foreign equities. About 65 per cent of world non-domestic equity turnover and 95 per cent of EU non-domestic equity turnover took place in London, with one-half of that activity being in Japanese and German shares, and another one-eighth in French shares. By contrast, the turnover of domestic equity on the German Stock Exchange was higher than London's turnover of domestic equity, while Paris was the largest of the European centres in terms of share issuance over the decade – reflecting the government's raising of funds for state-controlled corporations and the sale of state assets. London was also the main venue for mergers and acquisitions in the European time zone.[12] Political barriers to entry were low for inward acquisitions. Market capitalisation was high, equalling 98.1 per cent of GDP in the late 1980s compared to 25 per cent of GDP in Germany and France.

A Bank of England report in spring 1989 indicated that a European market in retail finance business was not an imminent prospect.[13] Financial institutions in the EU were embedded first and foremost in their domestic contexts. German banks and insurance used historic cost-accounting, held extensive portfolios of physical assets, feared competition from multibranch insurers and brokers, and were opposed to the entry of less well-capitalised investment houses into Germany's equity markets. They used the London markets, but they, or their governments, sought to protect their national markets from the 'cosmopolitan' influence of London.

Frankfurt by 1990 hosted 272 foreign banks,[14] which held 5 per cent of German bank assets. US and Japanese institutions led the pack, with the French in third place. Foreign banks accounted for one-half of Frankfurt stock-exchange members, with over one-half of new issues ending up in the hands of foreign investors. Foreigners had also begun to enter investment service business, but were kept on the sidelines of Germany's cross-shareholding nexus.[15] New share issues were restricted,[16] and the authorities remained vigilant against the introduction of new financial products.[17]

Paris was more open to foreign influence. In France, the number of foreign institutions had risen during the 1970s from 50 to 120, winning 19 per cent of banking business in the French market. Liberalisation measures during 1984–86 brought the number of foreign banks in Paris to 160 by 1989.[18] Of the fifty-five stockbrokers, thirteen were owned by US, Japanese or UK houses. These accounted for 30 per cent of trading in French equities.[19] The turnover was, however, heavily located in London,[20] until Paris – like Frankfurt – began to claw back trades from 1991 on, as their domestic reforms took effect.

As Europe's 'city of capital', it was not surprising that London and Commission should sing from the same neo-classical hymnal on the benefits of opening national financial markets to the cleansing effects of competition.[21] Liberalisation of capital movements, it was argued, would improve the allocation of global financial resources. Were the EU's twelve financial systems to become one, the EU would command commercial banking resources larger than the United States. Transaction costs across national boundaries and between different currencies were high. National capital markets were small, and new issues hobbled by the forty-odd exchanges, the variety of regulations and the lack of an efficient secondary market. Neither American nor Japanese investors were attracted by this tangle of systems. A liberal regime which prompted the equalisation of the cost of financial transactions across the EU would yield considerable efficiency gains for consumers and users. A more efficient market in corporate assets would tilt power away from corporate management in protected markets towards institutional shareholders.

The British government could only promote a market-opening programme through building an effective coalition within the EU. The liberal camp for financial services was heterogeneous, composed of financial institutions in London, the EU Commission, and (initially) the British, Dutch, Luxemburg and German governments. The alliance took recognisable shape in 1977, with the appointment of a new Commission, presided over by Roy Jenkins, and the formation of a centre-right coalition in the Netherlands. London established a mini Treasury-in-exile within the Commission's directorate-general for financial affairs. A serviceable policy doctrine was designed which aimed 'to secure acceptance of the equivalence of national legislations rather than their replacement by European law'.[22] The landmark case – discussed earlier – which enabled the Commission to elaborate the concept on the basis of an ECJ judgement, was that of Cassis de Dijon.[23] The Commission brought the protection of insurance markets to the Council's attention in 1981, during the Dutch and British Presidencies. The (British) Commissioner Christopher Tugendhat then took legal action against the member states. By 1986, the Dutch and British presided over an EU moving to free-capital movements, the internal market, freer insurance services and the GATT Uruguay round of trade negotiations. Lord Cockfield's financial services portfolio was inherited by Sir Leon Brittan in 1989.

Germany, the BIS and the internal market

With internationalisation growing apace, national regulatory authorities supervised a declining portion of bank activities. This proved a particularly serious development for German supervisors, and the Bundesbank, given the importance attached by the latter to tight control over financial institutions. Reestablishing controls in an international context, though, proved elusive – the German authorities proved eager to extend regulations internationally. But serving partners with differing interests yielded only partial results, while German financial institutions came to appreciate the freedom available in world financial markets. Deficiencies in existing arrangements became evident in 1974 with the failures of Bankhaus Herstatt and the Franklin National Bank. International business contracted rapidly, and in September the BIS issued a communiqué, which commercial banks read as providing lender-of-last-resort facilities for funds deposited short-term in London by oil-producing countries. The resulting boom in bank loans to governments contributed to a sharp deterioration in bank solvency. A Committee on Banking Regulations and Supervisory Practices was also set up, composed of representatives from the regulatory authorities of BIS participants. Its First Concordat was issued in December 1975, and stipulated the mutual responsibility of home and host country authorities for foreign banks on their soil. But host countries were to hold primary responsibility for the liquidity of foreign banks.

This expanded agenda for the BIS to cover matters of bank solvency, lender-of-last-resort facilities and mutual supervision provided a new purpose for bank regulators in EU member states. The 1970s widened the network of institutions concerned with regulation and provided an opportunity to deepen relations between member states. The EU contact group of regulatory authorities, set up in 1972, was placed on a permanent basis in the first banking directive of 1977 with the creation of the Bank Advisory Committee. One of its main tasks was to come up with common criteria for capital adequacy solvency ratios and supervision of banks on a consolidated basis, as proposed by the BIS. In parallel, the OECD Financial Markets Committee, also founded in 1972, began to systematically study bank regulatory systems, notably with the creation in 1980 of the Group of Banking Experts. The private sector established its own Group of Thirty to focus on problems of global financial markets, while a World Conference of Regulatory Authorities held its first meeting in 1979.

The trend to a reinforcement of coordinated supervision was confirmed in 1982 when the international banks were hit by crisis in their loans to Latin America. Failure that year in Luxemburg of Banco Ambrosiano Holdings dealt a further blow to the markets, not least because Banco Ambrosiano had not been accredited as a bank. Since the clash between the Bundesbank and German banks in 1976–78, when the banks in Luxemburg[24] intermediated a steady flight into the DM,[25] the Bundesbank had demanded an extension of controls over the lending of German banks registered there.[26] An EU directive, adopted by the Council of Ministers under the German presidency in June 1983,[27] introduced the principle of home-country control into EU legislation. It was to be coordinated by the Bank Advisory Committee, seven of whose members were among the twelve regulators in the BIS. The intention may have been to extend its application to banks based in third countries, in cooperation with the United States. Cooperation was forthcoming, but partial. The BIS Second Concordat, announced in July 1983, stipulated that the host country was to retain responsibility for the supervision of banking subsidiaries, but the parent held the responsibility for the bank as a whole. Nonetheless, the German Finance Ministry seized on the June 1983 EU directive on consolidated accounting, and the banks' scare over the collapse in November 1983 of the Luxemburg subsidiary of Schröder, Münchmeyer & Hengst Co. (SMH),[28] to tighten lending provisions, and to have banks raise their capitalisation levels.

This directive introduced the principle of supervision by the home country's authority, on which the EU's second banking directive later came to be based. Capital requirements were to relate to the bank's global balance-sheet position, thus preventing banks seeking to avoid capital adequacy requirements by booking business through less heavily regulated financial centres. The directive was complemented in December 1986 with another on annual and consolidated accounts that provided for supervision of capital adequacy of bank branches or subsidiaries along lines agreed in the BIS.[29]

A Federal Reserve proposal of January 1986 on solvency supervision provided the prime stimulus to move the BIS into the more troubled waters of regulating securities markets, whose main centre in Europe was London. But it was never clear whether governments were seeking to control the Euro-securities markets or to have capital markets opened more to non-resident firms competing in financial services-related activities.[30] The United States subsequently concluded a series of bilateral accords with Switzerland, Japan and the Cayman Islands on securities, and the SEC signed a 'memorandum of understanding' in September 1986 with the British government. The agreement set out the conditions for a confidential exchange of information between the US and UK authorities to serve as the basis for the world-wide policing of markets.[31]

Negotiations resulted eventually in the BIS 'Proposals for International Convergence of Capital Measurements and Capital Standards', published in July 1988. International banks in participating countries were to have capital equivalent to at least 8 per cent of their risk-weighted assets, by January 1993. The BIS proposals thus provided the broader standard for the EU's internal measures, accompanying the Second Banking Directive, on solvency and own funds. The main difference was that the EU's definition of own funds was softer, to allow France's undercapitalised banks to meet solvency standards.[32] Applying the tougher BIS criteria would have severely restricted their activities.

Meanwhile, the US Securities and Exchange Commission received a mandate from Congress to combat international fraud in securities markets. This meant developing an international regime dealing with insider trading, money laundering and other criminal activities.[33] The SEC secured bilateral memoranda of understanding, first with the United Kingdom and Switzerland, and then with France and the Netherlands. The SEC also mobilised the International Organisation of Securities Commissions (IOSCO) with ninety-one regulatory authorities. IOSCO's technical committee, headed by SEC chairman Richard Breeden, worked closely with the BIS Committee to extend capital adequacy ratios to investment houses and the Eurobond markets. This alliance between bank regulators, notably the SEC and the Bundesbank, to strengthen supervision over global capital markets raised the stakes in the struggle over the EU's Investment Services Directive. The supervisors meeting in the Basle Committee urged securities houses to hold additional capital against market risks. Securities houses complained that the central bankers failed to appreciate the difference between bank loans, requiring capital reserves to cover against bankruptcy, and the securities business, where risk was spread across a diversity of assets that were continually marked-to-market.

The UK found a ready ally in Commissioner Leon Brittan. The struggle between securities firms and regulators was then projected into the negotiations between the Basle Committee and IOSCO, the club of international securities regulators. The investment houses' two foes proved to be the SEC, in alliance with the Bundesbank, both lined up against the Bank of England and the French authorities. It was a Franco-British alliance in June 1992 which put through the comparatively light capital adequacy requirements for security houses in the EU – the 'modular approach' referred to in the previous chapter.

Member states' jealousy of their prerogatives became even more evident as the BCCI scandal on drugs, arms smuggling and money laundering moved into public view from 1988 on. Bank unions seized the opportunity to argue that criminal activities were facilitated by freer markets.[34] The twelve EU members agreed that banks and financial institutions should inform national authorities of suspect movements of funds above 15,000 ECUs.[35] In an intergovernmental declaration,[36] they vowed to make money laundering and drug dealing a criminal offence in national law. But the reluctance of the Luxemburg authorities to take responsibility for BCCI's parent's branch operations abroad, notably in London, posed the question whether home-country control could work in practice.[37] Luxemburg opted to preserve its tight bank secrecy laws. It was the United States which pushed for more aggressive action, through the UN 1988 Vienna Convention, the BIS, and the Financial Action Group established at the G-7 world economic summit at Paris in 1989. And it was the Council of Europe convention, declaring money laundering a criminal offence and urging that bank secrecy no longer be an obstacle to cooperation, that provided the legal framework for broader cooperation.[38]

The BCCI scandal also provided sound reasons to extend the EU's Consolidated Accounting Directive of 1983 to include 'mixed activity holding companies'.[39] But the likely impact of the measures was marred by the necessary concessions to member-state susceptibilities. A large loophole was opened in order to meet universal bank requests that their securities activities, exposed to market risk, be exempted from surveillance.[40] The directive urged competent authorities to exchange information, but prosecution under criminal law remained at the discretion of the member states (Article 7.2). This directive was closely associated with further measures on deposit guarantees and deposit insurance, traditionally a highly sensitive domain of state prerogatives.[41] The negotiators toned down the principle of home-country responsibility in a compromise reaffirming the *de-facto* powers of the host to exclude branches which did not comply with local regulations.[42]

The United Kingdom's vision of a Europe of the states, open to world business, found notable expression in the EU directive to outlaw insider trading.[43] The draft was revived in early 1987 with a view to providing an EU-wide law to protect investors. Professionals were not to use 'any information not known to the public' that could have a significant effect on the value of a security. Agreement was finally reached in the course of 1989. France, Belgium, Greece and Italy supported the measure,[44] despite the close intimacy of their own financial networks. The Germans, Dutch and Luxemburgers preferred that their own authorities police the markets.[45] The Spanish advanced a proposal which could have brought London off-market investors under EU surveillance.[46] The directive excluded actions related to monetary and exchange-rate policy (at Germany's insistence) and stipulated that member states did not have to provide information if there was a risk to sovereignty, security and public order of the state (Article 10.1). The EU insider-trading directive provided a platform for Germany to introduce its own legislation, as recounted in Chapter 6.

France and reciprocity in the EU

The BCCI scandal brought out into the open a major flaw of the new EU regime in financial services: the territorial jurisdiction of EU law was limited in relation to the global scope of international finance. Financial firms in national jurisdictions made decisions in the context of world markets. Internationalisation of markets therefore severely circumscribed the readiness of the various member states' authorities to reduce their powers to the benefit of new EU authorities. Rather, the legislation reserved discretionary powers to the member states, but also created the institutions and instruments for joint supervision policing of markets.

This aspect of cooperative federalism was also translated into the EU financial area's relations with non-members. EU powers on reciprocity increased the attraction for third-country institutions to set up shop within the EU, while serving the EU as a negotiating instrument in opening access to non-member markets. But supervision of markets remained in the main a national preserve, requiring cooperation within and also beyond the jurisdiction of the EU.

Use of the reciprocity concept[47] was advanced for the first time by the Commission in its draft proposal on the Second Banking Directive, presented to the Council in February 1988. Two main ideas inspired its inclusion: (1) to end recourse by member states to national reciprocity clauses; and (2) to exploit the EU's new powers to lever open financial markets world-wide. The Commission's ambitions inevitably attracted opposition. Member states opposed an increase in Commission powers, and some disapproved of introducing reciprocity as a principle in trade relations. Non-member states, notably the United States and Japan, decried EU protectionism. The draft was discussed by Finance Ministers and then went for a first reading to the European Parliament. In April 1989, the Finance Ministers agreed to negotiate a new draft, and arrived at a common position on July 24. The final draft then went to parliament for second reading, and definitive adoption by the Council on December 15, 1989.

As Lord Cockfield indicated on introducing the directive,[48] a major objective was to ensure that the EU be taken as a serious negotiating partner. Reciprocity provided the main policy instrument. EU Trade Commissioner Willy de Clerq was even more blunt. 'We see no reason why the benefit of our internal liberalisation should be extended unilaterally to third countries.'[49] The statement prompted a media outburst in the United States against the prospect of a 'Fortress Europe'[50] and evoked US Treasury statements against reciprocity on the grounds that it would lead to protectionism.[51] Meanwhile, Congress voted the 1988 Fair Trade Act,[52] granting the President powers to ensure that US firms 'have access to (major) foreign (financial) markets and receive national treatment', equivalent to that of their local competitors. The US administration later presented a list of exemptions from the GATT most favoured nation clause, mostly related to services, and offered to reduce the list if others improved their offers.

France was the main champion of a strict interpretation of reciprocity.[53] There were a number of reasons for the French position, all related to a shared view across French élites of the vulnerability of their financial institutions. The BIS capital ratios had exposed French banks as seriously undercapitalised in 1987, with the ratio of primary to total risk-adjusted assets for all banks at 1.91, compared to 4.42 for German banks, and 5.9 for Swiss.[54] Raising funds on the open markets could dilute their ownership and control; hence the French state's promotion of cross-shareholding arrangements between impregnable, state-owned insurance companies and banks (see Figure 10.1).[55] The formation of these cross-shareholding arrangements were all the more important as EU legislation required that the opening in 1988 of French stock exchange firms' capital to outsider capital be available to all foreign firms licensed in the EU. Mitterrand's re-election in May 1988 ended the prospect of further privatisations, which in any case had been suspended following the October 1987 stock-market crash. Sales of state properties under those conditions would undoubtedly have dispersed the equity of French state corporations into international markets.

An additional factor was the role of retail savings on the Paris financial markets, as channelled through the SICAVs and unit trusts. The savings nourished the institutions which lay at the heart of the web of cross-shareholdings among French conglomerates. If savings were to be stabilised in France under conditions of free-capital movement, then a number of precautions had to be taken. The public had to become convinced that its savings could be preserved in France without the risk of loss through favourable taxation, the rigorous pursuit of a hard-franc policy, and a fixed-exchange regime or a single currency in the EU. All of these objectives could best be achieved by extending centralised EU control over the markets in London.

In the EU, France and the Commission thus championed strict reciprocity, and proposed that the request for a licence should go first to the Commission. Draft provisions in Article 7 authorised the Commission to suspend a licence or an acquisition by financial firms from a non-member state country. The non-EU applicant would have to wait for a period of six months, during which the Commission would make enquiries about whether non-member countries granted analogous rights of access to EU banks. Such an EU veto power arguably

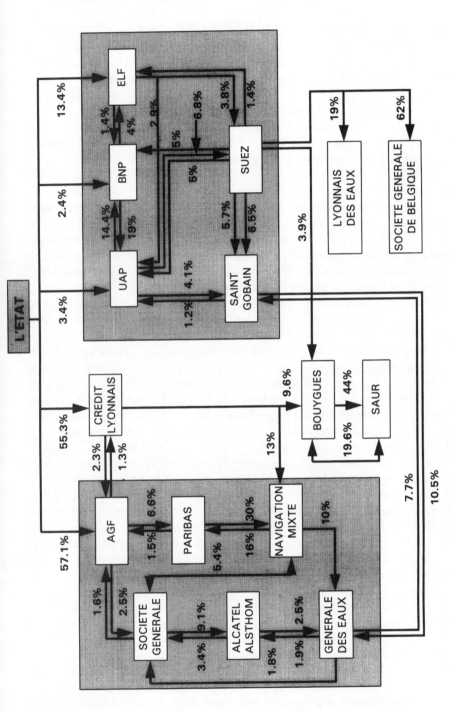

Figure 10.1 Selected French crossholdings, June 1995
Source: François Morin, University of Toulouse.

ran counter to Article 58 of the Rome Treaty, which ensured that non-EU firms be treated as EU nationals. After a major debate in autumn 1988 among the member states on third-country firms' access to the single market, the Commission published a communiqué, 'Europe, World Partner',[56] explaining that the ultimate aim was to ensure open world markets through multilateral negotiations. This position was reaffirmed by the European Council in December 1988.

This liberal orientation flowed from a compromise at the Finance Council meeting of November 1988. The UK and Luxemburg were determined to protect firms already in their markets; they were backed by the Federal Republic, which nonetheless favoured a stricter clause on reciprocity[57] – and US bankers lobbied hard to repeal the measure. Agreement was reached that credit institutions equipped with licences acquired prior to 1993 would not be affected by the measures[58] outlined in the draft Article 7. In theory, this meant that US and Japanese banks licensed in the UK could operate throughout the EU. The privilege, however, would only go to fully incorporated subsidiaries of non-member state firms. Branches of third-country banks were to fall under host-country law.[59] Most firms in London were branches, subject to the host-country authority and dependent on their parent bank's world-wide capital in calculations on debt ratios. They would have to alter their legal and capital structures to benefit from the new provisions.

Commissioner Brittan, who took over the financial services portfolio in January 1989, then suggested that the licence be given automatically without any prior demand for reciprocity. Only when a third country refused national treatment to EU institutions could the licence be restricted or withdrawn. Germany, the UK, the Netherlands and Luxemburg welcomed Brittan's suggestion. They sought to keep the power to deny licences to non-member state banks out of the hands of the Commission. That power was to reside with the states in Council and in the Bank Advisory Committee.[60] France, Italy, Spain and Greece, with strong support in the European parliament,[61] favoured extensive Commission powers for a single-bank policy to third countries. In April, a compromise was reached whereby the original draft Article 7, under the title 'Harmonisation of Authorisation Conditions', was broken into Articles 8 and 9, under a new title, 'Relations with Third Countries'. The power to deny licences was taken out of the hands of the Commission. The last word on reciprocity was to remain with the Council of Ministers and the Bank Advisory Committee.

Article 8 provided for close cooperation between Commission and Bank Advisory Committee on the supply of information regarding the granting of new licences, acquisitions, and group structures of third-country banks. This would provide the Commission with a significant database. Article 9 introduced a new procedure. Armed with the data, the Commission was to draw up a periodic report on the treatment afforded EU institutions in third countries. If the Commission considered that third parties were not granting 'effective market access comparable to that offered by the Community', it could seek a negotiating mandate from the Council under qualified majority voting. But as the basis of comparison was treatment extended to third-country banks in the EU, where national conditions remained diverse, comparability meant that EU policy was based on two principles.[62]

- Article 9.3 stipulated that the Commission could negotiate for reciprocal national treatment. This applied within the EU without exception as far as subsidiaries were concerned, though – as mentioned – the member states reserved discretionary powers with regard to the primary establishment. Negotiations were to be opened immediately in cases where third parties did not offer EU banks 'the same competitive possibilities as to national credit establishments'. Restrictive action to limit or suspend licences thus occurred when national treatment was not afforded to EU institutions. After three months, the Council would decide on qualified majority voting whether to continue the ban.
- Article 9.4 implied that the Commission could negotiate for more than reciprocal national treatment. The Commission could launch the procedure, described above, in the event that third countries did not provide EU banks with 'effective market access'. A maximum objective then was for the Commission to negotiate for 'reciprocity by equivalence'. If comparable access were not secured, the Commission could seek a mandate on the basis of qualified majority voting to negotiate for comparable treatment.

The EU's comparability clause linked member states' discretionary powers to legislative changes in the United States. For US international banks, this was no doubt an improvement on the earlier draft, whereby a US bank could be excluded from London if Paris was opposed.[63] The US Chambers of Commerce in Brussels had suggested that the EU drop the original reciprocity clause. But the amended Article 9 gave the EU powers to restrict their operations in view of the US law's ban on inter-state banking, the separation of commercial banking from investment services and restraints on banks' equity holdings in non-financial companies. Both US bankers and the Treasury therefore used the 'example'[64] of the EU's internal market as a goad to domestic legislative reforms in the course of 1991–92. The measures still fell short of the Commission's comparability test.[65]

Reciprocity was not just an outward-directed instrument. It was also a vehicle to ensure joint supervision of the market in corporate assets. This was notably the case for credit institutions, around whose ownership member states drew a protective ring. The Commission had no difficulty in 1987 in revising the earlier directive on listing stock-market requirements, through the application of mutual recognition.[66] But following Italian financier Carlo de Benedetti's hostile bid in early 1988 for the Société Générale de Belgique, EU legislation was introduced for bidders to notify shareholders of major holdings in a listed company.[67] The Second Banking Directive then stipulated that regulatory authorities be informed about the identity of bank shareholders (Article 5) and be consulted prior to a bid (Article 11.2). In the context of its reciprocity powers, the Commission was to examine any change in a branch bank's ownership, making it a subsidiary (Article 8). A subsidiary's EU expansion was to be through branches only (Article 18). As a further precaution, member states preserved their own array of reciprocity clauses with regard to licences for non-EU banks or insurance firms.[68] Their financial institutions retained a diversity of protectionist practices such as cross-shareholdings or restrictions on the percentage of equity capital to be held by non-nationals.

In parallel negotiations on applying the mutual-recognition principle to the directive on the prospectus required for listing publicly quoted companies, a similar blow was struck for retail investors who might be tempted to place their funds in higher-risk paper. The UK, Luxemburg, Germany and Ireland[69] rejected the proposal[70] – favoured by the French[71] – that the common prospectus should apply to Eurobonds as well. The six months that would be required to distribute a public prospectus would kill the market. The Commission's compromise applied the distinction of large and mass markets. The prospectus, said Lord Cockfield, would not be needed by 'governments, multinationals and multi-millionaires'.[72] It would only be required for securities sold to the general public. In fact, the directive of April 1989[73] exempted many retail savings instruments from the prospectus (Article 2), but required that the prospectus of a security on a regulated market must receive 'prior scrutiny' by the home state before being issued on the London or Luxemburg markets (Article 20). The measures left London's wholesale markets intact.

A similar struggle in defining the EU's 'specificity' was fought out over the Investment Services Directive, where France led a coalition in favour of reserving the financial services markets for European firms. The German Stock Exchange had backed London against the competing French proposal to dilute SEAQ's preeminence in equities trading through the 'interconnection' of price information on markets.[74] Compromises then were reached with France over on- and off-market trading, transparency and market access for institutions, while the Second Banking Directive provided the reference for reciprocity conditions.[75] Member states agreed to reject an application from a non-member state on a qualified majority basis. The Commission was to report regularly on access to third-country markets,[76] seek a mandate from the Council to negotiate an effective market for EU firms access, and initiate negotiations to ensure national treatment. Home-country supervision was restricted to subsidiaries of non-EU parent companies.

A non-accord in the EU was eventually reached in the course of 1992 and 1993. Capital adequacy again lay at the heart of the dispute. There was also the related directive on large exposures which the Eurobond dealers feared could curtail their exposure limits. France and Germany sought to tighten regulations, while Britain defended flexibility. The Commission proposed compromises for both directives.

- On large exposures, bank loans were to be limited to 40 per cent of capital as of 1994, coming down to 25 per cent by 1999 – the level permitted under German law.[77]

- The Capital Adequacy Directive defined different requirements for banks and investment houses,[78] using the different concepts of both credit, of primary concern to banks, and market risks, of primary concern to investment houses.

The complex compromise was hotly contested, as noted by the SEC and the central bankers. Not least, German universal banks remained bound by the BIS regulations of 1988. That implied that in 1996, when the EU directive on capital adequacy was to come into effect, there was a grey area as to whether the BIS took precedence over the EU measure.

With the US and Japanese commercial banks apparently turning inward, the EU came to champion multilateral trade in services. The US administration had pushed hardest to include financial services in the new round of GATT multilateral trade negotiations, which opened in September 1986. A partial reconciliation between the US and EU views on reciprocity was reached in winter 1988 at the Montreal mid-term negotiations over the Uruguay Round, defining reciprocity as 'effective market access'. But finance ministries and central banks of developing countries, led by India and Brazil, made clear in the course of 1989 their opposition to market-opening for financial services.

The opportunity was therefore seized to integrate GATT provisions into EU law. Article 9.6 was inserted in the Second Banking Directive to reassure third countries that action taken by the EU with regard to reciprocity would be in conformity with its international obligations. The services sector of the final GATT package, presented in December 1991, included a commitment to future GATT negotiations of financial services. As the Commission indicated, if GATT were successful in reducing barriers to trade in financial services, the EU could no longer unilaterally use its powers to limit or suspend decisions on licensing.[79] This EU support for a comprehensive multilateral agreement was thus in part designed to restrict its possible use of the reciprocity clause, but it failed to achieve this objective, not least because the US Congress failed to repeal legislation on banking that would have given *de-facto* reciprocal access for European institutions to US markets. In the event, the US in 1995 refused to endorse or participate in the Uruguay Round agreements on financial services, citing inadequate market-opening commitments on the part of various emerging-market countries. The negotiations were relaunched in 1997.

National legitimacy and Franco-German corporate governance

Fear, mixed with use of the 'cosmopolitan' markets in London, was common to both Germany and France. Germany's dramatic and volatile history as a unified state from 1870 to 1945 cast a long shadow over financial markets in the Federal Republic. Association between Jewishness and finance capital first erupted in the 1873 Berlin financial crash, following hectic speculation fuelled by the 5-billion-franc indemnity paid by France to Prussia for the war of 1870. Catastrophic losses were incurred.[80] As Fritz Stern has written, after 1873 Germans of the

Right and Left never lost a powerful sense of anti-capitalism. German economic policy turned to protection against foreign competition, and to state promotion of cartels. In the 1920s, war reparations, inflation and reconstruction kept the German banking system fragile and interest rates high. National Socialism derived much of its ferocity from the promise to deliver Germany from the tyranny of 'cosmopolitan' finance, symbolised in Berlin as Germany's financial metropolis. As the speaker of the Deutsche Bank said in 1994, both Communism and National Socialism saw the interest rate as a source of exploitation. 'The systems collapse and the prejudices survive.'[81]

Bank 'power' was a recurrent theme in the politics of the Federal Republic. The bank-power debates of the 1960s concluded in 1968 with the government deciding to bring the savings banks into competition with the 'big three'. Another was launched in 1971[82] at the height of Bonn's Ostpolitik, with calls by SPD militants and trade unions for bank nationalisation. The collapse of the Herstatt Bank in 1974, following ill-advised speculation on the currency markets, was then seized upon by the Helmut Schmidt government, with the banks' support, to shore up public confidence in the German banking system. A commission duly reported in 1979 that universal banking had not led to a concentration of bank power.[83]

The controversy was reopened in 1986, when the liberal and opposition parties, the trade unions and the Ministry of Economics launched a market-oriented critique of the Big Three.[84] Attention was thereby drawn to the banks' preeminent position in Frankfurt, even as the Bundesbank and the banks themselves initiated stock-market reforms in earnest. In the course of 1989, however, the Economics Ministry overrode the Cartel Office's veto of Deutsche Bank's promotion of the merger between Daimler-Benz and AEG, despite protestations by the Christian Democrats' liberal coalition partner. The coalition partners agreed on minimal legislation before the end of 1990, obliging banks to publish more information on their supervisory board seats.[85]

In effect, the major German banks' functions altered considerably from the 1970s on, as their securities' activities expanded and their corporate clients became flush with cash. By the early 1990s, Germany's ten largest banks had reduced the number of their equity participations over 10 per cent from a cumulative value of 1.3 per cent of all capital of non-banks in 1976 to 0.5 per cent in 1993.[86] The large banks held only 11 per cent of all German supervisory board seats.[87] But their major role in corporate affairs was as managers of proxy votes at the annual general meetings. One study on proxy votes in annual general meetings of thirty-two of the fifty largest firms showed that 72.7 per cent were wielded by the banks.[88] Banks, in other words, were part of a nexus of banks, insurance companies and industrial corporations,[89] which owned each other's shares and shared each other's supervisory board seats. Part of this nexus were Allianz and Munich Reinsurance, the two Munich insurance giants. As Wolfgang Schieren, the head of Germany's leading insurance firm, admitted at the time, 'Allianz is today a holding company, whose objective is to hold participations'.[90]

Protecting Germany's listed corporations from takeover by foreigners was a central function for the commercial banks,[91] and constituted the heart of their case in the permanent debate about 'bank power'.[92] Their legitimacy derived from their perceived vital protective function against foreign marauders. The argument was most clearly laid out by Alfred Herrhausen, speaker of the Deutsche Bank, in an address to the 'prominenz' of German politics and business in October 1989. It would be inadvisable, he declared, for legislation to oblige banks to sell their stakes. 'I can anticipate excited protests if banks sell our stakes in important German firms to foreigners on the grounds of the continuing and in principle welcome trend to the internationalisation and globalisation of the economy.'[93] Banks, he said, could abandon their voting and proxy powers. But who would replace them? 'I do not have to illustrate to you what would happen if, on the basis of a clear decline in attendance, annual general meetings were to become dominated by active minorities. We have repeated experience of such active minorities. God help us, if our economy should become their plaything.'[94] In other words, German capitalism was legitimate only within a tightly-specified, 'responsible' national community.

Walter Seipp, then Speaker of the Commerzbank, put the point more bluntly. 'If today you restrict or forbid stakeholding for German banks, the Federal Republic will become a sports arena for foreign banks, then you have Jimmy Goldsmith and other people here, and they will demonstrate to you how to buy, sell and strip industrial stakes in a market economy on the American model.'[95] In the German context, this argument was impregnable. It played to the fears of trade unions, the concerns of politicians, and the vehement hostility to an open market for corporate control. It was rooted in German labour, social or corporate law. It outlined government and business practices to stall foreign take-over bids. It appealed to national pride in the manufacturing strength that under-pinned the DM. It equated open share markets with the split banking systems of 'the Anglo-Saxons'.

German unity provided further evidence of the Big Three's fragile legitimacy. The process of German unification began as a joint bank–federation initiative. Treuhand, the state privatisation agency, was given the task by the Finance Ministry in February 1990 to take charge of the 4 million employees in the East German state conglomerates. Deutsche, Dresdner and Allianz promptly bought the commercial arms of the respective former state bank and insurer. The Treaty for monetary, economic and social union came into effect on July 1, 1990, based on a market-credit system 'operating by private economic principles and by competition between private, cooperative and public-law banks'.[96] But private-sector principles were not adequate for the task. The commercial banks insisted that Treuhand take over the debts on the East German corporate balance-sheets. In March 1991, the government launched its 'Upswing East' programme – up to two-thirds of outstanding loans in East Germany were covered by state guaran-tees.[97] The specialised federal credit institutes were mobilised to grant credit to small firms, for housing, and for investments by municipalities. The new states quickly established their own savings and *Landesbanken*. Chancellor Kohl joined the public in criticising the commercial banks for their inadequate contribution, and for their lending only to subsidiaries of West German corporations[98] – 89 per cent of East Germans polled in 1993 considered that the private sector had let them down.[99]

With German unity came dependence on imported capital, and the threat to national control of an increase in foreign ownership. Attendance at annual general meetings had remained at about 70 per cent until the 1970s, but then fell to turnouts below 50 per cent.[100] The main reason given by the banks was that, in purchasing German shares, foreign investors were more interested in receiving dividends than in attending meetings.[101] For the German advocates of shareholder rights, the problem was the continuance of cross-shareholdings as the norm in corporate Germany, and the lack of accountability to shareholders on the part of managers.[102] But the banks' response was that they were accountable to managers, workers and local communities, not only shareholders as the stakeholders of the German economy.

Meanwhile, financial institutions were a focus of political controversy and prejudice in France as well. Bank reforms undertaken in 1966 enabled two investment banks to form federations of companies, accounting in the aggregate for 48 per cent of French industrial value-added and 60 per cent of exports.[103] An alternative programme to this French version of the 'German model' had been forged with the signing in 1972 of a common programme between the Communists and the revived Socialist party.[104] Following his electoral victory of May 1981, President François Mitterrand opted for a 100 per cent nationalisation of thirty-six private banks, two investment banks and eleven industrial conglomerates. This extended public sector accounted for one-third of sales, one-fifth employment and over half of industrial investments in France. The state banking sector encompassed 90 per cent of all banking activity and employed 200,000 people. This state-led 'force de frappe'[105] was to foster investment, to promote new technologies, to reduce national dependence on foreign suppliers and to encourage greater risk-taking. State capital was to flow into a few publicly-owned groups, organised along Japanese *keiretsu* lines. But capital injections to industrial groups went on to the current budgets.[106] The state paid heavy indemnities to the owners. State corporations had to borrow from state banks. Corporations threatened closure unless state funds were made available.

Mitterrand's 'force de frappe' project was shelved in March 1983.[107] But the 1982 nationalisations led the conservative parties to favour sweeping privatisations, which the Socialist government initiated by stealth, by allowing state enterprises to issue non-voting preference shares in the capital market. The 1986–88 Conservative government's ambitious plan to privatise sixty-six public enterprises, worth a total of 300 billion francs, was interrupted by the October 1987 stock-market crash and by Mitterrand's second presidential victory,[108] by which time fourteen industrial and banking firms had been sold for a total of 70 billion francs. One-quarter of the holdings of these firms had been sold to institutional shareholders, and a discretionary limit had been placed on foreign share purchases. This was scarcely compatible with non-discrimination in the EU.[109] Mitterrand's defence of the status quo on ownership effectively starved state-owned companies of capital and prompted successive socialist governments to promote cross-shareholding, jointly-owned subsidiaries, and the sale or issue of state shares on the markets. With the return of the Conservatives in the April 1993 elections, privatisation was resumed, but the cross-shareholdings were maintained.

The driving motive behind the creation of cross-shareholding groups was to prevent nationally owned industries being 'dissolved in Europe'.[110] This view was widely held. The limits to France's commitment to the EU's internal market became evident when the Chirac government in 1986 imposed limits on foreign ownership of denationalised corporations. Re-elected in 1988, Mitterrand invited the legislature to protect French corporations against 'roving, predatory money which grabs everything without effort'.[111] The idea of national majority ownership in large corporate groupings took a number of forms.

- There was the old Gaullist idea of 'participation' whereby employees would own shares and acquire an indirect stake in management. The idea appeared in a variety of guises, such as the 1993 law offering shares to employees at a 20 per cent discount.
- Then came the modified socialist strategy of 1983–86 to constitute industrial poles centred around nationalised banks. As former Prime Minister Mauroy explained, the formula would enable nationalised firms 'to conquer foreign markets'.[112]
- A third variant was the 'hard-core' concept of the 1986–88 Conservative government, whereby the law reserved 25 per cent of privatised firms' capital to major bank or corporate shareholders, selected by the state.
- The socialist governments of 1988–93 sought to harness the big state insurers to the same purpose. The largest cross-shareholding pole in French capitalism was created in 1994, with the privatisation of UAP by, for, and with the support of the state.

The battle over nationalisation or privatisation was fought out in a France which lacked major pension funds or institutional investors. Social security was provided on a pay-as-you earn basis. As outlays rose, governments raised taxes from a total of 35 per cent of GDP in 1970 to an average of 47 per cent in the 1980s. Four-fifths of this increase went for welfare spending. The burden of financing additional welfare was regularly allocated to employers. Companies were not able to keep pension reserves as capital, as in Germany. In the absence of such a pool of capital, the task of creating a substitute was left to the French state.

The cause of cross-shareholding was promoted by the 1982 nationalisation law which allowed the shares of public sector enterprises to be held within the public sector. The Banking Act of 1984 then allowed banks to increase their stakes in companies, pointing further in the direction of a 'German model' of bank–industry relations. After the denationalisations of 1986–88, Finance Minister Bérégovoy had the Treasury promote *rapprochements* between banks and the state insurance companies. The insurance law was reformed in December 1989, enabling state insurers to have up to 25 per cent of capital held by private investors. French diplomacy in Brussels secured Article 12 in the December insurance directive, allowing bank–insurance tie-ups.[113] As the policy's defenders claimed, such cross-shareholdings created 'a powerful and organised financial heart' of corporate ownership.[114]

Given these national conditions in France and Germany, opportunities were limited for financial institutions to break into foreign markets. Few had the depth of Deutsche Bank's pockets to build up even the beginnings of a network through acquisitions abroad. Crédit Lyonnais tried, but fell a victim to its own ambitions. The prevalent approach in the European merger boom of the late 1980s and early 1990s was the formation of friendly cross-shareholding and market-sharing arrangements in banking. Eight such constellations were identified,[115] formed around core banks, three each in Germany and France, and two in Britain. The kernels of these constellations were national. The banks projected their competition on national markets into the constellations. Most acquisitions were of medium to small Spanish and Italian institutions by German or Swiss groups. Few bridges were built across the Rhine between the German and French-based constellations, with the exception of a strategic alliance between Dresdner Bank and Banque Nationale de Paris, and the acquisition of Bank für Gemeinwirtschaft by Crédit Lyonnais.

Continental alliances against and with 'the Anglo-Saxons'

The United Kingdom's internalisation of world financial markets combined with the government's EU strategy posed a major challenge to the French and German national cross-shareholding structures. In both Frankfurt and Paris, financial institutions felt the lure of London, whose markets stimulated their regulators to accelerate reforms at home. Their negotiators were most comfortable with the Second Banking Directive, presented by the Commission in January 1988, which enthroned the German-style universal bank as the model for the EU. They were most on the defensive over EU promotion of cross-border trade in insurance products and investment services. These were the two areas which brought Bonn into part-rivalry with Paris and especially with London. Britain was seen as ruthlessly exporting its 'Anglo-Saxon' preferences for 'casino' finance. The vehicle was the draft directive for investment services, which German bankers interpreted as providing exemptions to UK investment houses that would place them at an advantage in competition with the universal banks.[116] A conditional commitment to monetary union by Bonn to Paris proved one way to divide Paris from London. The constant concern was protection of the intricate arrangements of the German national social market economy, especially in the domain of finance.

The battle with Britain was engaged when Andrew Hugh-Smith, chairman of the International Stock Exchange, proposed the creation of a single European equity market in May 1989. London, he said, would also remain an open door to US and Japanese capital. If others did not join, London would go it alone.[117] What was to be done to keep abreast?[118] Frankfurt had to become the prime continental financial centre. That meant unravelling outdated regulations that had pushed business offshore. As Bundesbank President Pöhl stated in his speech of June 1989, Germany had to place its fragmented stock exchange under centralised state direction. 'I think here above all of Paris.'[119] London as an offshore centre would play a smaller part in an integrated EU market. As an 'active and constructive' partner in building up monetary union, Frankfurt had, the Bundesbank President implied, an evident claim to host the European Central Bank. That month, the Federation of German Labour Unions and the employer organisations agreed on a common strategy for EU social policy.[120] As Kohl urged, German employers and trade unions had to preserve and promote Germany's social practices.[121] Concern was heightened that German firms might fall victim in the ongoing merger wave to European predators.[122]

Germany could not accept the domestic consequences of Hugh-Smith's proposal for a central EU stock exchange. Germany's laws and institutions precluded an open and contestable market for corporate control. Banks dominated the fragmented stock exchanges, and held a monopoly on share-trading. Various other stakeholders received treatment preferential to that of shareholders. Companies in any case balked at disclosure requirements and the loss of control implied in any UK-style stock-exchange listing. The 'book-reserve system' for pensions provided companies with an alternative source of cheap capital and a large pool of retained funds to invest in the business. Co-determination laws made trade unions allies with management in preventing hostile takeovers. Not surprisingly, German banks opposed stricter disclosure laws and any access of less well-capitalised investment houses to German stock markets. The banks defended their industrial shareholdings, and galvanised parliamentary support in Bonn against Brussels' efforts to harmonise legislation on insider trading.[123]

Driving a wedge between the British government, and the City of London – and between London and Paris – was vital in order to protect German domestic arrangements. The task was relatively easy in the 'high politics' of social policy and monetary union, but not in the detailed maze of financial services negotiations. Where France differed from Britain was over monetary union. Mitterrand was eager for it, Thatcher was not. The City was in many minds. French ears, too, vibrated when Germany's senior bankers denounced the concept of a 'financial supermarket',[124] denigrated the 'Anglo-Saxon' division between commercial and investment banks[125] and excoriated 'the unbridled individualism of laissez-faire liberalism'.[126]

But these outbursts recorded German élites' anxiety at their combined failure to defend German interests in international forums.[127] In January 1990 the Finance Ministry hosted a round table to discuss national strategy with regard to the threat from London.[128] The round table's general tone was recorded in the Federation of German Stock Exchanges' annual report.[129] The Federation followed Pöhl's line – develop Finanzplatz Frankfurt on the centralised French model and have London uncouple itself from the European integration process. That meant Bonn mobilising common interests in all EU countries against the British.[130]

Driving a wedge between Britain and France was all the more important because of a series of British negotiating victories. France had supported Britain, but with a view to liberalising its partners' markets rather than its own. In late 1989, Germany's negotiators suffered a series of setbacks. On capital adequacy, the French EU Presidency had the definition watered down in order not to stifle French banks' lending activities.[131] The Federal Association of German Insurers warned the Ministry of Finance of the negative consequences to consumer protection of introducing competition in the EU at the expense of the German insurance industry.[132] But Commissioner Brittan swept ahead with his third wave of insurance directives. Germany's negotiators dropped their obstruction of EU legislation on insurance when France joined Britain and the Netherlands in late 1990 in order to open Germany's market to France's state insurers.[133] And Bonn was furious at being voted into a minority of eleven to one over an EU-wide deposit insurance regime.[134] Then British demands for different capital adequacy standards for securities firms found the German banks lobbying for a more lax definition so as not to be disadvantaged.[135] The banks won a partial victory.[136]

Nor were German interests readily aligned with Paris on the matter of collaboration between stock exchanges. The French Ministry of Finance had long sought to steer the European Federation of Stock Exchanges to adopt its proposals to link the markets. The aim was simply to provide an information and clearing service that would foster retail trade in equities between the various floors of the European stock exchanges. Retail trade on the floor of exchanges was amenable to continental corporate preference for stable shareholders.

The concept was revived in 1989 in modified form as the Price Information Project Europe (PIPE), to provide information on prices for 200–300 blue-chip companies. Rather than have different trading systems, dealers would trade on a single quotation and with one clearing procedure. It then reappeared under the name of EUROQUOTE, with the additional attraction of providing information in real time. An Anglo-German alliance voted it down on the grounds of cost.[137] A similar fate befell EUROLIST, whose more modest aim was to facilitate cross-border transactions while leaving the exchanges to decide their own market procedures. Priority went to domestic reforms, and to Frankfurt's aim to be the leading continental centre in close cooperation with London.[138]

During the course of discussions, German negotiators found many opportunities to vote with the British against the French. Both governments favoured complete freedom of capital movements as a precondition to progress in other areas. Both allied against French demands for an EU capital gains tax. The liberal camp fought hard to keep the power to deny banking licences out of the hands of the Commission, as urged by Paris.[139] German insurers welcomed the break-through in insurance.[140] Germany also resisted demands for the publication of a prospectus for every new issue of negotiable securities.[141] This was consistent with Bonn's opposition to Paris's request for strict regulation of off-floor markets on the grounds that operators should be left the greatest possible free-doms to conduct business in an optimum way. On investment services,[142] German negotiators conceded that British-type investment banks could operate on the Frankfurt stock market. On capital adequacy, the German and British nego-tiators compromised,[143] allowing the regulatory authorities to choose between the rules applying to banks or to investment houses. Germany and the UK, the two main protagonists, thus buried the hatchet over investment services in the course of 1992–93. The directives on investment services[144] and capital ade-quacy[145] entered into effect in January 1996. The directives in effect confirmed host regulators over their own territorial jurisdictions.

Franco-German compatible incompatibilities

Competition between financial centres followed the traditional principle of European balance-of-power politics. All were agreed to prevent any one from predominating. As London was the potential hegemonical centre, alliances had to be forged against it. The French had opened their futures market – the MATIF – in 1986, four years after London's LIFFE. The DTB – Germany's futures market – opened in January 1990. Negotiations between Germany and France to open a joint market for derivatives only began in late 1992 and a deal was announced in January 1993. Each was to have access to the market of the other. The idea was for MATIF members to gain access to DTB's DM derivative contracts, while DTB was to provide software to trade in ECU-denominated products. But it took until May 1994 for both to announce that their combined operation would be up and running by January 1996. The DTB and the MATIF were drawn closer by competition from London, but they also remained competitors. The project in effect faced a host of difficulties. One was the technical problem of linking an electronic trading system like the DTB to a floor-based system like MATIF. Another was that the deal added one further futures market to the seventeen already in operation in Europe. The Bundesbank remained sceptical about futures markets in general. Not least, MATIF products traded after hours in the United States, where the SEC had refused permission to the DTB's products. German accounting practices, quite simply, were not acceptable to the regulator of the world's primary financial market.

There was some small success, too, in strengthening the corporate sinews of the Franco-German relationship. Despite the talk of 'the internal market', national protectionist attitudes abounded. Both sides were aware that the only way to enter the others' protected markets for corporate assets was to negotiate the formation of friendly cross-shareholding and market-sharing arrangements. France's nationalised insurers UAP and AGF acquired stakes respectively in

Colonia and Aachener und Münchener (AMB). Sal. Oppenheim helped France's Victoire into the German insurance markets by selling its shares in Colonia to Victoire. UAP later became associated with this. AGF bought 25 per cent of AMB's shares, but had only 9 per cent of the votes on the board. AMB hid behind the device of nominative shares in order to continue to decide who had voting rights. AGF acquired its full shares of votes after getting Crédit Lyonnais to buy the loss-making German Bank für Gemeinwirtschaft from AMB. Deutsche, Dresdner, Allianz and Münchner Rück increased their share of AMB to insure its independence from the French. The boards of Dresdner and BNP decided to exchange personnel, and then extended the arrangement to buy a 10 per cent stake in each other.

The difficulty with France's 'German model' was also that it blocked 'integration' with Germany – the much-touted overarching objective of French policy. What was practised in France was found to be the French problem in penetrating German markets for corporate assets. There were only thirty-eight French firms listed on the German stock exchanges in 1991,[146] and French firms quoted on the Frankfurt market were fewer than in Munich. German corporates had a restricted presence in Paris. The Finance Ministry kept a wary eye over Allianz's efforts to buy its way into the French insurance market, while German insurers were equally protective of their national market. Crédit Lyonnais had to break off its discussions on a strategic alliance with Commerzbank because no agreement could be reached as to who would lead in their particular markets. BNP and Dresdner reached an agreement to cooperate in Spain and eastern Europe, an arrangement which worked precisely because it was limited to third countries. German institutions preferred to build up their presence in London, as did French banks. There were only 5 German banks in Paris in 1988, out of a total of 256 foreign financial firms, compared to 12 from the UK.[147] France had 32 bank entities in the UK in 1991, accounting for 29 per cent of French banking business in the EU, against 18 German banks accounting for 6 per cent.[148]

There was much selective imitation in France's 'German model', which envisioned long-term savings serving as the 'war sinews' of a 'modern Colbertism',[149] to finance projects with long gestation periods. Banque de France Governor Trichet had long been an advocate of 'German-style' bank–industry relations. Credit establishments with equity positions in companies would be co-responsible for corporate strategies. Stable ownership of large firms would enable French managers to invest in the development of their workforces and their products. National capital would be protected against unwanted takeovers, especially if state-owned as well as private capital was represented among the core shareholders on the board. Cross-shareholding, its proponents maintained, preserved management powers, but did not make them unaccountable. Board members remained responsible for their own institutions, as well as for the prosperity of the company, its suppliers, its workforce, its clients and its shareholders. The presence on boards of institutional investors assured a minimum of representation for shareholders. It was only when shareholdings were dispersed among a broad and fragmented public that managers ruled their corporate roosts unchecked.[150] In any case, withdrawal of the Trésor from refinancing banks meant that France's undercapitalised firms had to turn to other firms, banks and insurers to raise funds. A mixed economy, involving state and private capital, was essential to enable financial institutions to play a responsible role and pay attention to the longer-term requirements of their organisations.[151]

Not surprisingly, there were considerable penalties incurred by French capitalism in sustaining a mixed-purpose capital market. Listing terms were not attractive. The official market required that a minimum of 25 per cent of a listed company's capital broadly be held by the public, although the second market had less onerous terms. An OTC facility was available, but firms in general shunned it. Only 630 companies were listed in 1991 on the first market, and of the largest 200, two-thirds were family-controlled. The state presence was pervasive. Shared personnel across the blurred boundaries between ministries and corporations ensured a common cause among French corporations – that the state would retain discretionary powers to protect and promote their interests. Both family and state enterprises used similar devices to preserve ownership, despite the passage of laws against the use of reciprocal holdings within corporate groups to protect against external takeovers. These devices included statutory restrictions on shareholder voting rights, the rights of boards of directors to count abstentions in their favour, and the predominant influence of the state through cascade-holdings where minority owners could wield ultimate power. Most of the listed companies were held in this way, and were estimated to comprise about one-third of the 890 companies listed on the three German stock exchanges.[152] The equity market was hardly a discipline on corporations so much as an additional (albeit marginal) source of funding.

The high interest rates of the 1992–93 recession dealt the French 'German-style' bank policy a deadly blow. Between 1988 and 1993, Crédit Lyonnais had increased its industrial portfolio from FF5 billion to FF47 billion. That year, Crédit Lyonnais tipped into the red. Its chairman, Jean-Marie Haberer – who had been responsible for the 1966 bank reforms, and had introduced the banking reforms in the 1980s in his capacity as Directeur du Trésor – was dismissed. French opponents of France's 'German' model had for long pointed out the risks attending large bank exposures. Banks were responsible to their depositors, and were not necessarily well qualified to manage corporations. They became too much a prisoner of their clients' interests. Their participation in cross-share-holdings weighed on their market valuations, just as their capital base was too bound to the performances of their corporate owners. If the shareholder was the state, Crédit Lyonnais served as a prime example of the state's inability to fulfil its assigned role. Its management took risks which private shareholders would not have endorsed. Besides, the 'mixed economy' provided no clear ground rules. Too many of its resources had become locked into loss-making activities, as the threat of bankruptcy lessened. Entrenched interests received different treatment to that of relative outsiders. The state's direct involvement in ownership introduced bitter corporate battles for control into the heart of party politics and career prospects within the administration. And it made foreign or French private enterprises reluctant to be closely associated with state firms.

Meanwhile, German dependence on capital imports to finance unity prompted corporate Germany to close ranks to fend off the threat to their armoury of ownership posed by foreign investors as the marginal suppliers of funds in the early 1990s. Pension funds investing in German equities formed a broadening constituency in favour of more value for shareholders' money.[153] This constituency also sought reciprocal access to all possible markets. Frankfurt was no exception, with a surge in transactions volume on the exchange by a factor of 22 during the 1980s. In 1990, foreign investors owned 14 per cent of German equity market, and 50 per cent of freely-traded shares.[154] The most prominent of these investors were the Anglo-American institutions. Their target was Germany's corporate nexus of cross-shareholdings and their hidden value, in anticipation of an end to restrictions on shareholder voting. Their cause was furthered by EU legislation, the commercial banks' ambitions to build up the German Finanzplatz, and a more assertive German shareholder lobby. Influence over the direction and content of policy was heightened by their readiness to move their business away from Frankfurt if reforms were not forthcoming. And it was fostered by the German dependence in the early 1990s on imported capital, yet restricted by corporate Germany's view on stable ownership as a source of economic strength.

There was near-unanimous rejection by the German corporate sector of the SEC's efforts to export US accounting standards, aimed at providing unbiased and equal information for the benefit of all shareholders. The introduction of uniform accounts across all markets created the conditions for rational choice by investors. This in turn fostered heavy trading in shares, eagerly promoted by stockbrokers and investment bankers living off deals. They earned no income from loyal investors waiting forever for capital gains, as opposed to trading profits. Hence, US authorities' requests for reciprocal access of banks to bond markets complemented US institutions' demands for changes in the German law to one vote per share. In 1990, Deutsche Bank gained entry as a primary dealer to the US government bond market, but only after the Bundesbank had further eased access to the domestic bond underwriting consortium.[155] German companies improved disclosure of their holdings, and adopted more generous dividend policies. But they drew the line at any move to US-style transparency and contestability. Corporate Germany greeted Daimler-Benz's listing in October 1993 on the New York Stock Exchange as a betrayal of German principles of long-term commitments by investors.[156] Daimler-Benz's example was the sole German corporation among 594 foreign companies listed on the US exchanges.

More serious for corporate Germany's peace of mind were its own failings. German equity law stipulated a two-tier system of corporate governance. It postulated a strict division of tasks between the supervisory board (control) and the board (management). The supervisory boards were there to provide advice, information and experience. Yet in every recession, the supervisory boards were charged with incompetence. The electrical and electronic giant, AEG, was only salvaged from bankruptcy in 1982 with a combined bank, insurance, industrial and government-backed bailout. Similarly, the industrial conglomerate Metallgesellschaft had to be rescued with a financial package of DM3.4 billion in the winter of 1993–94, following losses in oil futures. In April, the Schneider construction group folded, with a debt of DM5 billion. In all of these cases, the impending disaster had not been monitored. The banks were seen as asleep at the wheel, ready to lend to large groups regardless or unaware of the risks, while supervisory boards were accused of operating as closed shops.[157] Yet for all the ritual of criticism, the beneficiaries of the German supervisory board system were too diverse for any coalition to form in favour of fundamental change. The varied nature of the board members' background symbolised the commitment to stakeholders in the corporation, rather than the priority to shareholders' interests encapsulated in Anglo-American corporate practice; this despite widespread lip-service to the alien concept of 'shareholder value'.

State financial systems and Maastricht Europe

The link between investment services and other policy areas in the EU points to alternative interpretations of the process leading to – and away from – the Maastricht Treaty.

- One interpretation is that the Treaty was the result of a marriage between traditional intergovernmental diplomacy and the practice of neo-functionalism by both member states and the Commission. The investment services directive was tied into negotiations in the EU on social policy, mergers and acquisitions, or monetary union.
- Another interpretation is that there was a strong dose of instrumentalism in Helmut Kohl's move in March and April 1990 to promote monetary and political union with President Mitterrand. Both agreed that the Anglo-Saxon thrust to open up equity markets had to be stymied, and that there was no better instrument to sink Thatcher than to promote a single currency.
- A third interpretation would hold that Kohl's motives were more circumstantial, in that the nexus of issues on the negotiating table in late 1989–90 required uniting Germany to shore up its relations with France.
- The final interpretation holds that Kohl had always been a convinced European federalist, and that the move to German unity had to go hand-in-hand with moves, together with France, toward European unity.

On April 19, 1990, Kohl and Mitterrand issued their joint declaration on European monetary and political union. The aim was 'to strengthen the democratic legitimacy of the union, to make the institutions more efficient, to ensure united and coherent action in the economic, monetary and political fields, and to bring about a common foreign and security policy'. The declaration opened the way to the negotiations on European union that led to the signing of the Maastricht Treaty in winter 1991–92.

As soon as the Treaty was signed, its flaws became apparent. A central flaw in Germany was the lack of support in the country for an 'irreversible' move to monetary union. The government's reasoning was therefore that German national prestige had to be satisfied as compensation for what *might* entail an abandonment of the DM. The campaign in favour of locating the ECB in Frankfurt had two dimensions. In the EU, Germany would be able to isolate the United Kingdom; in Germany, success would entrench Frankfurt as Germany's prime financial centre. The campaign was launched in January 1992, when Kohl made an official visit to Frankfurt for the first time in his ten years as Chancellor. He pledged to bring the ECB to Frankfurt and backed Finance Minister Theo Waigel's strategy to make the German Finanzplatz first among continental competitors. The 'Big Three' banks then threw their weight onto the scales in a public relations campaign, proclaiming monetary union as a logical consequence of the internal market,[158] and Germany as Europe's rising power, in contrast to Britain's decline.[159] In September, the combination of Bundesbank policy and developments on world financial markets had the pound sterling ejected from the exchange-rate mechanism, which it had joined only two years earlier. The Bundesbank then insisted that the pound sterling could only rejoin the exchange-rate mechanism at a rate agreed by all. As the British government was not prepared to have Germany determine sterling's 'correct' parity, and had not in any case signed up for the third phase of monetary union, London was effectively out of the running.

France's turn came next. The German government refused to discuss interest-rate policy with the French in June 1993, and rejected French proposals for a revaluation of the DM at the crisis meeting of EU Finance Ministers in Brussels in August. But the Bundesbank did intervene in the markets to sustain the franc. The reward came at the October 1993 EU summit in Brussels, when Kohl persuaded the majority of member states to locate the ECB in Frankfurt.

The breakdown in the exchange-rate mechanism was not unwelcome to the Bundesbank. At the level of symbolic politics, breakdown showed that it alone was 'the bank that rules Europe'.[160] More prosaically, the Bundesbank was relieved that it no longer had to support other currencies in the exchange-rate mechanism, at the risk of losing control over the German money supply. Each year, from 1990 to 1994, the Bundesbank's monetary target had been exceeded, and inflation had averaged 4 per cent a year. The Bundesbank's argument that 'special factors' accounted for its monetary problems was especially poignant in view of the fact that domestic conditions were scarcely separable from world markets. On the demand side, eastern German residents and eastern European neighbours turned eagerly to the DM in the months following the fall of the Berlin Wall. Government subsidies for bank loans in eastern Germany boosted credit expansion to private and public-sector borrowers. Higher interest rates attracted highly mobile funds from Germany or around the world. On the supply side, once the government in January 1994 taxed interest income associated with German holdings in Luxemburg, much of the money came home. More importantly, German corporations borrowed heavily abroad, since 80 per cent of private German savings were absorbed by government borrowing. Above all, the Bundesbank had to inject tens of billions of DM into the money supply in order to buy francs, pounds sterling and lira. In short, the exchange-rate mechanism leveraged Bundesbank control over European monetary aggregates.

Chancellor Kohl launched corporate Germany's effort to return to financial autonomy in September 1993, one month after the EU's latest financial melodrama. A government 'Report on Securing Germany's Economic Future', published on September 2, 1993, provided a catalogue of the country's ills, including high relative wages, an ageing population, over-regulation of markets and a government which absorbed nearly half the national income. As in 1982, the programme trumpeted control of labour costs, reduction in government expenditures, privatisation, increased flexibility, export expansion, and a return to healthier corporate financing through capital market reforms. Its announcement coincided with an inflection of Kohl's discourse away from a vision of a federal Europe, official requests for Germany to have a seat on the UN Security Council, and the Constitutional Court's judgement that the Maastricht Treaty created a 'confederation, which is sustained by the states'. Any future progress towards European Union, the Constitutional Court argued, would have to meet German parliamentary approval.

This half-way house in Germany's European policy was inherent in the process of the EU's transition from a 'confederation, sustained by the states' to a fully-fledged EU, with a much stronger federal content. On the one hand, Germany – as the EU's major power – had to deploy resources within and beyond the EU in order to achieve its objectives. On the other hand, deployment of those resources indicated the extent of Germany's new power to influence Europe in the way it felt appropriate.

But which way did Germany wish to go? The firm intention of German political, business or labour leaders was to ensure that capitalism in Germany would remain a national brand of its European variant. The hard core of Germany's social market economy was the stable structure of corporate ownership and power. That social market economy required corporate Germany to keep financial autonomy, to finance a generous welfare state, to sustain an export drive and to fund Germany's various international policies and commitments.

France's reforms amounted to 'Colbertisme' in modern guise. Reformers had borrowed from – but stopped well short of espousing – the Anglo-American approach. That would have meant establishing a truly liquid and transparent security market and a contestable market for corporate control. France had also borrowed from, but not imported, the German system. That would have required less 'Colbertisme'. The guiding principles for the modernisation of the French financial system was to improve the funding of the state, and the key objective of the related reforms of corporate financing was to ensure national ownership. The

French statist reforms led to a mercantilist conclusion in that its thrust was to seek to shift from consumption to investment and exports. In 1992, France moved back to trade surplus, in particular with Germany and the rest of the EU. National savings rates edged upwards. By 1994, the corporate sector was 113 per cent self-financing, dependent on neither banks nor equity markets.[161] France in the 1990s had become compatibly incompatible with Germany.

French and German policy demonstrated a cultural aversion to a more cosmopolitan approach to conducting financial affairs, and a marked propensity to export the costs of its own policies to neighbours. Both could only retain a none-too-comfortable status quo through perpetuating mercantilist practices. Yet both were engaged on a voyage to union, where universal banking was underwritten by the EU financial services regime and where shareholders across the EU would enjoy a free securities market. Beyond union stood the prospect of a 'British' Europe, where the European financial area would become an integral part of globalised financial markets, not only in London, but across the whole EU. The negotiated outcome of the EU Financial Area, though, also preserved the state system in Europe. Far from leading to an internal market, the relaunch of Europe in 1985 had therefore pointed straight towards a revival of European inter-state competition. At the heart of this competition lay the battles between different financial systems for hegemony in Europe. The completion of the transition from an inherited state system to an integrated Europe still lay ahead.

Notes

1 *Financial Times*, September 30, 1982.
2 *Financial Times*, April 9, 1984.
3 *Financial Times*, March 22, 1984.
4 Adrian Hamilton, *The Financial Revolution* (London: Adrian Hamilton, 1986); Charles Goldfinger, *La Géofinance* (Paris: Seuil, 1986).
5 Alfred Herrhausen, Deutsche Bank spokesperson, quoted in the *Financial Times*, November 28, 1984.
6 'London as an International Financial Centre', *Bank of England Quarterly Bulletin*, Vol. 29, No. 4, 1989.
7 'Europe's Capital Markets', *The Economist*, December 16, 1989.
8 *Europe*, Document No. 1800, October 3, 1992. 'Premier Rapport de la Commission Européenne au Conseil sur les Relations de la CEE avec les Pays Tiers dans les Secteurs des Banques et des Asurances'. The figures quoted are for 1990.
9 'Strategic Options in the EC '92 Market', *Bankers Magazine*, September–October 1991.
10 Switzerland and Hong Kong accounted for another 20 per cent of global exchange trading.
11 Figures quoted by Benn Steil, *Competition, Integration and Regulation in EC Capital Markets* (London: Royal Institute of International Affairs, 1993).
12 *Barriers to Takeovers* (London: Coopers & Lybrand, 1993).
13 'The Future of European Capital Markets', *Financial Times*, July 5, 1989.

14 'Mehr Marktorientierung der Bankenaufsicht Gefordert', *Handelsblatt*, January 24, 1991.
15 'Nur der Verband der Auslandsbanken ist für einen Beteiligungsabbau per Gesetz', *Handelsblatt*, December 8, 1993.
16 Deutscher Bundestag, Anhörung, *Macht von Banken und Versicherungen*, December 8, 1993, Verband der Auslandsbanken.
17 'Im vergleich schneidet Frankfurt nicht günstig ab', *Handelsblatt*, August 30, 1990.
18 'La France, Terre d'Accueil des Banquiers Etrangers', *Le Monde*, July 25, 1989.
19 'Small Bang Fall Out', *Financial Times*, December 12, 1991.
20 'France Presses on with Liberalisation', *Financial Times*, September 26, 1991.
21 Günther Bröker, *Competition in Banking* (Paris: OECD, 1989).
22 Statement of Robin Hutton, Director of banking, insurance and financial institutions in the Commission, quoted in *Financial Times*, December 5, 1977.
23 *Rewe-Zentral AG v. Bundesmonopolverwaltung für Branntwein (Cassis de Dijon)*, Case 120/78, 1979 Eur. Ct Repts 649, 1979 Common Mkt L. Repts 494.
24 'Closer Scrutiny of Euromarkets Sought', *Financial Times*, 9 August, 1979.
25 OECD Economic Surveys, *Germany*, 1979.
26 'Closer Scrutiny of Euromarkets Sought'.
27 J.O. L193, 17.8.1983.
28 'Fierce Debate on Likely Reforms', *Financial Times*, August 30, 1984.
29 J.O. L372, 8.12.1986.
30 *International Trade in Services: Securities* (Paris: OECD, 1987).
31 *Financial Times*, October 11, 1986.
32 The BIS defined own funds in terms of two tiers: tier one referred to basic equity, or core capital; tier two included supplementary capital, a varied assortment. The EC own-funds directive of April 1989 allowed for the inclusion into tier one of funds for general risks. Each member state remained free to accept the tougher BIS criteria. *Europolitique*, No. 1489, April 19, 1989.
33 *The Economist*, January 6, 1990.
34 *Europolitique*, No. 144, October 22, 1991.
35 J.O. L166/77, 28.6.1991.
36 J.O. L166/83, 28.6.1991.
37 Comments by Georges Zavvos, MEP, *Europolitique*, No. 1805, October 21, 1992.
38 The convention, open to ratification by the US, Canada and Australia, came into effect in May 1993. *Europolitique*, No. 1858, May 12, 1993.
39 J.O. L110/52, 28.4.1992.
40 *Journal de Genève*, April 8, 1991.
41 See the recommendation on deposit guarantees, J.O. L33/16, 9.2.1987; also the recommendation on bankruptcy, which sought to apply the home-country responsibility principle, languished in the entrails of the EC policy process. J.O. C36/1, 8.2.1988.
42 J.O. C178/14, 30.6.1993.
43 J.O. L334/30, 18.11.1989.
44 *Les Echos*, March 18, 1987.
45 *Europolitique*, No. 1502, June 7, 1989.
46 *Wall Street Journal*, June 19, 1989.
47 Philippe Vigneron and Aubry Smith, 'The Concept of Reciprocity in Community Legislation: The Example of the Second Banking Directive', *Revue du Marché*

Commun, No. 337, May 1990; Hal Scott, 'La Notion de Reciprocité dans la Proposition de 2è Directive Bancaire', *Revue du Marché Commun*, No. 323, January 1989.

48 *Europolitique*, No. 1372, January 16, 1988.
49 *Financial Times*, July 14, 1988.
50 'Who's Afraid of 1992?', *Newsweek*, October 31, 1988; 'Fortress Europe', *International Management*, December 1988.
51 Remarks by Governor R. H. Heller, Cato Institute Conference on *Governing Banking's Future: Markets Versus Regulation*, November 2, 1988.
52 Omnibus Trade and Competitiveness Act, P.L.100–418, 100th Congress, 2nd Session, 23.8.1988, Para. 3603.
53 Henri Froment-Meurice, 'L'Europe de 1992: Espace et Puissance', *Documentation Française*, March 1988. The report was written at the request of the French government.
54 Conseil Economique et Social.
55 Commission Bancaire, *Rapport 1994*, 'Dix Ans d'Activité et de Résultats des Banques Françaises'.
56 Press Information, 'Europe, World Partner', October 19, 1988.
57 *Le Monde*, November 9, 1988.
58 *European Community News*, October 20, 1988.
59 The European Parliament sought to restrict non-member state subsidiaries' rights under EC law. *Europolitique*, No. 14381, March 18, 1989; No. 1543, November 25, 1989. The concession was made to European Parliament demands, that branches of non-member banks may not benefit by the right of establishment. Lord Croham, 'Reciprocity and the Unification of the European Banking Market', for the Group of Thirty, December 18, 1989.
60 *Wall Street Journal*, June 20, 1989.
61 *Europolitique*, No. 1481, March 18, 1989.
62 Croham, 'Reciprocity and the Unification of the European Banking Market'. See also *Europe*, Documents, 'Premier Rapport de la Commission Européenne'.
63 'Financial Markets in Europe: Toward 1992', J. P. Morgan, *World Financial Markets*, Issue 5, September 9, 1988.
64 Sir Leon Brittan's speech to the European Parliament, *Information*, 14.4.1989.
65 *Europe*, Documents, 'Premier Rapport de la Commission Européenne', Chapter 3.
66 J.O. L185/81, 4.7.1987.
67 J.O. L348/62, 17.12.1988.
68 *Europe*, Documents, 'Premier Rapport de la Commission Européenne'.
69 *Europolitique*, No. 1446, November 9, 1988.
70 With the backing of Spain, Italy, Belgium and the Netherlands: *The Economist*, November 19, 1988.
71 Philippe Jaffré, Directeur Général de la Caisse Nationale, 'L'Intermédiation en Europe', *Le Figaro*, March 11, 1989.
72 *Europolitique*, No. 1446, November 9, 1988.
73 J.O. L124/8, 3.5.1989.
74 *Europolitique*, No. 1680, May 29, 1991.
75 *Europolitique*, March 7, 1990.
76 J.O. L141/35, 11.6.1993.
77 *Europolitique*, No. 1781, July 1, 1992.

78 *Europolitique*, No. 1789, March 15, 1993.

79 *Ibid.*

80 Fritz Stern, *L'or et le Fer: Bismarck et son Banquier Bleichröder* (Paris: Fayard, 1990).

81 'Kopper Gesteht Arroganz', *Handelsblatt*, June 15, 1994.

82 'Macht Ohne Aufsicht: Banken in Westdeutschland', *Der Spiegel*, January 18, 1971.

83 Gessler Kommission, 'Grundsatzfragen der Kreditwirtschaft, Bericht der Studienkommission', Shriftenreihe (Bonn, Bundesministerium für Finanzen: 1979).

84 'Grossbanken und Finanzgruppen', *WSI Mitteilungen*, 7 July 1986 provided an analysis of big three shareholdings. The Monopoly Commission report on the Daimler-Benz–AEB merger prompted the Bank Association to refute the allegations of bank power. 'Wir müssen in globalen Dimensionen denken: Commerzbank Vorstandsvorsitzender W. Seipp über die Macht der banken', *Der Spiegel*, July 14, 1986. The Academic Advisory Council, a permanent body attached to the Economy Ministry, supported the Monopoly Commission's perennial proposal to reduce any bank's equity stake in a non-bank to 5 per cent. 'Bonn economic advisers press for curb on banks in industry', *Financial Times*, December 22, 1986.

85 'Bonn unter Begrenzung der Bankenmacht uneinig', *Suddeutsche Zeitung*, September 7, 1989; 'Die Macht aus den Hinterzimmern', *Die Zeit*, October 27, 1989.

86 The banks' 'glasnost' came in the form of public communications from the Bundesverband der Deutschen Banken on July 25, 1987, March 29, 1989 and October 29, 1993.

87 *Supervisory Board Mandates in the Largest German 100 Corporations in 1988*, (Cologne: Bundesverband Deutscher Banken, 1990).

88 Arno Gottschalk, 'Bankeneinfluss und Depotstimmrecht', *WSI-Mitteilungen*, No. 5, 1988.

89 Rolf Ziegler, Donald Bender and Hermann Biehler, 'Industry and Banking in the German Corporate Network' in Frans N. Stokman, Rolf Ziegler and John Scott (eds), *Networks of Corporate Power: A Comparative Analysis of Ten Countries* (London: Polity Press, 1985). Josef Esser, 'Bank Power in West Germany Revisited', *West European Politics*, Vol. 13, No. 4, 1990; Tim Jenkinson and Colin Meyer, 'The Assessment: Corporate Governance and Corporate Control', *Oxford Review of Economic Policy*, Vol. 8, No. 3, 1993.

90 Interview with Wolfgang Schieren, *Die Zeit*, September 12, 1991.

91 Auschuss für Wirtschaft des Deutschen Bundestages, *Stellungnahme des Bundesverbandes der Deutschen Industrie zur öffentlichen Anhörung*, May 16, 1990.

92 'Kurzsichtige Kontroverse', *Die Zeit*, October 6, 1989.

93 Alfred Herrhausen, 'Es Riecht nach Komplott und Konspiration', *Die Welt*, October 27, 1989.

94 *Ibid.*

95 Ausschuss für Wirtschaft des Deutschen Bundestages, *Offentlicher Anhörung, Protokoll*, Nr. 74.

96 'Staatsvertrag zwischen Bundesrepublik and der DDR', *Die Welt*, May 16, 1990.

97 'Spearheading the Transition', *Financial Times*, July 1, 1992.

98 *Handelsblatt*, April 14, 1994.

99 'Verzerrtes Spiegelbild Deutscher Empfindungen', *Handelsblatt*, October 23, 1993.

100 *Anhörung*, Macht der Banken und Versicherungen, Bundesverband der Deutschen Industrie, November 30, 1993.

101 *Ibid.*

102 'Insider on the Outside', *Financial Times*, July 29, 1994.

103 Bertrand Bellon, *Le Pouvoir Financier et l'Industrie en France* (Paris: Seuil, 1980).

104 The new Socialist secretary-general told his party militants, in language redolent of the neo-socialist fascists of the 1930s, that 'the dominant phenomenon of capitalist concentration, money, enters everywhere and devours those whom it is supposed to assist'. Quoted in Catherine Nay, *Le Rouge et le Noir: Ou l'Histoire d'une Ambition* (Paris: Grasset, 1984).

105 'French industrial policy', *Financial Times*, January 8, 1982.

106 First Report of the High Council of the Public Sector, cited in *L'Année Politique, Economique, Sociale et Diplomatique* (Paris: Editeur du Moniteur, 1985).

107 Jacques Blanc and Chantal Brulé, *Les Nationalisations Françaises en 1982*, Notes et Etudes Documentaires, Nos. 4721–2, June 20, 1983.

108 Michel Bauer, 'The Politics of State-Directed Privatisation: The Case of France 1986–88', *West European Politics*, Vol. 11, No. 4, October 1988; Hervé Dumez and Alain Jeunemaitre, 'Privatisation in France' in Vincent Wright (ed.), *Privatisation in Western Europe, Pressures, Problems and Paradoxes* (London: Pinter, 1994).

109 In a letter of March 25, 1988 to Finance Minister Balladur, Lord Cockfield reproached France for the August 1986 legislation, reserving special treatment to French shareholders: *Le Figaro*, April 7, 1988.

110 The expression is that of Olivier Pastré, consultant to the Trésor: 'Pastré: le reveil des ZINvestisseurs', *La Tribune de l'Expansion*, September 7, 1992.

111 'Taste for Regulation Revived', *Financial Times*, November 2, 1989.

112 *L'Année Politique, Economique, Sociale et Diplomatique.*

113 Commission Bancaire, Rapport 1993, 'La Bancassurance en France'.

114 'La Logique du Coeur Financier', *Le Monde*, October 8, 1991.

115 'Liberating Capital', *International Management*, February 1990.

116 'Genug Kapital für Moderne Infrastruktur in der DDR', *Handelsblatt*, December 12, 1989.

117 *Financial Times*, September 11, 1989.

118 Bank Association Chairman Röller, 'Wir müssen den Anschluss an die internationale Entwicklung behalten', *Frankfurter Allgemeine Zeitung*, September 20, 1989.

119 Karl Otto Pöhl, 'Frankfurt im Konkurrenzkampf der Finanzplätze neue Rahmenbedingungen sind schnell erforderlich', *Frankfurter Allgemeine Zeitung*, June 24, 1989.

120 See Bundesvereinigung der Deutschen Arbeitgeberverbände, *Jahresbericht*, 1989.

121 See Presse und Informationsamt der Bundesregierung, Nr. 40/S 333 (Bonn: March 22, 1988). Ansprache des Bundeskanzlers, 'Europas Zukunft-Vollendung des Binnenmarktes 1992', Nr. 172/S 1525 (Bonn: December 9, 1988). Erklärung des Bundeskanzlers zur Eröffnung, Nationale Europa-Konferenz in Bonn. Also 'Europakonferenz: Kohl will Mitbestimmungsmodell Offensiv Vertreten', *Handelsblatt*, August 31, 1989.

122 *Frankfurter Allgemeine Zeitung*, January 20, 1989. Economy Minister Haussman stated, in the Bundestag Europe debate, that the merger wave must not sweep away Mittelstand firms, on which the vitality of the German economy depended.

123 'Les Délits d'Initiés au Régime de l'Honneur', *Journal de Genève*, January 28, 1989.

124 Interview with Dr Ulrich Ramm, Chief Economist, Commerzbank, in *Asian Finance*, September 19, 1989.

125 Deutsche Bank Spokesperson Alfred Herrhausen had a hard exchange with Sir Leon Brittan over the Investment Services Directive: 'Können Deutsche Banken Künftig nur noch mit Londoner EG-Pass operieren?', *Handelsblatt*, October 26, 1989.

126 Former Deutsche Bank Spokesperson, Dr Wilfried Guth, in 'Auf ein Wort', *Die Welt*, October 17, 1989.

127 'Können Deutsche Banken künftig nur noch mit Londoner EG-Pass operieren?', *Handelsblatt*, October 26, 1989.

128 *Handelsblatt*, January 31, 1990.

129 *Handelsblatt*, March 15, 1990.

130 'Auch für die Unternehmen steht viel auf dem Spiel', *Handelsblatt*, May 12, 1990.

131 'Ein fauler Kompromiss', *Handelsblatt*, December 21, 1989.

132 *Frankfurter Allgemeine Zeitung*, May 26, 1989.

133 'Insurers Still Face Problems in Pursuit of a Real Single Market', *Financial Times*, June 29, 1992.

134 'Bank Deposit Plan Angers Bonn', *Financial Times*, September 14, 1993.

135 'Einschränkung bei der Anerkennung von Reserven dringend notwendig', *Handelsblatt*, October 29, 1992.

136 'German banks win modification to capital rules', *Financial Times*, November 26, 1992.

137 *Financial Times*, July 5, 1991.

138 'Bank Chief's Sights Set on Central Role for Germany', *Financial Times*, June 10, 1992.

139 *Wall Street Journal*, June 20, 1989.

140 *International Herald Tribune*, September 24, 1990.

141 *Europolitique*, No. 1446, November 9, 1988.

142 Commission Information, November 25, 1990.

143 *Europolitique*, No. 1776, June 13, 1992.

144 J.O. L141/27, 11.6.1993.

145 J.O. L141/1, 11.6.1993.

146 'Frankfurt, Une Place Financière Incontournable', *Le Monde,* March 8, 1991.

147 Commission Bancaire, *Rapport 1991*, 'L'Implantation des Principaux Etablissements de Crédit Francais à Vocation Internationale dans les Autres Pays de la Cté Economique Européenne'.

148 Commission Bancaire, *Rapport 1988*, 'L'integration Financière Européenne et la Concurrence Bancaire Analyse Rétrospective (1978–1988)'.

149 Denis Kessler, 'Le Nerf de la Guerre du Capitalisme', *Le Monde*, March 15, 1994.

150 Jean Peyrevelade, 'Le Rôle des Investisseurs Institutionnels', *Cadres CFDT*, December 1990.

151 Interview with Michel Albert, 'La Nouvelle Guerre Froide', *Option Finance*, August 30, 1991.

152 'Reform Marred by Contradictions and Confusion', *Financial Times*, July 3, 1989.

153 See *Board Directors and Corporate Governance: Trends in the G7 Countries Over the Next Ten Years* (Oxford: Oxford Analytica, 1992).

154 'Frankfurt's Role Consolidating', *Financial Times*, May 31, 1994.

155 'Wall Street Yields to Deutsche Bank', *Financial Times*, December 20, 1990.

156 'Feeling of Betrayal in Corporate Germany', *Financial Times*, October 22, 1993.

157 'Bonn in New Move to Avert AEG Collapse', *Financial Times*, July 7, 1982; 'Club der Amateure', *Manager Magazin*, August 1993; 'Der Zusammenbruch des

Bauimperiums Schneider: Eine schwere Schlappe für die deutschen banken', *Die Zeit*, April 22, 1994.

158 'Absage an die Kritischen Thesen zu Maastricht', *Neue Zurcher Zeitung*, June 17, 1992.

159 'Frankfurt: Germany's Financial Capital Prepares to Meet the Single Market', *The Economist*, December 17, 1992.

160 David Marsh, *The Bundesbank: The Bank that Rules Europe* (London: Heinemann, 1992).

161 Commission Bancaire, *Rapport 1994*, 'La Situation du Système Bancaire Français'.

11

Epilogue

Given the long and painful path towards financial integration in Europe, it remains to suggest a few conclusions and signposts for the future.

EMU and financial integration

Completion of the transition from discrete and competing financial systems embedded in the institutional and political fabric of the member states, to a European financial area under a common regulatory framework and authorities, still lies ahead. As in earlier decades, the states of Western Europe have sought to reconcile the maintenance of a stable exchange-rate regime with residual discretion in national policy. But in contrast to previous attempts at monetary union, the criteria and timetable was this time ratified by all EU member states as a token of their commitment to 'an ever-closer union' of states and peoples. The broad design was for a single currency, managed by one central bank, with sole responsibility for a monetary policy that in turn required extensive coordination of fiscal policy. As envisaged by many, this macro-stream for Europe was to end in one unified financial market regime, largely inspired by 'Anglo-Saxon' criteria of consumer sovereignty, shareholder-orientation market and transparency, with world markets operating to reinforce convergence on common ground-rules in what promised to be the world's largest internal market.

With the political commitments made, the project's supporters would argue that the train has left the station. Most likely, the start of the new millennium will see a Europe of the ins and outs, with the former benefiting from lower transaction costs, improved capital allocation and the economic dynamism likely to come with it, hopefully including a vibrant pan-European equity market and a much more active market for venture capital that will help to propel Europe once again to the front ranks of some of the world's cutting-edge industries. This will come at a price, as the exchange-rate disappears as a policy tool, as monetary policy is subordinated to the interests of the whole, as fiscal policy migrates from national environments to the level of the EU, and as the political costs of these developments become increasingly evident. But some of these costs have already been incurred, and the system has been stress-tested during the recession and currency crises of the early 1990s. So the remaining hurdles seem surmountable.

Our analysis of the national financial regimes, and the complex negotiations to create the European financial area, hint at an alternative future. In this view, national regimes continue to evolve within their own logic, rooted in specific historic constellations and the cumulative layers of reforms and adaptations through which they have passed. Lessons from history in each EU country vary according to fashion or to the problems of the hour, while initiatives imported from other regimes and systems remain inevitably partial. National financial regimes imply national financial systems, which have in turn been characterised by specific forms of regulation, corporate governance, and bank–industry relations. They function optimally in their own governmental structures and labour markets, such as Germany's inclusive stakeholder arrangements or the hire-and-fire approach introduced in the United Kingdom in the 1980s. They are anchored in their particular national currencies, which stand against each other on the global foreign-exchange markets. World markets in such conditions help to perpetuate national forms of capitalism, rather than to lead them to 'converge' on a single norm. An international regulatory regime covering a diverse mosaic of financial systems such as exists in Europe is much more likely to resemble the detailed and ambiguous negotiated outcome of the European Financial Area than an idealized caricature.

Indeed, the durability of national financial systems and regimes suggests scepticism about the prospect of a rapid break from past experiences, especially when efforts to sustain stable exchange regimes – whether in their own right or as preludes to union – have regularly broken down. There is no obvious reason to consider as credible the claim that the achievement of nominal convergence on the basis of the Maastricht criteria among a select group of member states presupposes an ability of national polities to adapt their institutions one to another without great difficulty. Financial systems and corporate practices are more likely to converge under the pressure of competition in the global markets and through the implementation of the European financial area legislation over the coming decades. That lengthy convergence is likely to be extremely turbulent, given that the EU's social policies remain national rather than supranational in content, form and identity. Clinging to nominal convergence criteria while maintaining existing national systems implies continued high unemployment across the EU. The pools of nationally unemployed that are likely to persist within a fragmented economic space under a single currency, are resented and fought over. The fundamentals of the EU project are thus both shaky and speculative.

Furthermore, Western Europe, as the first chapter suggests, over the past decades has been prone to progress by muddling through, postponing settlement of differences, settling on incremental changes and resisting temptations to dramatise disagreements. If differences were deep and required settlement, they could always be reintroduced in more favourable political circumstances. Playing on the factor of time proved to be a crucial ingredient in the dynamic consensus which went under the broad concept of 'integration'. With German unity, as discussed in Chapter 3, all that changed. Maastricht made 'irreversible' the commitment to move to a single currency, where the Germans would surrender the DM in return for French support for a constitutional design in the EU compatible with the principles laid down in Germany's Basic Law. This was to be accompanied by progress in the definition of a common foreign and security policy, and in implementing a common social policy. Progress on all fronts has been elusive. But the commitment to a timetable suggests that all major unsettled business in Europe must be resolved by 1999–2002. Maastricht, quite simply, has deprived the weary EU policy process of its necessarily opportunistic use of the future to focus on present disagreements. The EU policy process is, therefore, quite likely to deprive Maastricht of some of its promise.

Sources of change in national financial systems

National financial systems in the EU remain distinct but dynamic in response to broader changes in society and markets, in the composition of national policy communities, in the style of public or corporate policy, and in the context of world politics and markets.

* They have adapted as occupational structures, evolving technologies and ageing populations have produced more demanding clienteles. They have been transformed by inflationary growth policies which undermined the fixed exchange-rate regime of the 1960s, and diverged as a result of differing streams of policy that led to restraints on the development of Germany's equity markets, to the inflation-cum-devaluation cycle of France's overdraft economy, and to the undermining of the United Kingdom's archipelago of financial cartels by the evolution of parallel markets, followed by empirical efforts to regain control.
* The composition of national policy communities has changed over time, with alterations in bank–industry financing, in government regulation, and in the growth of capital markets. A shared trend in Germany and France has been towards the bank cross-shareholding system presented in stylised form in Chapter 5, while Great Britain from 1979 at the latest confirmed its equity-based system. Germany's stakeholder institutions and laws have been adapted as the savings and cooperative banks have moved to the fore, the 'Big Three' banks have campaigned to make Frankfurt Germany's pre-eminent Finanzplatz, and Allianz and Munich Re have occupied centre-stage in Germany's tangled web of bank–industry cross-shareholding. France's state-led financial system has evolved from its segmented and bank-based format inherited from the 1940s to a hybrid predicated on a dominant capital market in Paris, and mixed ownership bank–industrial cross-shareholdings, where French insurers also occupy a central place in the 'inextricable interpenetration' of state and corporate interests that lies at the heart of France's political

market-place. By contrast, the transformation of Britain's lightly regulated financial cartels into regulated and competitive retail and wholesale markets has confirmed London as Europe's 'city of capital', host to financial institutions from the EU, the United States, Japan and the rest of the world.

- Styles of public policy and market discourse have evolved as regulators and market participants adapted to opportunities, learnt from past mistakes, and indulged in the process of selective emulation. Great Britain's public discourse of competitive and regulated markets, absorbed in part from US experience, became the standard fare of the EU's internal-market programme, but modified in practice by the public policy style of experimental learning by doing, referred to in Chapter 8, and by the Treasury's preference for host-country control and international regulatory cooperation that flowed from British goals of internalising global markets in London. Germany's 'organised liberalism' was also injected into the regulatory discourse of the EU's internal-market programme, while the inclusiveness of Germany's federal policy process and stakeholder system drove the pace and content of financial market reforms, as discussed in Chapter 6. As in France, the thrust of German policy was to preserve a national brand of European capitalism while negotiating the foundations for an EU-wide regime. France's idiosyncrasy was to introduce its own version of 'the German model' into its own potent brew of corporatist, nationalist and Marxist policy strands, while borrowing from US experience on capital market development.

- The changing context of world politics and markets provided national financial systems with opportunities to survive and permanent incentives to adapt. The rhythm of national policies and performances – presented in Chapter 2 – has been dictated first and foremost by the dollar, as the world's key currency, which provided the enabling conditions for a stable exchange-rate regime in the 1950s and 1960s, the shift under President Nixon's administration towards a world of floating exchange-rates and dollar-based world financial markets, and then, starting in the 1980s, the swift turnaround in those markets from credit-based activities to securities markets. Latin American debt crises of August 1982 reinforced the shift in British, French and German financial policies to adapt financial markets to new conditions in London, Paris and Frankfurt. The exponential development of wholesale capital markets was driven by the growth of government and corporate-bond markets, as the US and European states vied for world savings. This was the context in which the DM emerged as the world's second reserve currency, the Bundesbank became Europe's *de-facto* central bank and power in the economic policy debates shifted to Germany.

Growth and transition in the EU financial regime

The founders of the EU insisted on the creation of institutions which could outlive anyone toiling in the fields of European integration, and could embody the determination of the EU's founders to overcome the Continent's fragmentation, identified by many as the source of the Continent's ever more savage wars. The history of establishing a financial service regime bears witness to their conviction, as the 1961 EU Council programme, discussed in Chapter 2, in effect had to wait until 1985–86 before acquiring programmatic form and content. The reasons for delay lie in the aforementioned multiple incentives for financial systems to survive and adapt. The French and Italian financial policy communities, for instance, were unprepared to relinquish control over new issues on national capital markets, while initially there was adamant opposition in London to regulation from Brussels. As a result, the EU's mercantilist states were unprepared to jointly confront the world of competing currencies, frenetic bank lending to developing countries, inadequate monetary controls and struggles for market-share which followed on Nixon's crucial decision in August 1971 to put an end to the dollar's convertibility into gold, thereby terminating the US economy's role as anchor of the world financial system. EU member states responded in their own ways to new conditions. Germany successfully isolated its financial system by floating the DM freely on foreign-exchange markets, clamping down on domestic consumption, raising exports, and incorporating trade unions into corporate decisions. But the member states also cooperated in the development of EU institutions, such as the European Council or the Bank Advisory Committee.

When did this pre-transitional period end, out of a 'non-system' – as French commentators called the post-1971 years – towards a negotiated pact to create the foundations for a new EU-wide financial regime? The year 1982–83 marked the turning-point, with the rapid shift to securities on world financial markets, the creation of the Internal Market Council, the changes in government in Bonn and of policy in Paris, capped by the re-election of a radical Tory administration in 1983. The German Finance Ministry and the Bundesbank, with the support of the 'Big Three' universal banks, began their prolonged campaign to revitalise equity markets in Germany. Meanwhile, Mitterrand's first government, faced by an explosion of foreign debt and a collapse in national savings, accelerated bank and financial-market reforms in order to ease the constraints on financing France's extensive public sector and its welfare commitments. And the British government, facing no effective opposition and politically defenceless brokers, jobbers, merchant banks and discount houses, pushed through a set of radical regulatory reforms which transformed the inner workings of the British financial system. With varying motives, the EU Commission, member states and major corporations allied on a common platform, based on the Commission's 'new approach' to reduce non-tariff barriers within the EU.

The decision phase marking the transition from discrete national regimes to an EU-wide regime spans the decade of negotiations between 1983 and 1993. The results of these prolonged and complex negotiations yielded benefits for national regulatory authorities, big institutional investors, the wholesale financial markets, and London in particular. They provided an additional incentive for France and Germany to accelerate reforms of domestic markets and practices, and opened up banking, securities and non-life insurance to cross-border trade. As measures moved towards retail financial markets, the sensitivities of national authorities became more evident. Arguably, none of the legislation saw a clear victory for the home-country principle, as the member states negotiated a host of clauses into the directives reserving host-country authorities' discretion. As we have argued, member states were not prepared to surrender powers over financial firms making decisions within their national jurisdictions that might affect 'the public interest' or the ability to compete in world markets. But they were prepared to 'pool' joint powers of supervision of markets within the EU infrastructure of committees, while keeping the Commission at arm's length.

One aspect of the multi-dimensional chessboard on which the commitment to move to an EU-wide regime was played out was in the bureaucratic battles in the EU, in bilaterals, or in other multilateral forums. There was broad agreement to promote universal banking, to foster bank–securities–insurance universals, to legislate extension of regulatory reach beyond the national level, and to negotiate for transition periods which provided time for necessary domestic changes in market structures to be pushed through.

All participants, with the notable exception of the British, sought to ease access to others' markets while limiting access to their own. Their positions were riddled with internal contradictions, which stood in often stark contrast to their vaunted role as champions of EU integration, and which derived from their need to protect or to promote a host of domestic interests. The fundamental flaw in the French negotiating position was to seek to prevent the internal consolidation of a financial system for a united Germany, while continuing to implement the French version of the 'German model' in order to protect national rights of ownership and ensure the Treasury continued access to its privileged financial circuits. The United Kingdom negotiated to open the EU markets to investment services, but balked when the French and German joined to promote a federal EU, requiring extensive surrender of national powers to joint EU institutions. Germany vaunted its European vocation on monetary union and a common foreign policy, but plied a distinctly national path with regard to financial markets.

There was no let-up during the definitional phase in the competition for market share between London, Paris and Frankfurt. London had the advantage of first mover in the introduction of futures markets, and then of SEAQ International, pulling away trades from the secluded and less efficient continental markets. This galvanised competing centres to update their technologies, their settlement systems or their regulatory frameworks. Paris, like London, opened its markets to Anglo-American financial firms, sought to expand the liquidity of the markets and moved slowly to privatisation of French state enterprises. German financial reforms progressed more slowly because of the multiple interests that demanded attention, but were driven forward by the determination of Frankfurt's reforming coalition of banks, by the continued growth of the bond market, and by fear of losing equity and derivatives trading to rival centres. But institutional sensitivities circumscribed reforming zeal in both continental centres. Corporate governance in both Germany and France was ill at ease with the signs of growing shareholder activism, which placed in doubt the prerogatives of managers and workforces. Sources of financial-market liquidity were hindered by broad political resistance to any tampering with inherited pay-as you-go pension schemes. Indeed, one of the major reasons cited for continued national protection of retail banking markets and life insurance was avoidance of foreign-exchange risk for small investors.

Both France and Germany therefore were in accord to protect their national brands of European capitalism, pending the big leap to monetary union. Up to that moment, their financial systems would remain – as they had been in the past – service providers for retail customers and national corporations competing on European or world markets. Both financial systems provided incentives for firms to compete for market share, rather than profitability, and translated into national mercantilist priorities. All key candidates for the first wave of monetary union, led by France and Germany, run persistent trade surpluses. Once in monetary union, though, the urgency of shifting corporate policies rapidly in the direction of a pronounced emphasis on shareholder value is likely to be accentuated. The resulting turmoil in labour markets is likely to be extreme unless monetary union is swiftly followed by a surge in growth, as business people respond to new opportunities. Equally, monetary union may well spell the death of national bank–industrial cross-shareholding structures, given that the EU principle of non-discrimination on nationality grounds is bound to be upheld in law, with regard to ownership structures, and the search for cheaper equity capital opens up shareholdings to new and more performance-oriented global investors. It is in this sense that Great Britain's is by far the most 'European' of all national financial regimes.

Europe and the structure of global banking firms

Financial integration in Europe will proceed quite irrespective of the movement towards EMU. The reason is that wholesale finance has progressed far down the globalisation path, and obstacles such as national currencies can be easily surmounted, and in some cases present as many opportunities as challenges for financial institutions. Banks and securities houses thrive on imperfect markets, and market imperfections are often the products of government policies that create fault-lines across markets. Yet exploitation of market imperfections itself carries with it an inevitable progress towards more competitive markets, and this dynamic will prevail regardless of the specific features of EMU.

We have concluded that the universal bank has emerged as the dominant form of financial organisation in Europe, the only exception being the British tradition of merchant banking and the French *banques d'affaires*. By 1996, however, most of the British merchant banks had been acquired by European universals –

Morgan Grenfell by Deutsche Bank, Kleinwort Benson by Dresdner Bank, S. G. Warburg by Swiss Bank Corporation, Hoare Govett by ABN Amro, and Barings by ING Groep. With Smith New Court having been acquired by Merrill Lynch, this left only Robert Fleming, Schroders and Rothschilds as the remaining merchant banks, with the latter having established a strategic alliance with ABN Amro. In France, the sale of Banque Indosuez to Crédit Agricole left only Banque Paribas and Lazard Frères as the remaining *banques d'affaires*, and the major French universals consolidating their positions in the domestic investment-banking business. In Spain and Italy too, such institutions as Santander and San Paolo di Torino are developing their securities activities.

So universal banking as a structural form of providing financial services seems to have captured Europe.[1] As is often the case, however, every victory is only a ticket to a new and even more challenging contest, and now the European universals will be in a battle for dominance with the major US integrated investment banks, as well as commercial banks that have made the transition to investment banking, notably Bankers Trust and J. P. Morgan. And if US restrictions separating commercial and investment banking are repealed or further undermined by judicial or regulatory actions, there will be more of these. The resurgent Japanese banks and securities houses, likewise subject to deregulation at home, will likely be back in the global fray in force toward the end of the 1990s as well.

So far, the Americans have dominated the field. Data on market shares and league tables of firms engaged in international wholesale banking is necessarily partial in coverage. However, available information suggests that much of the market is highly competitive and contestable, even though in some areas market structure is quite concentrated. Tables 11.1 and 11.2 show 1995 market shares and their evolution over the period 1990–95 in international investment banking (underwriting of equities and fixed-income securities plus mergers and acquisitions) and international syndicated lending, respectively, for the leading banks and securities firms. This composite league-table represents a rough guide to the various banks' prominence or visibility in the market. Note that, of the top ten firms, all were American except for one (CS First Boston), which was partially American. The top-twenty listing contains a more varied mix of US, European and Japanese firms – but again with three-fourths wholly or partially American.

US securities firms have achieved a disproportionately large share of international business in this industry. How this will develop in the years ahead as the industry consolidates globally remains to be seen. The Herfindahl Index[2] shows that market concentration has roughly doubled for the top ten firms during 1990–95, and increased by about 50 per cent from 1992 to 1995 for the top twenty firms. Note that the European universals are far more heavily represented in the second ten than in the top ten firms, and each of them has expressed an interest, either explicitly or implicitly, in being among the top global players early in the new millennium. As mergers and acquisitions in the industry occur, including further purchases of investment banks by universals and development of selected lending capabilities by the major US investment banks, many observers believe

Table 11.1 Global wholesale banking and investment banking, 1995 (full credit to book running manager only; $ billions)

Firm	Global debt & equity securities underwriting & placement (a)	Global M&A advisory (b)	International loans arranged (c)	Medium-term notes lead-managed (d)	Total	% of industry total
Merrill Lynch	173.43	34.76	2.00	208.80	418.99	10.8
CS/First Boston	109.58	66.22	45.90	69.00	290.70	7.5
Chemical/Chase	11.30	—	272.40	—	283.70	7.3
J.P. Morgan	76.32	53.72	128.60	—	258.64	6.7
Morgan Stanley	104.52	113.77	—	18.00	236.29	6.1
Goldman Sachs	96.44	83.64	2.00	39.06	221.14	5.7
Lehman Brothers	91.15	46.17	—	55.00	192.32	5.0
Salomon Brothers	82.28	39.34	—	21.40	143.91	3.7
Citicorp	10.70	—	116.50	10.30	137.50	3.6
Bear Stearns	38.31	47.81	—	31.50	117.62	3.0
SBC Warburg	36.75	31.50	11.30	—	79.55	2.1
Deutsche MG	23.87	21.35	20.40	12.50	78.12	2.0
UBS	30.06	15.81	31.10	—	76.97	2.0
Lazard Houses	—	75.45	—	—	75.45	2.0
NationsBank	18.40	—	38.90	13.00	70.30	1.8
Smith Barney	29.33	25.75	—	5.96	61.04	1.6
ABN/Amro	20.94	—	23.10	7.50	51.54	1.3
Bank of America	7.00	—	42.20	—	49.20	1.3
Nomura	48.32	—	—	—	48.32	1.2
DLJ	32.26	14.83	—	—	47.09	1.2
Total industry	1535.1	575.80	1098.40	656.70	3866.00	100.0
Top 10% as % of total	51.72	84.31	51.66	68.99	59.49	59.49
Top 20% as % of total	67.81	116.38	66.86	74.92	75.98	75.98

Notes:
(a) Global rankings, top 25, completed deals only, including all US private placements; Securities Data Corp.
(b) By market value of completed global transactions, full credit to both advisers, top 25 advisers; Securities Data Corp.
(c) Full credit to book manager, top 25 managers as reported, *IFR International Financing Review*, Jan. 20, 1996.
(d) Global MTNs, top 25 managers; Securities Data Corp.

Table 11.2 Global wholesale banking: market concentration, 1990–1995

	1990	1991	1992	1993	1994	1995
Top ten						
% of market	40.6	46.1	56.0	64.2	62.1	59.5
Herfindahl Index	171.6	230.6	327.8	459.4	434.1	403.0
No. of firms from:						
USA	5	7	5	9	9	9
Europe	5	3	5	1	1	1
Japan	0	0	0	0	0	0
Top twenty						
% of market			80.5	75.6	78.1	76.0
Herfindahl Index			392.7	478.4	481.4	439.5
No. of firms from:						
USA			8	15	15	14
Europe			11	4	5	5
Japan			1	1	0	1

that universal banking will be the dominant form of organisation of global financial institutions in the years ahead. If so, the European form of organisation will have won again – this time in global wholesale financial markets – and with it will come all of the strengths and weaknesses associated with universal banking. Even for the United States this will represent a trip 'back to the future', returning to the universal form of financial institutions (appropriately adapted to today's conditions) that existed before 1933.

Europe and the global pattern of corporate governance

Whereas the European form of financial institution structure may well become dominant among global firms in the twenty-first century, this is unlikely to be repeated with regard to the continental European approach to corporate governance and state exercise of management influence through government and bank shareholdings. This is not inconsistent with financial liberalisation and the wider use of securities markets by continental European corporations or with increasingly performance-oriented portfolio management on the part of mutual funds, insurance companies and other institutional investors. Both appear to be leading toward a gradual shift away from bank finance, and a weakening of tight industry–bank relationships.

There have already been the beginnings of unwanted takeover attempts in continental Europe through acquisition of shareholdings by unaffiliated (often foreign) investors.[3] There have also been a number of embarrassing lapses in the role of banks on supervisory boards of non-financial corporations in continental Europe, casting doubt on the efficacy of the classic 'insider' relationships between banks and industry. At the same time, easing of bank activity-limits in the United Kingdom and the United States is allowing them to play a larger role in industrial restructuring transactions, and to exploit some of the information and relationship advantages they have as lenders. Gradual convergence of Anglo-American style capital-market orientation and Euro-Japanese style bank–firm linkages will test the relative merits of outsider and insider systems – that is, the importance of information asymmetries against the free market's capability of allocating and pricing capital both within and across national frontiers. And the rapidly growing role of mutual funds and pension funds in the United States and in Europe, where the unviability of existing pension arrangements in coping with onrushing demographic changes will be a challenge of epic proportions, will challenge the European pattern of corporate control with much greater activism and orientation to shareholder value on the part of institutional investors. It is here that the Anglo-American approach is likely to undermine the traditional continental European ways of doing things within an increasingly integrated European financial playing-field.

Meanwhile, the transformation economies of Eastern Europe are casting around for appropriate models to speed economic recovery after half a century of failed experimentation with command economics. They too are likely to 'buy into' the emerging pattern of universal banking and contestable patterns of corporate control likely to characterise Europe and the United States.

Timing of the transition

We have sketched some of the many facets of fundamental changes that would have to sweep through the EU as national monetary and financial regimes are supplanted by a wider EU-wide regime. When is that likely to occur? The official timetable indicates that the starting date for consolidation of a European financial area will be at the latest January 2002. But between now and 2002 the member states will navigate in waters that simultaneously promise to sweep them forward into a new and qualitatively different EU, or to keep them swirling around in the repetitive cycles of the past fifty years, punctuated by efforts to promote a fixed exchange-rate regime or monetary union and constantly undermined by divergent policies and performances among competing mercantilisms.

The following conclusions would appear to be compelling, and point the way forward.

- In the past, German universal banks have had a lock on DM bonds, both domestically and offshore. UK and French financial institutions have not had a comparable advantage. If EMU goes through, such distinctions will disappear and all banks will be competing in a highly liquid market.
- The future European financial market-place will be composed of vigorously competing centres, which will have to provide a broad range of services or disappear into niche positions. This is a major problem for Frankfurt as an end

to the DM bond market means that institutions operating in that environment will have to offer financial services equivalent to competitors elsewhere. That already means that the Bundesbank has yielded to pressure to allow development of active money markets – not least because of the funding requirements of government.

- There is no indication so far that financial markets have had consistent success in effectively pressuring governments toward fiscal balance. Under a single currency and with a relatively independent central bank, as we have argued, German, French or UK bonds will be rated and priced as if they were New York or California bonds in the US municipal markets. This will place significant constraints on public financing throughout the EU.
- Highly liquid markets and contestable financial markets will provide corporations throughout the EU with a new range of opportunities for external financing, but those opportunities are likely to go hand in hand with greater scrutiny of management and workforce performances. Shakeouts, downsizing, management accountability and shareholder value along Anglo-American lines will thus continue to permeate Europe.
- Social policies remain national. So intensified competition spells dissolution of national cross-shareholdings, and an end to quasi-permanent credits given generously to corporations, on a relationship basis, which fail to earn adequate returns for performance-oriented shareholders.
- In turn, the pressures for greater accountability spell further moves in France and Germany to Anglo-American accounting, intensified political debates on corporate governance, growing pressures to develop Europe-wide interest groups and political parties to martial demands and convert them into policy through the Euro-policy process, and increasingly tough bargaining in the Council of Ministers.

In short, financial integration and EMU represent a revolutionary programme which promises to denationalise market structures, and blow open national bond markets/ cross-shareholdings, impact labour markets and transform national politics. Are today's European political and business leaders quite so revolutionary? Probably not. Germany does not go for 'Big Bangs', and prefers to do things consensually. France is ambitious, but existing arrangements and commitments weigh heavily. The United Kingdom is probably the best prepared, but lacks political support for the leap into the full set of EU commitments. Meanwhile, France wants to Europeanise Germany, whose political leadership in turn wants to oblige business leaders and the general public who abhor financial instability and the prospects of inflationary Euro-policies beyond their control, even as Britain is having to choose to be in on the ground floor or wait and be nudged sideways in what promises to be a political struggle to decide who wins in the 'battle of systems'.

The prospect of repetitive cycles stretching into an indefinite future provides a central motivation to cash in the political capital invested in the EU's most ambitious project to date. Indeed, monetary union is seen as a catalyst for future initiatives toward political union. By contrast, the Bundesbank has argued that for monetary union to succeed, it has to be sustained by a polity capable of absorbing the inevitable and perhaps extreme tensions associated with such a revolutionary step. Only the existing states now have the legitimacy which enables them to answer the central political question: By what right do you rule? The EU institutions have little to none. It is therefore reasonable to argue that a less ambitious path to a more integrated Europe, one that resorts to the tried and tested EU negotiating technique of using the future as a place to locate present disagreements, may prove more capable of sustaining the prolonged passage which lies ahead to consolidation of the EU's single financial area. Between these two positions there is no obvious meeting ground. Faith and reason are no longer distinguishable in the politics of the EU financial area and monetary union.

Notes

1 See Anthony Saunders and Ingo Walter (eds.), *Universal Banking* (Oak Brook, IL: Richard D. Irwin, 1996); and Anthony Saunders and Ingo Walter, *Universal Banking in the United States* (New York: Oxford University Press, 1994).
2 The Herfindahl Index is the sum of the squares of the market shares, i.e. $H=\Sigma s^2$, which lies somewhere below 10,000 (pure monopoly) and zero, with the index declining as the number of competitors rises and, for a given number of competitors, the index declining as market shares are more evenly distributed. This is the most powerful available statistic describing market structures.
3 Ingo Walter and Roy C. Smith, *Investment Banking in Europe* (Oxford: Basil Blackwell, 1990).

Index

Note: 'n' after a page reference indicates the number of a note on that page. Information relating to a particular country is indexed under that country's entry.

Aachener und Münchner Beteiligungs Gesellschaft (AMB), 169, 204–5, 300
Accepting Houses Committee, 226
Action Programme for Employment and Growth, 17–18, 90
AEG, 292, 303
A. G. Becker, 201
agency problems, 139
agricultural policy, 34–5
Air France, 207
Alexanders Laing & Cruickshank, 204
Allianz, 169, 170, 205, 292
Alphandéry, Edmond, 66
Al Saudi bank, 212
Altus Finance, 202, 207
American Express, 170
Arbeitsgemeinschaft der deutschen Wertpapierbörsen, 176
arbitrage, 119
Ardant, Henri, 219–20, 220n.8
Association Française des Banques (AFB), 192, 196, 212
Association Française des Etablissements de Crédit (AFEC), 197
Association of Foreign Banks, 175
Association of Future Brokers and Dealers (AFBD), 241, 249n.64
Association of International Bond Dealers (AIBD), 242
Assurances Générales de France (AGF), 204–5, 299–300
Atlantic Council, 4

Australia, 4
Austria-Hungary, 33
Automobile Association, 170

Baker, James, 54
balance of payments, 40, 42
Balladur, Edouard, 80, 200, 215
Banco Ambrosiano Holdings, 282
Banco Commercial Español, 204
Banco de Santander, 206
Banco di Roma, 205
Banco Hispano Americano (BHA), 205–6
Banco Jover, 204, 205
Bank Advisory Committee, 15, 21, 282, 288
bank-based system, corporate control, 140–2
Bank Credit Laws, Germany, 164, 165, 171, 176
Bankers Trust, 320
Bank for International Settlements (BIS), 4–5, 22, 27, 35, 196, 237, 243, 261, 275, 281–5
Bank für Gemeinwirtschaft (BfG), 204, 205, 296, 300
bank-industrial crossholding system, corporate control, 142
Banking Act (1979, UK), 235
Banking Act (1984, France), 193, 197, 201, 210, 212, 295–6
Banking Act (1985, France), 194
Banking Act (1987, UK), 235, 236, 237
Banking Securities Act (1987), 242, 245

Bank of Credit and Commerce
International (BCCI), 24, 212, 235,
243, 245, 284, 285
Bank of England, 55, 224–5, 226, 232,
234–7, 278
Bank of England Act (1946), 225
Bank of Italy, 50
Bank of Japan, 146
bank-subsidiary structure, 137–8
Bank Supervisory Office, Germany, 170
Banque de France, 35, 65, 66, 67, 190–1
'German model', 217–18, 219
reforms, 197, 212, 214, 215
Banque Française de Commerce
Extérieure (BFCE), 194
Banque Indosuez, 121, 192, 204
Banque Nationale de Commerce et
d'Industrie (BNCI), 199
Banque Nationale de Paris (BNP), 197,1
99, 206, 207, 296, 300
Banques Arabes et Françaises (UBAF), 199
banques d'affaires, 150, 320
Banques de Dépôts, 199
Barclays Bank, 198, 225, 229
Barclays de Zoete Wedd, 230
Barre, Raymond, 48, 191
Basel-Nyborg Agreements (1987), 54
Bayerische Hypo, 170
Bayerische Landesbank, 169
Belgium, 4, 12, 14, 63, 203–4, 258, 267
Benedetti, Carlo de, 289
Bérégovoy, Pierre, 201, 206, 211, 214, 296
Berrill, Sir Kenneth, 240
Bingham, Justice, 243, 245
Bloch-Lainé, François, 199
Bloomberg, 116
Blum, Norbert, 83
bond underwriting, 118–19
bonds, EU, 69
Bonn accord (1978), 11
BOSS, 181
Bourse, 212–13
Boyer, Miguel, 80
Brandt, Willy, 10, 76
Breeden, Richard, 268, 283
Breit, Ernst, 83
Bretton Woods system 33–6
Breuer, Rolf E., 181
British Insurance Brokers Association,
238
Brittan, Leon, 22, 267–8, 281, 284, 288,
298

brokerage, 119
brokers, 227
Brussels Treaty (1948), 4
budgets, 42
building societies, 225–6, 229, 241
Bundesbank
capital movements, liberalisation, 20
as central bank of Europe, 32, 45, 50
Delors' negotiations with, 76
economic and monetary union, 84,
87–8
ECU, 49
EMS, 49, 51, 54
exchange-rates, 46, 48, 50
export surplus, 44–5, 50
financial services, 162, 163, 164, 168,
171, 172, 175–7, 178, 180
German unity and tension in the ERM,
61–2, 65, 66–7
Maastricht Treaty, 97
political integration, 43
role in ECB, 85, 86
termination of currency intervention to
support the dollar, 10
unemployment blamed on, 11
Burani, Umberto, 27, 250
Bush, George, 82
business sector, financial intermediation,
110
buy-side assignments, 120

CAC, 215
Caisse des Depôts et Consignations
(CdC), 150, 192, 193, 208, 211, 212
Caisse Nationale du Crédit Agricole
(CA), 193
Callaghan, James, 234
Canada, 4
capital gains tax, 174
Capital Issues Committee, 227
Capital Market Committee, 22
capital movements, 1, 8, 18, 20, 24, 254–7
Cartel Office, Germany, 168, 170
Carter, Jimmy, 51–4
Cassis de Dijon, 15–16, 251, 281
Cecchini report, 28
Cedel, 215
Central Capital Market Committee, 44
Central Credit Committee, 166
central securities deposits (CSDs), 121
Chaine, Jacques, 199
China, 10

Chinese walls, 138
Chirac, Jacques, 77, 78, 86, 200, 213
Cholet-Dupont Michaux, 201, 202
Citibank, 170
clearing banks, 225, 228
Clerq, Willy de, 286
Clindus, 203
Clinvest, 203
Cockfield, Arthur, 1, 16, 24, 89, 252, 259, 281, 285, 290
collective investment vehicles, 110, 121, 257–9
Colombo, 12, 13
Colonia Versicherungs AG, 169, 204, 300
Comité de la Réglementation Bancaire (CRB), 197
Comité des Etablissements de Crédit (CET), 197
Comité des Organisations Professionelles du Crédit (COC), 22
Commerzbank, 166, 205, 206, 300
Commission Bancaire (CB), 197, 212
Commission des Opérations du Bourse (COB), 210–11, 216, 219, 257
Committee of Central Bank Governors, 19–20, 35, 81, 82, 86, 87
Committee of Stock Exchanges, 22
Committee on Banking Regulation and Supervisory Practices, 237, 282
Commodity Futures Trading Commission (CFTC), 243, 276
Common Agricultural Policy (CAP), 35
Common External Tariff (CET), 6
Common Programme of the Left, 189–90
Communauté Financière Africaine (CFA), 195
Communist Party of the Soviet Union (CPSU), 77
Compagnie Française pour la Commerce Extérieur (COFACE), 194
Companies Act (1980), 239
Company Securities (Insider Trading) Act (1985), 244–5
competition, 4, 25, 118–22, 254, 262
   France, 197
   Germany, 165, 167, 168, 171
   UK, 228, 229, 234
Competition Commission, 197
Completing the Internal Market (1985 White Paper), 250–1
Comptoir National d'Escomptes de Paris (CNEP), 199

computerisation, German financial services, 179–80, 181–2
Congress, 3
Conseil des Bourses de Valeurs (CBV), 216, 218
Conseil du Marché à Terme (CMT), 215
Conseil National de Crédit (CNC), 191
Conseil National des Assureurs (CNA), 211
Constitutional Court, 163–4, 168
consumer sector, financial intermediation, 110
consumption, 11–12
Contact Committee, 21–2
contracting, financial, 110–12
Control Commission, France, 211
control medium, 140
Cooke committee, 222n.35
cooperative banks, Germany, 167, 169
corporate tax, 174
Council for Economic and Finance Ministers (ECOFIN), 19
Council for Mutual Economic Assistance (COMECON), 45, 172
Council for the Securities Industry (CSI), 238, 239
Council of Europe, 5, 22
counterparty risk, 38
County NatWest, 230
Crédit Agricole, 192, 193
credit cards, 170
Crédit Commerciale de France, 206
credit institutions, 118
Credit Law (1976), 44
Credit Law (1985), 45
Crédit Lyonnais (CL), 197–210, 296, 300, 301
Crédit Médical de France, 202
Crédits Populaires, 199
Cresson, Edith, 209
CREST, 237
Criminal Justice Act (1987), 245
Cruise missiles, 12
currency swaps, 38
Czechoslovakia, 4

Daimler-Benz, 292, 302
Daiwa, 121
DAX, 182
Debré, Maurice, 191, 192
Defence and Security Council, 80
Deflassieux, Jean, 199, 200

Delors, Jacques, 76
  Action Programme for Employment
    and Growth, 18
  Crédit Lyonnais saga, 201
  EMS, 91
  ERM, 51
  European Financial Area, 254, 255,
    256
  financial market reforms, 86
  internal market, 18, 75
  monetary union, 20, 21, 75, 80, 81, 94
  political union, 1
  Presidency of Commission, 13, 196
  securities markets, 213
  'social dimension', 80
demand for money and credit, 39
Denmark, 10, 25, 63, 65, 66, 261, 264
Department of Trade and Industry (DTI),
    225, 239, 240, 243, 244
Deutsche Bank, 166, 168, 170, 179, 180,
    183, 198, 278, 302
Deutsche Börse AG, 181
Deutsche Genossenschaftbank, 169, 176
deutschemark, 36, 44, 46, 55–9, 60, 61–2,
    84–5
Deutscher Kassenverein, 182
Deutsche Terminbörse (DTB), 181, 299
Deutsche Wertpapierdatenzentrale GmbH
    (DWZ), 181
DG Bank, 169, 176
disclosure rules, Germany, 183
discount houses, 226
dollar, 5, 10, 35, 36
  exchange-rates, 55–6, 59, 60, 61
  as world's key currency, 3, 11, 33–4, 45
Dresdner Bank, 166, 170, 205, 206, 296
Dupont, Xavier, 215
dynamic efficiency, financial systems,
    114–15

East Germany, 45
  see also Germany, reunification
Ecole Nationale d'Administration (ENA),
    191
Ecole Polytechnique, 191
Economic and Financial Council, 54, 77,
    80
Economic Policy Committee, 20
efficiency, financial systems, 112–15
electronic data interchange (EDI), 125
Elysée Treaty (1963), 80
Emminger, Otmar, 73n.25

employment and unemployment, 11–12,
    34, 40, 75, 96, 190
Equity Law (1966), 175
equity-market system, corporate control,
    139–40
establishment, right of, 7, 8, 9, 19
Euro, 97
Eurobond market, 70
Eurocard, 170, 211
Euroclear, 215
Euro-Clinvest, 203
Eurodollar market, 224
Eurofiet, 22
EUROLIST, 298
Europartners, 205–6
European Atomic Agency Community
    (Euratom), 6, 9
European Banking Confederation, 21
European Central Bank (ECB)
  arguments for, 51
  competition to host, 63–5, 66, 67, 304
  currency, 85
  differing views, 94
  France and Germany, different views,
    87–8
  Germany attitudes, 61, 84, 86
  Maastricht Treaty, 93
  monetary union, implications, 79
  proposals for, 80
  role, 67–9, 71
European Coal and Steel Community
    (ECSC), 5, 9
European Company Statute, 25, 80, 84,
    91–2
European Convention of Human Rights,
    5
European Council, 11
European Currency Unit (ECU), 48, 49,
    55–6, 59, 81, 85, 256
European Defence Community (EDC), 5
European Free Trade Area (EFTA), 9
European Investment Bank (EIB), 197
European Monetary Area (EMA), 7
European Monetary Cooperation Fund
    (FECOM), 48, 49
European Monetary Institute (EMI), 93,
    97–8
European Monetary System (EMS), 2, 11,
    15, 48–9, 50, 256
European Parliament, 11, 13, 95
European Payments Union (EPU), 4–5, 35
European Political Cooperation (EPC), 13

European Recovery Programme Special
    Fund, 167
European System of Central Banks
    (ESCB), 61, 81, 83
European Unit of Account (EUA), 48
EUROQUOTE, 298
exchange-control liberalisation, 7
Exchange Rate Mechanism (ERM), 26,
    48, 50, 51–70, 80, 91, 233
exchange-rate policies, 7, 32–59, 91, 277
Executive Life, 202
export surplus, 43–5

Fair Trade Act (1988), 286
Fair Trading Act (1973), 238
Federal Association of German Insurers,
    298
Federal Bank Supervisory Office, 164
Federal Bond Consortium, 166, 169
Federal Cartel Office, 165
Federal Monopoly Commission, 43
Federal Reserve, 4, 35, 46, 49, 60, 276
Federal Supervisory Office for Insurance,
    165
Federation Française des Sociétés
    d'Assurance (FFSA), 192, 193
Federation of German Stock Exchanges,
    179
Finance Act (1920), 227
Finance Council, 61
Finance Ministry, Germany, 164, 165,
    177–8, 180, 181
Financial Markets, Laws to Promote, 180,
    182–3
Financial Services Act (1986), 236, 240,
    244
Finanzplatz Deutschland, 65, 172–80
Finland, 65
firewalls, 138
Fisher, Sir Henry, 238, 239
fixed exchange rates, 8, 36–43
Flemings, 230
Fond de Développement Economique et
    Social (FDES), 191, 195
franc, French, 36, 55, 56, 65, 66
France
    agricultural policy, 35
    banking proposals, 14
    banque d'affaires, 121
    battle of the systems, 275–6, 280,
        285–303
    Brussels Treaty, 4

capital movements, 1, 8
champion of European integration, 13
collective investment instruments,
    257–9
cooperative diplomacy, desire to go
    beyond, 5
corporate control, 142, 150–1, 155–7,
    160
Council of Europe, 5
deepening of EU, 10
dollar holdings converted to gold, 35
economic and monetary union, 75
ECSC, Rome Treaty and Euratom
    institutions, fusion of, 9
EDC, 5
elections (1993), 66
EMS, 15, 50, 256
European Financial Area, 254
exchange-rates, 33, 46, 48, 50, 54–5
financial services, 189–220, 315–16
foreign and security policy, 94, 95
German foreign policy, reconciliation
    with, 10–11
German unity, 59–60, 61, 66, 82, 83,
    88–9
insurance, 14, 263, 264, 265
investment services directives, 267
Maastricht Treaty, 65, 96, 304, 305–6
monetary union, 20, 77, 87–8
mutual recognition principle, 15–16
NATO, detachment from, 9
nuclear weapons, 78, 88–9, 95
Second Banking Directive, 259–60, 261,
    262
shares, controls, 8
single market, 26, 62, 63
Socialist governments, falling support,
    63
social protection, 86–7
sovereignty, changing perception 10
Spain's entry to EU, 13
support for internal market, 12
taxation, 255–6, 258
transition, 317–19
UN Security Council, 94
vetoes of British entry to EU, 9
France Télécom, 211
Frankfurt Stock Exchange, 181
Franklin National Bank, 281
Freiburg school, 163
fringe banks, 235
fully-integrated universal banks, 137

functional linkages, financial contracting, 111
futures trading, 179, 214–15, 299

Gaulle, Charles de, 35, 190, 231
General Agreement on Tariffs and Trade (GATT), 3, 18, 22, 250, 291
General Code of Insurance, 193
Genscher, Hans-Dieter, 12, 13, 80, 84
geographic linkages, financial contracting, 111
German Unity Fund, 60, 172
Germany
    Atlantic Council, 4
    banking proposals, 14
    battle of the systems, 275–6, 278, 280, 281–5, 291–303
    Bonn accord, 11
    brokers and cross-border payments, 269
    CAP, 35
    capital flows, 10
    corporate control, 140, 150–5, 157, 159–60
    Council of Europe, 5
    Crédit Lyonnais, 204
    door-to-door selling, 258, 264
    ECB, 63–5, 67
    economic and monetary union, 20, 75, 80, 84–6, 94
    EDC, 5
    EMS, 50, 51, 256
    exchange-rates, 33, 34, 46, 48, 49, 50, 54–5
    export surplus, 43–5
    financial services, 162–85, 233–4, 315–16
    foreign and security policy, 94–5
    framework of European security, pivotal role, 9
    French foreign policy, reconciliation with, 10–11
    growth, 43
    insurance, 14, 252, 262–3, 264–5
    investment services directives, 266, 267, 268–9
    Maastricht Treaty, 93, 96–7, 304–6
    mutual recognition principle, 15–16
    NATO, 5
    nuclear disarmament, 77–8
    Ostpolitik, 10, 45, 292
    power, 12–13

reunification, 27, 55, 59–67, 82–3, 88–9, 172
Second Banking Directive, 254, 259–60, 261, 262
shares, liberalisation, 8
single market, delays, 26
social policy, 83–4, 91–2
speculative capital flows, 20
support for internal market, 12
transition, 317–19
universal banking, 122, 123
and US, 82, 92
Gesellschaft für Zahlungssysteme (GZS), 170
Gewerkschaft Handel, Banken und Versicherungen, 166
gilts market, 236
Girobank, 229
Giscard d'Estaing, Valéry, 48, 199
global banking firms, 319–22
Goldman Sachs, 121
gold standard, 32, 33
Gonzalez, Filipe, 81
Goodison, Sir Nicholas, 239
Gorbachev, Mikhail, 27, 77, 82
government deficits, 70, 71
government sector, financial intermediation, 110
Great Britain
    Action Programme for Employment and Growth, 17
    banking proposals, 14
    battle of the systems, 275, 276–81
    Brussels Treaty, 4
    CAP, 35
    'City revolution', 26
    Commonwealth trade, 3
    consumption, 35, 55
    Crédit Lyonnais, 204
    direct marketing, 258
    economic and monetary union, 80
    EFTA, 9
    EMS, 49
    entry to EU, 9, 10, 23
    European Central Bank, 65, 66, 304
    European Payments Union, support for, 4
    exchange rates, 33, 55
    free-market ideals, promotion of, 12
    insurance directives, 262
    internal market, 62
    NATO, 5

Great Britain (*cont.*)
  Second Banking Directive, 259, 262
  Social Charter, 82
  supranational deals, hostility to, 5
  universal banking, 122, 123
  UN Security Council, 94
  wartime alliance with the US, 2–3
  see also United Kingdom
Greece, 4, 10, 24, 62, 255, 261, 263, 264,
  265
Grindlays Bank, 226
Grossbanken, 155
gross domestic product (GDP), 28, 78
Groupe Financière de Paribas, 200
Groupe Victoire, 204
growth rates, 11, 43, 75, 78, 190, 316–19
guilder, 55, 58
Guinness, 245
Gulf states, 10, 62
Gulf War, 62

Haberer, Jean-Yves, 192, 193, 197–8,
  200–1, 203, 204, 205, 207, 209–10,
  301
Hachette, 207
Hades nuclear missiles, 88
Hausbanken, 150, 151, 155, 162
hedging, 119–20
Hermes export insurance schemes, 43, 45,
  170
Herrhausen, Alfred, 293
Herstatt Bank, 44, 237, 281, 292
Hoare Govett, 230
holding-company structure, 138
home-country principle, 17, 19, 27, 250,
  251
Hong Kong and Shanghai Bank (HSBC),
  226, 236
Hugh-Smith, Andrew, 297

India, 231
inflation, 38–9, 50–1, 61–2, 70, 177, 191,
  233
infrastructure, financial systems, 115–17
Innolion, 203
innovations, financial systems, 114
insider dealing, 182, 183, 238, 239, 244–5
insider systems, 138
Instituto Bancaria San Paolo di Torino,
  198
Insurance Act (1989), 211
Insurance Brokers Act (1977), 238

Insurance Committee, 21, 266
Insurance Federation, 166
Inter-bank Information System (IBIS),
  182
Inter-Bourse Data Information System
  (IDIS), 257
Interest Equalisation Tax, 276
interest rate parity theorem (IRPT), 37–8
interest rates, 44, 48, 49, 62, 69, 70, 72,
  177
  and exchange-rates, 37–8, 39, 40–2, 50,
  51
Inter-Fimo, 202
intermediation, financial, 108–10, 122–7
Internal Market Council, 16, 21
International Bank for Reconstruction
  and Development (IBRD), 3
International Banking Facilities (IBF),
  276–7
International Dealerships, 279
International Federation of Stock
  Exchanges (IFSE), 22
International Monetary Fund (IMF), 3, 7,
  11, 232
International Organisation of Securities
  Commissions (IOSCO), 22, 243, 283,
  284
International Securities Regulatory
  Organisation (ISRO), 242, 243
International Stock Exchange (ISE), 279
investment, 1, 12, 27, 49, 121
investor services, 121
Iran, 45, 46, 49
Ireland, 10, 17, 24, 62, 65, 204, 254, 255,
  263, 264
Italy
  Action Programme for Employment
    and Growth, 17
  banking proposals, 14
  brokers and cross-border payments, 269
  capital movements liberalisation, 1, 8
  elections (1992), 63
  EMS, 49
  ERM, 51
  European Financial Area, 254, 255
  insurance directives, 263
  investment services directives, 267
  public finances, reforms, 94
  Second Banking Directive, 259
  support for EU, 62
  support for internal market, 12
  taxation, 255

Japan
  banking, 24
  banks in Germany, 175
  benchmarking against, 144–9
  Bundesbank's relationship with, 50
  corporate control, 156, 159–60
  EU delegations, 22
  exchange-rates, 54
  financial flows to US, 49–50
  investments, 49, 234, 277
  job creation, 11
  keiretsu, 142, 145, 147, 148, 150, 151,
    152–3, 154
  OEEC membership, 4
  securities companies, 121
  trade with EU and US, 1
  UK financial services, 279
  UK as offshore production base, 90
  world order, new, 77
Jenkins, Roy, 281
jobbers, 227
Johnson, Lyndon B., 35
Johnson Matthey Bankers (JMB), 235,
    245
joint-stock companies, 172, 174, 175
J. P. Morgan, 155, 320

keiretsu, 142, 145, 147, 148, 150, 151,
    152–3, 154
Kennedy, Paul, 231
KISS, 181
Kleinwort Benson, 230
Kohl, Helmut
  assertiveness, 82
  Bundesbank intervention to support
    franc, 65
  commercial banks, criticism, 294
  Cruise and Pershing missiles, 12
  economic and monetary union, 17, 75,
    81, 87–8, 303
  electoral victory (1990), 63
  ERM, 82
  European Central Bank, 65, 67, 181,
    304
  European Parliament, powers, 95
  financial autonomy, 305
  financial services, 162, 181
  German unity, 59, 61, 82–3, 88–9
  government reshuffle (1989), 178
  Maastricht Treaty, 97
  nuclear disarmament, 77
  popularity, 63

  pro-business platform, 26
  security policy, 92, 94–5
  social policy, 83–4, 91, 297
Korean War, 4
Kreditanstalt für Wiederaufbau, 167
krone, Danish, 65

La Fondaria, 204–5
Lambsdorff, Count Otto von, 183
Lamfalussy, Alexandre, 80
Landesbanken, 168–9
Landeszentralbank, 164
Latin Monetary Union, 33
Lawson, Nigel, 91, 92, 233, 240
lend-lease, 3, 231
Lévêque, Jean-Maxime, 200
Lion Assurances, 202
Lion Expansion, 203
Lipper Analytics, 116
Liquidity Consortium Bank, 44
lira, 55, 58, 65
Lloyd's Act (1982), 239, 244
Lloyds Bank, 225, 229
Lloyd's of London, 14, 225, 227–8, 238,
    239, 244, 245, 263
lobbies, 22
London Clearing House, 225
London International Commodities
    Clearing House, 278
London International Financial Futures
    Exchange (LIFFE), 278–9
Louvre accords (1987), 61
Luxemburg
  Banco Ambrosiano Holdings, 282
  banking proposals, 14
  bank secrecy laws, 256, 284
  Brussels Treaty, 4
  door-to-door selling, 258
  German banks in, 44–5, 171
  protectionism, 288
  Second Banking Directive, 261
  support for internal market, 12, 63
  taxation, 256, 258–9

Maastricht Treaty, 1, 67–70, 86, 93–6, 180,
    303–6, 315
  referenda, 63, 65, 66
Major, John, 63, 65, 96
majority voting rule, 13
Marketing Investments Board (MIB), 241
Marshall, George, 3
Marshall Plan, 3–4, 167

MATIF, 212, 214–15, 299
Mauroy, Pierre, 295
Maxwell, Robert, 207, 245
merchant banking, 120, 230, 319–20
mergers and acquisitions (M&As), 91, 120
Merrill Lynch, 121
Metallgesellschaft, 303
MGM/UA Communications, 207, 208
Midland Bank, 225, 229
Ministry of Economics, Germany, 165
Ministry of Finance
    France, 189, 193, 194
    Japan (MoF), 145, 146, 147, 148
Ministry of International Trade and
    Industry (MITI), 146
Ministry of Telecommunications, 211
Minitel, 21
Mittelstand firms, 150
Mitterand, Francois
    corporate governance, 294–5
    Cruise and Pershing missiles, 12
    domestic economic policy, 12
    economic and monetary union, 17, 75,
        82, 87, 88, 94, 297, 303
    elections, 66, 78, 86, 87, 196, 199, 206,
        294
    ERM, 26, 50
    European unity, 13
    financial services, 189, 191, 194, 195,
        200, 201, 211, 213, 216
    German unification, 83
    'hard franc' policy, 59–60
    Maastricht Treaty referendum, 65, 217
    nationalisation, reflation and income
        distribution experiment, 16, 50, 196
    security policy, 88, 89
    social protection, 86, 87
Monetary Committee, 19–20, 35, 66, 81
Monnet, Jean, 190
Monopoly Commission, Germany, 169
Moody's investor Services, 79, 116, 208
Morgan Grenfell, 278
Morgan Stanley, 121
Morningstar, 116
mortgage banks, Germany, 167
multinational companies, 34
Munich Reinsurance, 169, 170, 205, 292
mutual recognition principle, 15–16, 17,
    251, 253–4

NASDAQ, 237
National Association of Securities

Dealers and Investment Managers
    (NASDIM), 230
National Girobank, 226
National Investment Bank, 228
National Savings banks, 226
National Westminster Bank, 225, 229
Nederlands Credietbank, 204
Netherlands, 4, 14, 25, 61, 261, 264, 267, 269
    Crédit Lyonnais, 204, 205
    support for internal market, 12, 63
net regulatory burden (NRB), 130–3
New Zealand, 4
Nikko, 121
Nixon, Richard, 10, 36, 316, 317
Nölling, Wilhelm, 185
Nomura, 121
non-discrimination, 252
Non-Proliferation Treaty, 95
non-tariff barriers, 12, 16
NordLB, 169
North Atlantic Treaty Organization
    (NATO), 5, 6, 9, 13, 78, 82, 83, 89
nuclear weapons, 77–8, 88–9, 95
Nyborg agreements (1987), 77

Office of Fair Trade (OFT), 238, 239
oil shocks, 11, 45, 49
Olympia & York, 207
Organisation for Economic Cooperation
    and Development (OECD), 4, 22, 34,
    46, 282
Organisation for Economic European
    Cooperation (OEEC), 3, 4
Organization of Petroleum-Exporting
    Countries (OPEC), 45
outsider systems, 138, 140

Padoa-Schioppa, Tomasso, 51
Paribas, 121, 192, 201
Paris Club, 195
Paris Treaty (1952), 5
Parkinson, Cecil, 239
Parretti, Giancarlo, 205, 207
partially-integrated financial
    conglomerates, 137
pensions, 174, 264
Permanent Conference of Insurance
    Regulators, 15
Pershing missiles, 12, 77
Personal Investment Authority (PIA), 241
peseta, 65
Pöhl, Karl-Otto, 61, 84–5, 86, 297, 298

Poland, 4, 45
Policyholder's Protection Act (1974), 238
Polly Peck, 245
Pompidou, Georges, 10
Portugal, 10, 18, 24, 62, 65, 255, 263, 264, 265
Price Information Project Europe (PIPE), 298
private limited-liability companies, 172, 175
privatisation, 79
processes, financial system, 106, 107
process innovations, financial systems, 114
product innovations, financial systems, 114
profitability, 12
public debt, 70, 71
public interest, 253, 254
public officials, and corporate control, 143–4
punt, 65
purchasing power parity (PPP), 38, 55–9

qualified majority voting, 18, 21

Reagan, Ronald, 27, 54, 77, 177, 277
real estate, 120
recapitalisations, 120
Recognised Investment Exchange (RIE), 242
regimes, financial system, 106, 107
Regional Scope of Credit Institutions, Law on (1952), 166
Registrar of Friendly Societies, 225, 226
regulatory tradeoffs, financial system, 127–9
RELIT, 215
research, financial system,s 119
reserves, central bank, 40, 42
Reuters, 116
REX, 182
Ridley, Nicholas, 104n.82
risk, 117, 119–20
Robert Fleming, 121
Rocard, Prime Minister, 87
Rome Treaty (1957), 6–9, 12, 13, 26
RONA, 215
Roosevelt, Franklin D., 33
Rothschilds, 121, 230
Round Table of European Industrialists, 12

Royal Bank of Scotland, 206, 236
Russia, 33

Sal Oppenheimer, 300
Santer, Jacques, 258
Saturn network, 215
Saudi Arabia, 46
savings, 11, 18, 26, 48, 108–10, 170–1, 174, 194–5, 286
savings banks, Germany, 166–7, 168, 169, 171
Schieren, Wolfgang, 292
Schioppa, Padoa, 81
Schlesinger, Hans, 65
Schmidt, Helmut, 46, 233, 292
Schneider, 303
Schroders, 121, 230
Schröder, Münchmeyer & Hengst Co. (SMH), 45, 282
Schuman, Maurice, 5
SEAQ International, 237, 279
secondary market trading, 119
Securities and Exchange Commission (SEC), 243, 276, 283
Securities and Futures Securities Association Authority (SFA), 242
securities firms, 118–21
Securities Investment Board (SIB), 240, 241, 242, 243–4
securities markets, 21–2, 26, 72, 212–17
securitisation, 122
Security Council, Franco-German, 78
Séguin, Philippe, 102n.48
Seipp, Walter, 293
self-regulation, 165–6
sell-side assignments, 120
Serious Fraud Office, 245
services, freedom to supply, 7, 8, 18–19
S. G. Warburg, 230
share-ownership, 172–5
shares, 8
Single European Act (SEA), 1, 13, 17, 18, 23, 28, 75, 77, 251
Slavenburgs Bank, 204, 205
Smithsonian Agreement, 36
'snake', 36, 46, 47
Social Action Programme, 76
Social Affairs Council, 82
Social Charter, 25, 81, 82, 84, 90–1
Social Democratic Party, Germany (SPD), 183
social market economy, 163

Soisson, Jean-Pierre, 102n.48
social security, 11
Société des Bourses Françaises (SBF), 216
Société Générale, 197, 199, 200
Sociétés de Bourse (SDB), 215
Sociétés de Développement Regionale,
   196
Solemn Declaration on European Union,
   12
Sorenson, Knud, 27
South Africa, 45
Soviet Union, 3, 9, 10, 77, 83
Spain
   Atlantic Council, 4
   brokers and cross-border payments, 269
   capital liberalisation, 24
   Crédit Lyonnais, 204, 205–6
   ERM, 55, 65
   EU membership, 10, 12, 13, 18, 62
   European boom, 54
   European Financial Area, 255
   funds demanded by, 80, 94
   insurance directives, 263, 264, 265
   investment services directives, 267
   labour costs, 55
   OEEC membership, 4
   Second Bank Directive, 261
Special Drawing Rights (SDRs), 11, 35
Stability and Growth Law (1967), 34
Stalin, Joseph, 3–4
Standard & Poors, 79, 116
Standard Chartered Bank, 169, 226, 236
state-led financial market system,
      corporate control, 142–3
static efficiency, financial systems, 112–15
sterling, 3, 33, 35, 36, 55, 56, 65, 66
Stern, Fritz, 291–2
Stock Corporation Act, 183
stock exchanges
   France, 196, 212–13, 280
   Germany, 181, 280, 290
   United Kingdom, 225, 226–7, 229, 230,
      237, 238, 242, 278–80
   United States, 276
stock underwriting, 119
Strauss, Franz-Josef, 77
subsidies, 79
Supervisory Office for Securities, 182–3
supply of money and credit, 38–9
Sweden, 55, 65
Switzerland, 62
systems, financial, 106, 107

takeovers, 183
taxation, 42, 174, 177–8, 255–6, 258–9
Telerate, 116
Thatcher, Margaret
   'City revolution', 26
   ERM, 256
   financial services, 224, 233
   Germany, attitude towards, 93
   internal market, 89
   monetary union, 17, 88, 92, 297
   resignation, 63, 91
   Social Charter, 90–1
   social policy, 88
   US and Japanese multinational
      companies, 90
Thomson, 208
Thygessen, Niels, 80
Tietmeyer, Hans, 60
Todai, 149
too-big-to-fail (TBTF) banks, 155
trade associations, Germany, 65
trades unions, 34, 83, 84
Transfer and Automated Registration of
      Uncertified Stock (TAURUS) 182,
      237
transfer risk, 38
transition in financial systems, 156–8
travellers' cheques, 170
Treasury bills, 52
Treasury circuit, 191
Trésor, 189, 191–2, 195, 196, 197, 210,
      214, 215, 216
Treuhand, 293
Trichet, Governor, 300
Truman, Harry S., 4
Trustee Savings Bank, 229, 241
trustee savings banks, 225–6
Tugendhat, Christopher, 15, 281
Turkey, 4, 45

underwriting, 118–19
unemployment, *see* employment and
      unemployment
Union Assurance de Paris (UAP), 204,
      295, 299–300
Union of Soviet Socialist Republics, 3, 9,
      10, 77, 83
United Kingdom
   battle of the systems, 284, 296–9
   brokers and cross-border payments, 269
   corporate control, 139, 149–54, 156,
      159

EMS, 256
financial service, 224–47, 315–16
insurance directives, 264, 265
investment services directives, 266, 267, 268
liberalism, 89–93
protectionism, 288
Second Banking Directive, 260, 261
transition, 318
see also Great Britain
United Nations (UN), 3, 22, 94, 95
United States of America
agricultural policy, 34–5
banking, 24
bilateral accords, 282
boom, 49
Bundesbank's relationship with, 50
Common External Tariff, 6
consumption, 35
corporate control, 139, 151–5, 159
disillusionment with Western European events, 9–10
EPU, 5
EU delegations, 22
European savings flows, 26
exchange-rates, 32, 33, 34, 49–50
financial contracting, alternative modes, 111
financial services sector, 113, 124, 126
GATT, 18
German macroeconomic policy, 54
German unity, 62
Germany's relationship with, 92, 175, 177, 302
Gulf presence, 10, 62
Iran and Saudi Arabia, deals with, 46
job creation, 11
loans, ending of restrictions, 46
Marshall Plan, 3–4
net regulatory burden, 130
non-convertibility of dollars, 35–6
nuclear disarmament, 77

OEEC membership, 4
protectionism, 286
and reciprocity, 289, 291
trade deficits, 49
trade with EU and Japan, 1
UK as offshore production base, 90
UK financial services, 231, 238, 242–3, 245–6, 276–7
universal banking, 122, 123
wartime alliance with Britain, 2–3
Washington Treaty, 4
Western European security, 4, 6
as world's banker, 3
unit trusts, 18, 180
universal banks, 122, 123, 137, 162, 171
Usinor-Sacilor, 207, 209

value, financial contracting, 111
Vietnam War, 35
Visa, 170, 211
von Rosen, Rudiger, 179
von Siemens, Georg, 166
von Weizäcker, Richard, 85

wages and salaries, 11, 177
Waigel, Theo, 65, 66, 178, 180, 181, 304
Washington Treaty (1949), 4
Washington Treaty (1987), 77, 78
Werner Report, 10, 36, 81
Western European Union (WEU), 78, 94
West Germany, *see* Germany
WestLB, 169
White Book (1985), 1, 15, 16–17, 23, 27, 89
Wilson Committee, 234
Woodchester, 204

Yamaichi, 121
yen, 55, 56
Yugoslavia, 45

zaibatsu, 145